WITHDRAWN
LVC BISHOP LIBRARY

POTENTIAL

The High School Comic Chronicles of
ARIEL SCHRAG

A Touchstone Book
Published by Simon & Schuster
New York   London   Toronto   Sydney

 Touchstone
A Division of Simon & Schuster, Inc.
1230 Avenue of the Americas
New York, NY 10020

Copyright © 1997 by Ariel Schrag
Originally published by SLG Publishing

All rights reserved, including the right to reproduce
this book or portions thereof in any form whatsoever.
For information address Touchstone Subsidiary Rights Department,
1230 Avenue of the Americas, New York, NY 10020.

First Touchstone trade paperback edition May 2008

TOUCHSTONE and colophon are registered trademarks of Simon & Schuster, Inc.

For information about special discounts for bulk purchases,
please contact Simon & Schuster Special Sales at
1-800-456-6798 or business@simonandschuster.com.

Manufactured in the United States of America

10 9 8 7 6 5 4 3 2 1

Library of Congress Cataloging-in-Publication Data
Schrag, Ariel.
    Potential : the high school comic chronicles of Ariel Schrag.
      p. cm.
    "A Touchstone Book."
    ISBN-13: 978-1-4165-5235-2
    ISBN-10:   1-4165-5235-9
  I. Graphic novels.   I. Title.
    PN6727.S287P68 2008
741.5'973—dc22

                                                                    2007060443

For Jessica

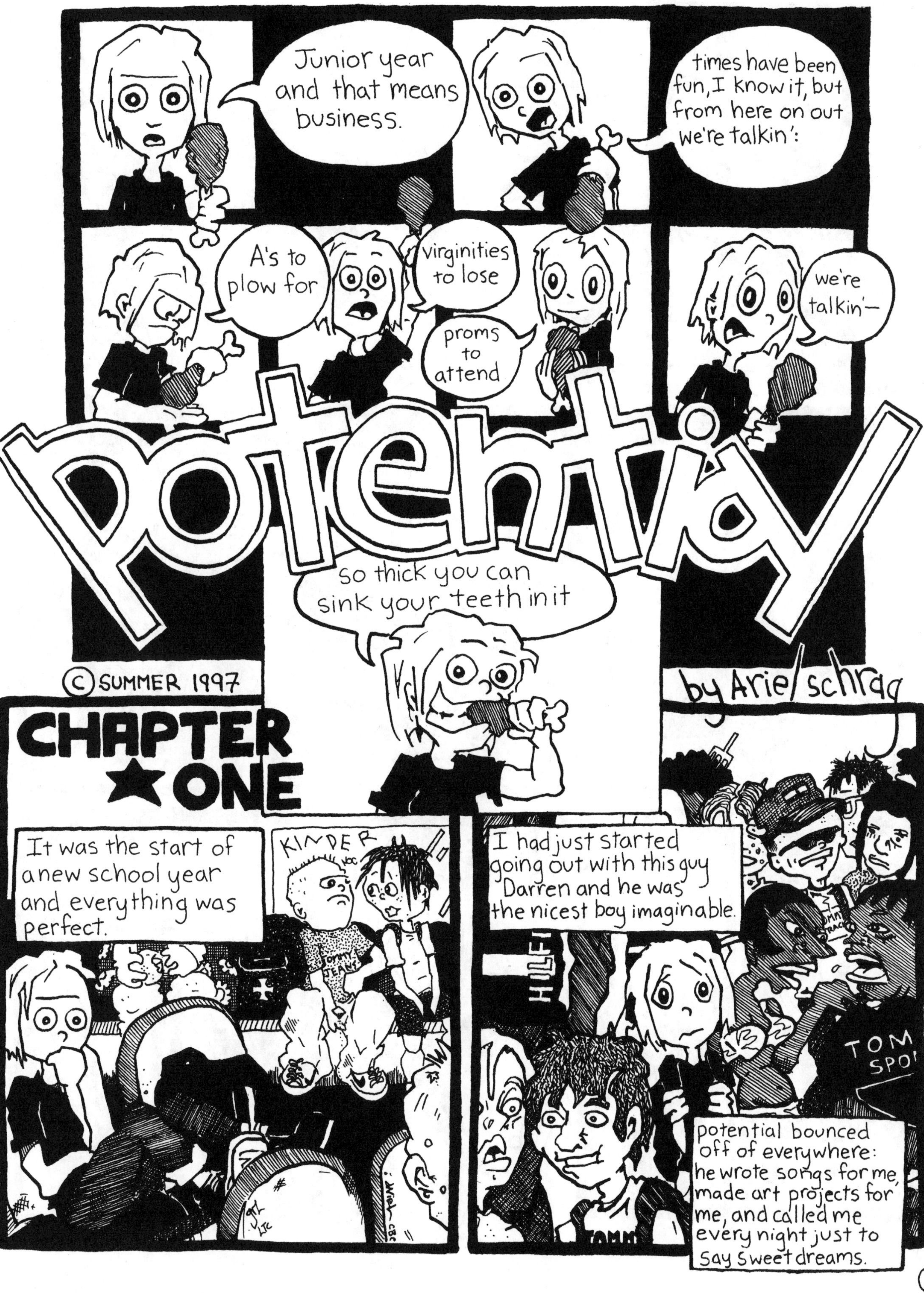
Junior year and that means business.
times have been fun, I know it, but from here on out we're talkin':
A's to plow for
virginities to lose
proms to attend
we're talkin'—
potentiaLy
so thick you can sink your teeth in it
© SUMMER 1997
by Ariel Schrag
CHAPTER ★ ONE
It was the start of a new school year and everything was perfect.
KINDER
TOMMY JEANS
I had just started going out with this guy Darren and he was the nicest boy imaginable.
potential bounced off of everywhere: he wrote songs for me, made art projects for me, and called me every night just to say sweet dreams.

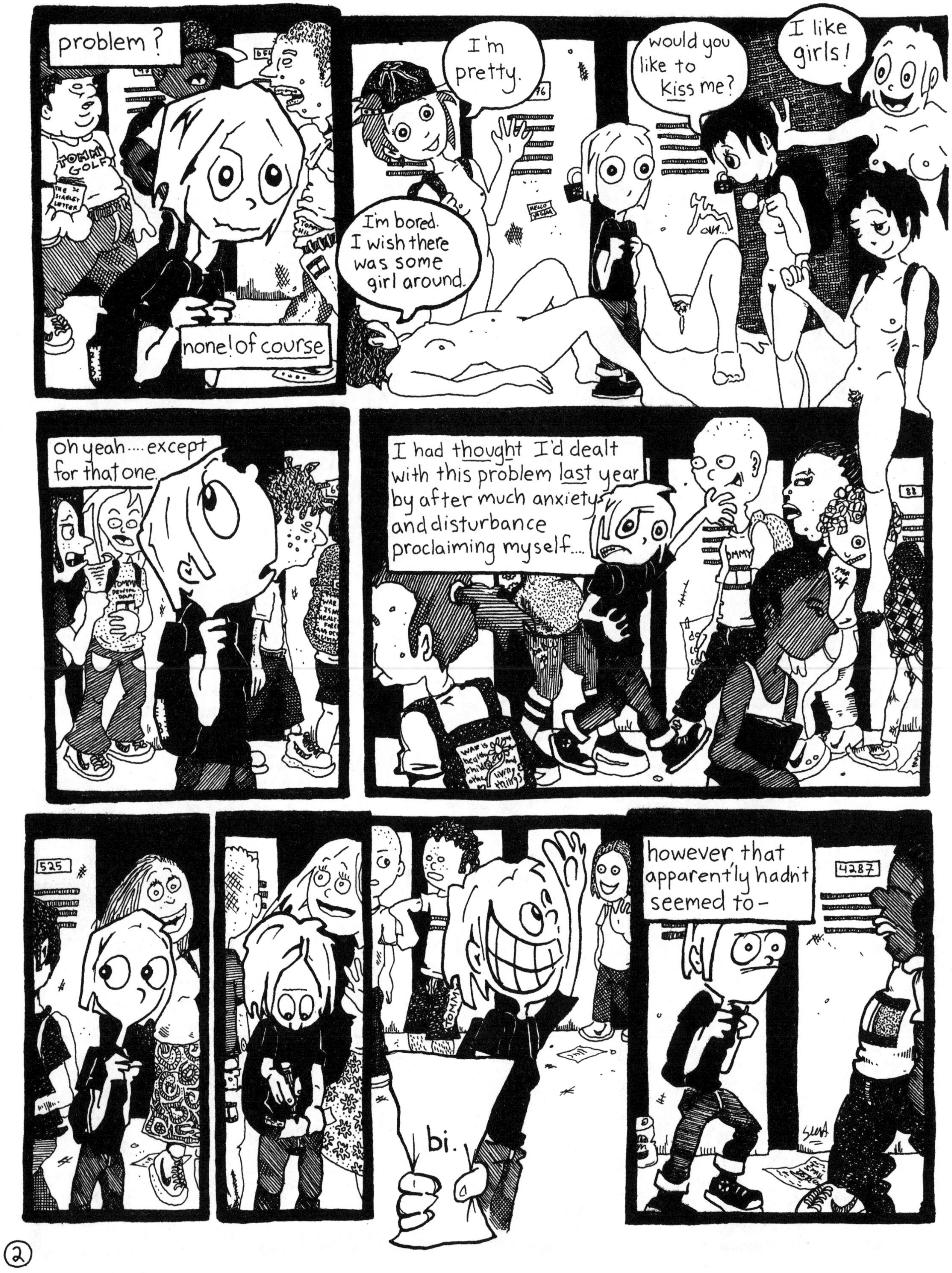
problem ?
TOMMY GOLF
THE SCARLET LETTER
none! of course
I'm pretty.
I'm bored. I wish there was some girl around.
would you like to kiss me?
I like girls!
oh yeah.... except for that one.
I had thought I'd dealt with this problem last year by after much anxiety and disturbance proclaiming myself....
525
bi.
however that apparently hadn't seemed to -
4287

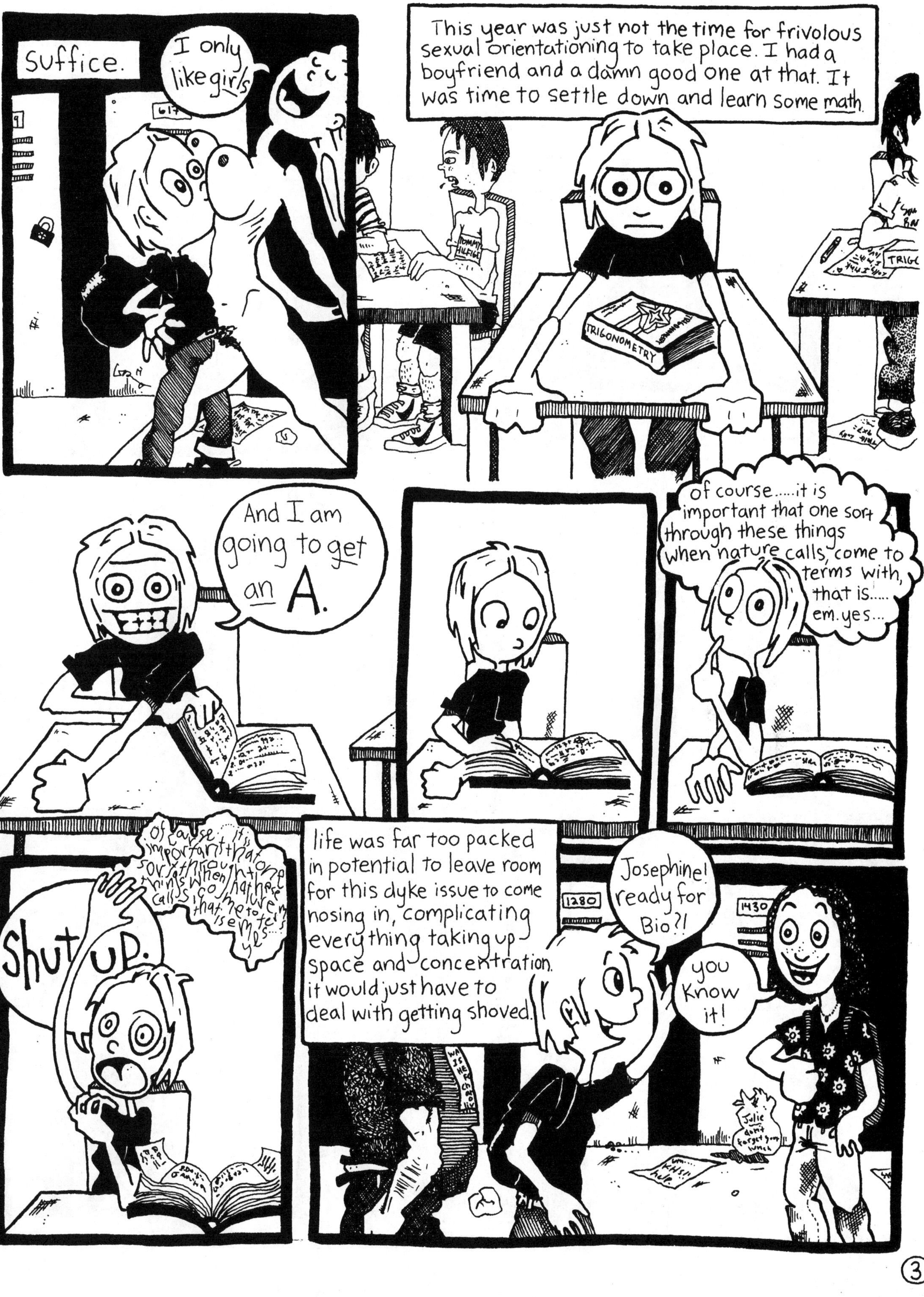

Suffice.
I only like girls
This year was just not the time for frivolous sexual orientationing to take place. I had a boyfriend and a damn good one at that. It was time to settle down and learn some math.
TOMMY HILFIGER
TRIGONOMETRY
And I am going to get an A.
of course.....it is important that one sort through these things when nature calls, come to terms with, that is..... em. yes...
of course... it's important that one sort through these things when nature calls, come to terms with, that is em. yes
Shut up.
life was far too packed in potential to leave room for this dyke issue to come nosing in, complicating everything taking up space and concentration. it would just have to deal with getting shoved.
1280
1430
Josephine! ready for Bio?!
you know it!

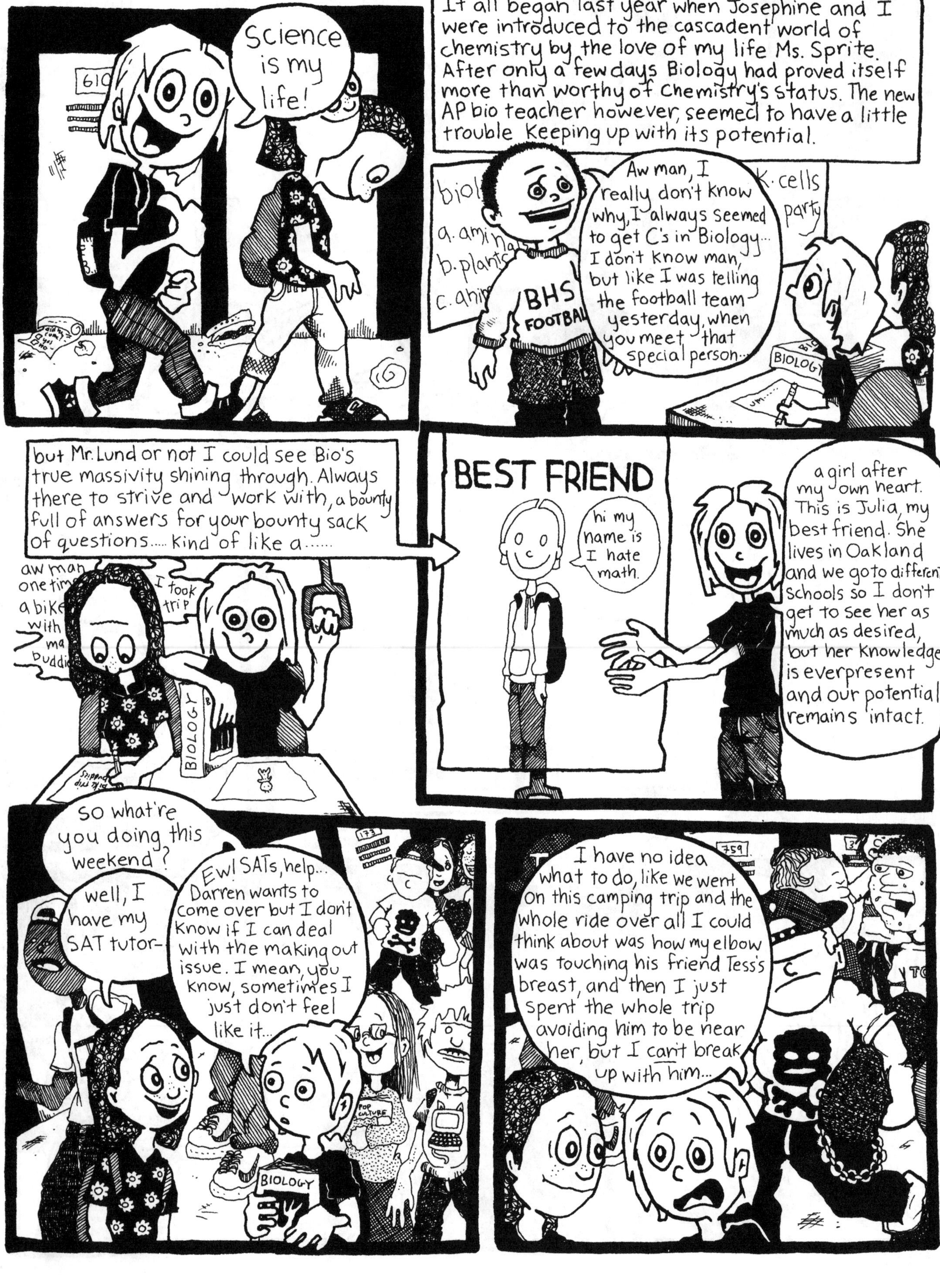
Science is my life!
It all began last year when Josephine and I were introduced to the cascadent world of chemistry by the love of my life Ms. Sprite. After only a few days Biology had proved itself more than worthy of Chemistry's status. The new AP bio teacher however, seemed to have a little trouble keeping up with its potential.
Aw man, I really don't know why, I always seemed to get C's in Biology... I don't know man, but like I was telling the football team yesterday, when you meet that special person...
BHS FOOTBALL
BIOLOGY
but Mr. Lund or not I could see Bio's true massivity shining through. Always there to strive and work with, a bounty full of answers for your bounty sack of questions..... kind of like a......
I took trip
BIOLOGY
BEST FRIEND
hi my name is I hate math.
a girl after my own heart. This is Julia, my best friend. She lives in Oakland and we go to different schools so I don't get to see her as much as desired, but her knowledge is everpresent and our potential remains intact.
So what're you doing this weekend?
well, I have my SAT tutor-
Ew! SATs, help... Darren wants to come over but I don't know if I can deal with the making out issue. I mean, you know, sometimes I just don't feel like it...
POP CULTURE
BIOLOGY
I have no idea what to do, like we went on this camping trip and the whole ride over all I could think about was how my elbow was touching his friend Tess's breast, and then I just spent the whole trip avoiding him to be near her, but I can't break up with him...

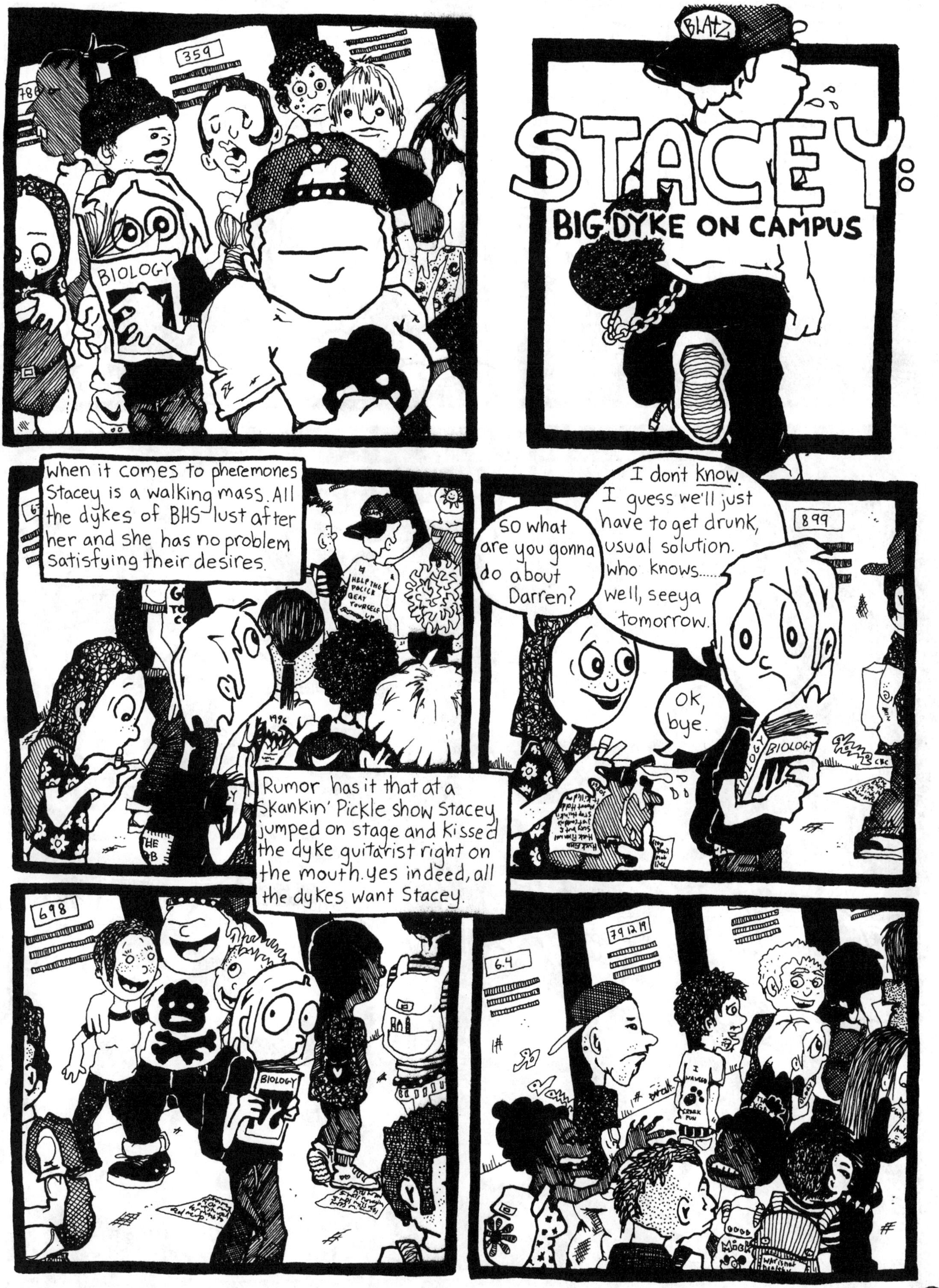
STACEY:
BIG DYKE ON CAMPUS
BLATZ
BIOLOGY
When it comes to pheremones Stacey is a walking mass. All the dykes of BHS lust after her and she has no problem satisfying their desires.
HELP THE POLICE BEAT YOURSELF UP
So what are you gonna do about Darren?
I don't know. I guess we'll just have to get drunk, usual solution. who knows...... well, seeya tomorrow.
OK, bye.
BIOLOGY
Rumor has it that at a Skankin' Pickle show Stacey jumped on stage and kissed the dyke guitarist right on the mouth. yes indeed, all the dykes want Stacey.
BIOLOGY
I WANTED

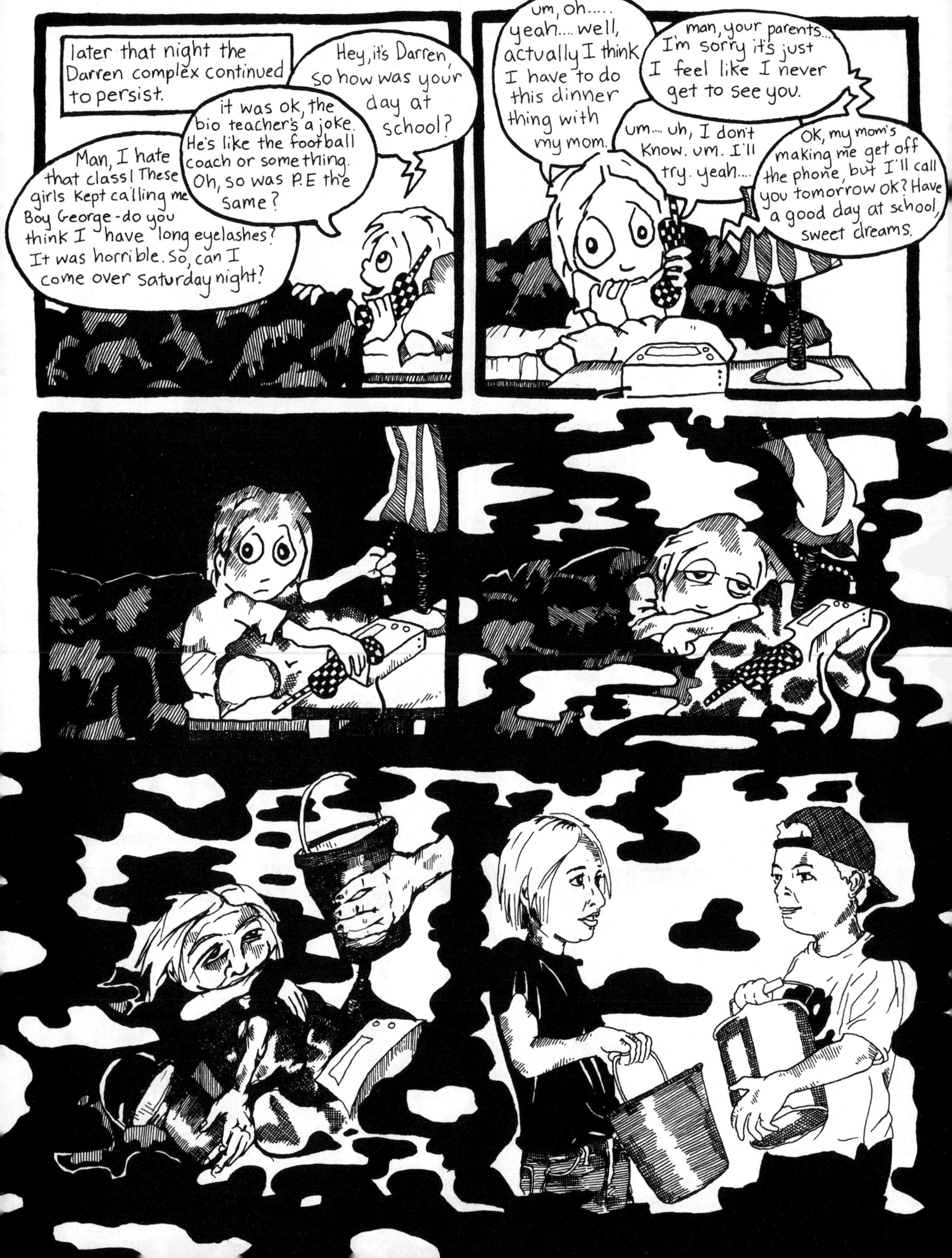
later that night the Darren complex continued to persist.
Hey, it's Darren, so how was your day at school?
it was ok, the bio teacher's a joke. He's like the football coach or something. Oh, so was P.E the same?
Man, I hate that class! These girls kept calling me Boy George - do you think I have long eyelashes? It was horrible. So, can I come over saturday night?
um, oh..... yeah.... well, actually I think I have to do this dinner thing with my mom.
man, your parents... I'm sorry it's just I feel like I never get to see you.
um.... uh, I don't know. um. I'll try. yeah....
OK, my mom's making me get off the phone, but I'll call you tomorrow ok? Have a good day at school, sweet dreams.

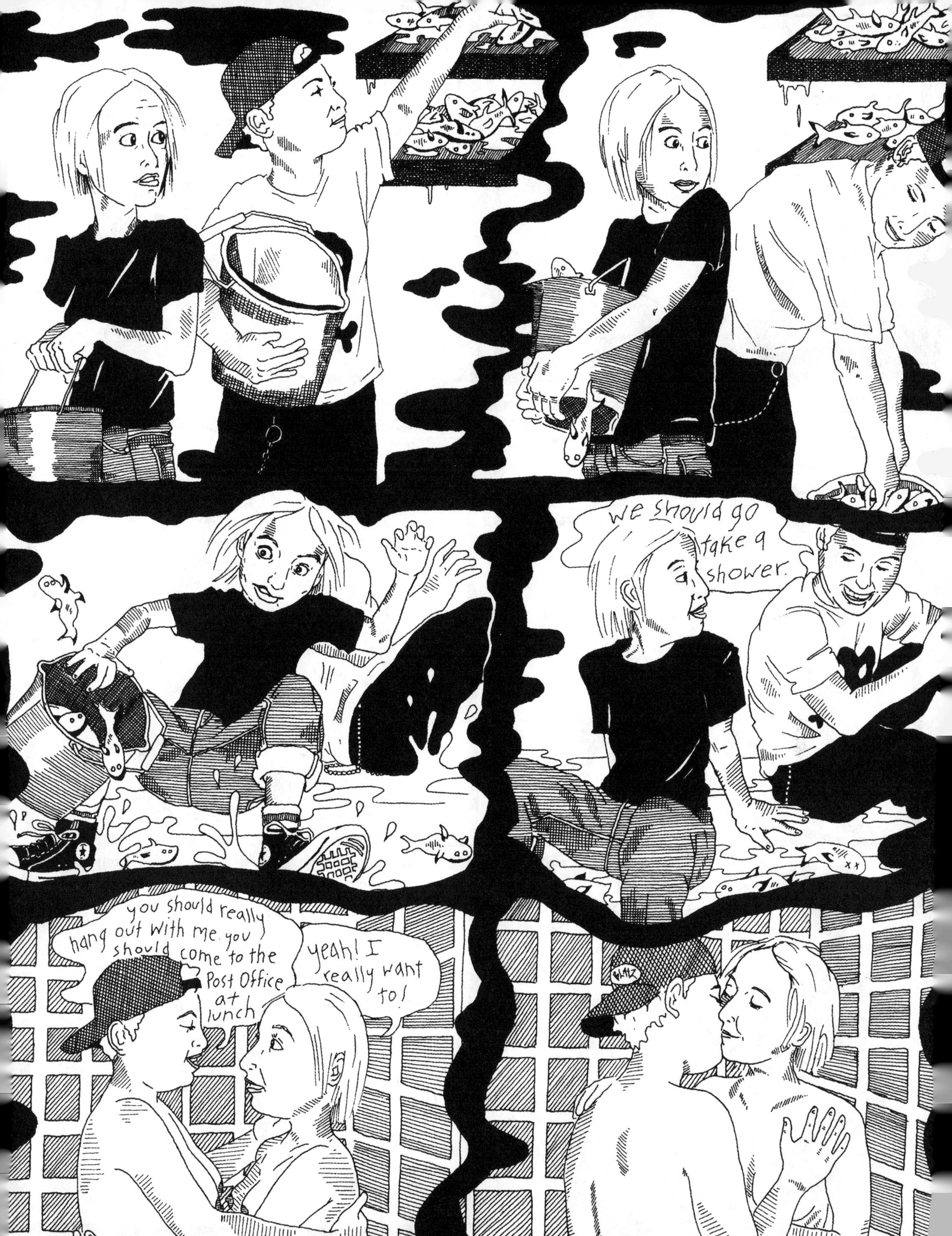
we should go take a shower.
you should really hang out with me. you should come to the Post Office at lunch
yeah! I really want to!

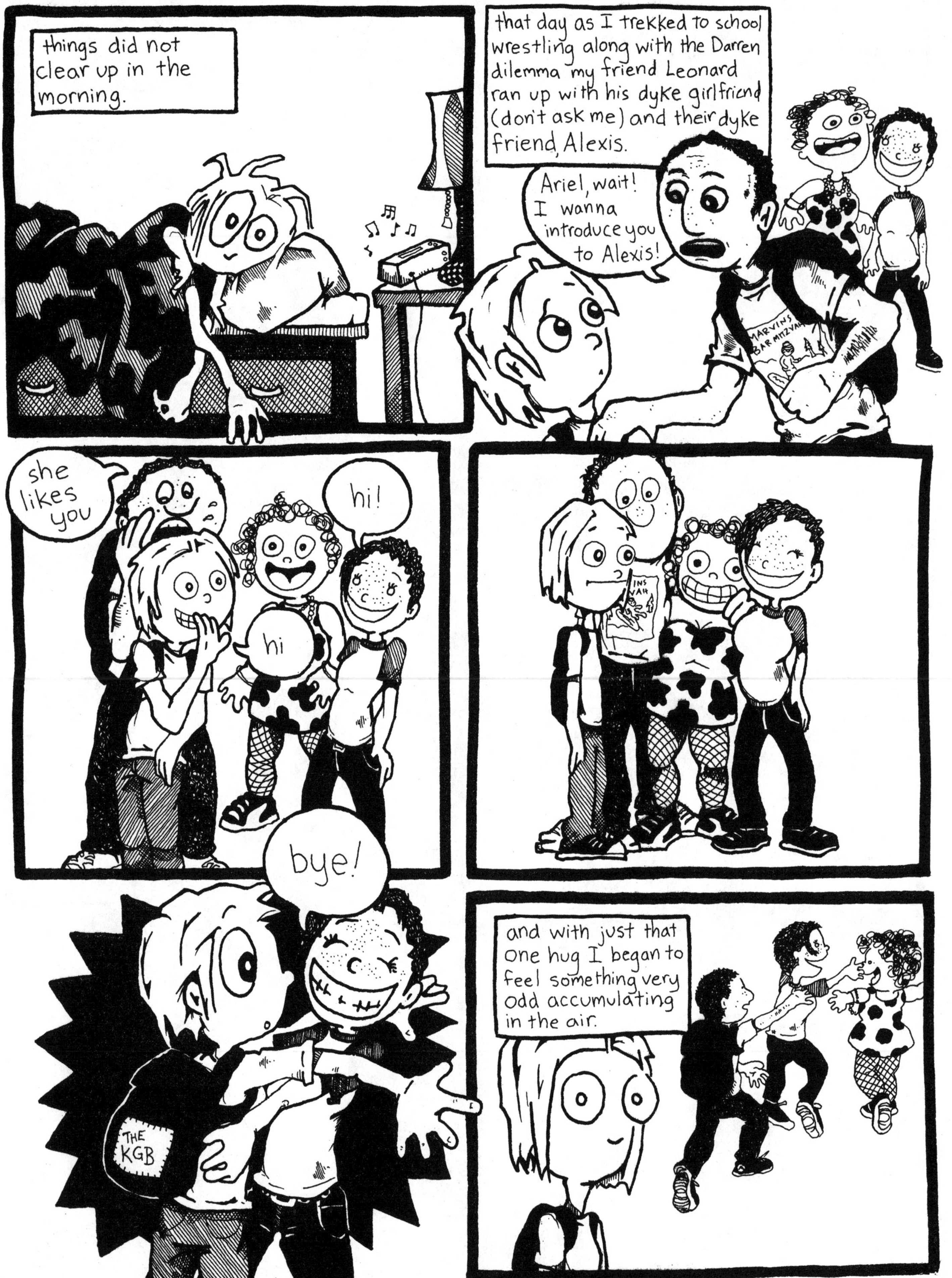
things did not clear up in the morning.
that day as I trekked to school wrestling along with the Darren dilemma my friend Leonard ran up with his dyke girlfriend (don't ask me) and their dyke friend, Alexis.
Ariel, wait! I wanna introduce you to Alexis!
MARVINS BAR MITZVAH
she likes you
hi!
hi
bye!
THE KGB
and with just that one hug I began to feel something very odd accumulating in the air.

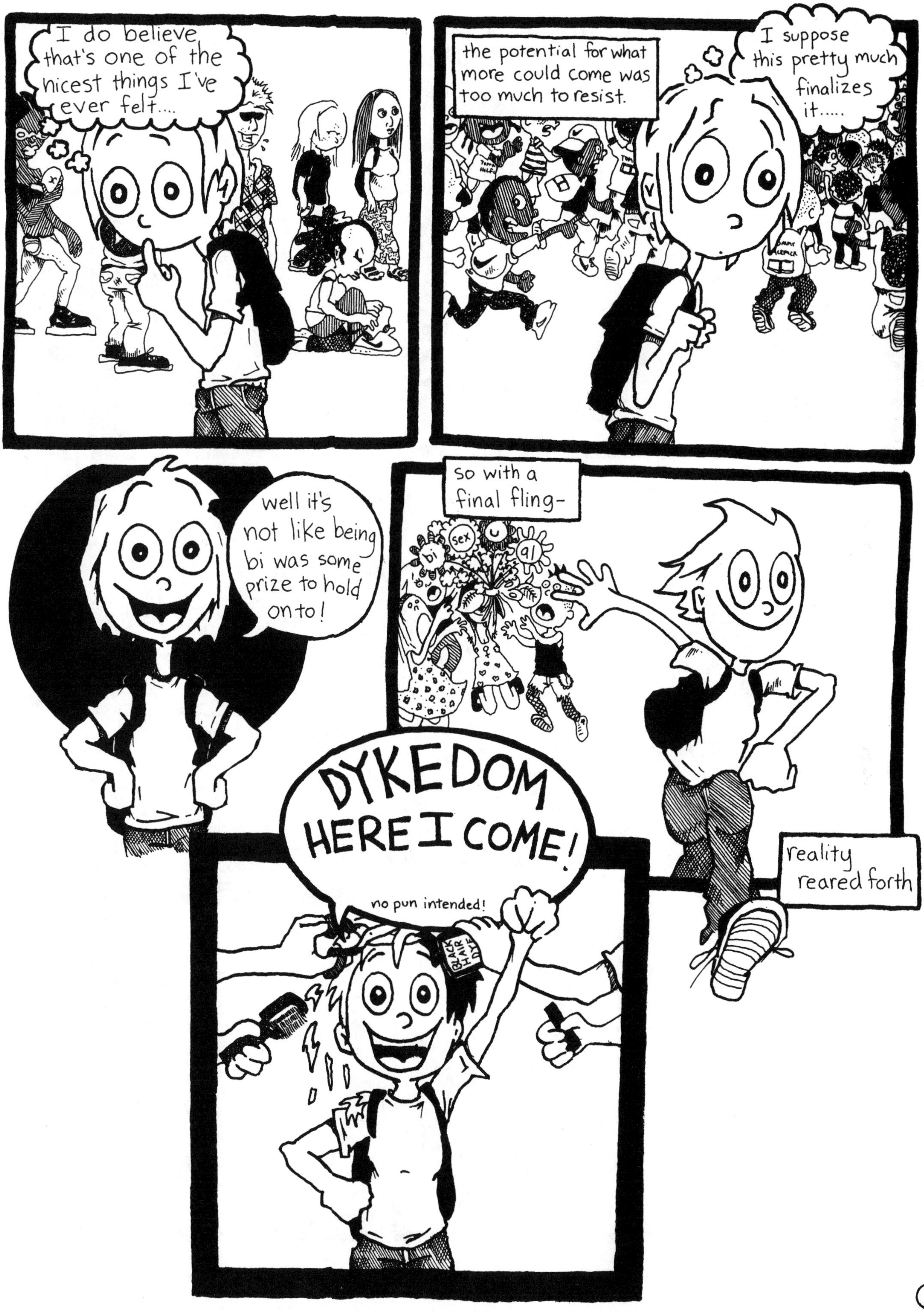
I do believe that's one of the nicest things I've ever felt....
the potential for what more could come was too much to resist.
I suppose this pretty much finalizes it.....
well it's not like being bi was some prize to hold on to!
so with a final fling-
bi
sex
u
gl
reality reared forth
DYKEDOM HERE I COME!
no pun intended!
BLACK HAIR DYE

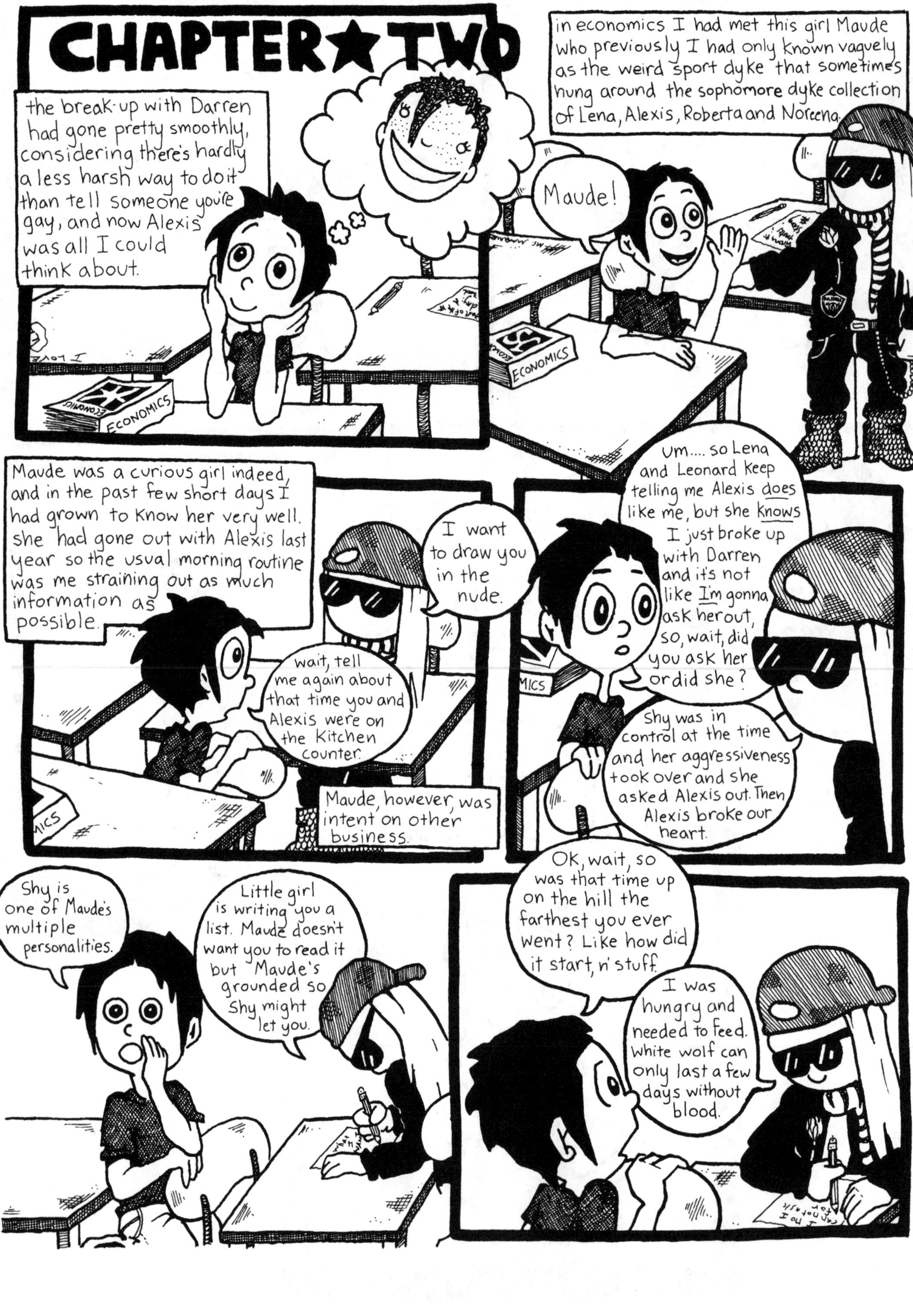
CHAPTER★TWO
the break-up with Darren had gone pretty smoothly, considering there's hardly a less harsh way to do it than tell someone you're gay, and now Alexis was all I could think about.
ECONOMICS
in economics I had met this girl Maude who previously I had only known vaguely as the weird sport dyke that sometimes hung around the sophomore dyke collection of Lena, Alexis, Roberta and Noreena.
Maude!
ECONOMICS
Maude was a curious girl indeed, and in the past few short days I had grown to know her very well. she had gone out with Alexis last year so the usual morning routine was me straining out as much information as possible.
I want to draw you in the nude.
wait, tell me again about that time you and Alexis were on the Kitchen counter.
Maude, however, was intent on other business.
Um.... so Lena and Leonard Keep telling me Alexis does like me, but she knows I just broke up with Darren and it's not like I'm gonna ask her out, so, wait, did you ask her or did she?
Shy was in control at the time and her aggressiveness took over and she asked Alexis out. Then Alexis broke our heart.
Shy is one of Maude's multiple personalities.
Little girl is writing you a list. Maude doesn't want you to read it but Maude's grounded so Shy might let you.
Ok, wait, so was that time up on the hill the farthest you ever went? Like how did it start, n' stuff.
I was hungry and needed to feed. White wolf can only last a few days without blood.

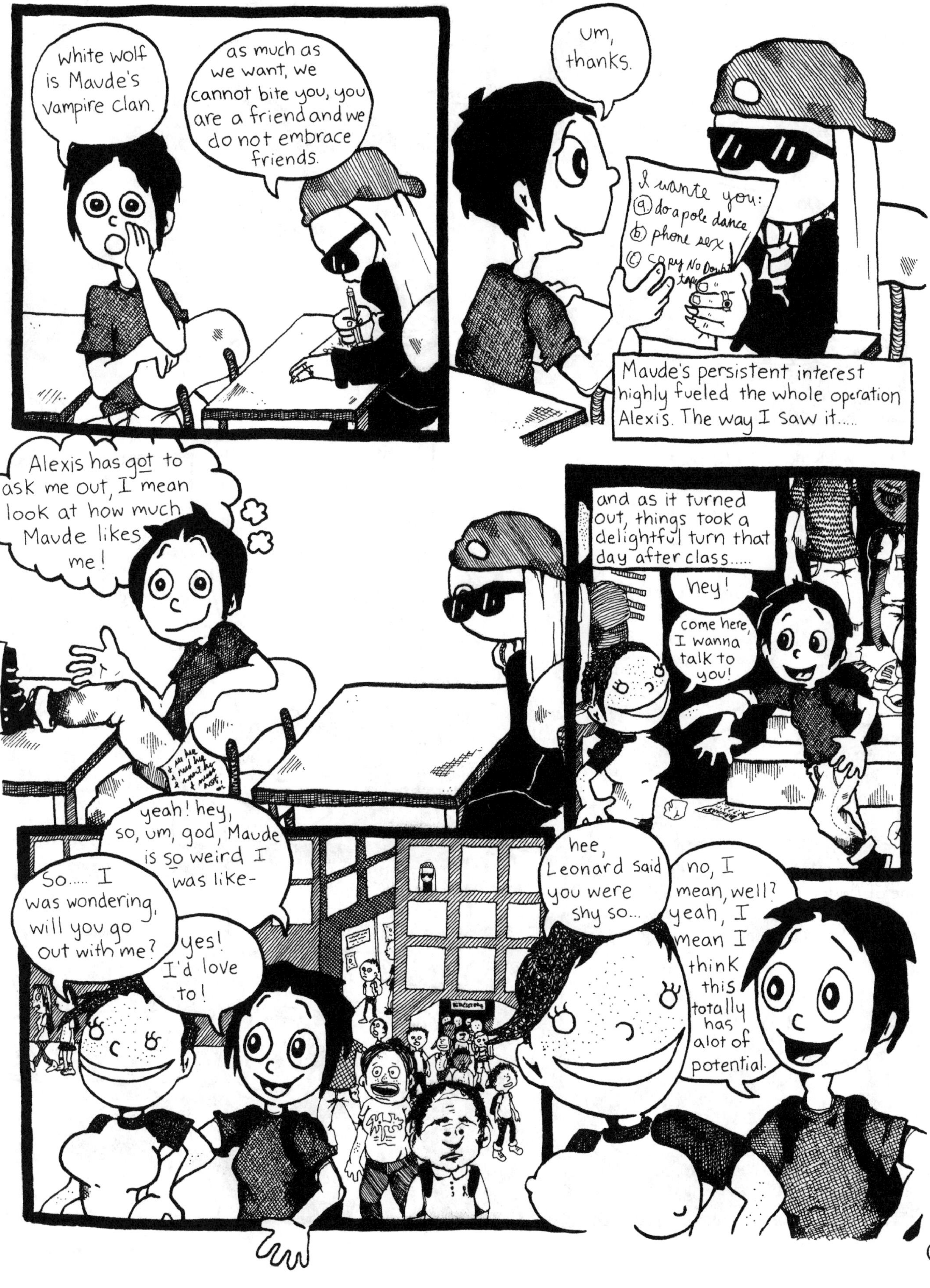
white wolf is Maude's vampire clan.
as much as we want, we cannot bite you, you are a friend and we do not embrace friends.
um, thanks.
I wante you:
a) do a pole dance
b) phone sex
c) copy No Doubt
Maude's persistent interest highly fueled the whole operation Alexis. The way I saw it.....
Alexis has got to ask me out, I mean look at how much Maude likes me!
and as it turned out, things took a delightful turn that day after class.....
hey!
come here, I wanna talk to you!
yeah! hey, so, um, god, Maude is so weird I was like-
So..... I was wondering, will you go out with me?
yes! I'd love to!
hee, Leonard said you were shy so...
no, I mean, well? yeah, I mean I think this totally has alot of potential.

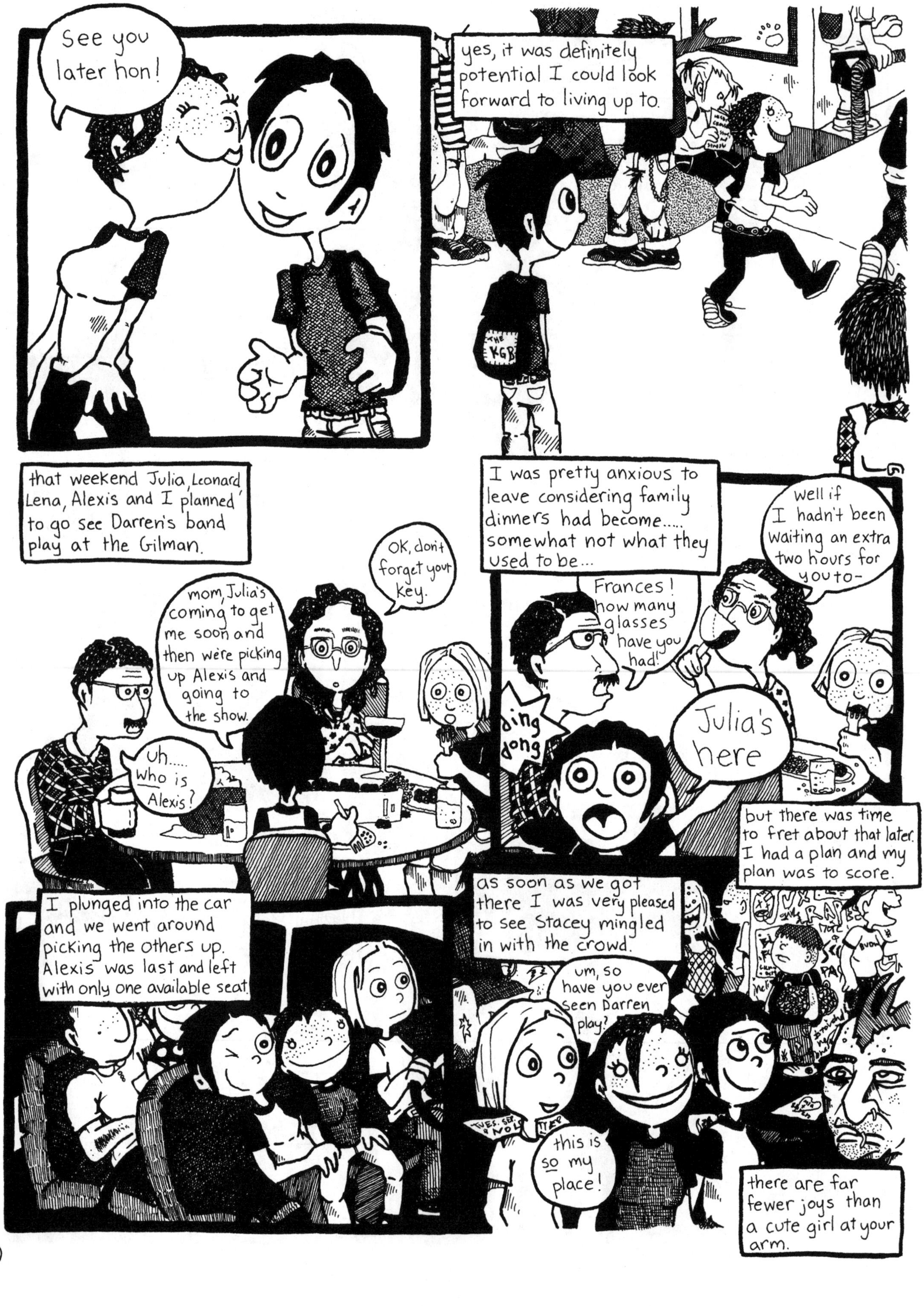
See you later hon!
yes, it was definitely potential I could look forward to living up to.
that weekend Julia, Leonard Lena, Alexis and I planned to go see Darren's band play at the Gilman.
mom, Julia's coming to get me soon and then we're picking up Alexis and going to the show.
OK, don't forget your key.
uh..... Who is Alexis?
I was pretty anxious to leave considering family dinners had become..... somewhat not what they used to be...
Frances! how many glasses have you had!
well if I hadn't been waiting an extra two hours for you to-
ding dong
Julia's here
but there was time to fret about that later. I had a plan and my plan was to score.
I plunged into the car and we went around picking the others up. Alexis was last and left with only one available seat.
as soon as we got there I was very pleased to see Stacey mingled in with the crowd.
um, so have you ever seen Darren play?
this is so my place!
there are far fewer joys than a cute girl at your arm.

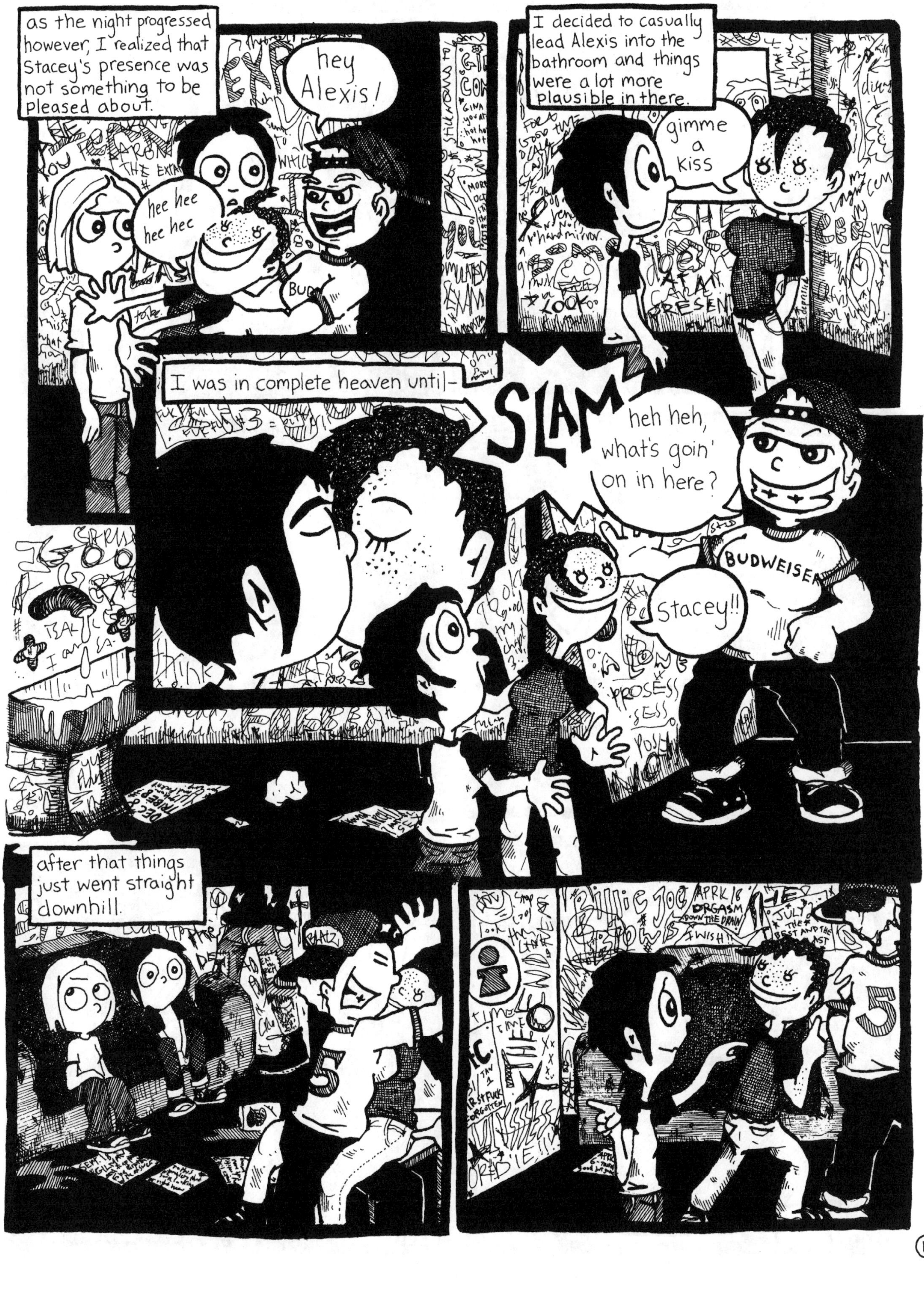

as the night progressed however, I realized that Stacey's presence was not something to be pleased about.
hey Alexis!
hee hee hee hee
I decided to casually lead Alexis into the bathroom and things were a lot more plausible in there.
gimme a kiss
I was in complete heaven until-
SLAM
heh heh, what's goin' on in here?
BUDWEISER
Stacey!!
after that things just went straight downhill.

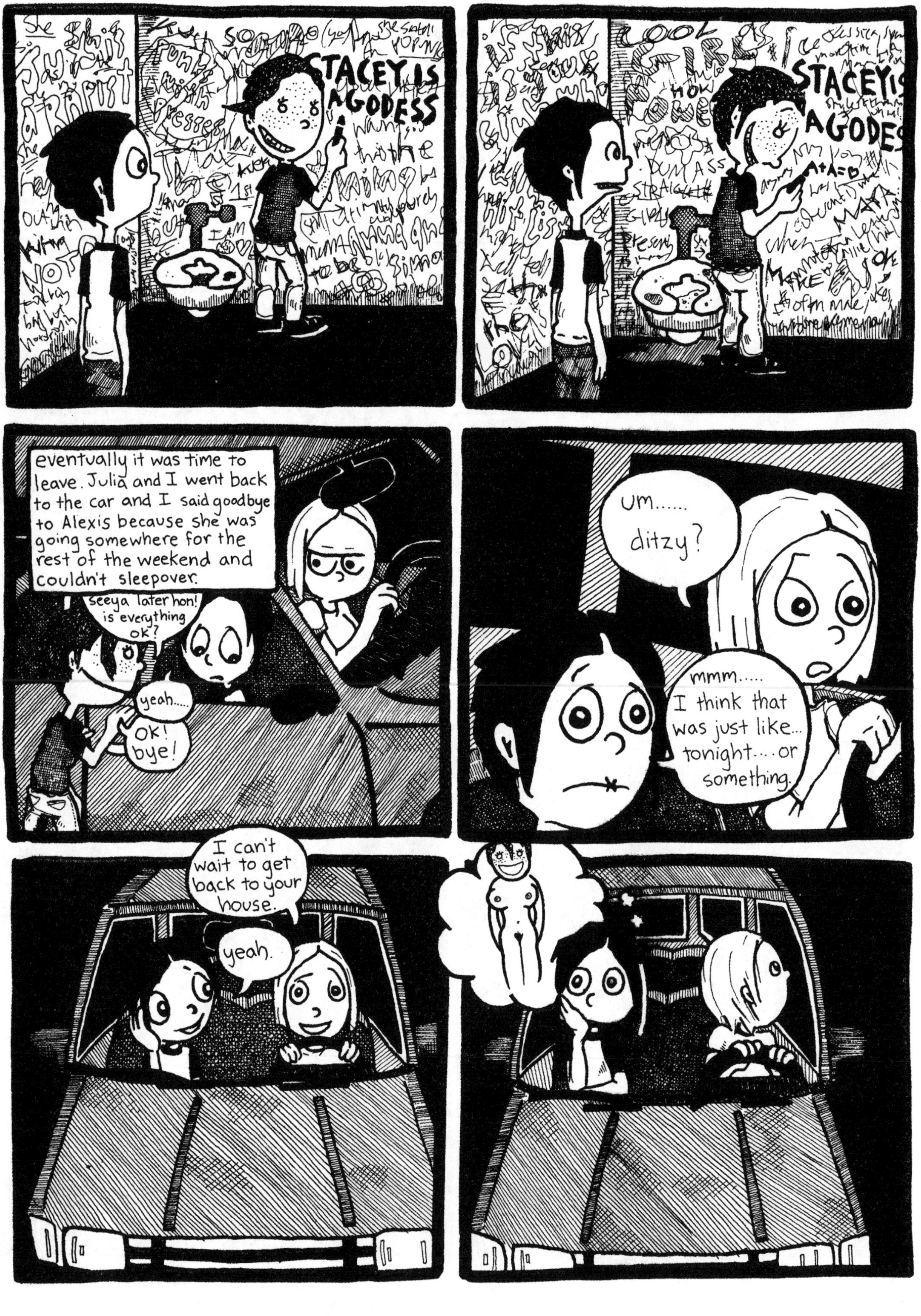
STACEY IS A GODESS
eventually it was time to leave. Julia and I went back to the car and I said goodbye to Alexis because she was going somewhere for the rest of the weekend and couldn't sleepover.
seeya later hon! is everything ok?
yeah.....
OK! bye!
um...... ditzy?
mmm..... I think that was just like... tonight.... or something.
I can't wait to get back to your house.
yeah.

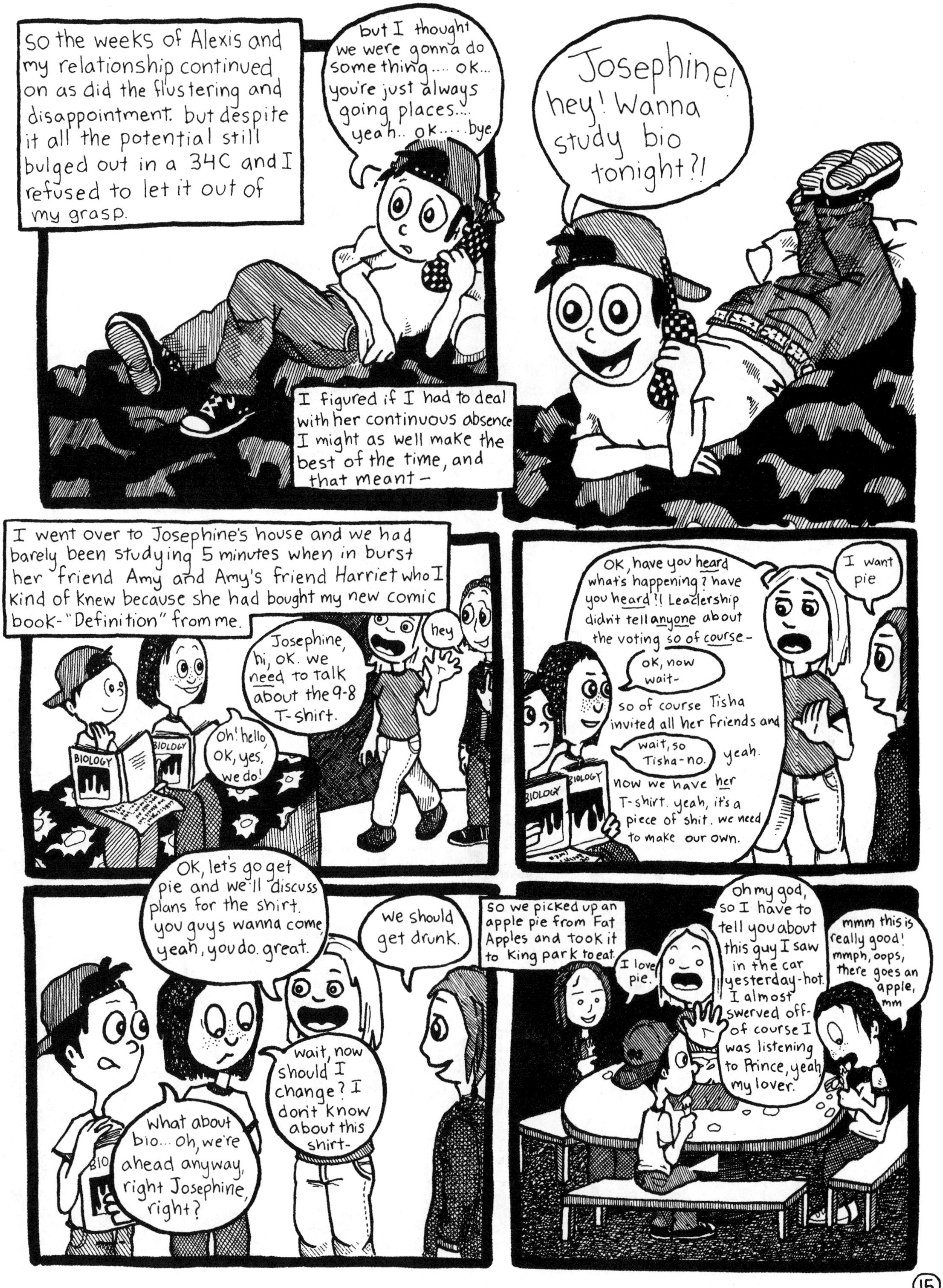

So the weeks of Alexis and my relationship continued on as did the flustering and disappointment. but despite it all the potential still bulged out in a 34C and I refused to let it out of my grasp.
but I thought we were gonna do something.... ok... you're just always going places.... yeah.. ok..... bye.
I figured if I had to deal with her continuous absence I might as well make the best of the time, and that meant –
Josephine! hey! Wanna study bio tonight?!
I went over to Josephine's house and we had barely been studying 5 minutes when in burst her friend Amy and Amy's friend Harriet who I kind of knew because she had bought my new comic book- "Definition" from me.
BIOLOGY
BIOLOGY
Josephine, hi, OK. we need to talk about the 9-8 T-shirt.
hey
Oh! hello, OK, yes, we do!
OK, have you heard what's happening? have you heard!! Leadership didn't tell anyone about the voting so of course-
ok, now wait-
so of course Tisha invited all her friends and
wait, so Tisha- no.
yeah.
now we have her T-shirt. yeah, it's a piece of shit. we need to make our own.
I want pie
BIOLOGY
BIOLOGY
OK, let's go get pie and we'll discuss plans for the shirt. you guys wanna come yeah, you do. great.
We should get drunk.
wait, now should I change? I don't know about this shirt-
what about bio... oh, we're ahead anyway, right Josephine, right?
So we picked up an apple pie from Fat Apples and took it to King park to eat.
I love pie.
oh my god, so I have to tell you about this guy I saw in the car yesterday- hot. I almost swerved off- of course I was listening to Prince, yeah my lover.
mmm this is really good! mmph, oops, there goes an apple, mm

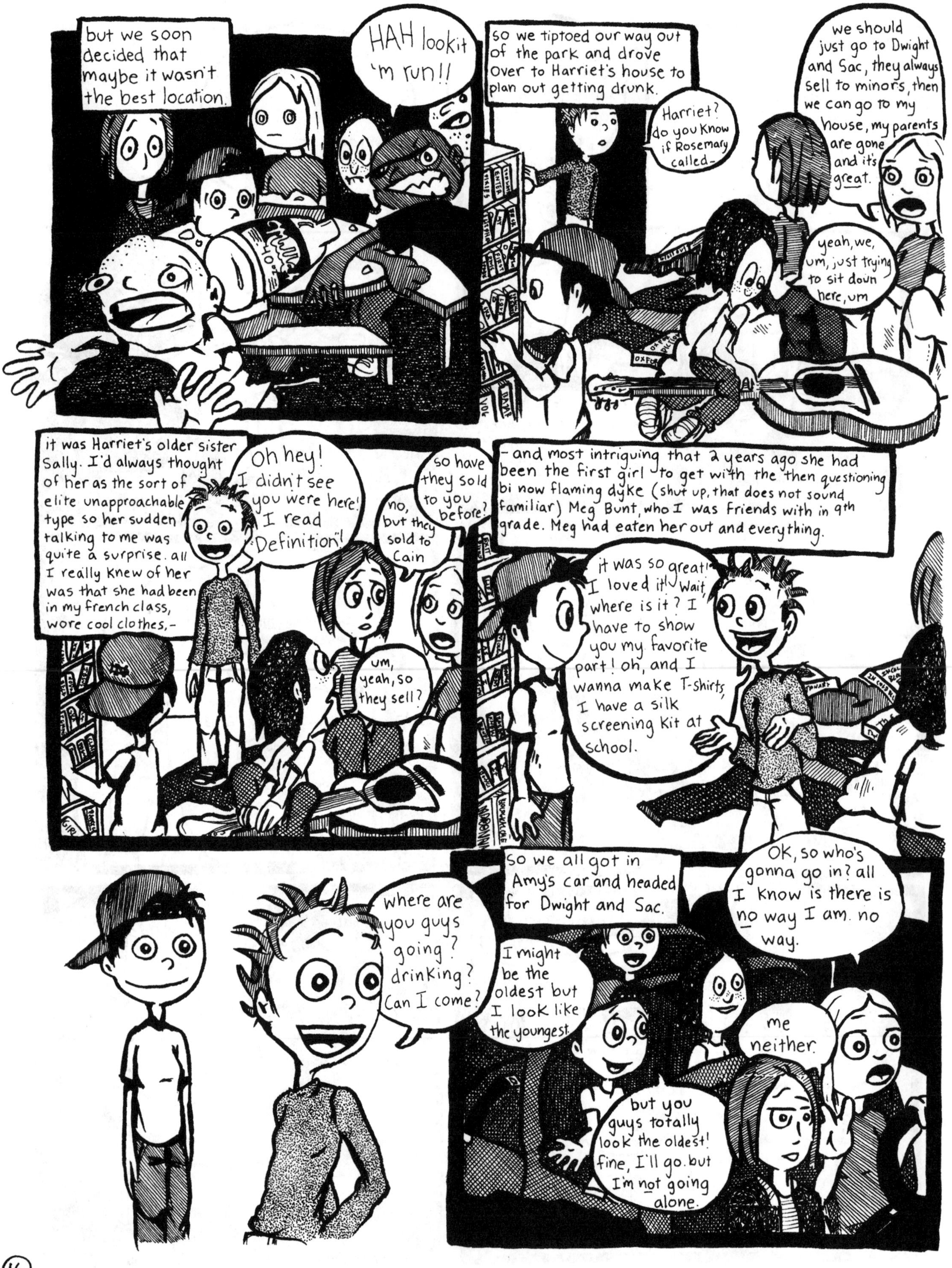
but we soon decided that maybe it wasn't the best location.
HAH lookit 'm run!!
so we tiptoed our way out of the park and drove over to Harriet's house to plan out getting drunk.
Harriet? do you know if Rosemary called-
we should just go to Dwight and Sac, they always sell to minors, then we can go to my house, my parents are gone and it's great.
yeah, we, um, just trying to sit doun here, um
it was Harriet's older sister Sally. I'd always thought of her as the sort of elite unapproachable type so her sudden talking to me was quite a surprise. all I really knew of her was that she had been in my french class, wore cool clothes,-
Oh hey! I didn't see you were here! I read "Definition"!
so have they sold to you before?
no, but they sold to Cain
um, yeah, so they sell?
-and most intriguing that 2 years ago she had been the first girl to get with the then questioning bi now flaming dyke (shut up, that does not sound familiar) Meg Bunt, who I was friends with in 9th grade. Meg had eaten her out and everything.
it was so great! I loved it! wait, where is it? I have to show you my favorite part! oh, and I wanna make T-shirts, I have a silk screening kit at school.
where are you guys going? drinking? Can I come?
so we all got in Amy's car and headed for Dwight and Sac.
OK, so who's gonna go in? all I know is there is no way I am. no way.
I might be the oldest but I look like the youngest.
me neither.
but you guys totally look the oldest! fine, I'll go. but I'm not going alone.

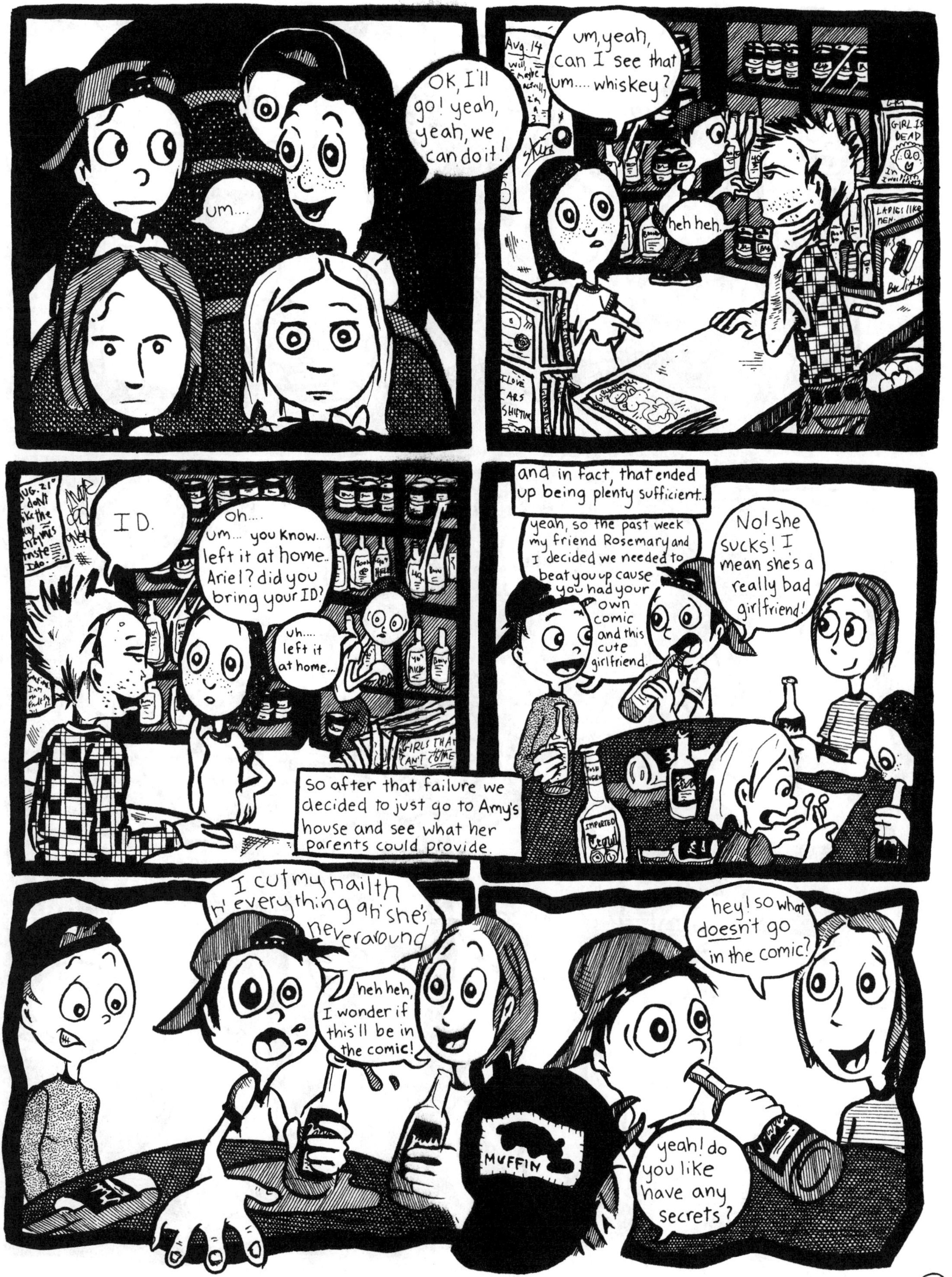

Ok, I'll go! yeah, yeah, we can do it!
um....
um, yeah, can I see that um.... whiskey?
heh heh.
I.D.
oh.... um... you know... left it at home.. Ariel? did you bring your ID?
uh.... left it at home...
So after that failure we decided to just go to Amy's house and see what her parents could provide.
and in fact, that ended up being plenty sufficient..
yeah, so the past week my friend Rosemary and I decided we needed to beat you up cause you had your own comic and this cute girlfriend.
No! she sucks! I mean she's a really bad girlfriend!
IMPORTED
I cut my nail th n' everything an' she's never around
heh heh, I wonder if this'll be in the comic!
MUFFIN
hey! so what doesn't go in the comic?
yeah! do you like have any secrets?

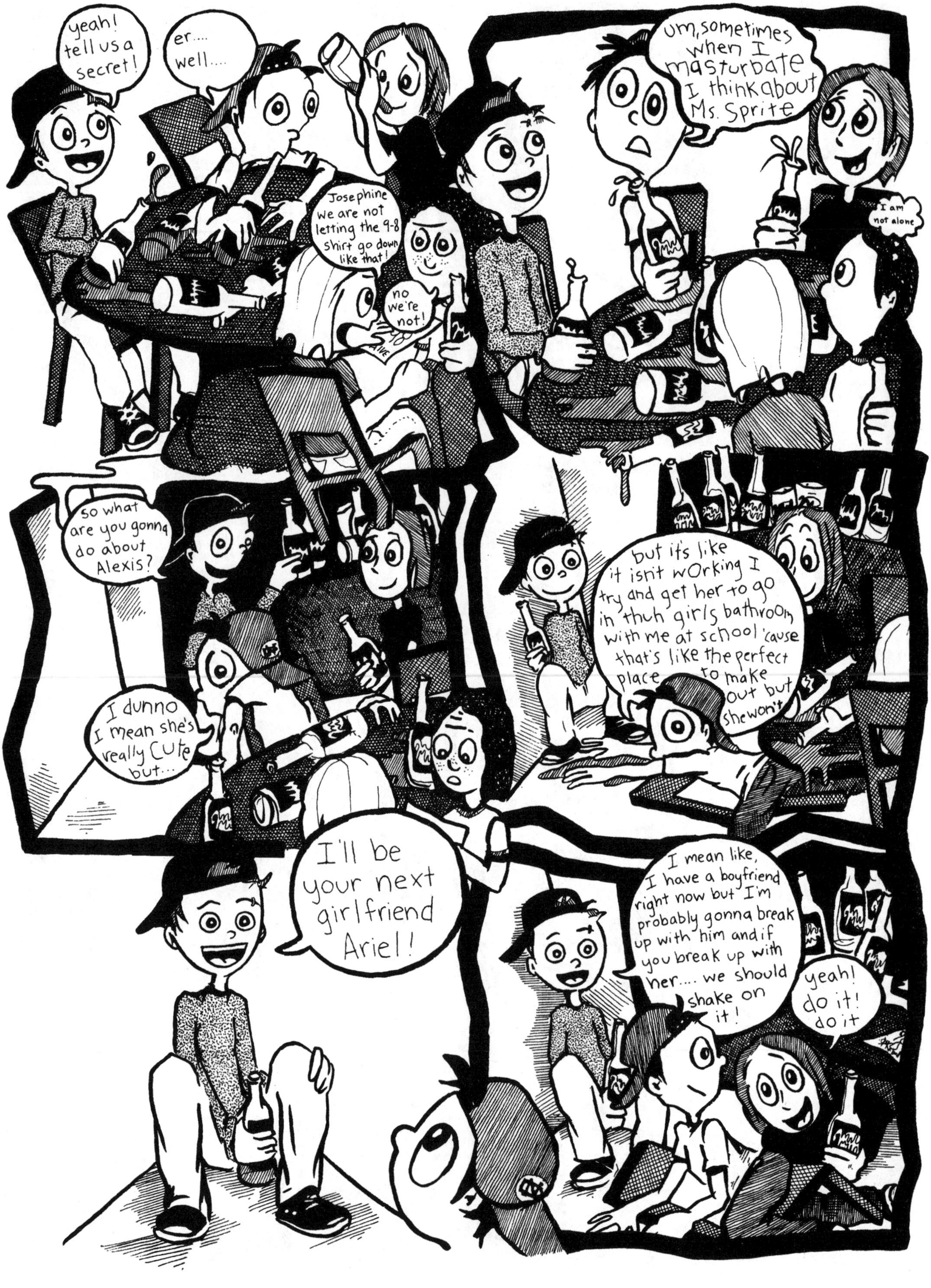
yeah! tell us a secret!
er.... well....
Um, sometimes when I masturbate I think about Ms. Sprite
Josephine we are not letting the 9-8 shirt go down like that!
no we're not!
I am not alone
so what are you gonna do about Alexis?
I dunno I mean she's really Cute but...
but it's like it isn't working I try and get her to go in thuh girls bathroom with me at school 'cause that's like the perfect place to make out but she won't
I'll be your next girlfriend Ariel!
I mean like, I have a boyfriend right now but I'm probably gonna break up with him and if you break up with her.... we should shake on it!
yeah! do it! do it

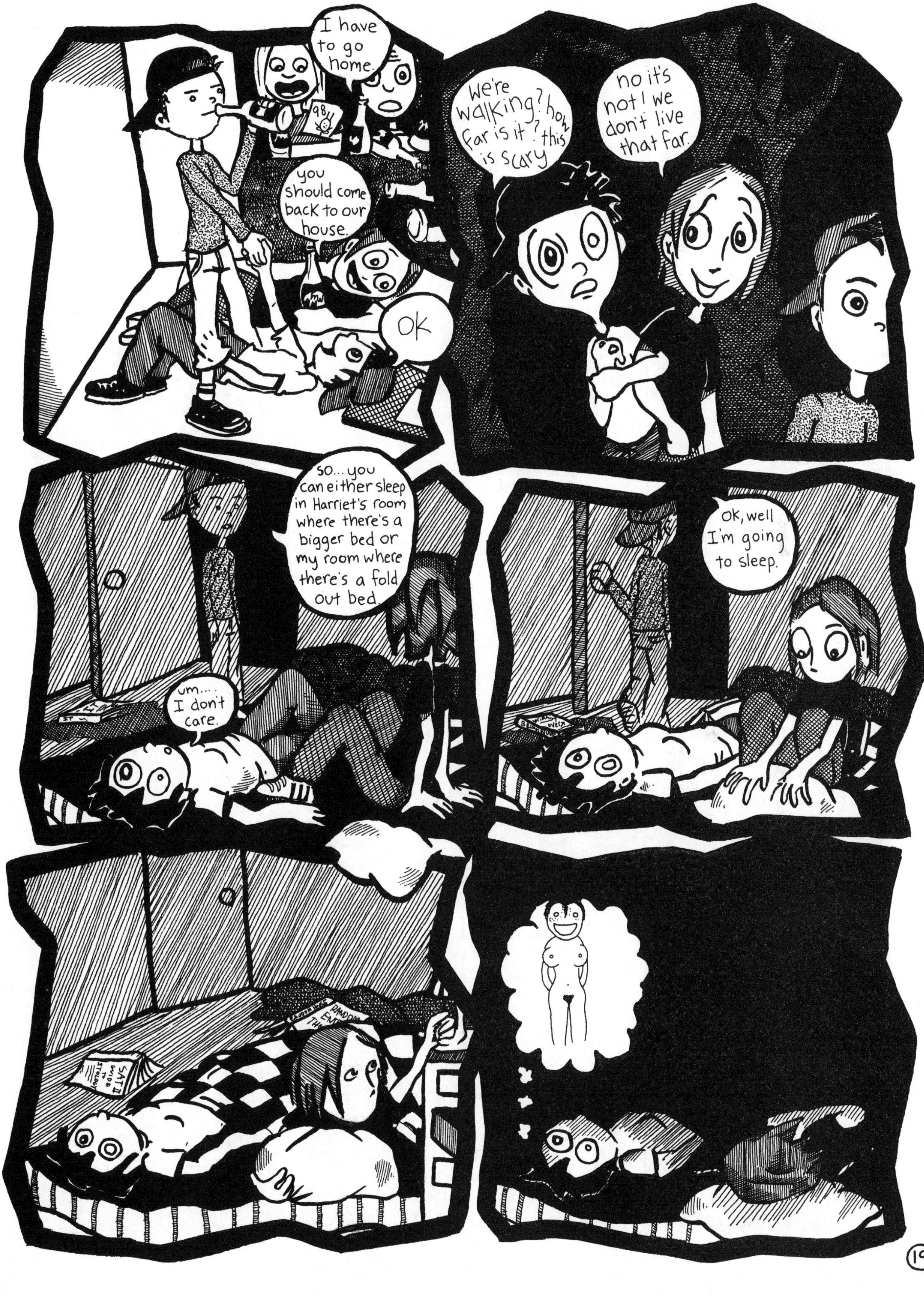
I have to go home.
you should come back to our house.
OK
we're walking? how far is it? this is scary
no it's not! we don't live that far.
so... you can either sleep in Harriet's room where there's a bigger bed or my room where there's a fold out bed.
um.... I don't care.
Ok, well I'm going to sleep.
SAT II Guide to Italian

today was Alexis and my one-month anniversary, and sure maybe I still barely knew who she was and every conversation was still awkward, an anniversary is an anniversary and that means potential secreting all over the place. We were gonna go to dinner and a movie, and as for the rest of the night, well, there's only so much you can do on an anniversary. yes indeed, the potential was so strong I could practically taste it.

OCTOBER

the plan was for Alexis and I to meet on Shattuck around 4:00, go do our dinner/movie thing and then meet Roberta, Noreena, and some others.

hi!

hey hon!

so what movie are we seeing again?

"Bound"! it's about two dykes that take on the mob! I can't wait!

SUNDAY BREAKFAST. EGGS OVER EASY!...

once we were in the theater Alexis started getting very into the movie, she sat with her legs spread wide open and proud.

I wondered if I too, could be so proud, and tried slowly parting my legs.

somehow I just couldn't seem to pull it off.

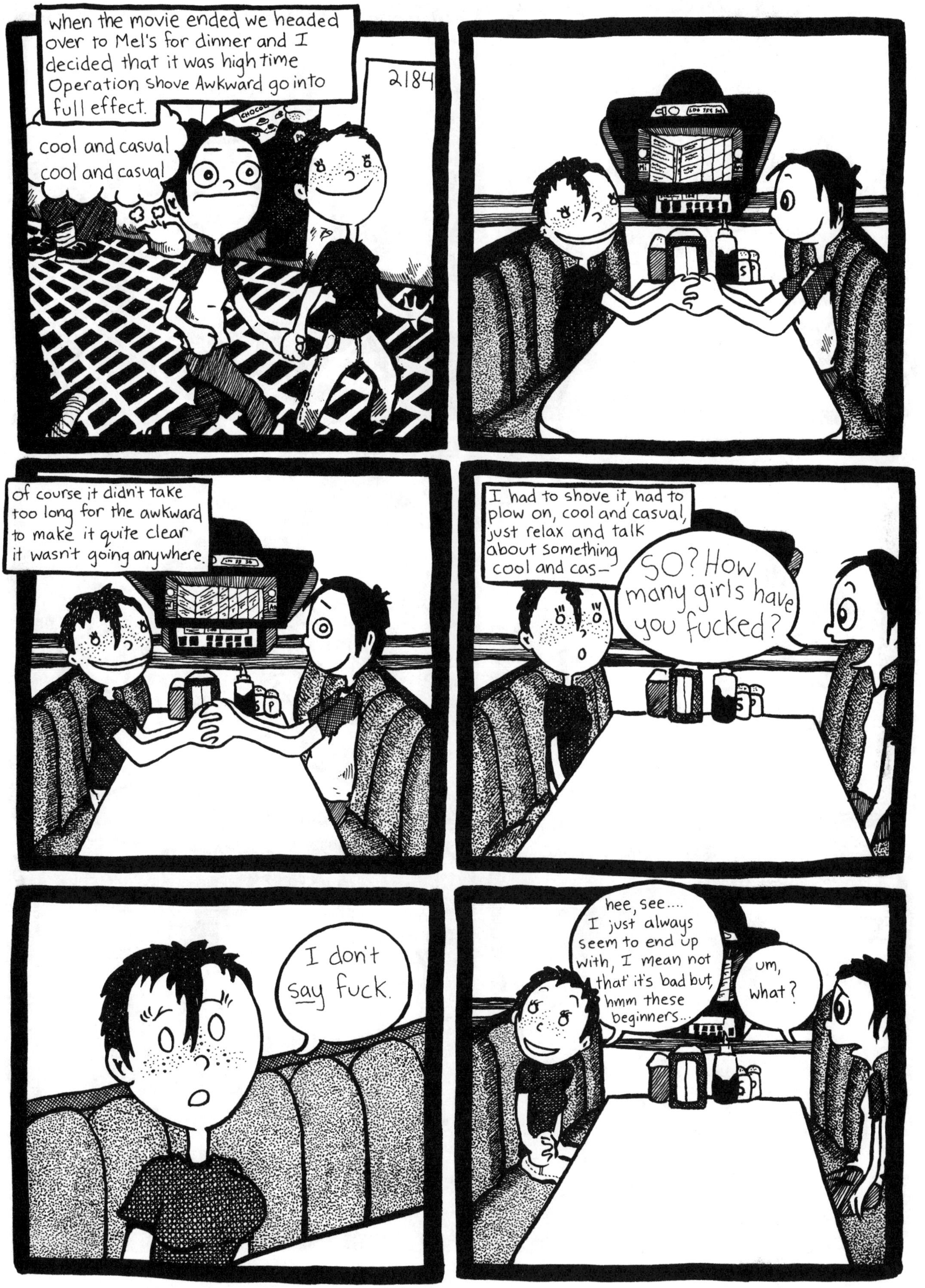

when the movie ended we headed over to Mel's for dinner and I decided that it was high time Operation shove Awkward go into full effect.
2184
cool and casual cool and casual
of course it didn't take too long for the awkward to make it quite clear it wasn't going anywhere.
I had to shove it, had to plow on, cool and casual, just relax and talk about something cool and cas–
SO? How many girls have you fucked?
I don't say fuck.
hee, see.... I just always seem to end up with, I mean not that it's bad but, hmm these beginners...
um, what?

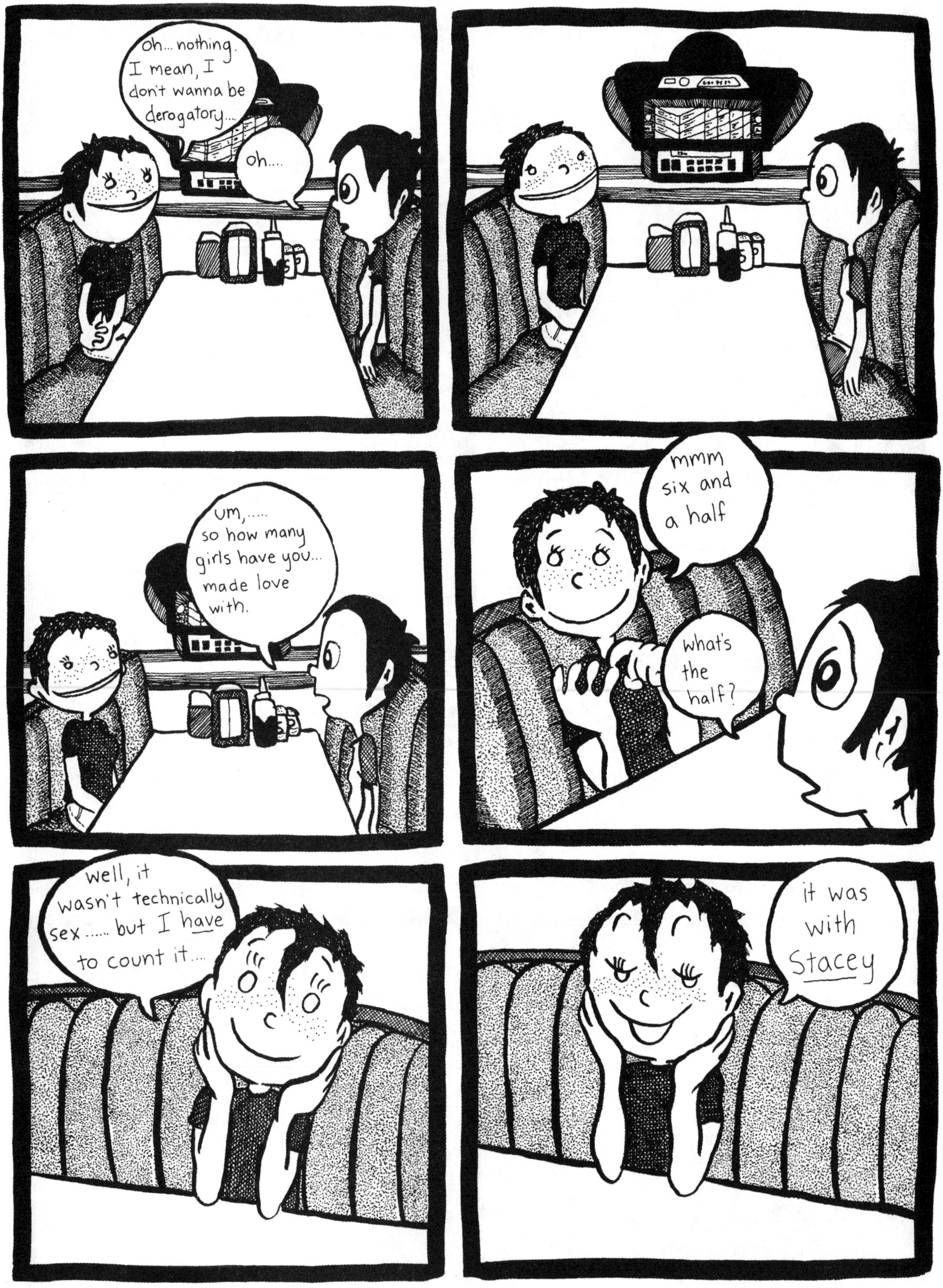
Oh... nothing. I mean, I don't wanna be derogatory....
oh....
Um,..... so how many girls have you... made love with.
mmm six and a half
what's the half?
well, it wasn't technically sex ...... but I have to count it....
it was with Stacey

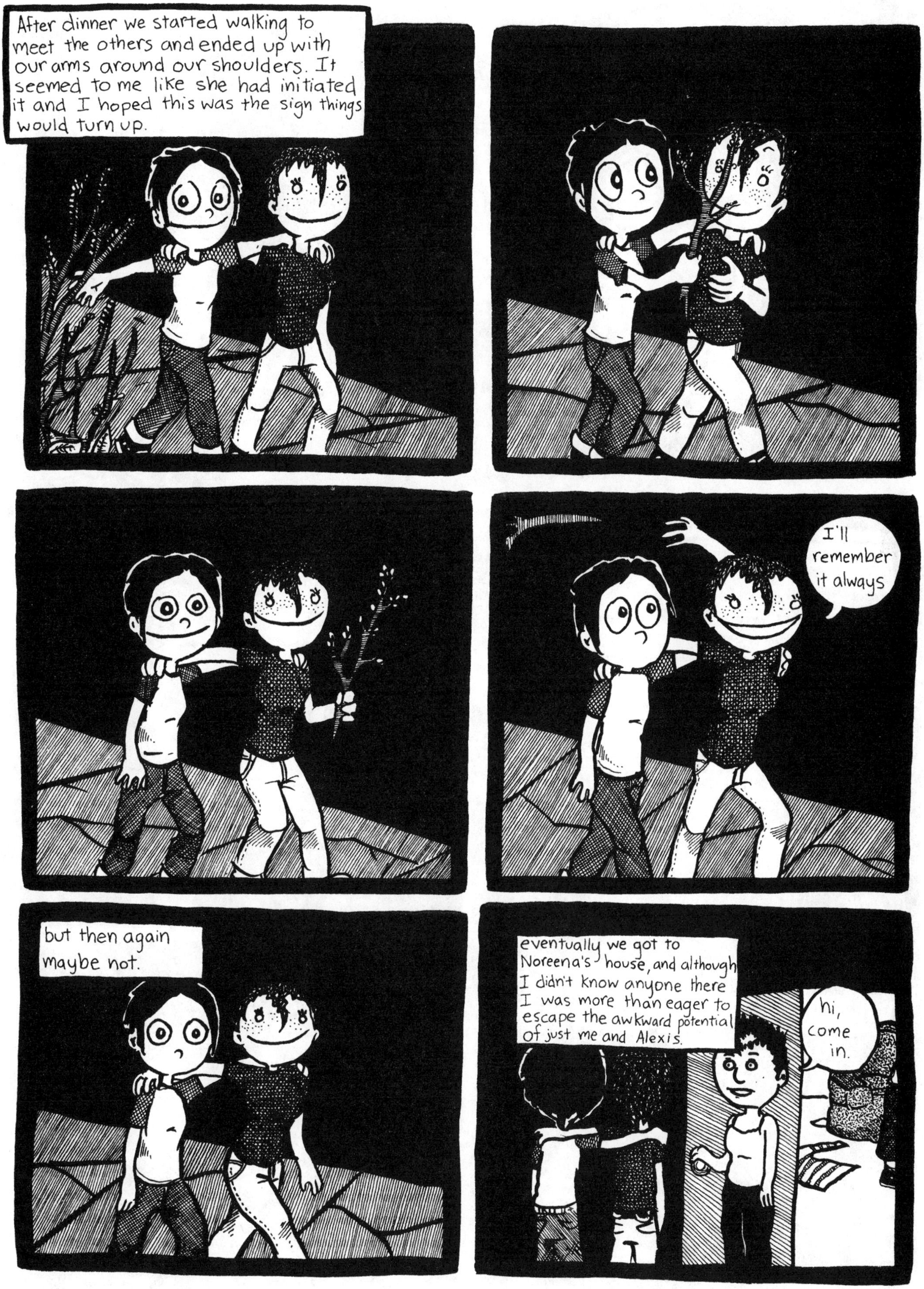
After dinner we started walking to meet the others and ended up with our arms around our shoulders. It seemed to me like she had initiated it and I hoped this was the sign things would turn up.
I'll remember it always
but then again maybe not.
eventually we got to Noreena's house, and although I didn't know anyone there I was more than eager to escape the awkward potential of just me and Alexis.
hi, come in.

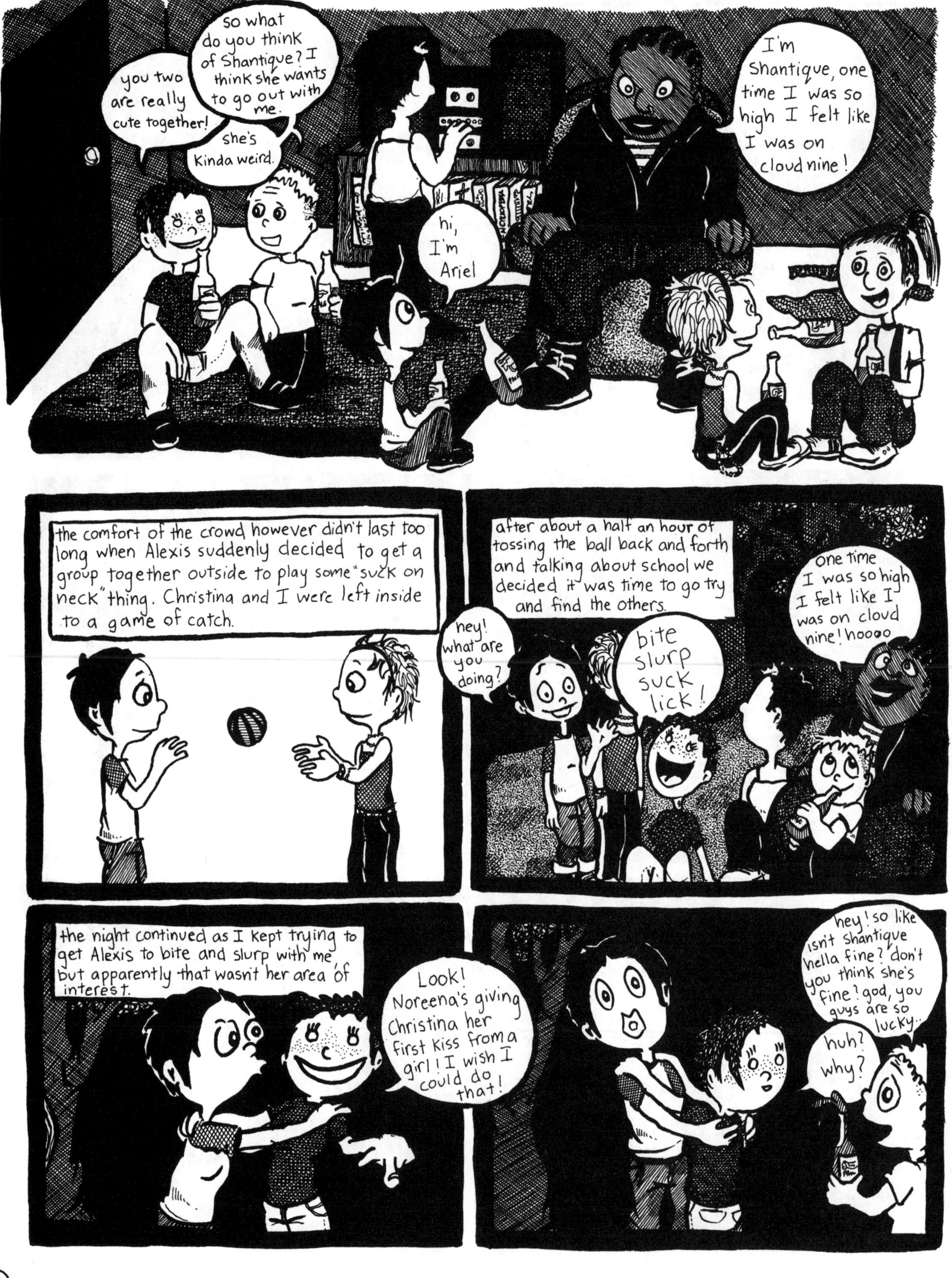
you two are really cute together!
so what do you think of Shantique? I think she wants to go out with me.
she's Kinda weird.
I'm Shantique, one time I was so high I felt like I was on cloud nine!
hi, I'm Ariel
the comfort of the crowd however didn't last too long when Alexis suddenly decided to get a group together outside to play some "suck on neck" thing. Christina and I were left inside to a game of catch.
after about a half an hour of tossing the ball back and forth and talking about school we decided it was time to go try and find the others.
hey! what are you doing?
bite slurp suck lick!
one time I was so high I felt like I was on cloud nine! hoooo
the night continued as I kept trying to get Alexis to bite and slurp with me, but apparently that wasn't her area of interest.
Look! Noreena's giving Christina her first kiss from a girl! I wish I could do that!
hey! so like isn't Shantique hella fine? don't you think she's fine? god, you guys are so lucky..
huh? why?

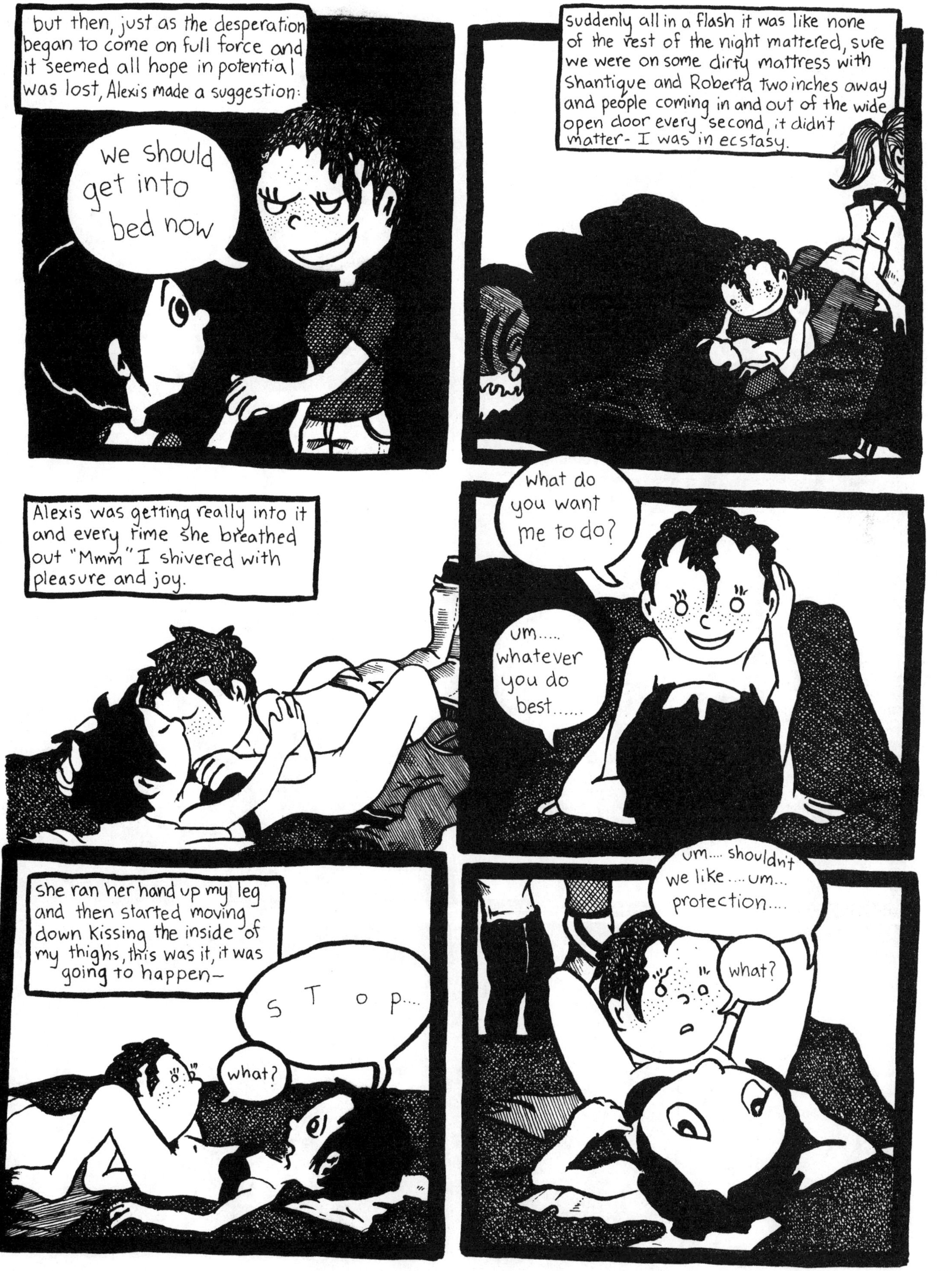
but then, just as the desperation began to come on full force and it seemed all hope in potential was lost, Alexis made a suggestion:
we should get into bed now
suddenly all in a flash it was like none of the rest of the night mattered, sure we were on some dirty mattress with Shantique and Roberta two inches away and people coming in and out of the wide open door every second, it didn't matter- I was in ecstasy.
Alexis was getting really into it and every time she breathed out "Mmm" I shivered with pleasure and joy.
what do you want me to do?
um..... whatever you do best......
she ran her hand up my leg and then started moving down kissing the inside of my thighs, this was it, it was going to happen-
S T O P....
what?
um.... shouldn't we like....um... protection....
what?

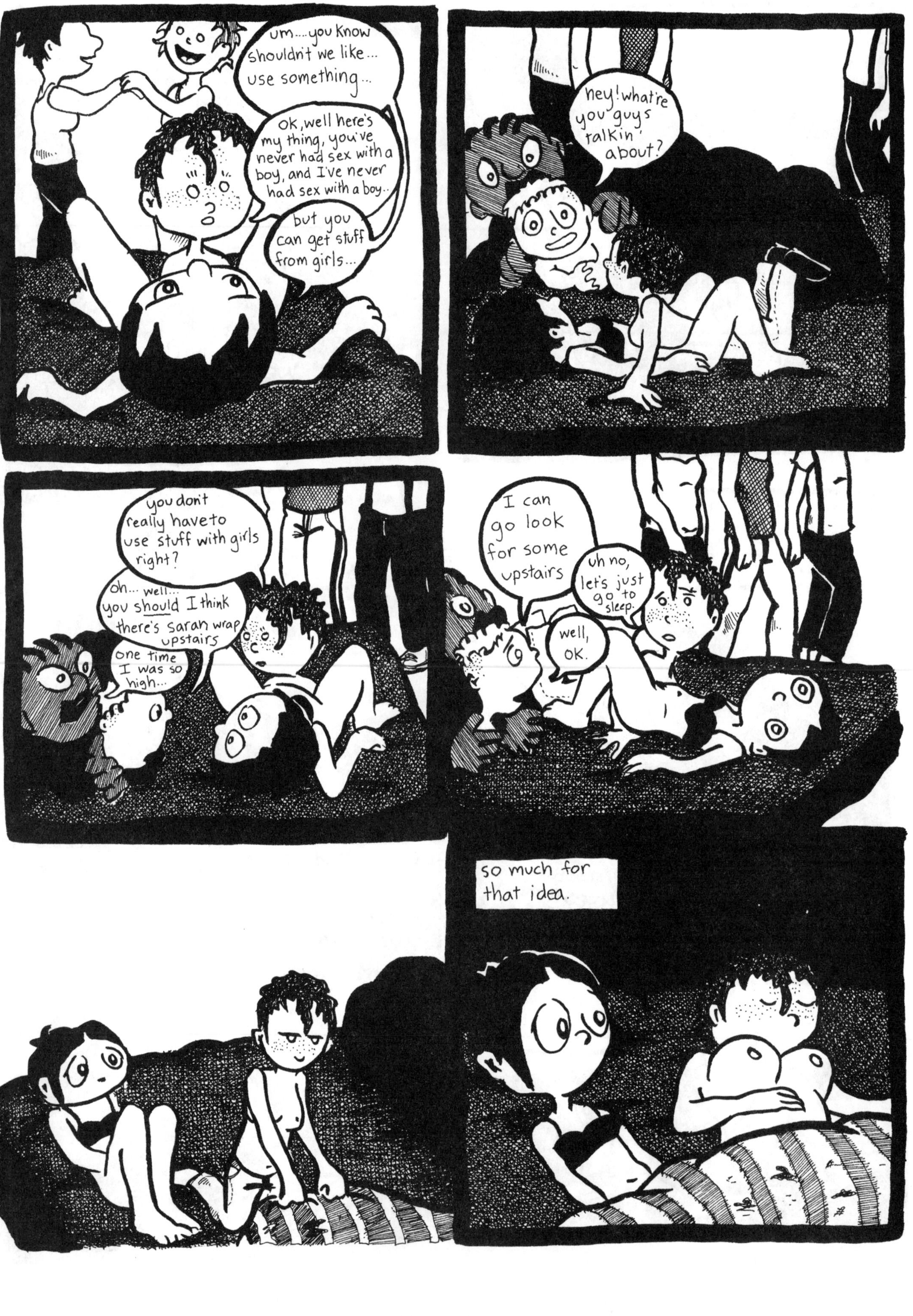
um....you know shouldn't we like... use something...
ok, well here's my thing, you've never had sex with a boy, and I've never had sex with a boy..
but you can get stuff from girls...
hey! what're you guys talkin' about?
you don't really have to use stuff with girls right?
oh... well... you should I think there's saran wrap upstairs
one time I was so high...
I can go look for some upstairs
uh no, let's just go to sleep.
well, OK.
so much for that idea.

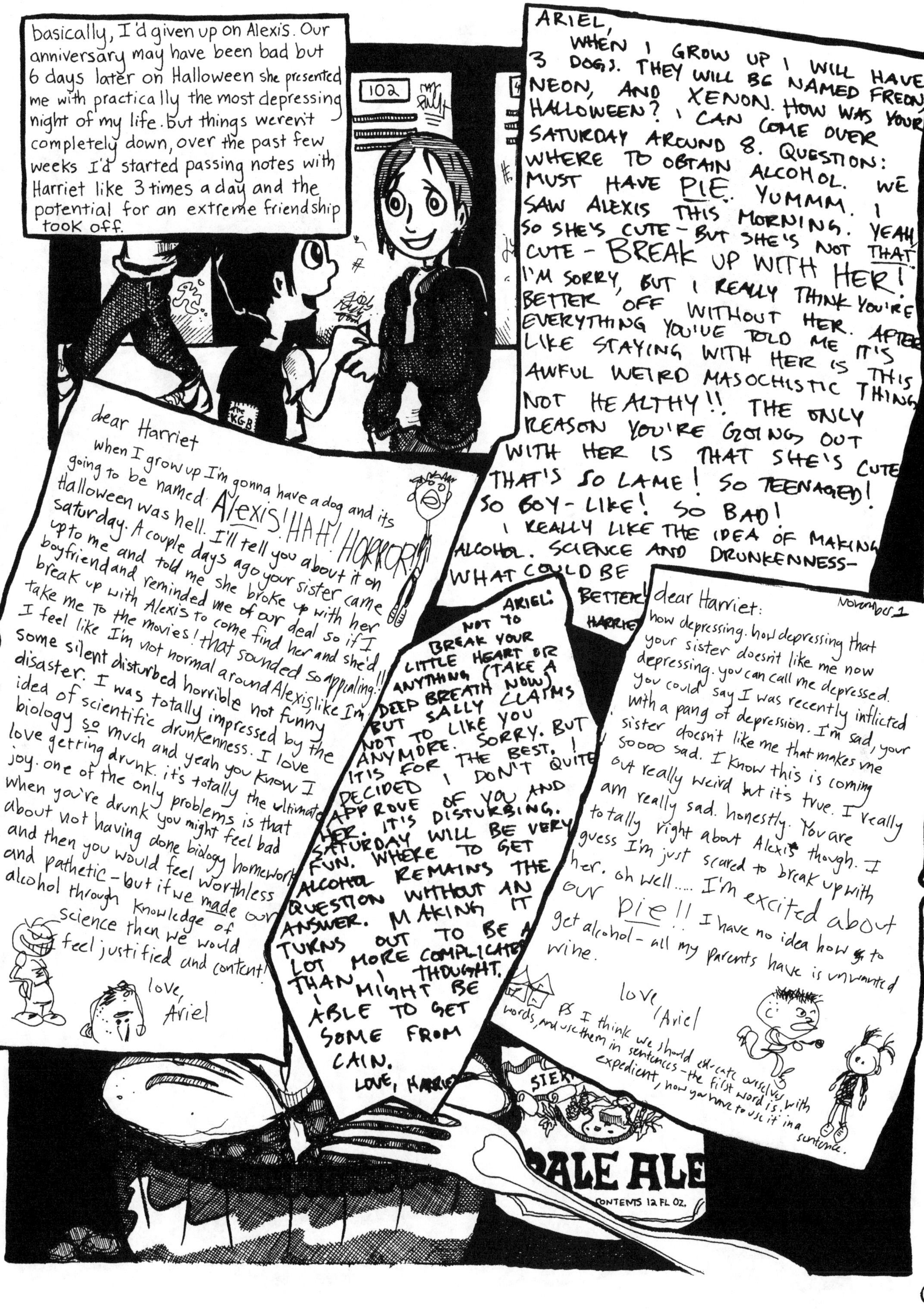
basically, I'd given up on Alexis. Our anniversary may have been bad but 6 days later on Halloween she presented me with practically the most depressing night of my life. But things weren't completely down, over the past few weeks I'd started passing notes with Harriet like 3 times a day and the potential for an extreme friendship took off.
102
ARIEL,
WHEN I GROW UP I WILL HAVE 3 DOGS. THEY WILL BE NAMED FREON, NEON, AND XENON. HOW WAS YOUR HALLOWEEN? I CAN COME OVER SATURDAY AROUND 8. QUESTION: WHERE TO OBTAIN ALCOHOL. WE MUST HAVE PIE. YUMMM. I SAW ALEXIS THIS MORNING. YEAH, SO SHE'S CUTE - BUT SHE'S NOT THAT CUTE - BREAK UP WITH HER! I'M SORRY, BUT I REALLY THINK YOU'RE BETTER OFF WITHOUT HER. AFTER EVERYTHING YOU'VE TOLD ME IT'S LIKE STAYING WITH HER IS THIS AWFUL WEIRD MASOCHISTIC THING. NOT HEALTHY!! THE ONLY REASON YOU'RE GOING OUT WITH HER IS THAT SHE'S CUTE. THAT'S SO LAME! SO TEENAGED! SO BOY-LIKE! SO BAD!
I REALLY LIKE THE IDEA OF MAKING ALCOHOL. SCIENCE AND DRUNKENNESS - WHAT COULD BE BETTER!
HARRIET
dear Harriet
when I grow up I'm gonna have a dog and its going to be named Alexis! HAH! HORROR!! Halloween was hell. I'll tell you about it on saturday. A couple days ago your sister came up to me and told me she broke up with her boyfriend and reminded me of our deal so if I break up with Alexis to come find her and she'd take me to the movies! that sounded so appealing!! I feel like I'm not normal around Alexis, like I'm some silent disturbed horrible not funny disaster. I was totally impressed by the idea of scientific drunkenness. I love biology so much and yeah you know I love getting drunk. it's totally the ultimate joy. one of the only problems is that when you're drunk you might feel bad about not having done biology homework and then you would feel worthless and pathetic - but if we made our alcohol through knowledge of science then we would feel justified and content!
love,
Ariel
ARIEL:
NOT TO BREAK YOUR LITTLE HEART OR ANYTHING (TAKE A DEEP BREATH NOW) BUT SALLY CLAIMS NOT TO LIKE YOU ANYMORE. SORRY. BUT IT IS FOR THE BEST. I DECIDED I DON'T QUITE APPROVE OF YOU AND HER. IT'S DISTURBING. SATURDAY WILL BE VERY FUN. WHERE TO GET ALCOHOL REMAINS THE QUESTION WITHOUT AN ANSWER. MAKING IT TURNS OUT TO BE A LOT MORE COMPLICATED THAN I THOUGHT. I MIGHT BE ABLE TO GET SOME FROM CAIN.
LOVE, HARRIET
dear Harriet:
November 1
how depressing. how depressing that your sister doesn't like me now depressing. you can call me depressed. you could say I was recently inflicted with a pang of depression. I'm sad, your sister doesn't like me that makes me soooo sad. I know this is coming out really weird but its true. I really am really sad. honestly. You are totally right about Alexis though. I guess I'm just scared to break up with her. oh well..... I'm excited about our pie!! I have no idea how to get alcohol - all my parents have is unwanted wine.
love,
Ariel
PS I think we should educate ourselves with words, and use them in sentences - the first word is: expedient, now you have to use it in a sentence.
PALE ALE
CONTENTS 12 FL OZ.

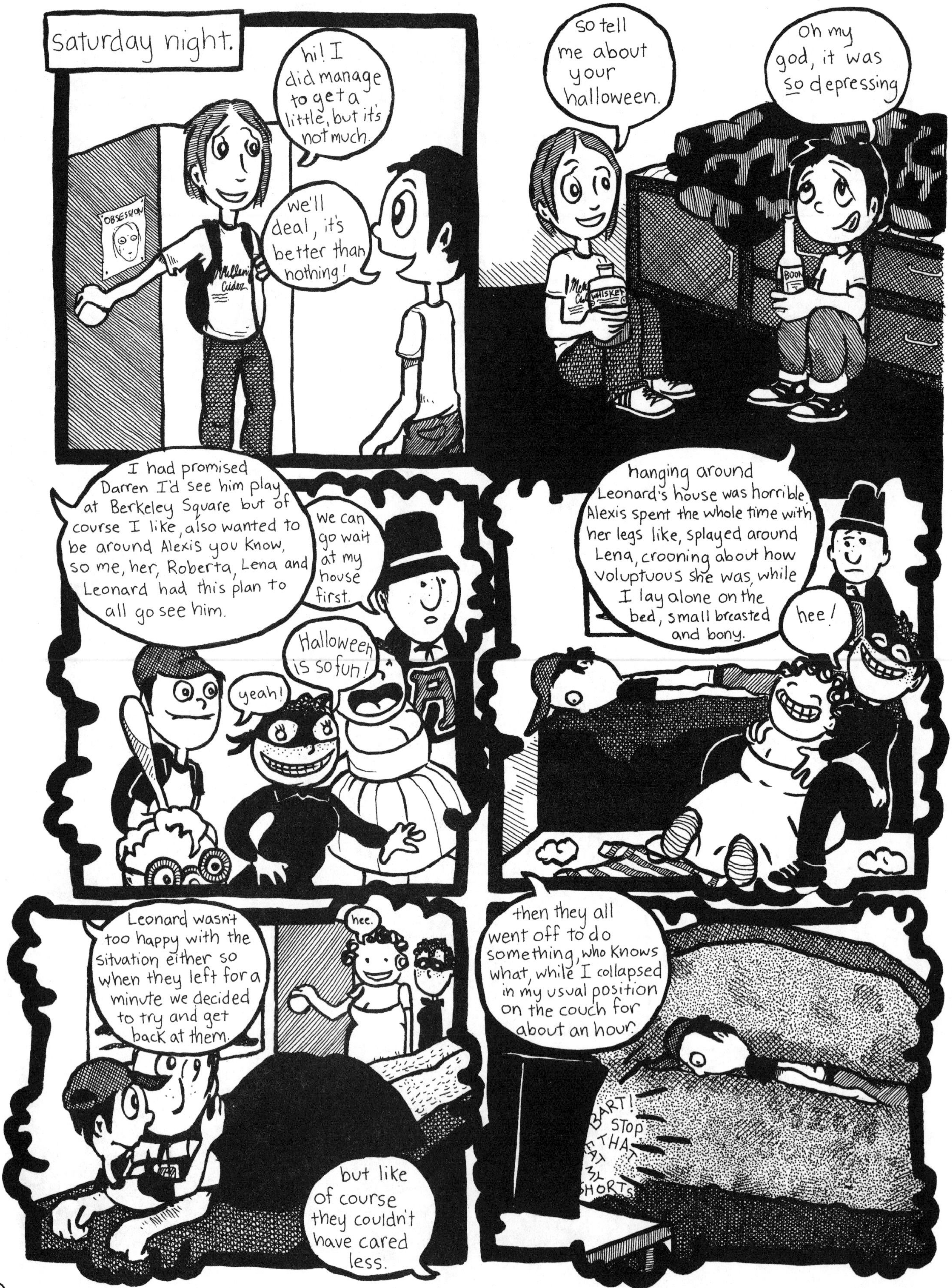
saturday night.
hi! I did manage to get a little, but it's not much.
we'll deal, it's better than nothing!
OBSESSION
Millenia Cidez
so tell me about your halloween.
Oh my god, it was so depressing
WHISKEY
BOON
I had promised Darren I'd see him play at Berkeley Square but of course I like, also wanted to be around Alexis you know, so me, her, Roberta, Lena and Leonard had this plan to all go see him.
We can go wait at my house first.
Halloween is so fun!
yeah!
hanging around Leonard's house was horrible. Alexis spent the whole time with her legs like, splayed around Lena, crooning about how voluptuous she was, while I lay alone on the bed, small breasted and bony.
hee!
Leonard wasn't too happy with the situation either so when they left for a minute we decided to try and get back at them.
hee.
but like of course they couldn't have cared less.
then they all went off to do something, who knows what, while I collapsed in my usual position on the couch for about an hour.
BART! STOP THAT EAT MY SHORTS

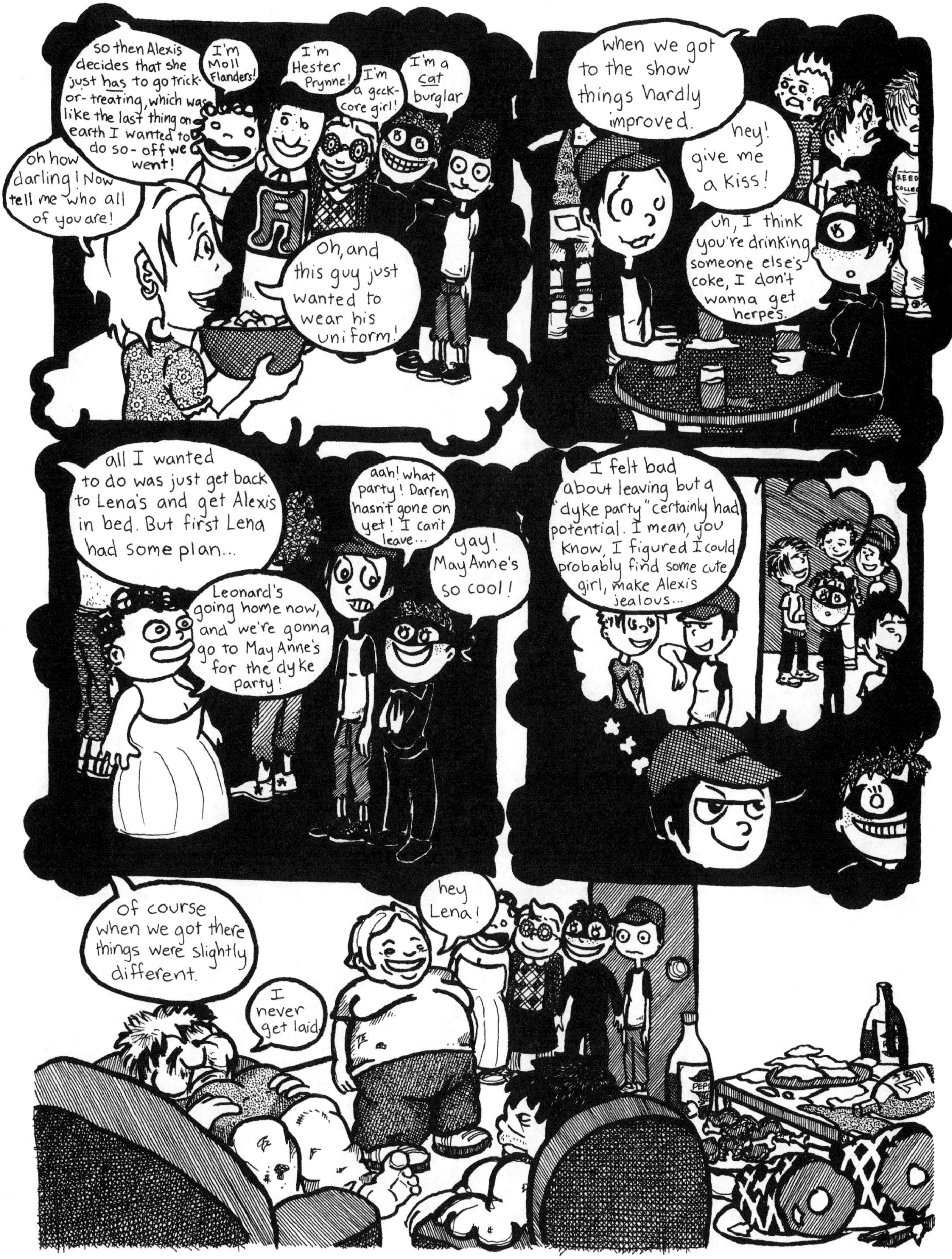
so then Alexis decides that she just has to go trick-or-treating, which was like the last thing on earth I wanted to do so- off we went!
I'm Moll Flanders!
I'm Hester Prynne!
I'm a geek-core girl!
I'm a cat burglar
oh how darling! Now tell me who all of you are!
Oh, and this guy just wanted to wear his uniform!
when we got to the show things hardly improved.
hey! give me a kiss!
uh, I think you're drinking someone else's coke, I don't wanna get herpes.
REED COLLEGE
all I wanted to do was just get back to Lena's and get Alexis in bed. But first Lena had some plan...
aah! what party! Darren hasn't gone on yet! I can't leave...
yay! May Anne's so cool!
Leonard's going home now, and we're gonna go to May Anne's for the dyke party!
I felt bad about leaving but a "dyke party" certainly had potential. I mean, you know, I figured I could probably find some cute girl, make Alexis jealous...
of course when we got there things were slightly different.
hey Lena!
I never get laid

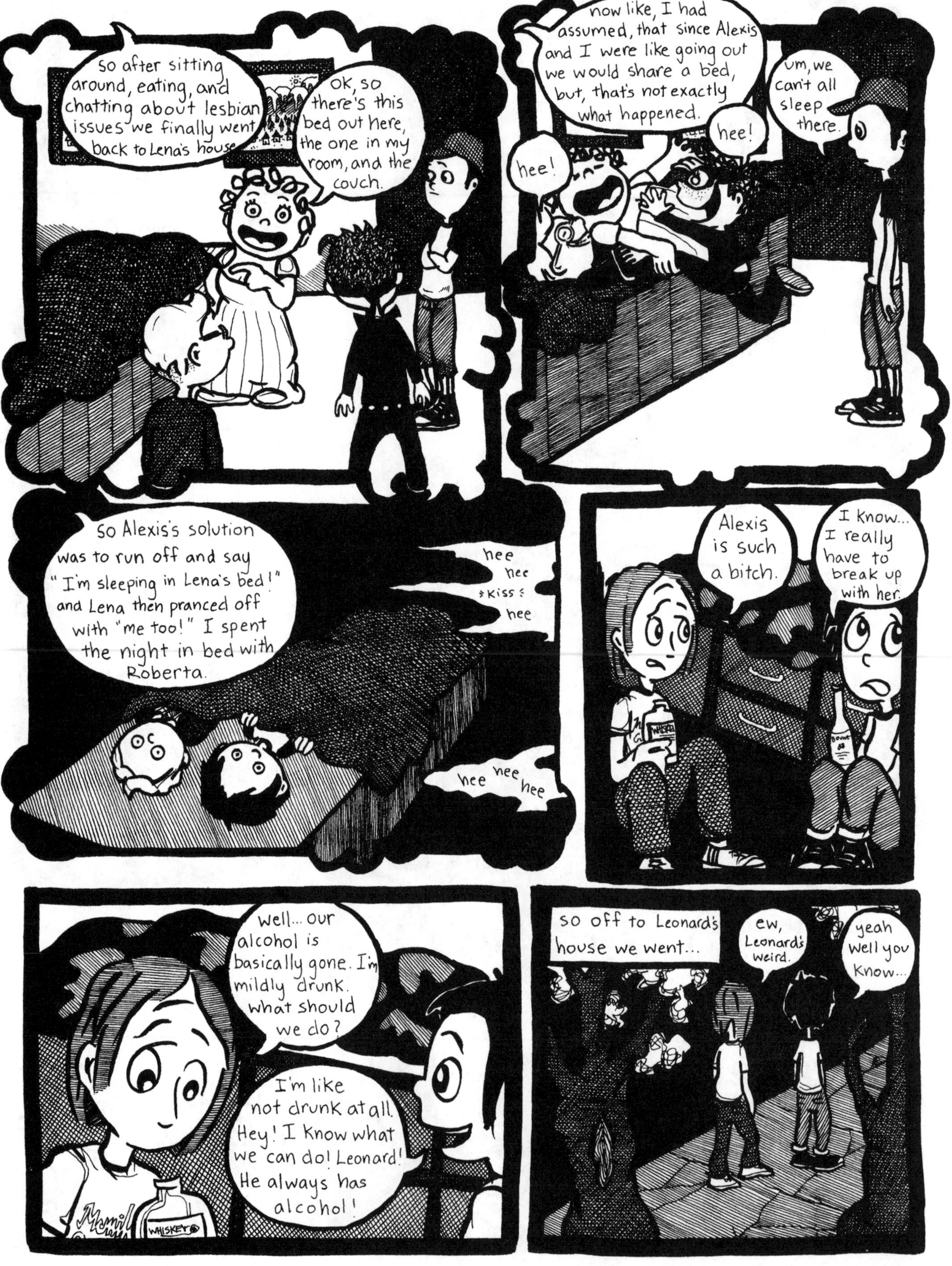
so after sitting around, eating, and chatting about lesbian issues we finally went back to Lena's house.
Ok, so there's this bed out here, the one in my room, and the couch.
now like, I had assumed, that since Alexis and I were like going out we would share a bed, but, that's not exactly what happened.
hee!
hee!
um, we can't all sleep there.
So Alexis's solution was to run off and say "I'm sleeping in Lena's bed!" and Lena then pranced off with "me too!" I spent the night in bed with Roberta.
hee
hee
kiss
hee
hee hee hee
Alexis is such a bitch.
I know... I really have to break up with her.
well... our alcohol is basically gone. I'm mildly drunk. what should we do?
I'm like not drunk at all. Hey! I know what we can do! Leonard! He always has alcohol!
so off to Leonard's house we went...
ew, Leonard's weird.
yeah well you know...

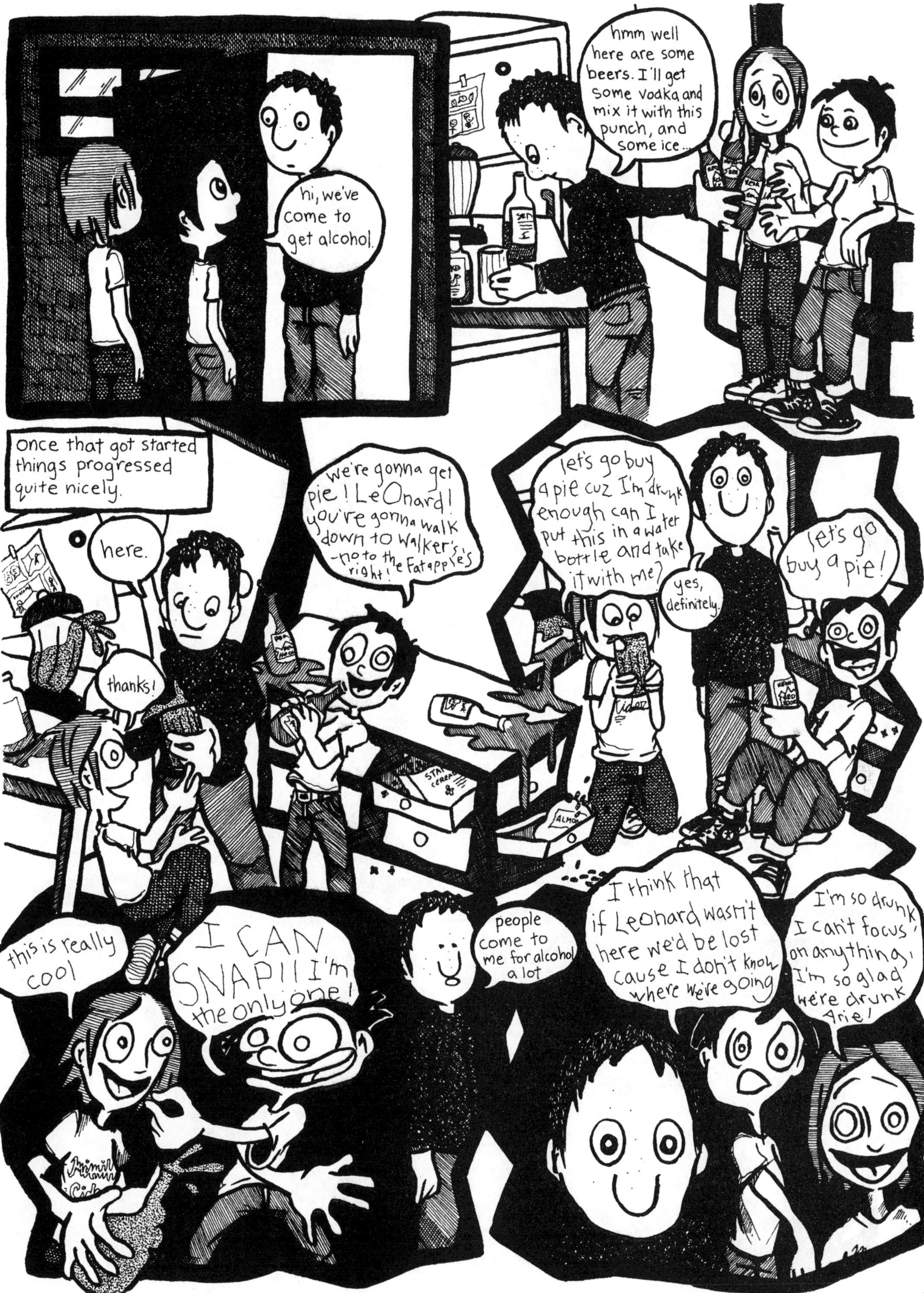
hi, we've come to get alcohol.
hmm well here are some beers. I'll get some vodka and mix it with this punch, and some ice...
once that got started things progressed quite nicely.
here.
thanks!
we're gonna get pie! LeOnard! you're gonna walk down to Walker's -no to the Fatapple's right!
let's go buy a pie cuz I'm drunk enough can I put this in a water bottle and take it with me?
yes, definitely.
let's go buy a pie!
this is really cool
I CAN SNAP!! I'm the only one!
people come to me for alcohol a lot
I think that if Leonard wasn't here we'd be lost cause I don't know where we're going
I'm so drunk I can't focus on anything, I'm so glad we're drunk Arie!

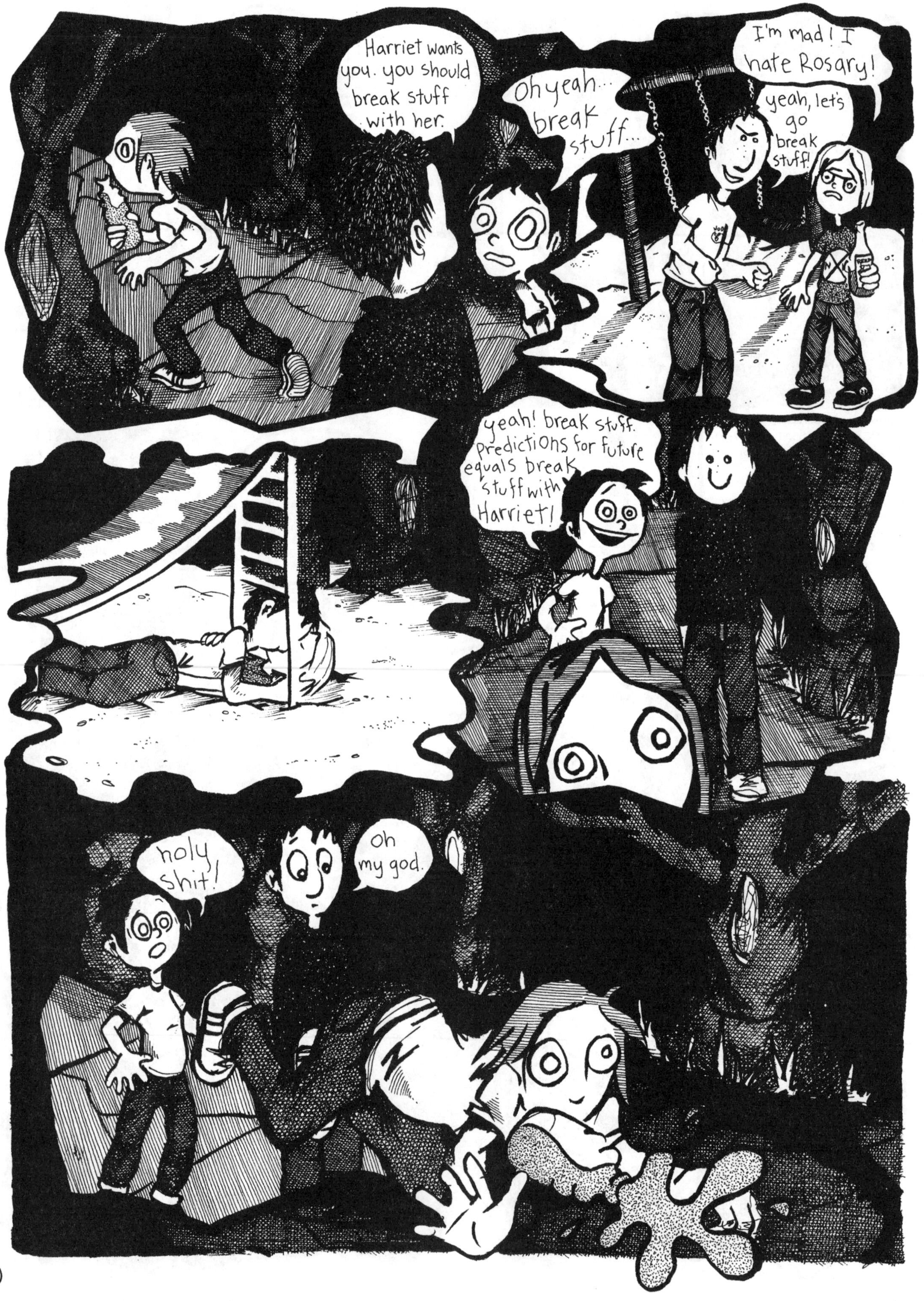
Harriet wants you. you should break stuff with her.
Oh yeah... break stuff...
I'm mad! I hate Rosary!
yeah, let's go break stuff!
yeah! break stuff. predictions for future equals break stuff with Harriet!
holy shit!
oh my god.

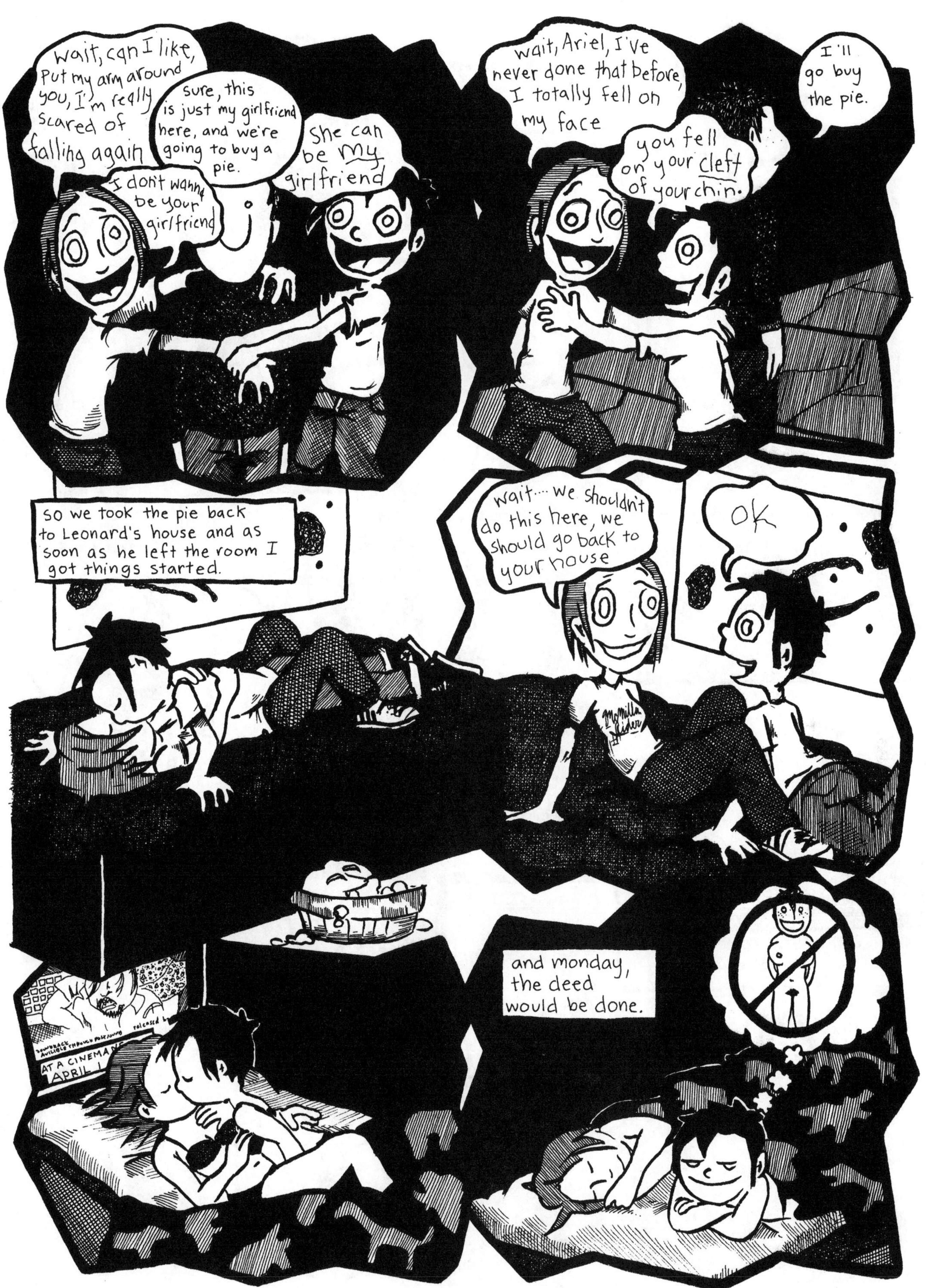
wait, can I like, put my arm around you, I'm really scared of falling again
Sure, this is just my girlfriend here, and we're going to buy a pie.
She can be my girlfriend
I don't wanna be your girlfriend
wait, Ariel, I've never done that before, I totally fell on my face
you fell on your cleft of your chin.
I'll go buy the pie.
so we took the pie back to Leonard's house and as soon as he left the room I got things started.
wait.... we shouldn't do this here, we should go back to your house
OK
and monday, the deed would be done.

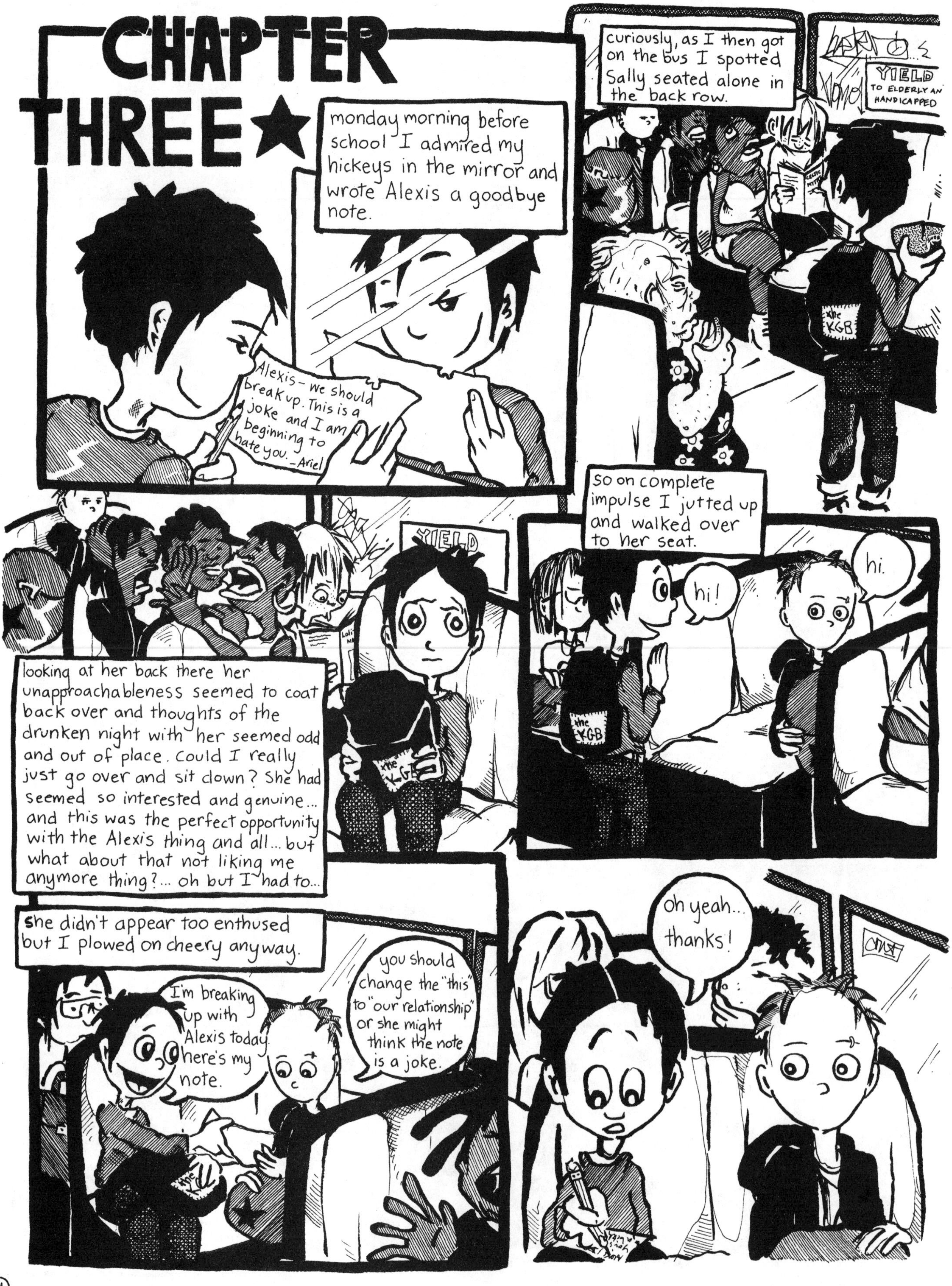
CHAPTER THREE
monday morning before school I admired my hickeys in the mirror and wrote Alexis a goodbye note.
Alexis- we should break up. This is a joke and I am beginning to hate you. -Ariel
curiously, as I then got on the bus I spotted Sally seated alone in the back row.
YIELD TO ELDERLY AND HANDICAPPED
the KGB
YIELD
looking at her back there her unapproachableness seemed to coat back over and thoughts of the drunken night with her seemed odd and out of place. Could I really just go over and sit down? She had seemed so interested and genuine... and this was the perfect opportunity with the Alexis thing and all... but what about that not liking me anymore thing?... oh but I had to...
the KGB
so on complete impulse I jutted up and walked over to her seat.
hi!
hi.
the KGB
She didn't appear too enthused but I plowed on cheery anyway.
I'm breaking up with Alexis today. here's my note.
you should change the "this" to "our relationship" or she might think the note is a joke.
oh yeah.. thanks!

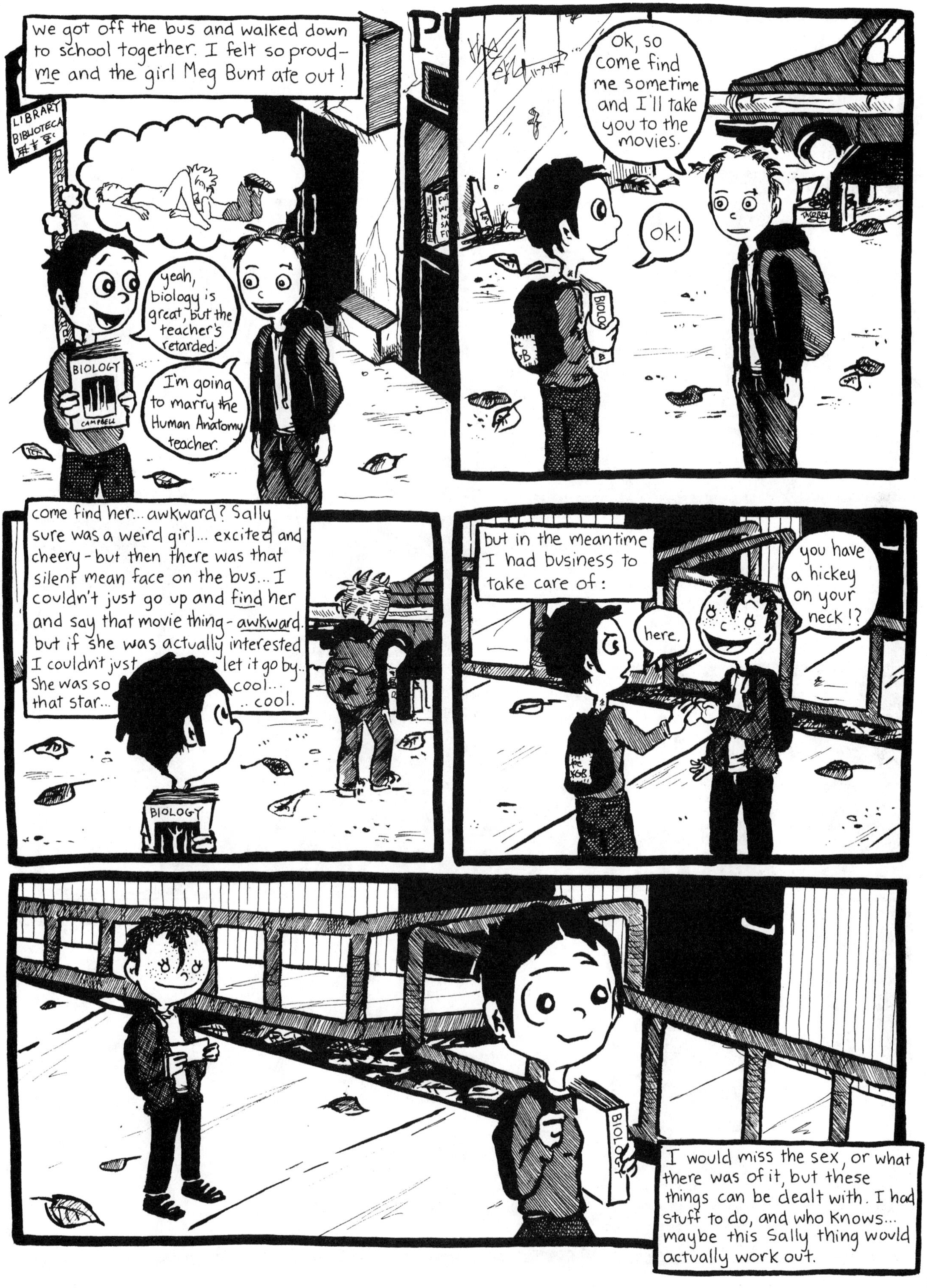
we got off the bus and walked down to school together. I felt so proud- me and the girl Meg Bunt ate out!
LIBRARY
BIBLIOTECA
yeah, biology is great, but the teacher's retarded.
I'm going to marry the Human Anatomy teacher.
BIOLOGY
CAMPBELL
Ok, so come find me sometime and I'll take you to the movies.
OK!
come find her... awkward? Sally sure was a weird girl... excited and cheery - but then there was that silent mean face on the bus... I couldn't just go up and find her and say that movie thing - awkward. but if she was actually interested I couldn't just let it go by.. She was so cool... that star... ..cool.
BIOLOGY
but in the meantime I had business to take care of:
here.
you have a hickey on your neck!?
I would miss the sex, or what there was of it, but these things can be dealt with. I had stuff to do, and who knows... maybe this Sally thing would actually work out.

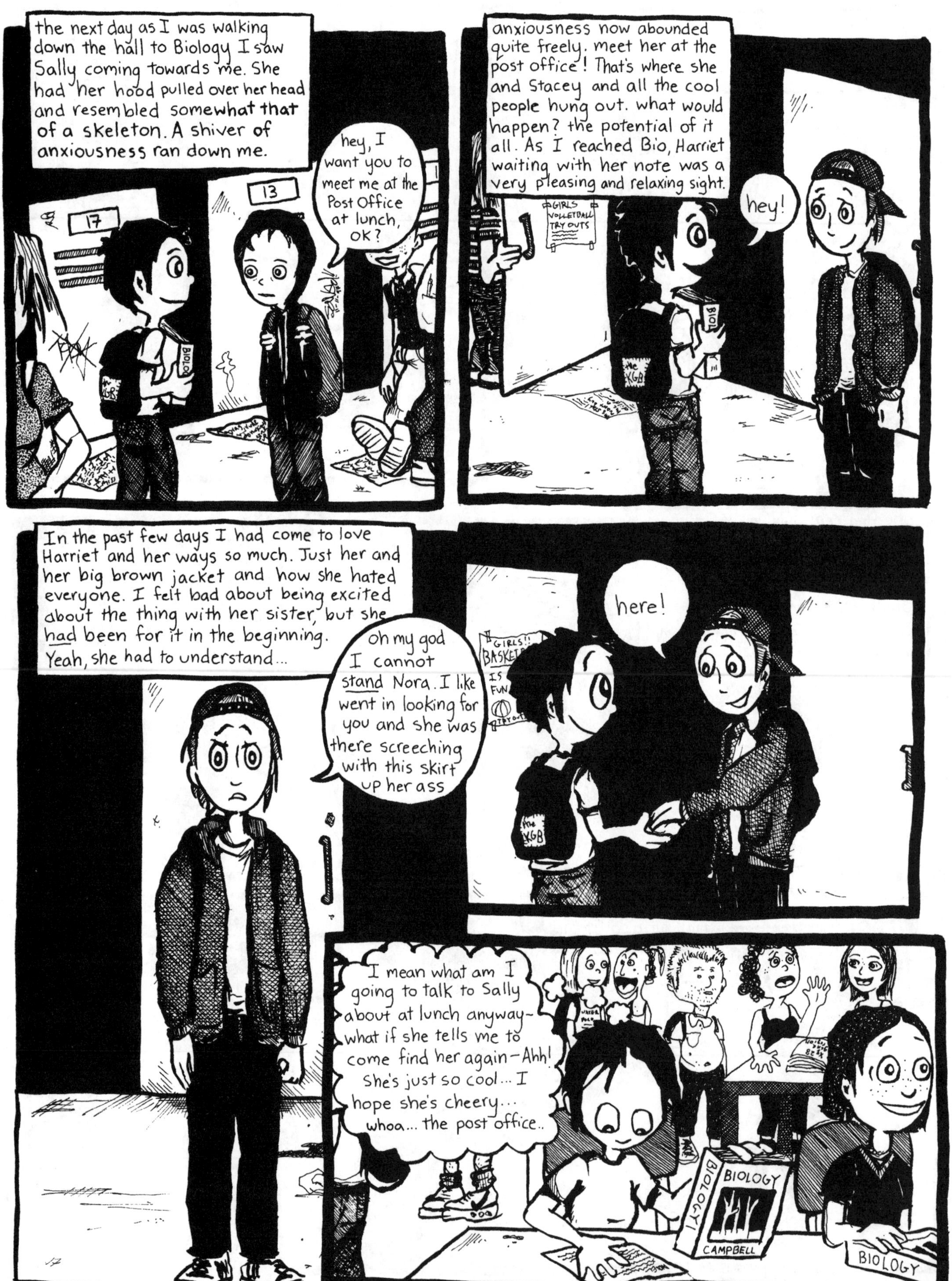
the next day as I was walking down the hall to Biology I saw Sally coming towards me. She had her hood pulled over her head and resembled somewhat that of a skeleton. A shiver of anxiousness ran down me.
17
13
hey, I want you to meet me at the Post Office at lunch, ok?
anxiousness now abounded quite freely. meet her at the post office! That's where she and Stacey and all the cool people hung out. what would happen? the potential of it all. As I reached Bio, Harriet waiting with her note was a very pleasing and relaxing sight.
GIRLS VOLLEYBALL TRY OUTS
hey!
In the past few days I had come to love Harriet and her ways so much. Just her and her big brown jacket and how she hated everyone. I felt bad about being excited about the thing with her sister, but she had been for it in the beginning. Yeah, she had to understand...
oh my god I cannot stand Nora. I like went in looking for you and she was there screeching with this skirt up her ass
here!
I mean what am I going to talk to Sally about at lunch anyway- what if she tells me to come find her again-Ahh! She's just so cool... I hope she's cheery... whoa... the post office..
BIOLOGY
CAMPBELL
BIOLOGY

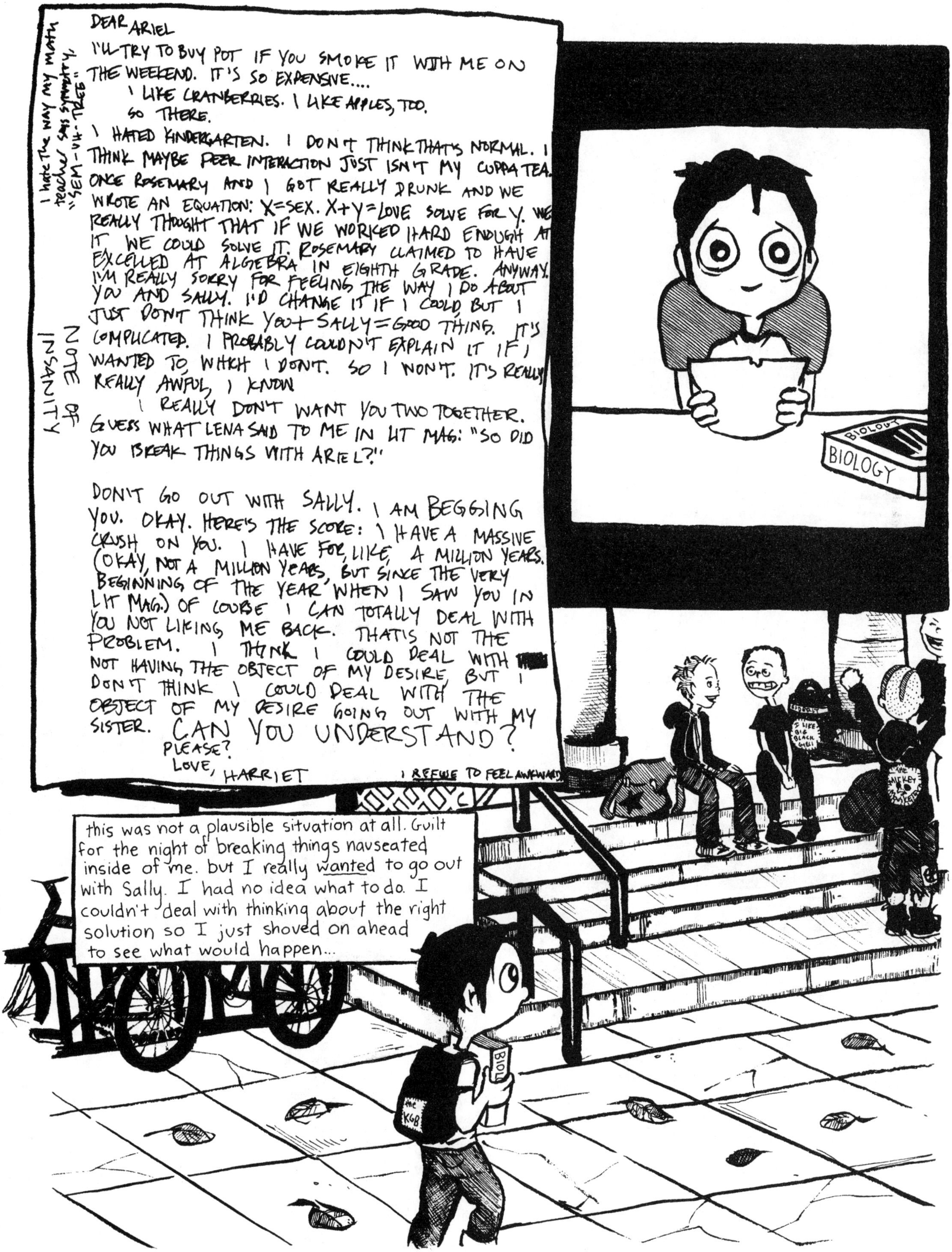
DEAR ARIEL
I'LL TRY TO BUY POT IF YOU SMOKE IT WITH ME ON THE WEEKEND. IT'S SO EXPENSIVE....
I LIKE CRANBERRIES. I LIKE APPLES, TOO. SO THERE.
I HATED KINDERGARTEN. I DON'T THINK THAT'S NORMAL. I THINK MAYBE PEER INTERACTION JUST ISN'T MY CUPPA TEA. ONCE ROSEMARY AND I GOT REALLY DRUNK AND WE WROTE AN EQUATION: X=SEX. X+Y=LOVE SOLVE FOR Y. WE REALLY THOUGHT THAT IF WE WORKED HARD ENOUGH AT IT WE COULD SOLVE IT. ROSEMARY CLAIMED TO HAVE EXCELLED AT ALGEBRA IN EIGHTH GRADE. ANYWAY. I'M REALLY SORRY FOR FEELING THE WAY I DO ABOUT YOU AND SALLY. I'D CHANGE IT IF I COULD BUT I JUST DON'T THINK YOU+SALLY=GOOD THING. IT'S COMPLICATED. I PROBABLY COULDN'T EXPLAIN IT IF I WANTED TO, WHICH I DON'T. SO I WON'T. IT'S REALLY REALLY AWFUL, I KNOW.
I REALLY DON'T WANT YOU TWO TOGETHER. GUESS WHAT LENA SAID TO ME IN LIT MAG: "SO DID YOU BREAK THINGS WITH ARIEL?"
DON'T GO OUT WITH SALLY. I AM BEGGING YOU. OKAY. HERE'S THE SCORE: I HAVE A MASSIVE CRUSH ON YOU. I HAVE FOR, LIKE, A MILLION YEARS. (OKAY, NOT A MILLION YEARS, BUT SINCE THE VERY BEGINNING OF THE YEAR WHEN I SAW YOU IN LIT MAG.) OF COURSE I CAN TOTALLY DEAL WITH YOU NOT LIKING ME BACK. THAT'S NOT THE PROBLEM. I THINK I COULD DEAL WITH NOT HAVING THE OBJECT OF MY DESIRE, BUT I DON'T THINK I COULD DEAL WITH THE OBJECT OF MY DESIRE GOING OUT WITH MY SISTER. CAN YOU UNDERSTAND?
PLEASE?
LOVE, HARRIET
I REFUSE TO FEEL AWKWARD
I hate the way my math teacher says symmetry, "SEM-uh-TREE"
NOTE OF INSANITY
BIOLOGY
BIOLOGY
this was not a plausible situation at all. Guilt for the night of breaking things nauseated inside of me. but I really wanted to go out with Sally. I had no idea what to do. I couldn't deal with thinking about the right solution so I just shoved on ahead to see what would happen...

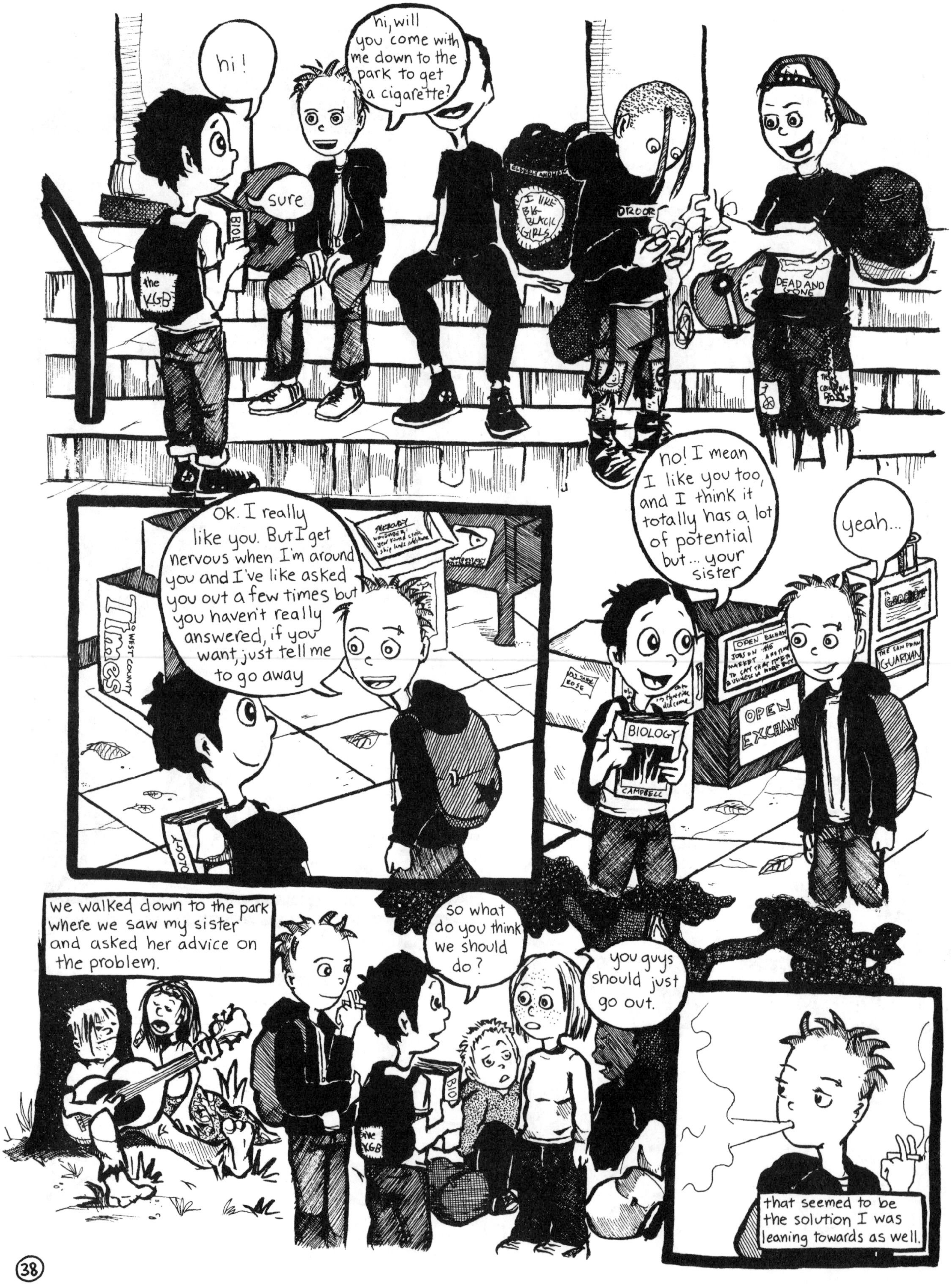
hi!
hi, will you come with me down to the park to get a cigarette?
sure
OK. I really like you. But I get nervous when I'm around you and I've like asked you out a few times but you haven't really answered, if you want, just tell me to go away
no! I mean I like you too, and I think it totally has a lot of potential but... your sister
yeah...
BIOLOGY
CAMPBELL
OPEN EXCHANGE
We walked down to the park where we saw my sister and asked her advice on the problem.
so what do you think we should do?
you guys should just go out.
that seemed to be the solution I was leaning towards as well.

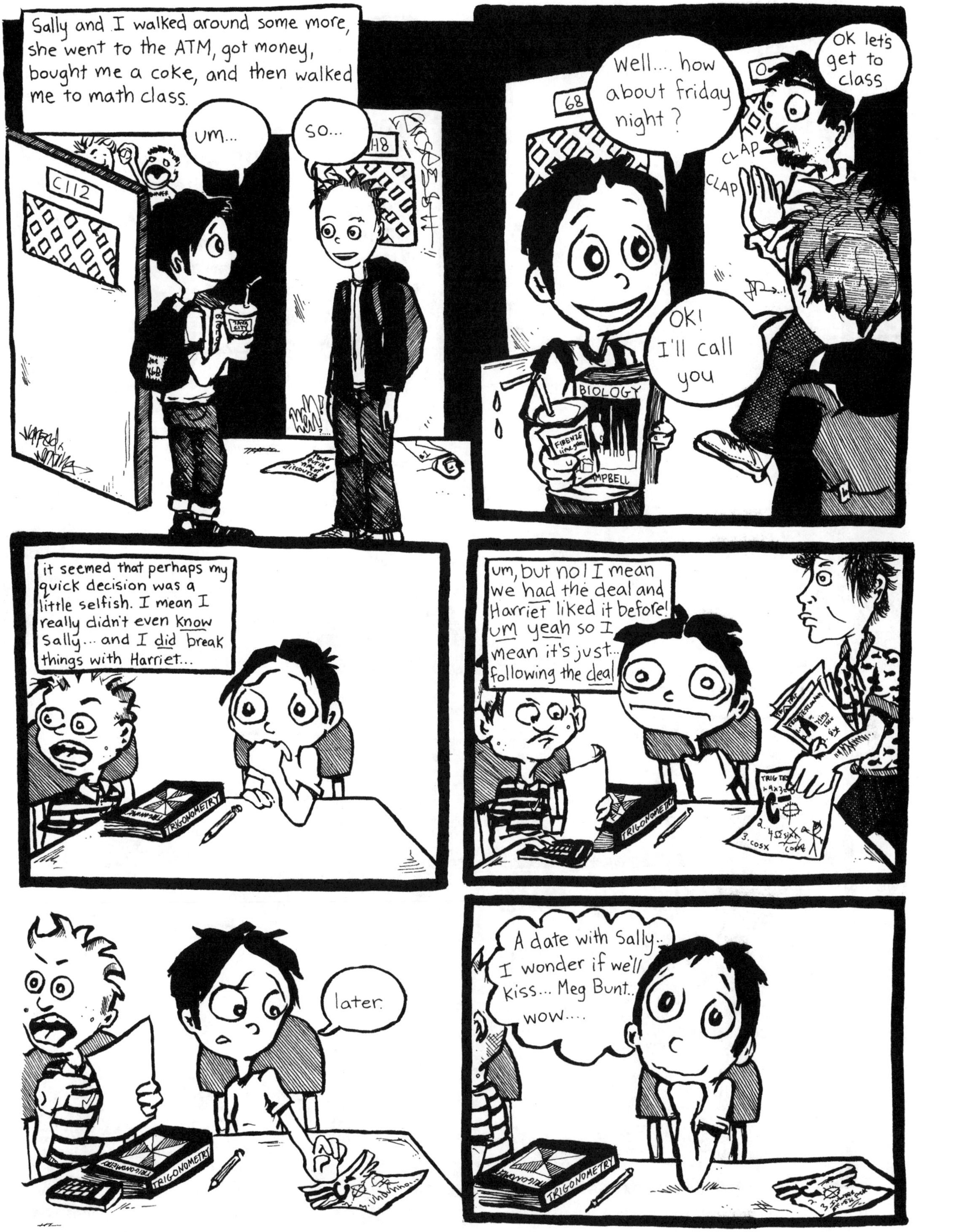
Sally and I walked around some more, she went to the ATM, got money, bought me a coke, and then walked me to math class.
um...
so...
Well.... how about friday night?
OK let's get to class
CLAP
CLAP
OK! I'll call you
BIOLOGY
it seemed that perhaps my quick decision was a little selfish. I mean I really didn't even know Sally... and I did break things with Harriet...
TRIGONOMETRY
um, but no! I mean we had the deal and Harriet liked it before! um yeah so I mean it's just... following the deal
TRIGONOMETRY
later.
TRIGONOMETRY
A date with Sally.. I wonder if we'll kiss... Meg Bunt.. wow....
TRIGONOMETRY

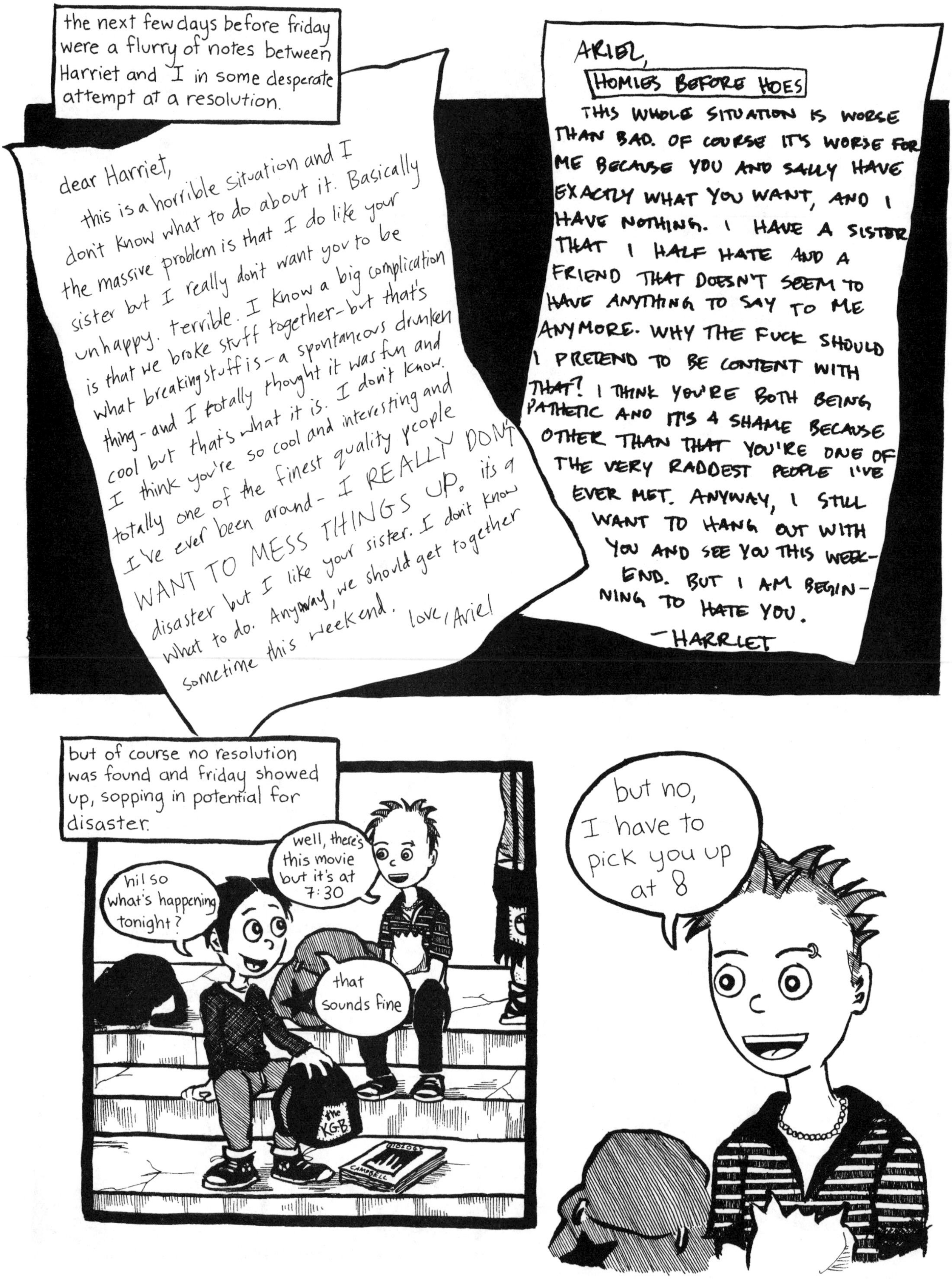

the next few days before friday were a flurry of notes between Harriet and I in some desperate attempt at a resolution.
dear Harriet,
this is a horrible situation and I don't know what to do about it. Basically the massive problem is that I do like your sister but I really don't want you to be unhappy. terrible. I know a big complication is that we broke stuff together - but that's what breaking stuff is - a spontaneous drunken thing - and I totally thought it was fun and cool but that's what it is. I don't know. I think you're so cool and interesting and totally one of the finest quality people I've ever been around - I REALLY DON'T WANT TO MESS THINGS UP. its a disaster but I like your sister. I don't know what to do. Anyway, we should get together sometime this weekend.
love, Ariel
ARIEL,
HOMIES BEFORE HOES
THIS WHOLE SITUATION IS WORSE THAN BAD. OF COURSE IT'S WORSE FOR ME BECAUSE YOU AND SALLY HAVE EXACTLY WHAT YOU WANT, AND I HAVE NOTHING. I HAVE A SISTER THAT I HALF HATE AND A FRIEND THAT DOESN'T SEEM TO HAVE ANYTHING TO SAY TO ME ANYMORE. WHY THE FUCK SHOULD I PRETEND TO BE CONTENT WITH THAT? I THINK YOU'RE BOTH BEING PATHETIC AND IT'S A SHAME BECAUSE OTHER THAN THAT YOU'RE ONE OF THE VERY RADDEST PEOPLE I'VE EVER MET. ANYWAY, I STILL WANT TO HANG OUT WITH YOU AND SEE YOU THIS WEEK-END. BUT I AM BEGIN-NING TO HATE YOU.
-HARRIET
but of course no resolution was found and friday showed up, sopping in potential for disaster.
hi! so what's happening tonight?
well, there's this movie but it's at 7:30
that sounds fine
the KGB
BIOLOGY
CAMPBELL
but no, I have to pick you up at 8

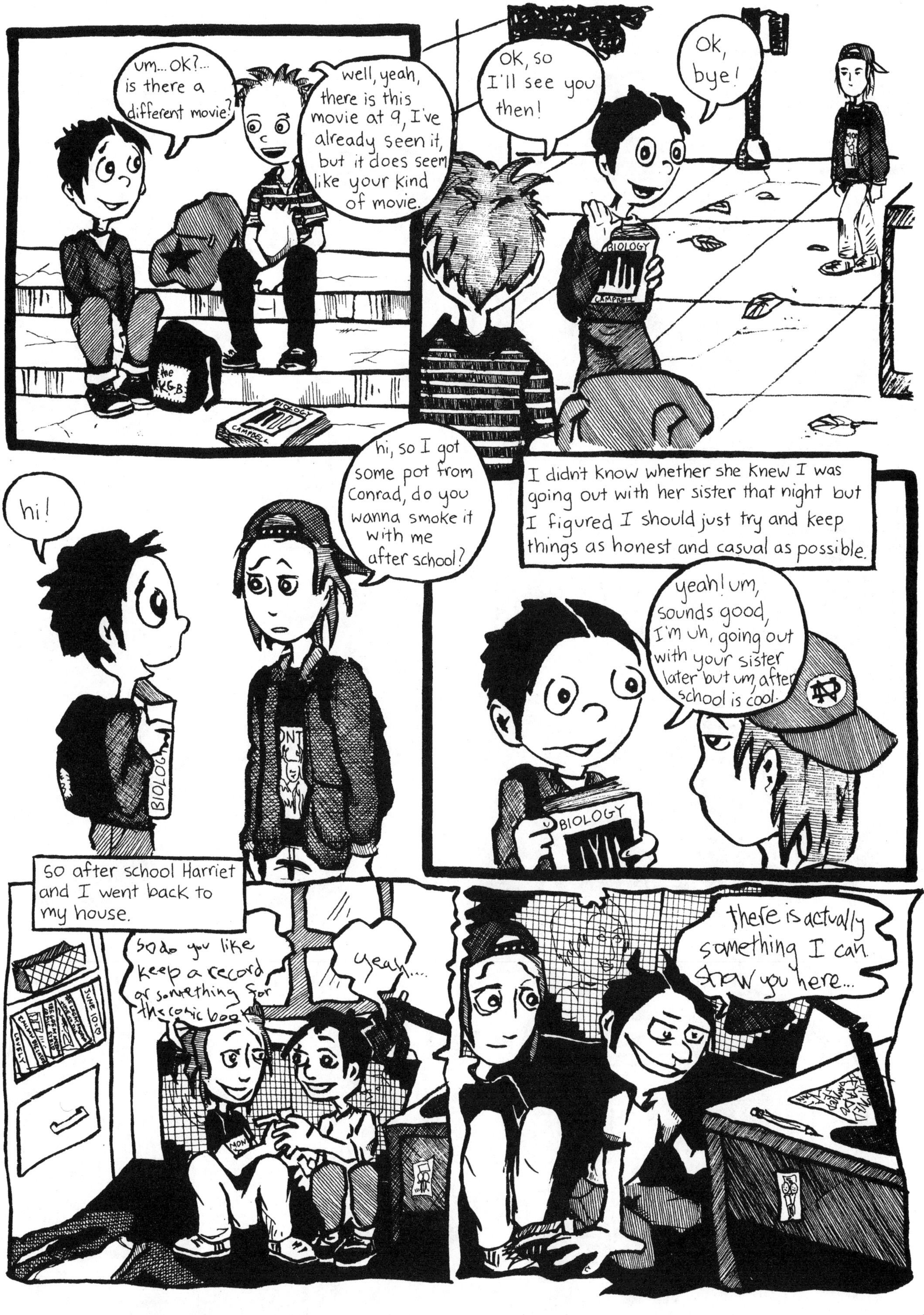

um... OK?... is there a different movie?
well, yeah, there is this movie at 9, I've already seen it, but it does seem like your kind of movie.
the KGB
BIOLOGY
CAMPBELL
OK, so I'll see you then!
Ok, bye!
BIOLOGY
CAMPBELL
hi!
hi, so I got some pot from Conrad, do you wanna smoke it with me after school?
BIOLOGY
I didn't know whether she knew I was going out with her sister that night but I figured I should just try and keep things as honest and casual as possible.
yeah! um, sounds good, I'm uh, going out with your sister later but um, after school is cool.
BIOLOGY
So after school Harriet and I went back to my house.
so do you like keep a record or something for the comic boo
yeah...
there is actually something I can show you here...

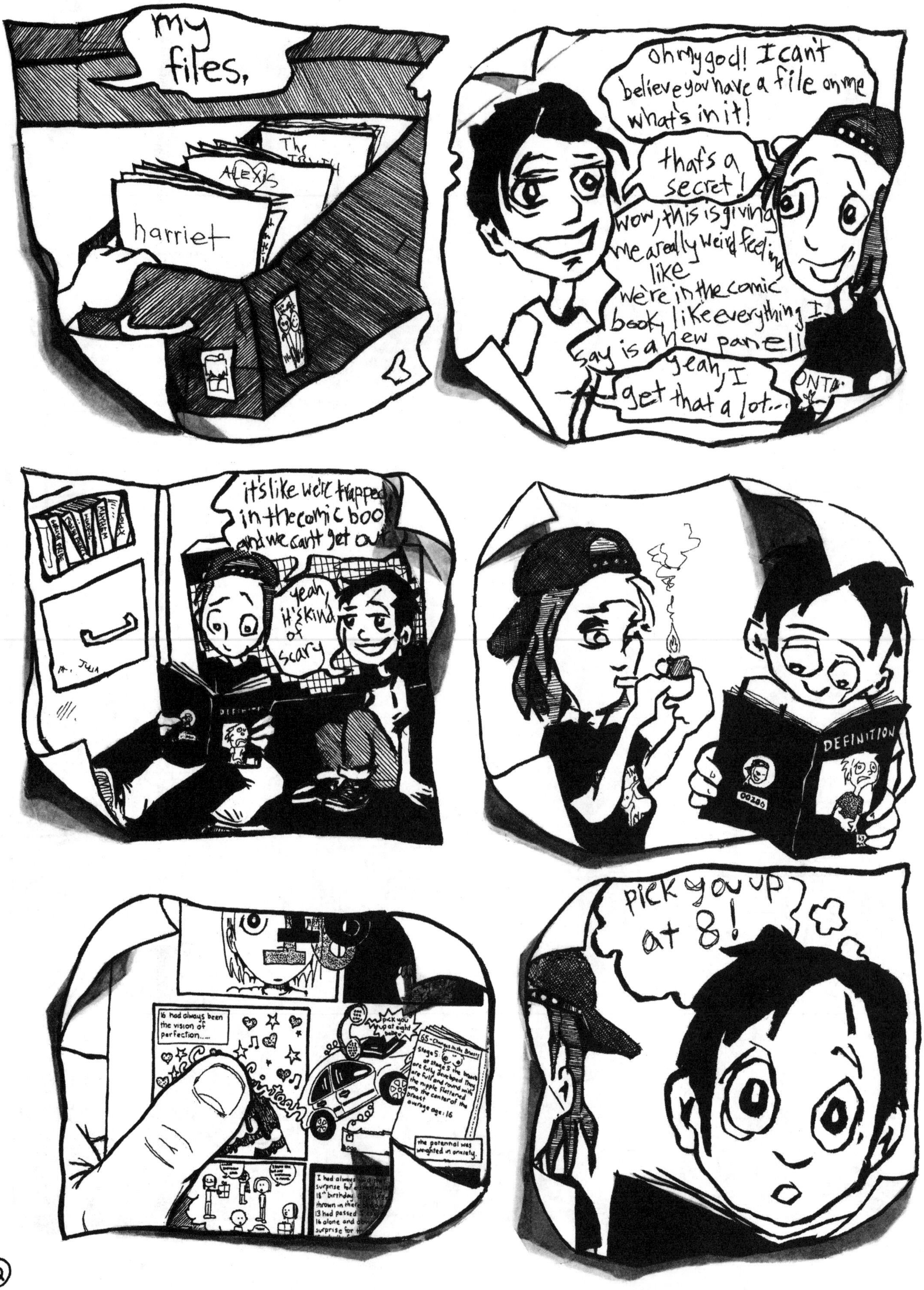
my files,
harriet
ALEXIS
oh my god! I can't believe you have a file on me what's in it!
that's a secret!
wow, this is giving me a really weird feeling like we're in the comic book, like everything I say is a new panel!
yeah, I get that a lot...
it's like we're trapped in the comic book and we can't get out
yeah, it's kind of scary
DEFINITION
16 had always been the vision of perfection.....
pick you up at 8!

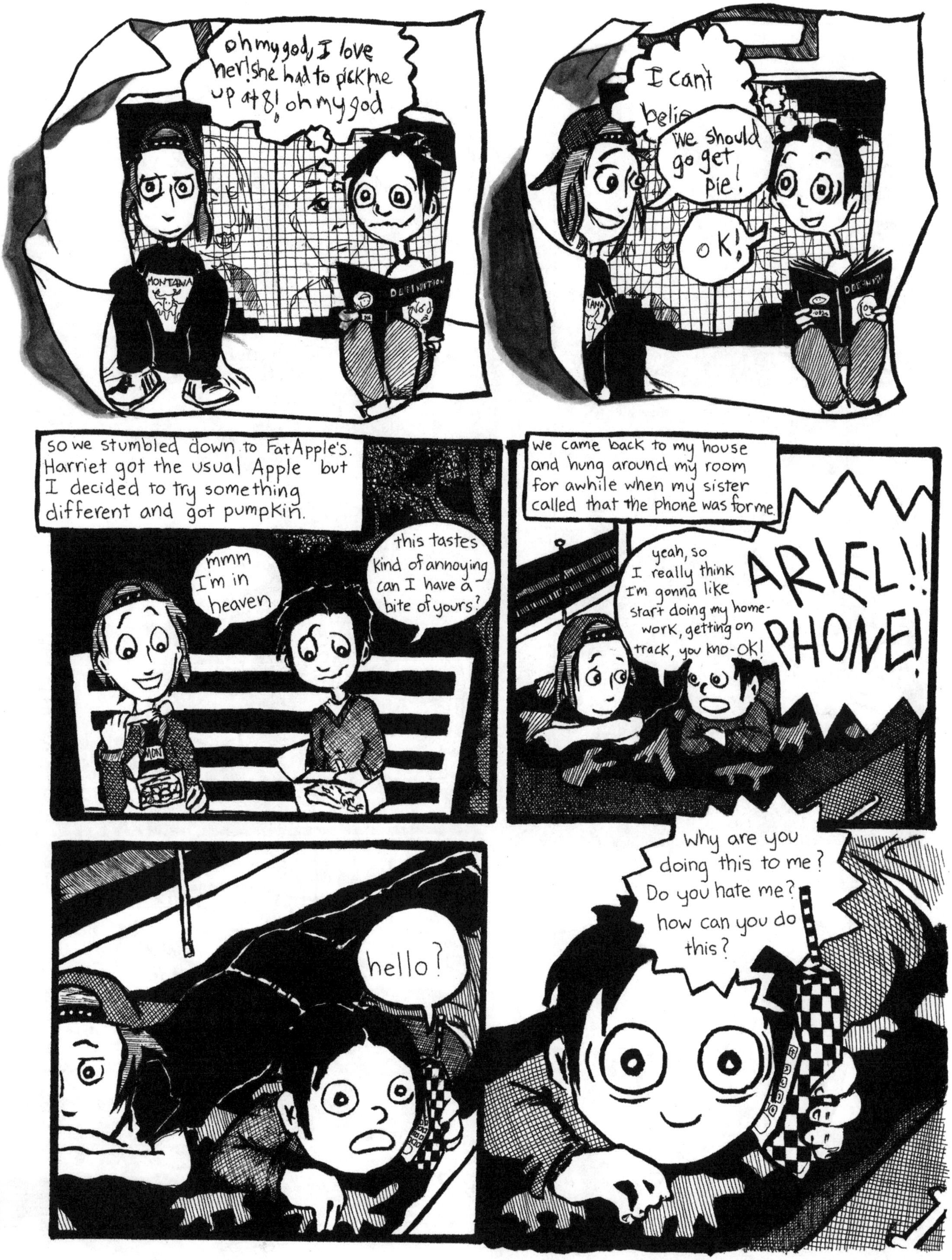
oh my god, I love her! she had to pick me up at 8!, oh my god
I can't belie
We should go get pie!
OK!
so we stumbled down to Fat Apple's. Harriet got the usual Apple but I decided to try something different and got pumpkin.
mmm I'm in heaven
this tastes kind of annoying can I have a bite of yours?
we came back to my house and hung around my room for awhile when my sister called that the phone was for me.
yeah, so I really think I'm gonna like start doing my homework, getting on track, you kno-OK!
ARIEL!! PHONE!
hello?
why are you doing this to me? Do you hate me? how can you do this?

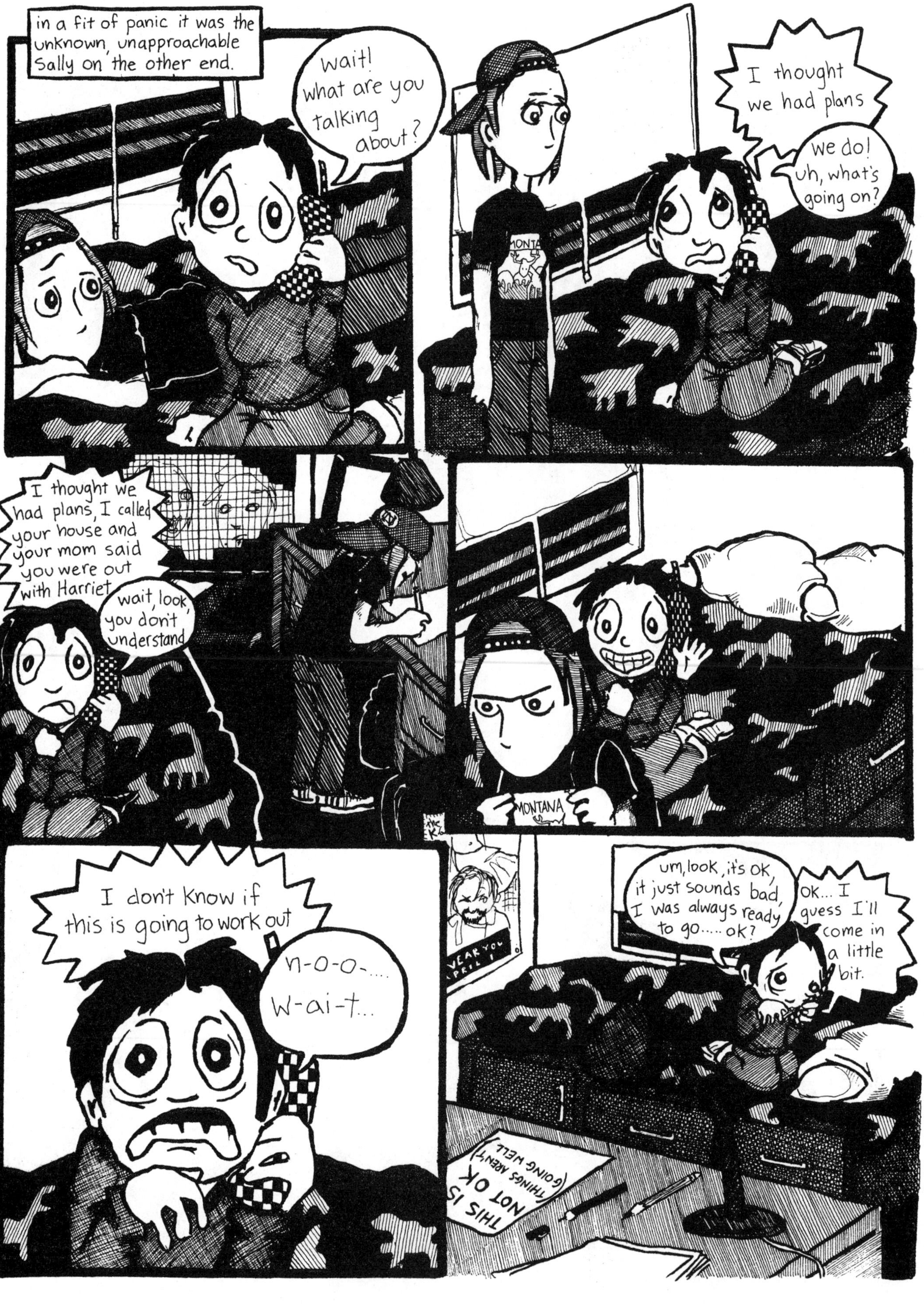
in a fit of panic it was the unknown, unapproachable Sally on the other end.
Wait! what are you talking about?
I thought we had plans
We do! uh, what's going on?
I thought we had plans, I called your house and your mom said you were out with Harriet
wait, look, you don't understand
MONTANA
I don't know if this is going to work out
n-o-o-....
w-ai-t...
um, look, it's OK, it just sounds bad, I was always ready to go.....ok?
OK... I guess I'll come in a little bit.
THIS IS NOT OK
(THINGS AREN'T GOING WELL)

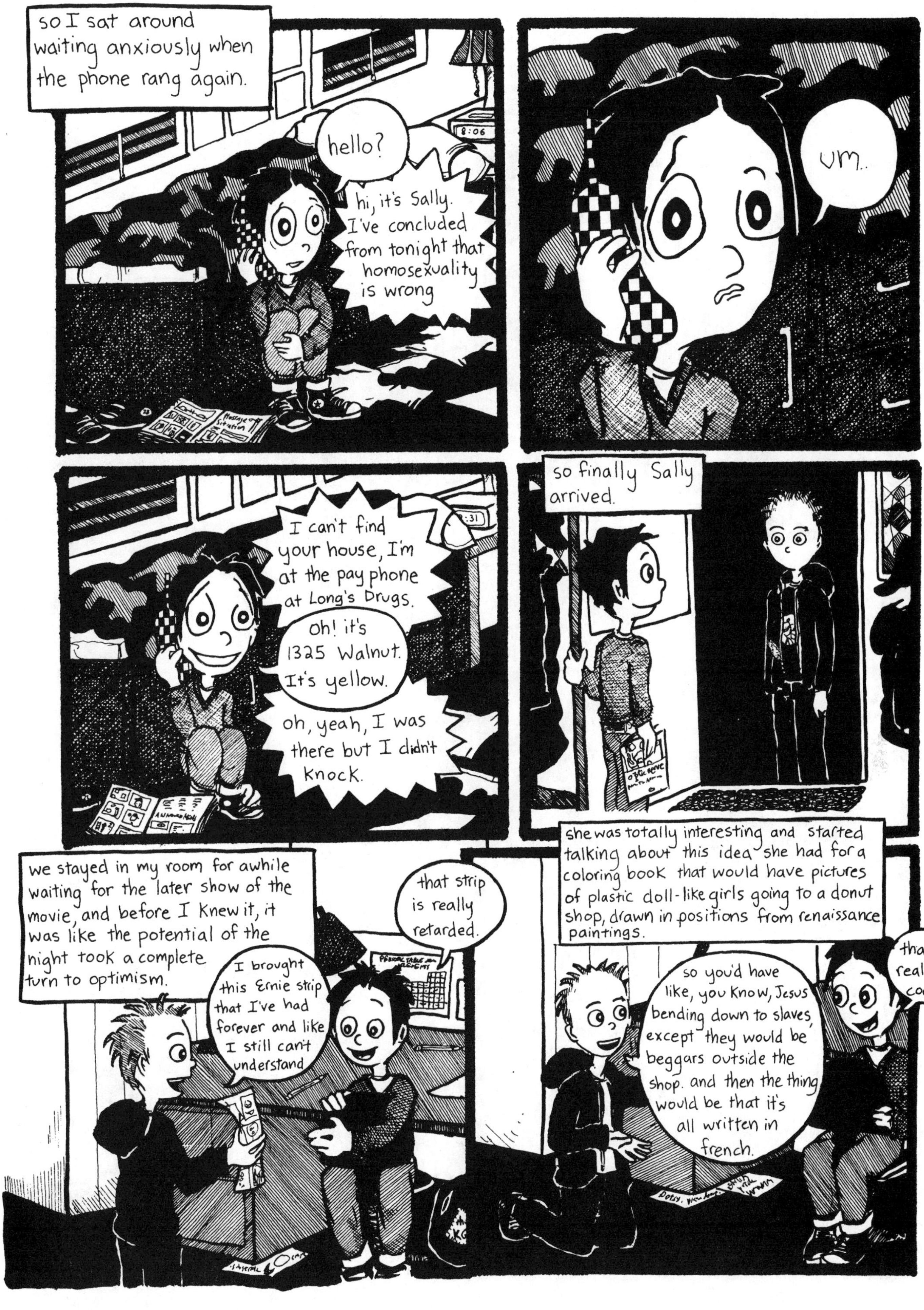
so I sat around waiting anxiously when the phone rang again.
8:06
hello?
hi, it's Sally. I've concluded from tonight that homosexuality is wrong
um..
I can't find your house, I'm at the pay phone at Long's Drugs.
oh! it's 1325 Walnut. It's yellow.
oh, yeah, I was there but I didn't knock.
so finally Sally arrived.
we stayed in my room for awhile waiting for the later show of the movie, and before I knew it, it was like the potential of the night took a complete turn to optimism.
I brought this Ernie strip that I've had forever and like I still can't understand
that strip is really retarded.
she was totally interesting and started talking about this idea she had for a coloring book that would have pictures of plastic doll-like girls going to a donut shop, drawn in positions from renaissance paintings.
so you'd have like, you know, Jesus bending down to slaves, except they would be beggars outside the shop. and then the thing would be that it's all written in french.
that's really cool!

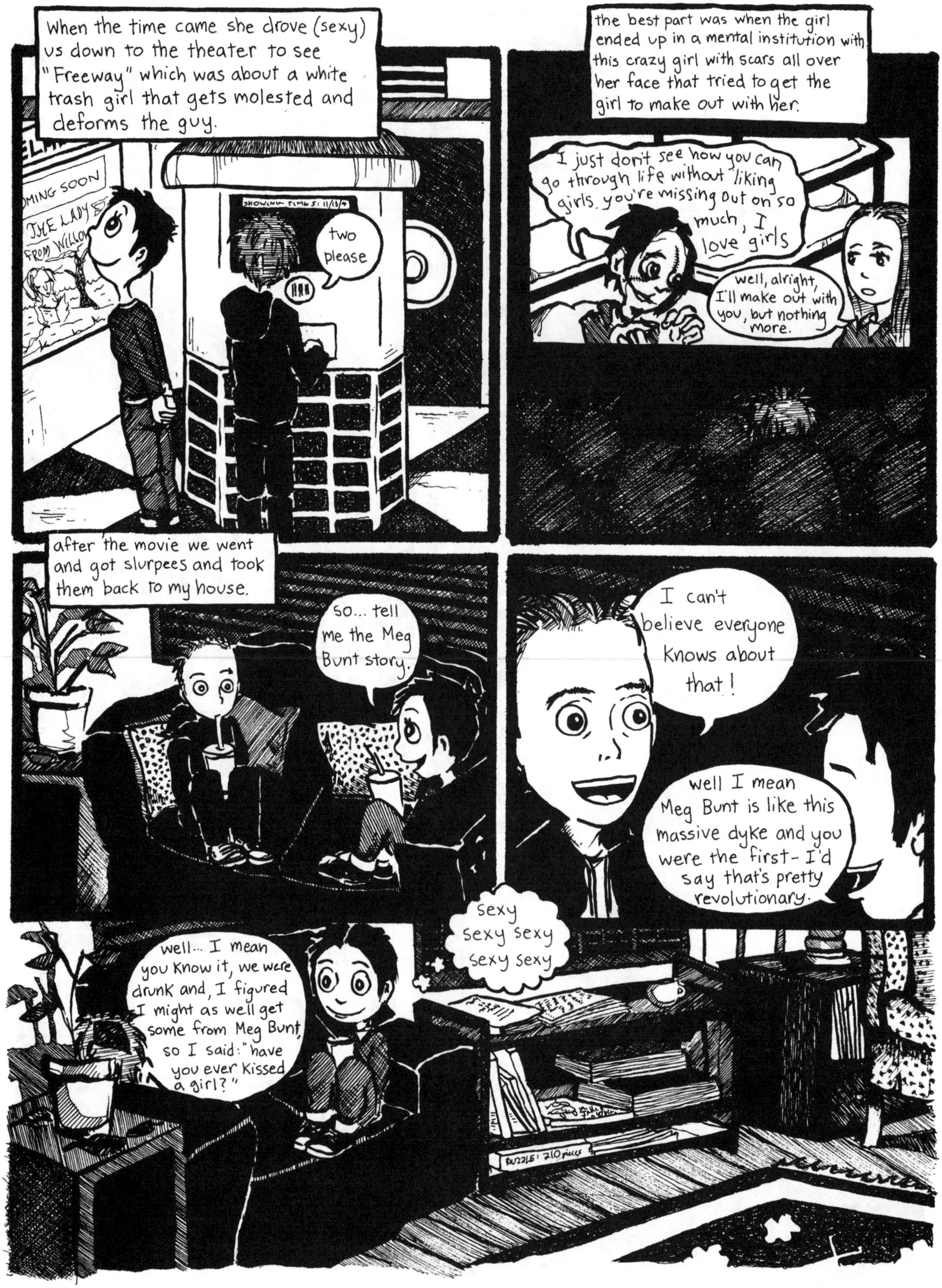

When the time came she drove (sexy) us down to the theater to see "Freeway" which was about a white trash girl that gets molested and deforms the guy.
COMING SOON
THE LADY FROM WILLOW
SHOWING TIMES: 11/13/4
two please
the best part was when the girl ended up in a mental institution with this crazy girl with scars all over her face that tried to get the girl to make out with her.
I just don't see how you can go through life without liking girls. you're missing out on so much, I love girls
well, alright, I'll make out with you, but nothing more.
after the movie we went and got slurpees and took them back to my house.
so... tell me the Meg Bunt story.
I can't believe everyone knows about that!
well I mean Meg Bunt is like this massive dyke and you were the first- I'd say that's pretty revolutionary.
well... I mean you know it, we were drunk and, I figured I might as well get some from Meg Bunt, so I said: "have you ever kissed a girl?"
sexy sexy sexy sexy sexy
PUZZLE: 210 pieces

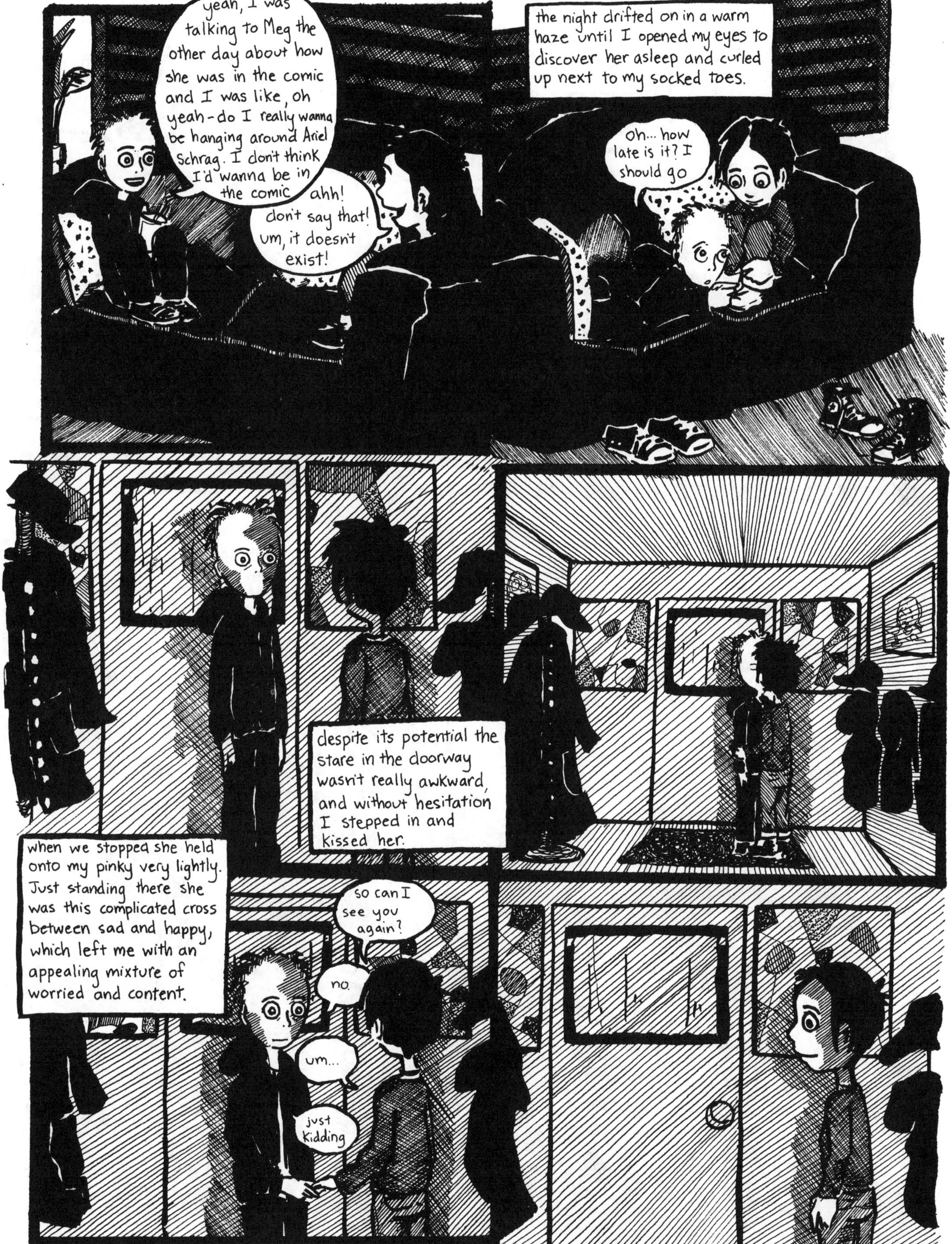
yeah, I was talking to Meg the other day about how she was in the comic and I was like, oh yeah - do I really wanna be hanging around Ariel Schrag. I don't think I'd wanna be in the comic
ahh! don't say that! um, it doesn't exist!
the night drifted on in a warm haze until I opened my eyes to discover her asleep and curled up next to my socked toes.
oh... how late is it? I should go
despite its potential the stare in the doorway wasn't really awkward, and without hesitation I stepped in and kissed her.
when we stopped she held onto my pinky very lightly. Just standing there she was this complicated cross between sad and happy, which left me with an appealing mixture of worried and content.
so can I see you again?
no.
um...
just kidding

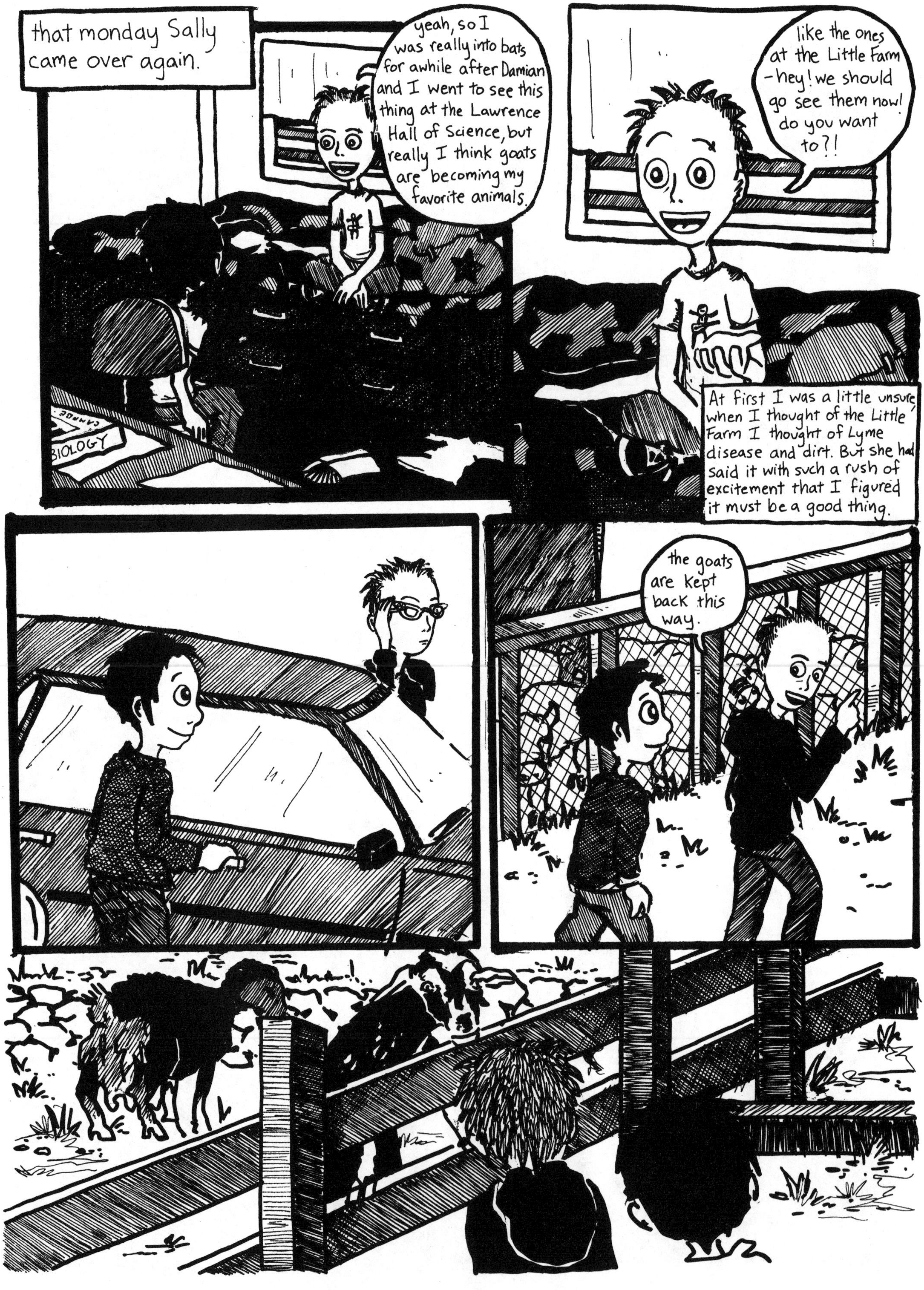
that monday Sally came over again.
yeah, so I was really into bats for awhile after Damian and I went to see this thing at the Lawrence Hall of Science, but really I think goats are becoming my favorite animals.
BIOLOGY
like the ones at the Little Farm -hey! we should go see them now! do you want to?!
At first I was a little unsure, when I thought of the Little Farm I thought of Lyme disease and dirt. But she had said it with such a rush of excitement that I figured it must be a good thing.
the goats are kept back this way.

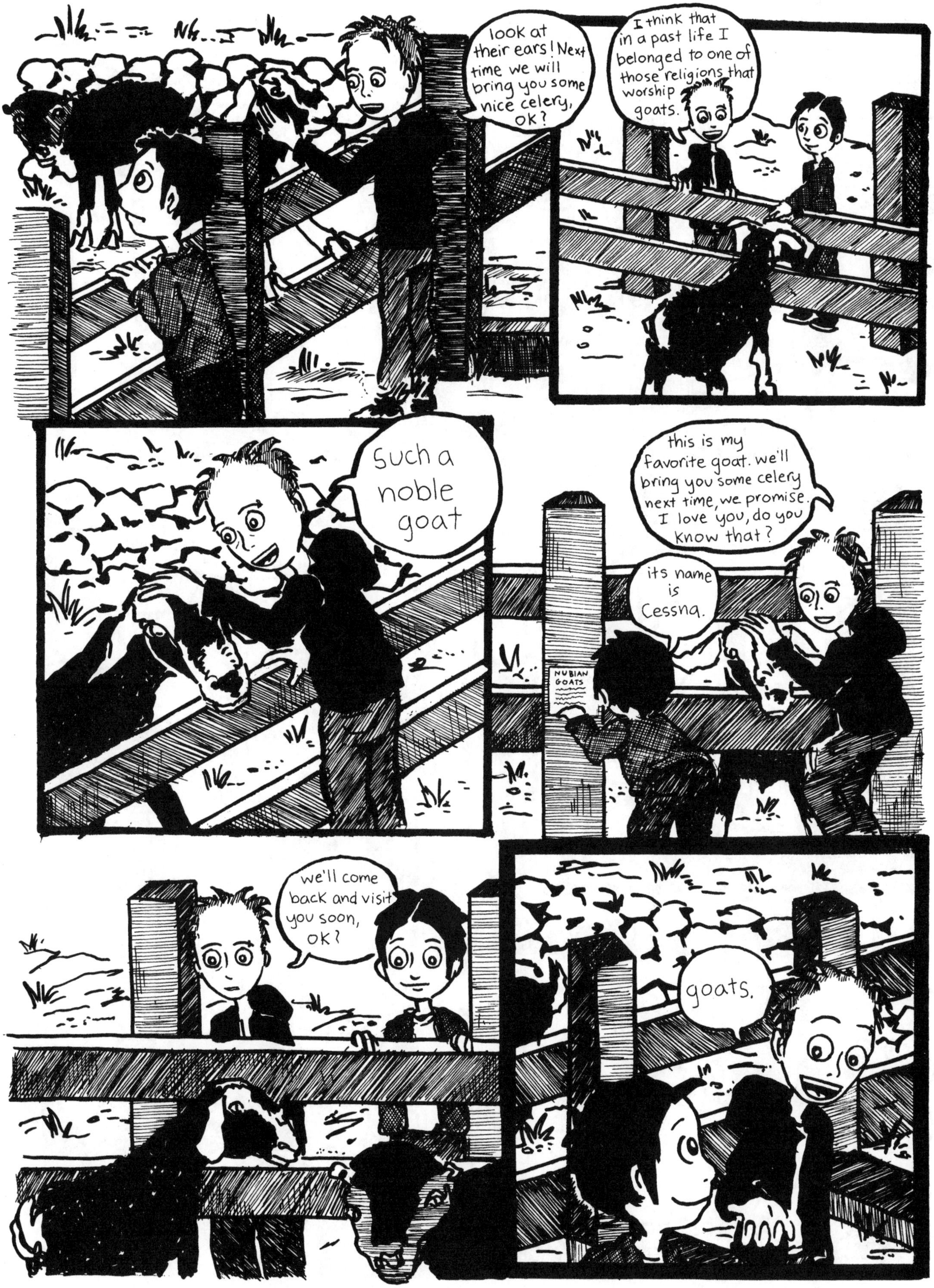
look at their ears! Next time we will bring you some nice celery, OK?
I think that in a past life I belonged to one of those religions that worship goats.
Such a noble goat
this is my favorite goat. we'll bring you some celery next time, we promise. I love you, do you know that?
its name is Cessna.
NUBIAN GOATS
we'll come back and visit you soon, OK?
goats.

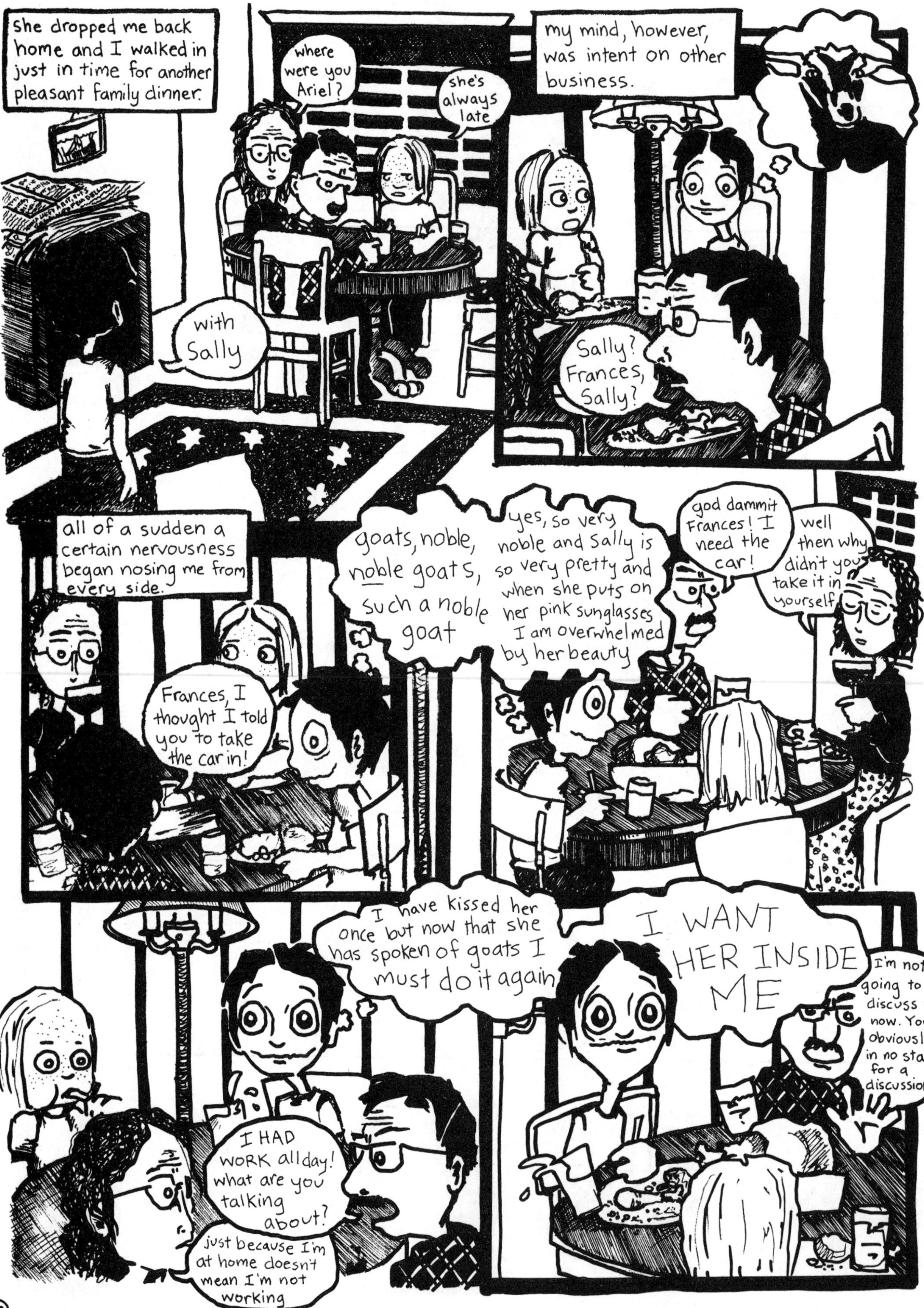

she dropped me back home and I walked in just in time for another pleasant family dinner.
where were you Ariel?
she's always late
with Sally
my mind, however, was intent on other business.
Sally? Frances, Sally?
all of a sudden a certain nervousness began nosing me from every side.
goats, noble, noble goats, such a noble goat
Frances, I thought I told you to take the car in!
yes, so very noble and Sally is so very pretty and when she puts on her pink sunglasses I am overwhelmed by her beauty
god dammit Frances! I need the car!
well then why didn't you take it in yourself
I have kissed her once but now that she has spoken of goats I must do it again
I HAD WORK all day! what are you talking about?
just because I'm at home doesn't mean I'm not working
I WANT HER INSIDE ME
I'm not going to discuss this now. You're obviously in no state for a discussion.

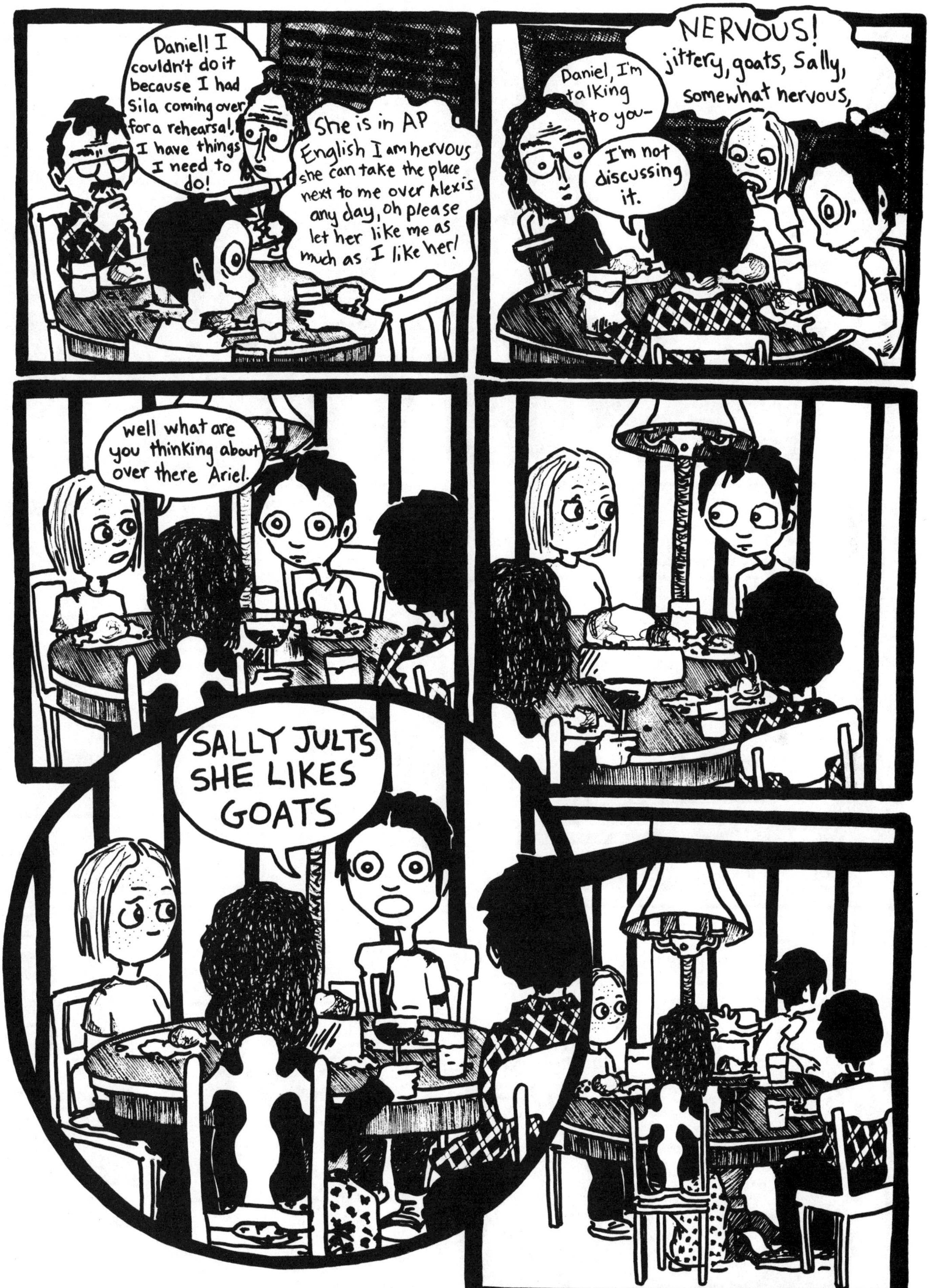

Daniel! I couldn't do it because I had Sila coming over for a rehearsal! I have things I need to do!
She is in AP English I am nervous she can take the place next to me over Alexis any day, oh please let her like me as much as I like her!
NERVOUS! jittery, goats, Sally, somewhat nervous,
Daniel, I'm talking to you-
I'm not discussing it.
well what are you thinking about over there Ariel.
SALLY JULTS SHE LIKES GOATS

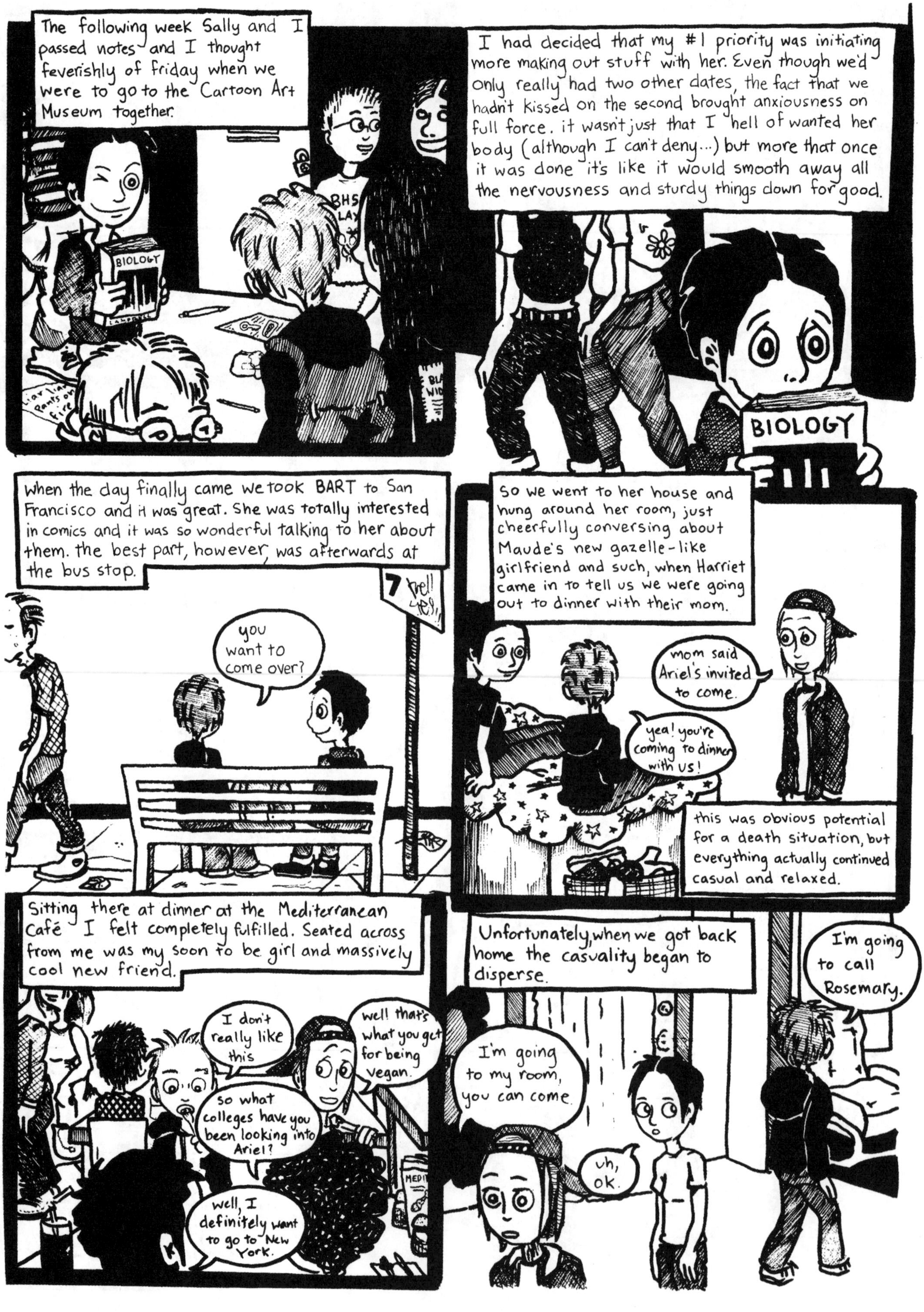

The following week Sally and I passed notes and I thought feverishly of friday when we were to go to the Cartoon Art Museum together.
BIOLOGY
BHS
Liar Liar Pants on Fire
I had decided that my #1 priority was initiating more making out stuff with her. Even though we'd only really had two other dates, the fact that we hadn't kissed on the second brought anxiousness on full force. it wasn't just that I hell of wanted her body (although I can't deny...) but more that once it was done it's like it would smooth away all the nervousness and sturdy things down for good.
BIOLOGY
when the day finally came we took BART to San Francisco and it was great. She was totally interested in comics and it was so wonderful talking to her about them. the best part, however, was afterwards at the bus stop.
7
hell yes!
you want to come over?
So we went to her house and hung around her room, just cheerfully conversing about Maude's new gazelle-like girlfriend and such, when Harriet came in to tell us we were going out to dinner with their mom.
mom said Ariel's invited to come.
yea! you're coming to dinner with us!
this was obvious potential for a death situation, but everything actually continued casual and relaxed.
Sitting there at dinner at the Mediterranean Café I felt completely fulfilled. Seated across from me was my soon to be girl and massively cool new friend.
I don't really like this
well! that's what you get for being vegan.
so what colleges have you been looking into Ariel?
well, I definitely want to go to New York.
Unfortunately, when we got back home the casuality began to disperse.
I'm going to call Rosemary.
I'm going to my room, you can come
uh, ok.

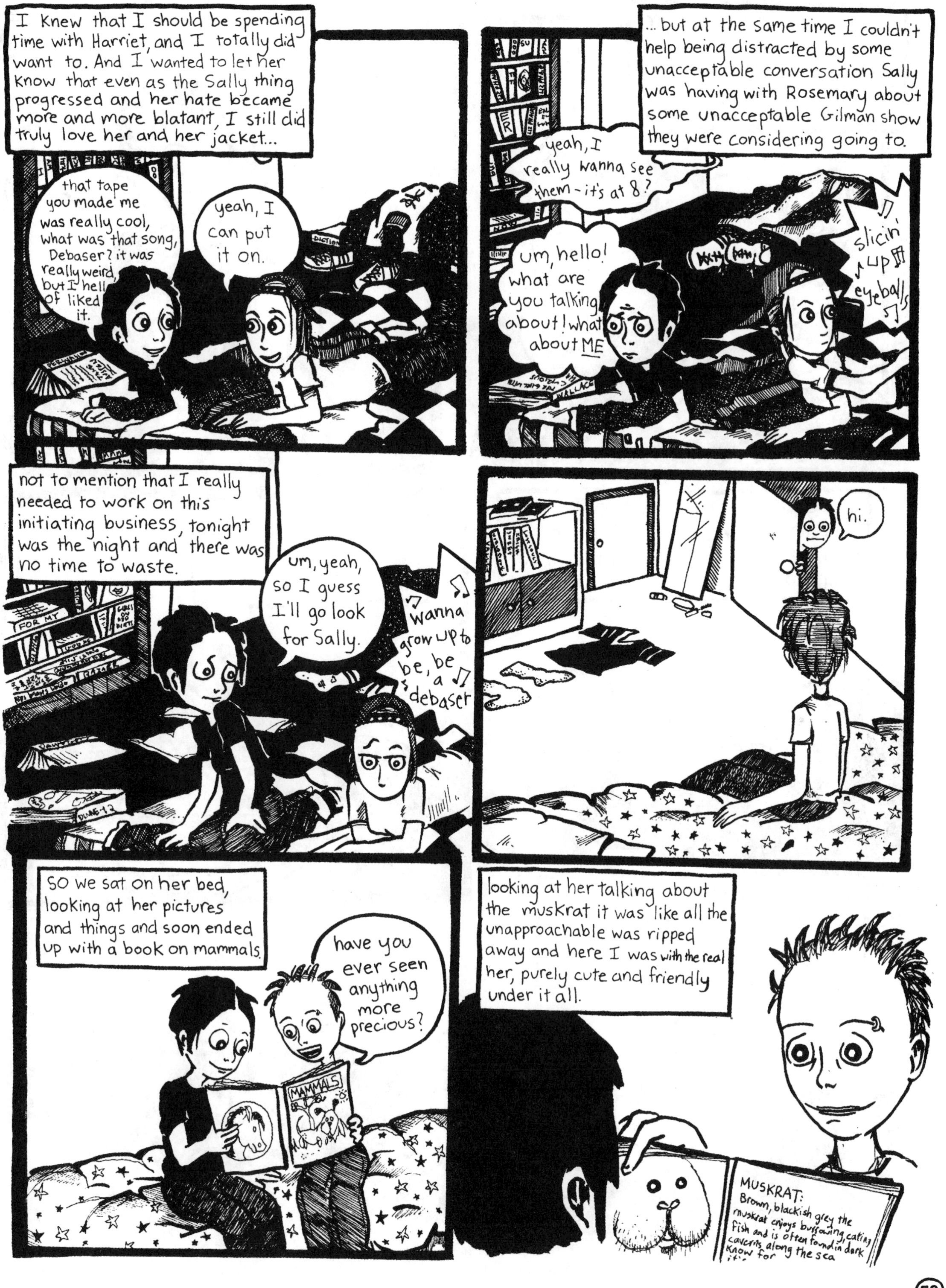
I knew that I should be spending time with Harriet, and I totally did want to. And I wanted to let her know that even as the Sally thing progressed and her hate became more and more blatant, I still did truly love her and her jacket...
that tape you made me was really cool, what was that song, Debaser? it was really weird, but I hell of liked it.
yeah, I can put it on.
... but at the same time I couldn't help being distracted by some unacceptable conversation Sally was having with Rosemary about some unacceptable Gilman show they were considering going to.
yeah, I really wanna see them - it's at 8?
um, hello! what are you talking about! what about ME
slicin' up eyeballs
not to mention that I really needed to work on this initiating business, tonight was the night and there was no time to waste.
um, yeah, so I guess I'll go look for Sally.
wanna grow up to be, be a debaser
hi.
SO we sat on her bed, looking at her pictures and things and soon ended up with a book on mammals.
have you ever seen anything more precious?
MAMMALS
looking at her talking about the muskrat it was like all the unapproachable was ripped away and here I was with the real her, purely cute and friendly under it all.
MUSKRAT:
Brown, blackish grey the muskrat enjoys burrowing, eating fish and is often found in dark caverns along the sea

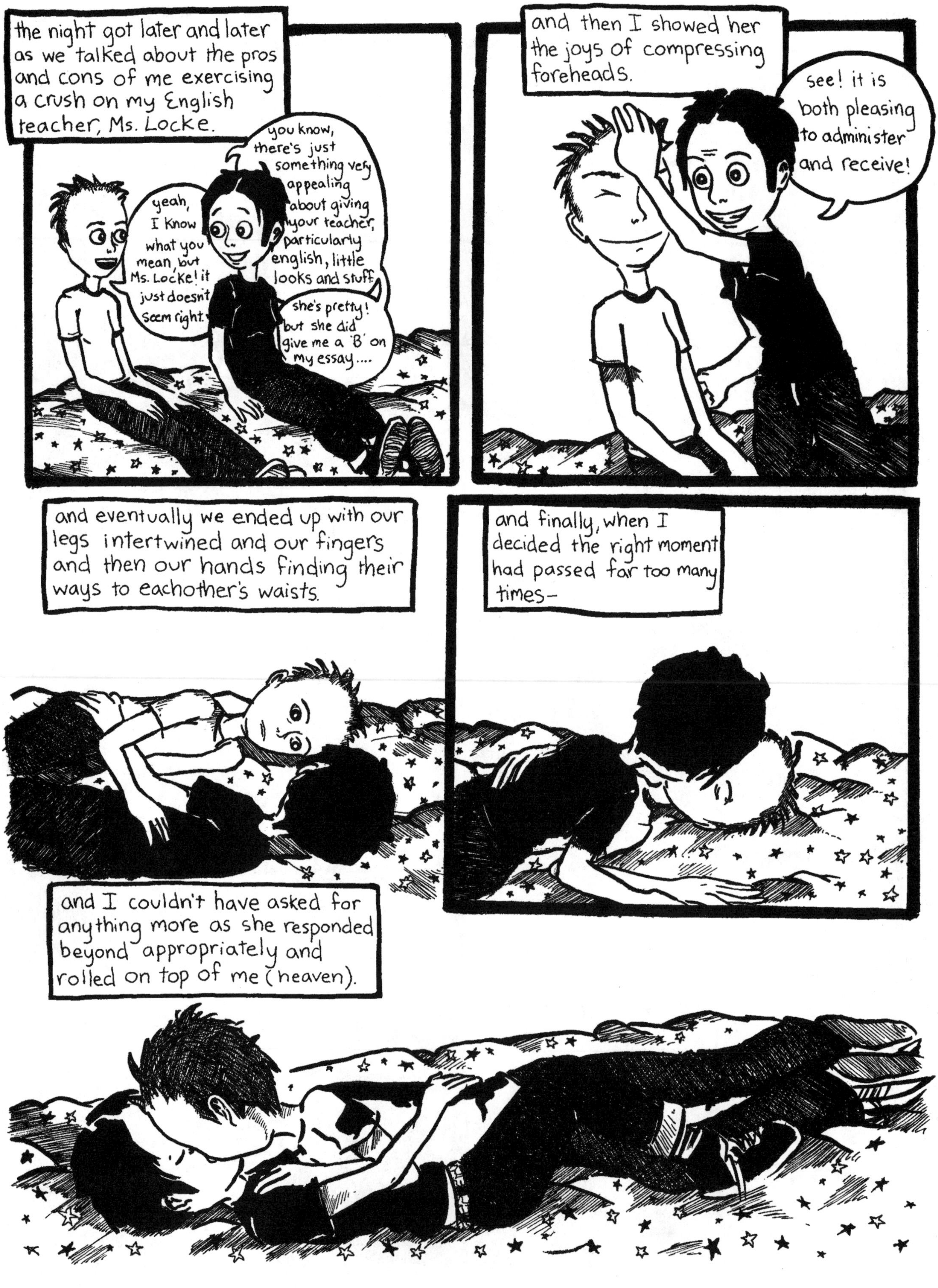

the night got later and later as we talked about the pros and cons of me exercising a crush on my English teacher, Ms. Locke.
you know, there's just something very appealing about giving your teacher, particularly english, little looks and stuff.
yeah, I know what you mean, but Ms. Locke! it just doesn't seem right.
she's pretty! but she did give me a 'B' on my essay....
and then I showed her the joys of compressing foreheads.
see! it is both pleasing to administer and receive!
and eventually we ended up with our legs intertwined and our fingers and then our hands finding their ways to eachother's waists.
and finally, when I decided the right moment had passed far too many times–
and I couldn't have asked for anything more as she responded beyond appropriately and rolled on top of me (heaven).

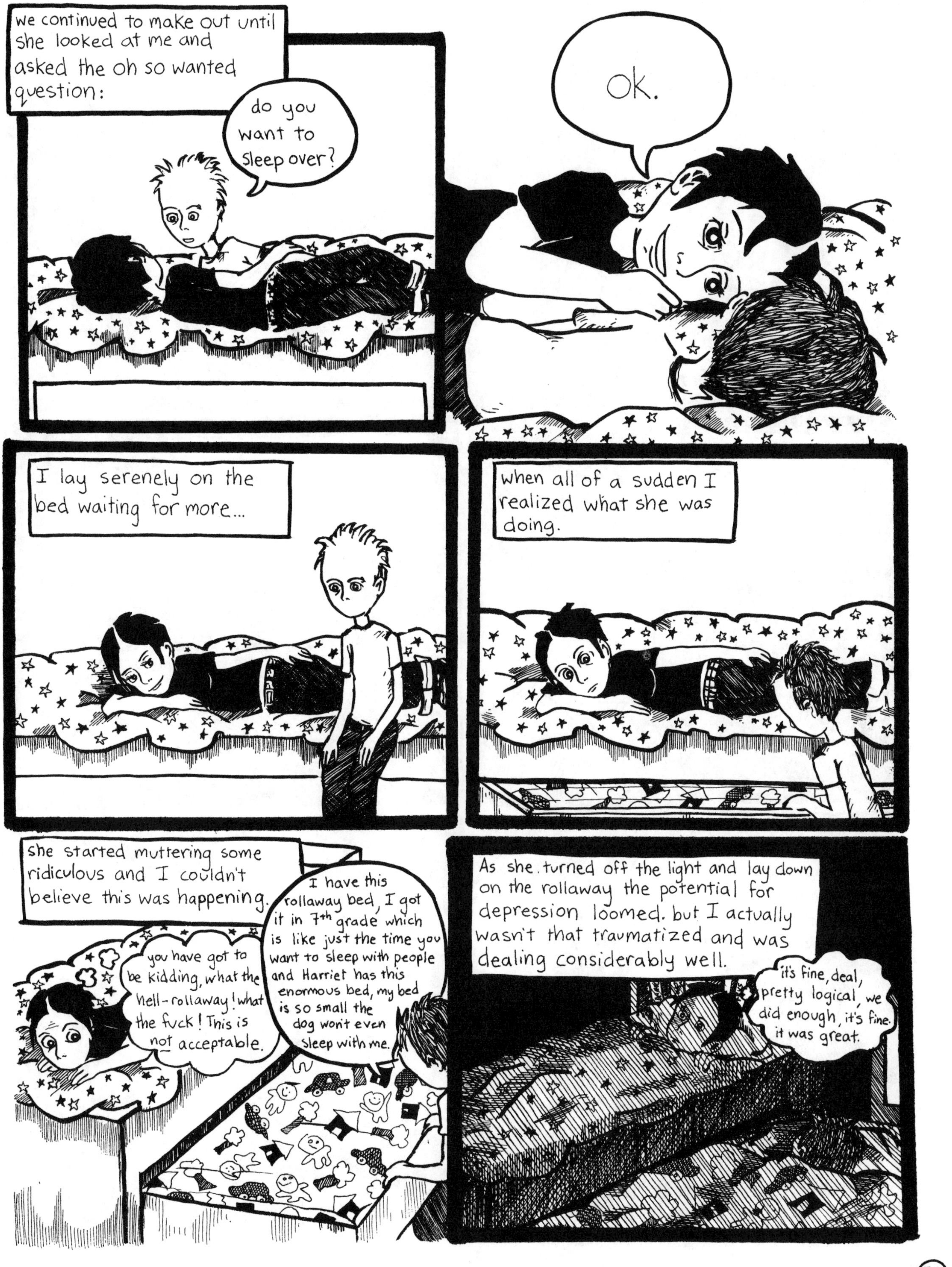
we continued to make out until she looked at me and asked the oh so wanted question:
do you want to sleep over?
ok.
I lay serenely on the bed waiting for more...
when all of a sudden I realized what she was doing.
she started muttering some ridiculous and I couldn't believe this was happening.
you have got to be kidding, what the hell-rollaway! what the fuck! This is not acceptable.
I have this rollaway bed, I got it in 7th grade which is like just the time you want to sleep with people and Harriet has this enormous bed, my bed is so small the dog won't even sleep with me.
As she turned off the light and lay down on the rollaway the potential for depression loomed. but I actually wasn't that traumatized and was dealing considerably well.
it's fine, deal, pretty logical, we did enough, it's fine. it was great.

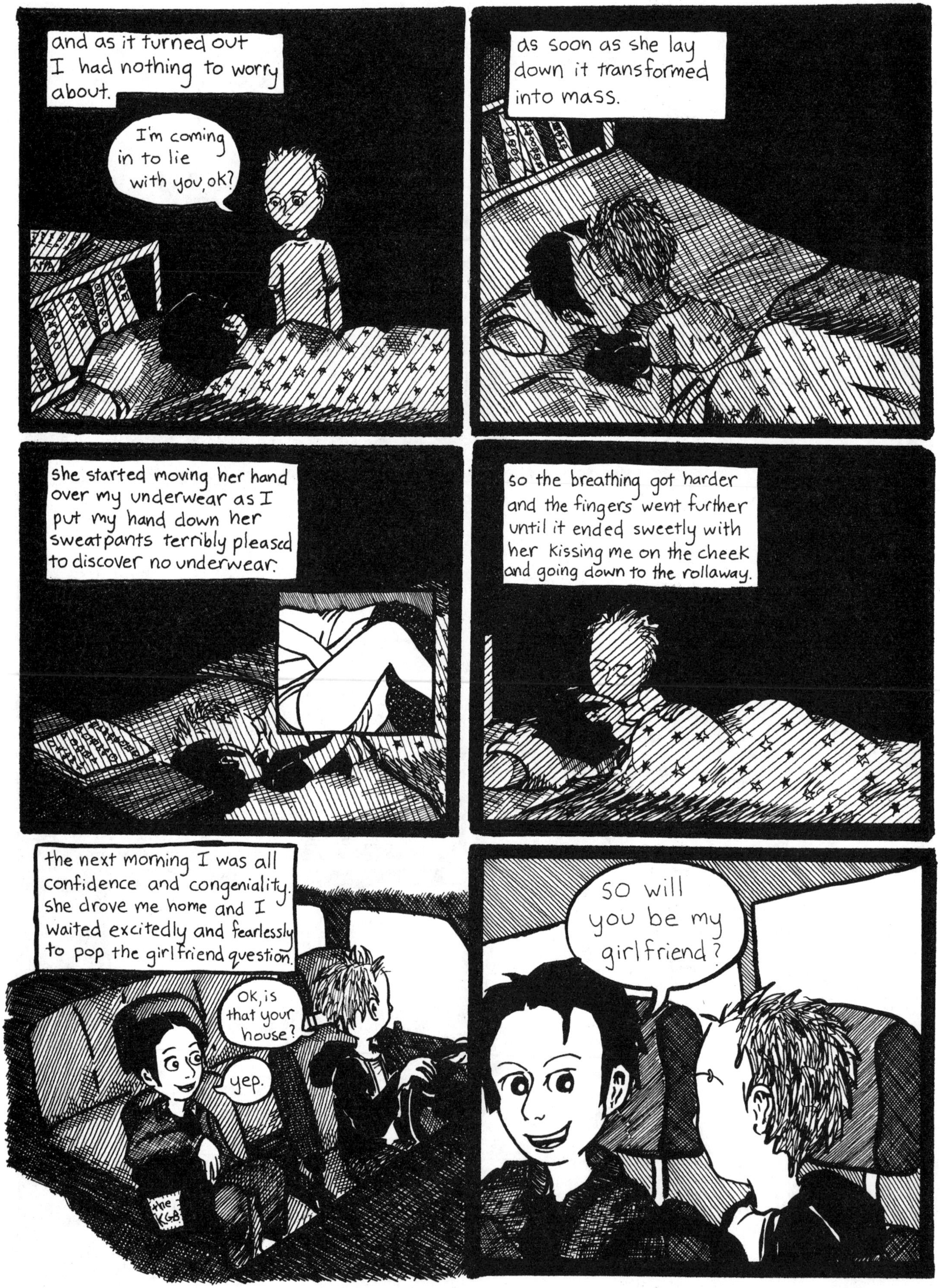
and as it turned out I had nothing to worry about.
I'm coming in to lie with you, ok?
as soon as she lay down it transformed into mass.
she started moving her hand over my underwear as I put my hand down her sweatpants terribly pleased to discover no underwear.
so the breathing got harder and the fingers went further until it ended sweetly with her kissing me on the cheek and going down to the rollaway.
the next morning I was all confidence and congeniality. she drove me home and I waited excitedly and fearlessly to pop the girlfriend question.
Ok, is that your house?
yep.
the KGB
so will you be my girlfriend?

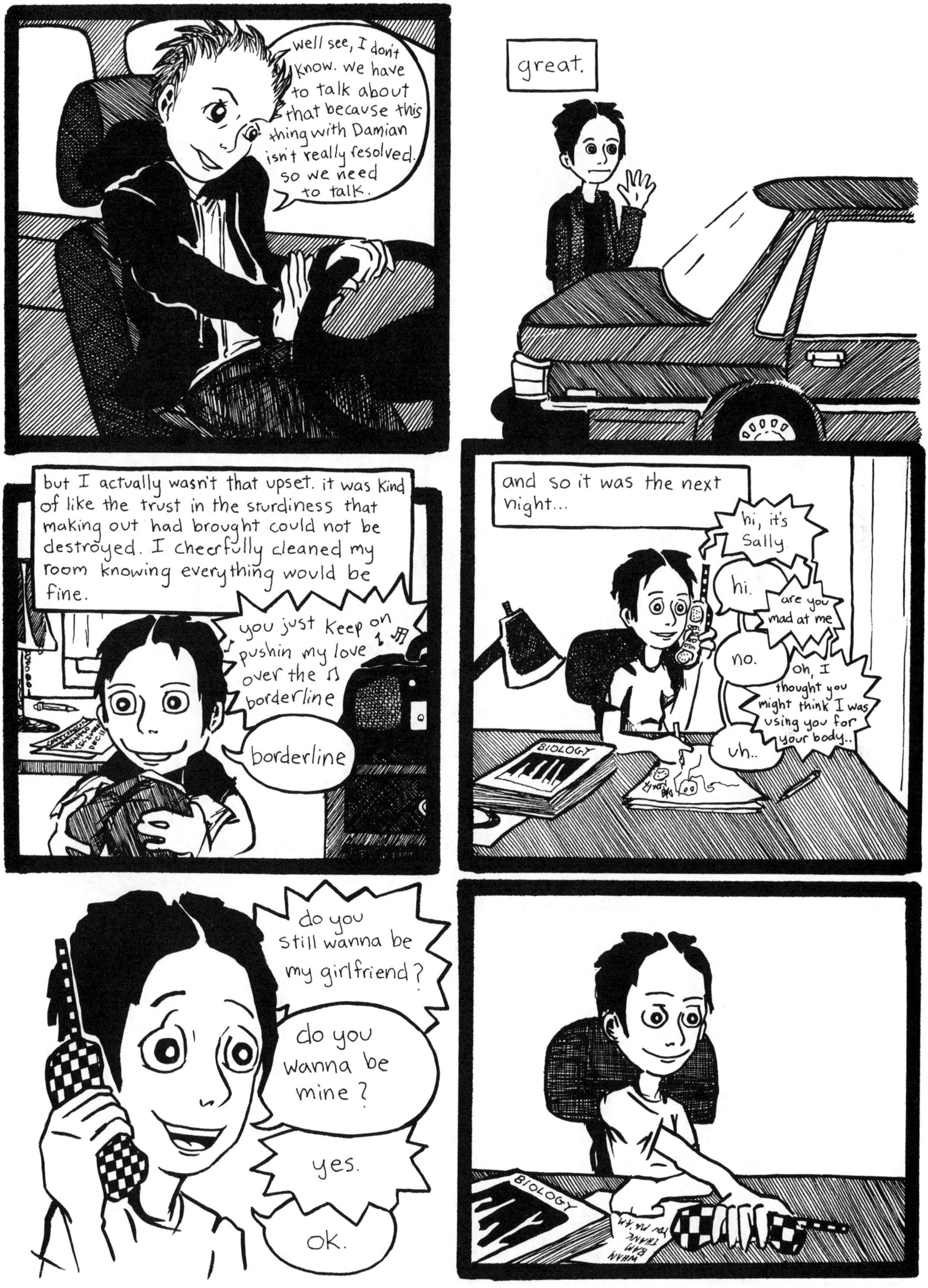
well see, I don't know. we have to talk about that because this thing with Damian isn't really resolved. so we need to talk.
great.
but I actually wasn't that upset. it was kind of like the trust in the sturdiness that making out had brought could not be destroyed. I cheerfully cleaned my room knowing everything would be fine.
you just keep on pushin my love over the borderline
borderline
and so it was the next night...
hi, it's Sally.
hi.
are you mad at me
no.
oh, I thought you might think I was using you for your body..
uh..
BIOLOGY
do you still wanna be my girlfriend?
do you wanna be mine?
yes.
ok.
BIOLOGY

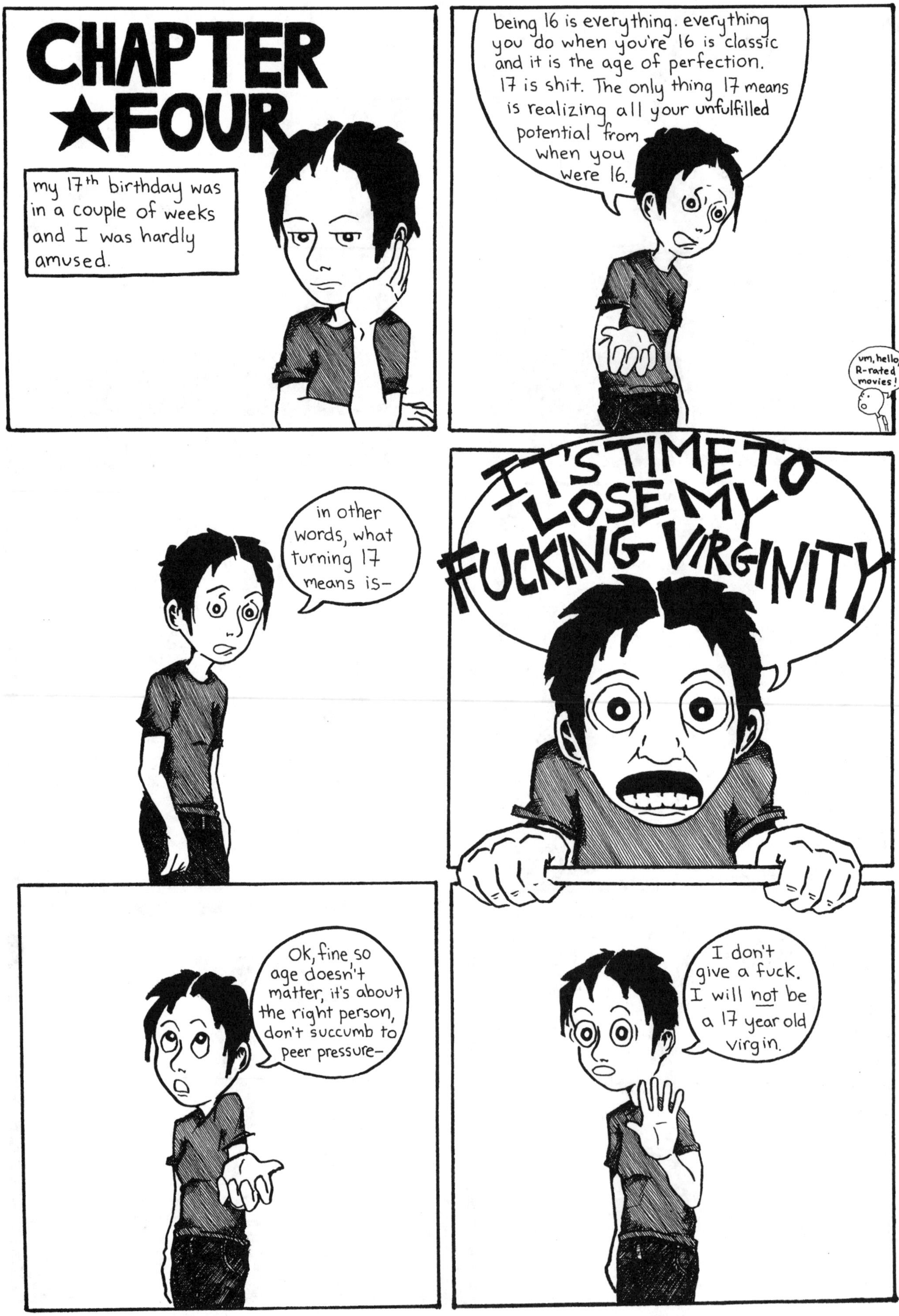
CHAPTER ★FOUR
my 17th birthday was in a couple of weeks and I was hardly amused.
being 16 is everything. everything you do when you're 16 is classic and it is the age of perfection. 17 is shit. The only thing 17 means is realizing all your unfulfilled potential from when you were 16.
um, hello, R-rated movies!
in other words, what turning 17 means is—
IT'S TIME TO LOSE MY FUCKING VIRGINITY
Ok, fine so age doesn't matter, it's about the right person, don't succumb to peer pressure—
I don't give a fuck. I will not be a 17 year old virgin.

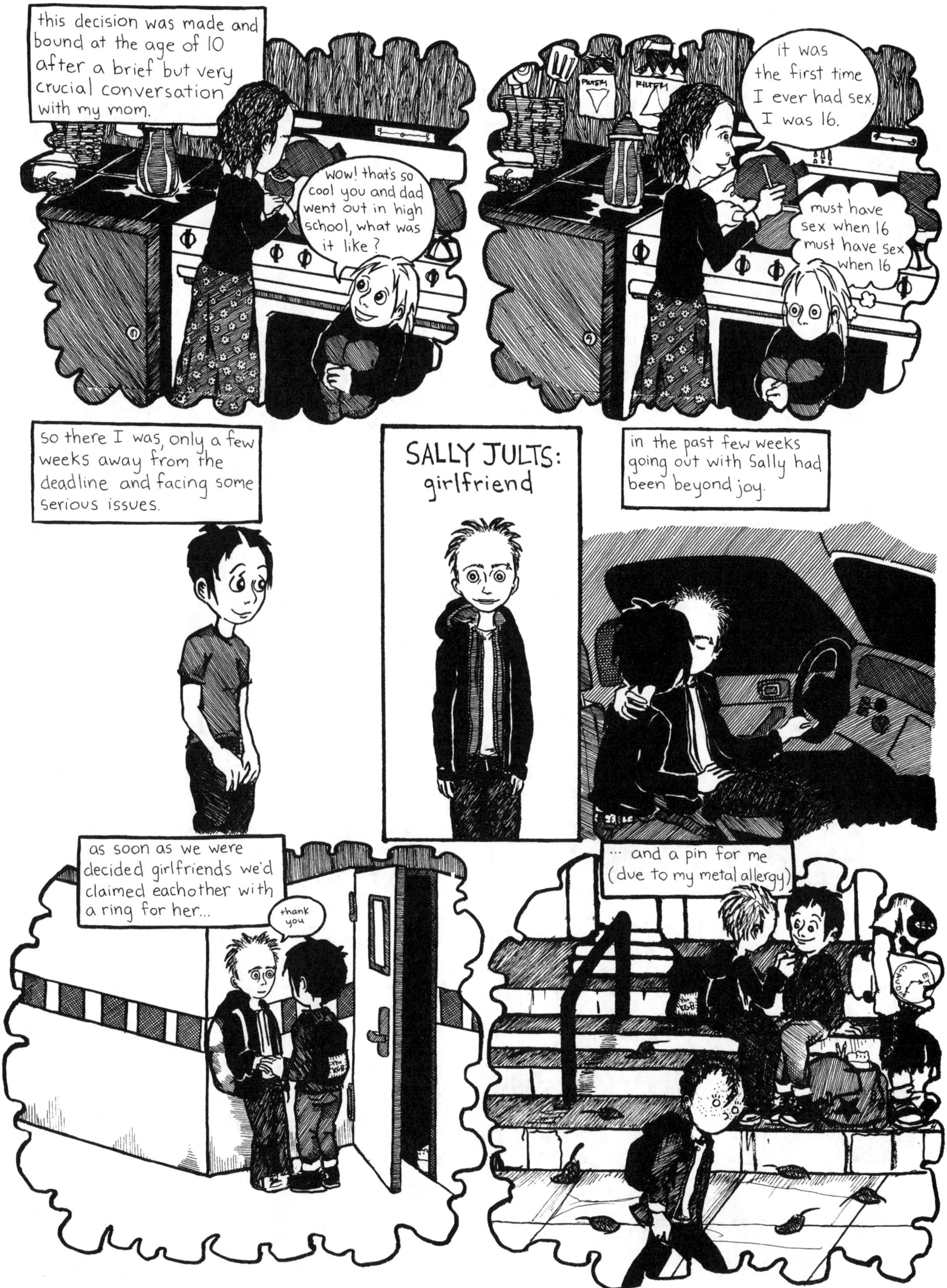
this decision was made and bound at the age of 10 after a brief but very crucial conversation with my mom.
wow! that's so cool you and dad went out in high school, what was it like?
it was the first time I ever had sex. I was 16.
must have sex when 16 must have sex when 16
so there I was, only a few weeks away from the deadline and facing some serious issues.
SALLY JULTS: girlfriend
in the past few weeks going out with Sally had been beyond joy.
as soon as we were decided girlfriends we'd claimed eachother with a ring for her...
thank you
... and a pin for me (due to my metal allergy)

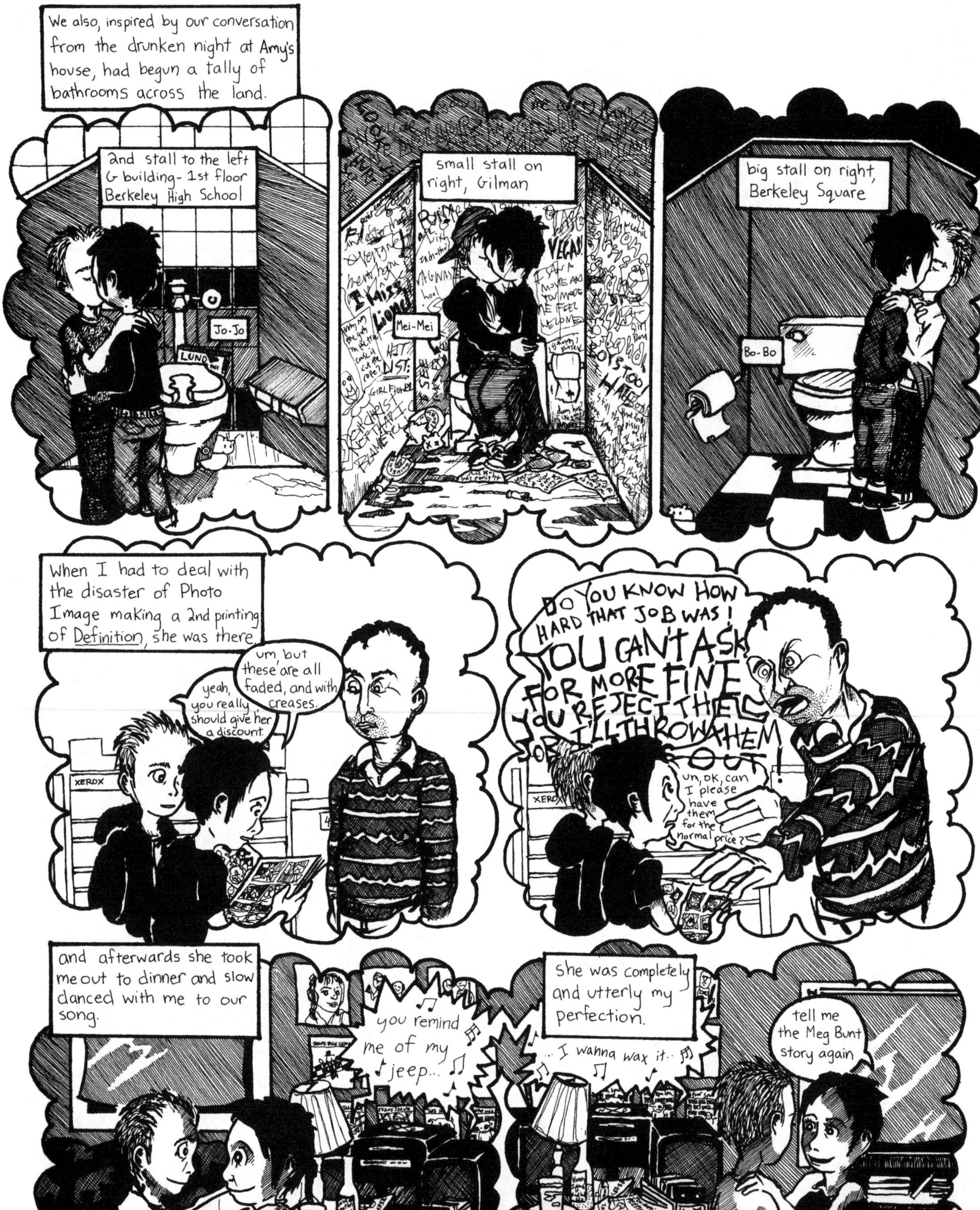
We also, inspired by our conversation from the drunken night at Amy's house, had begun a tally of bathrooms across the land.
and stall to the left G building- 1st floor Berkeley High School
Jo-Jo
small stall on right, Gilman
Mei-Mei
big stall on right, Berkeley Square
Bo-Bo
When I had to deal with the disaster of Photo Image making a 2nd printing of Definition, she was there.
yeah, you really should give her a discount.
um, but these are all faded, and with creases.
XEROX
DO YOU KNOW HOW HARD THAT JOB WAS!
YOU CAN'T ASK FOR MORE
un, ok, can I please have them for the normal price?
and afterwards she took me out to dinner and slow danced with me to our song.
you remind me of my jeep...
She was completely and utterly my perfection.
... I wanna wax it...
tell me the Meg Bunt story again

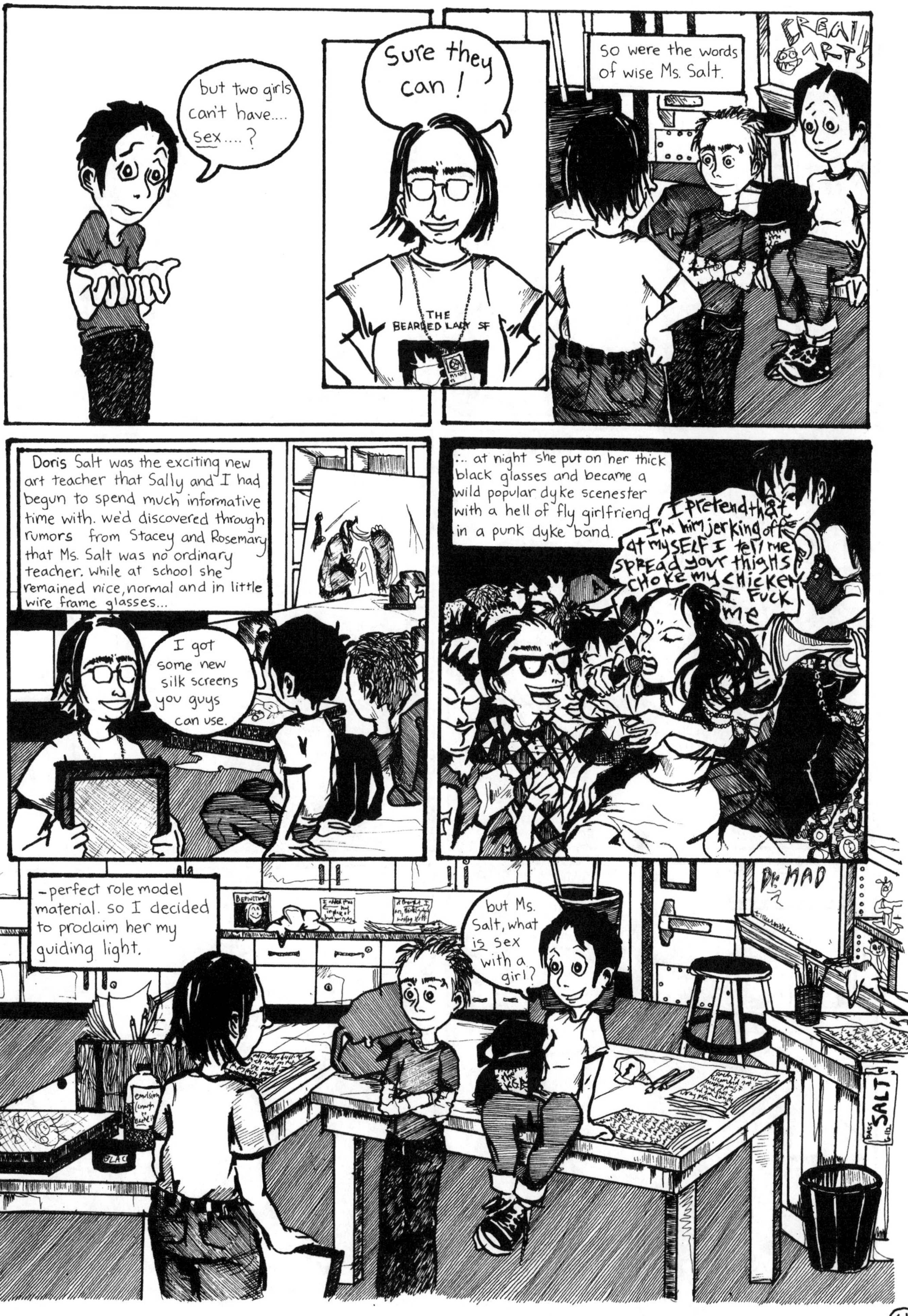

but two girls can't have.... sex.... ?
Sure they can!
THE BEARDED LADY SF
So were the words of wise Ms. Salt.
Doris Salt was the exciting new art teacher that Sally and I had begun to spend much informative time with. we'd discovered through rumors from Stacey and Rosemary that Ms. Salt was no ordinary teacher. While at school she remained nice, normal and in little wire frame glasses...
I got some new silk screens you guys can use.
... at night she put on her thick black glasses and became a wild popular dyke scenester with a hell of fly girlfriend in a punk dyke band.
I pretend that I'm him jerking off at mySELF I tell me
SPREAD your thighs
CHOKE my chicken
I FUCK me
-perfect role model material. so I decided to proclaim her my guiding light.
but Ms. Salt, what is sex with a girl?
Dr. MAD
SALT

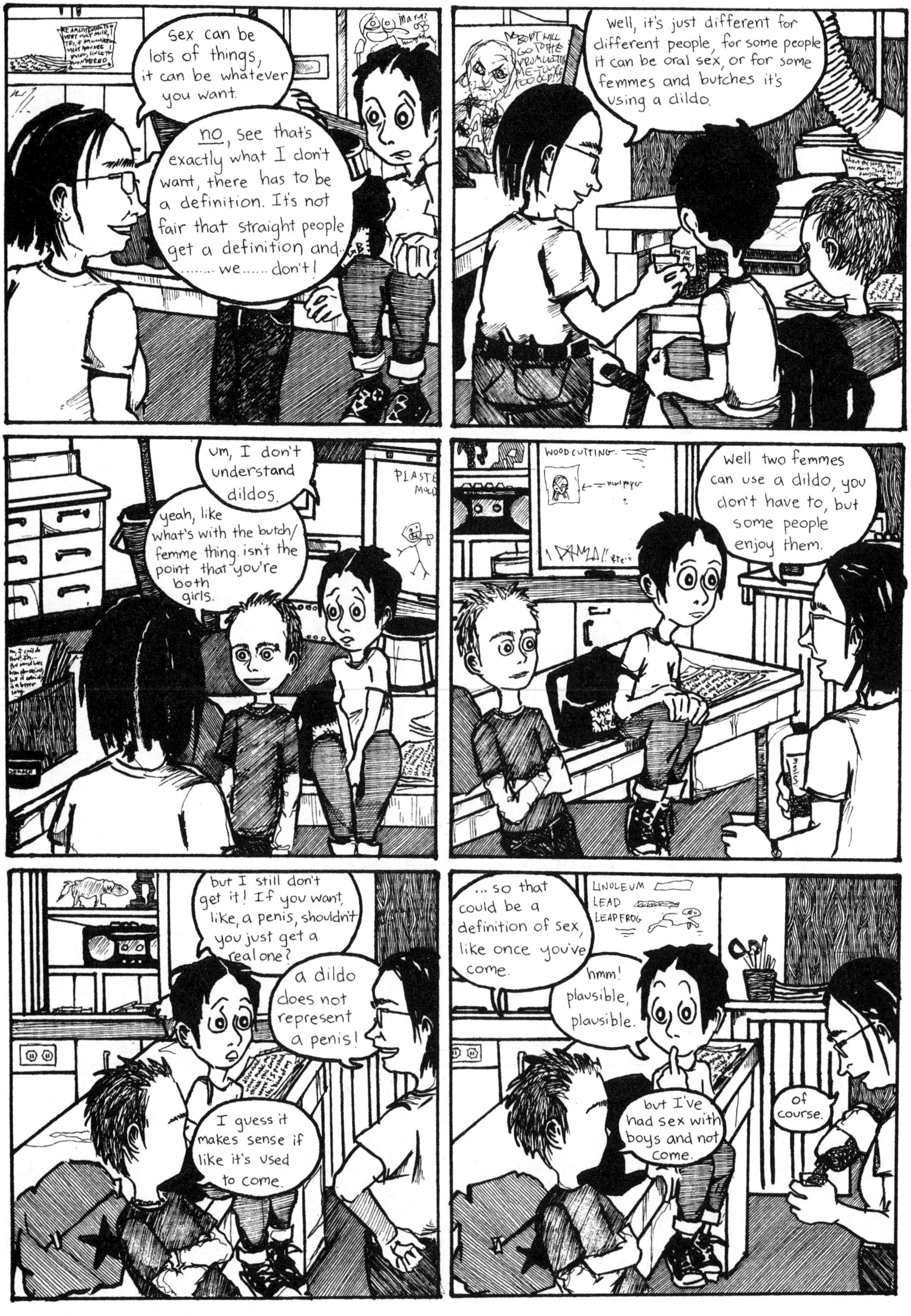

Sex can be lots of things, it can be whatever you want.
no, see that's exactly what I don't want, there has to be a definition. It's not fair that straight people get a definition and... ....we...... don't!
Well, it's just different for different people, for some people it can be oral sex, or for some femmes and butches it's using a dildo.
um, I don't understand dildos.
yeah, like what's with the butch/femme thing. isn't the point that you're both girls.
PLASTER MOLD
WOOD CUTTING
Well two femmes can use a dildo, you don't have to, but some people enjoy them.
but I still don't get it! If you want, like, a penis, shouldn't you just get a real one?
a dildo does not represent a penis!
I guess it makes sense if like it's used to come.
...so that could be a definition of sex, like once you've come.
LINOLEUM
LEAD
LEAPFROG
hmm! plausible, plausible.
but I've had sex with boys and not come.
of course.

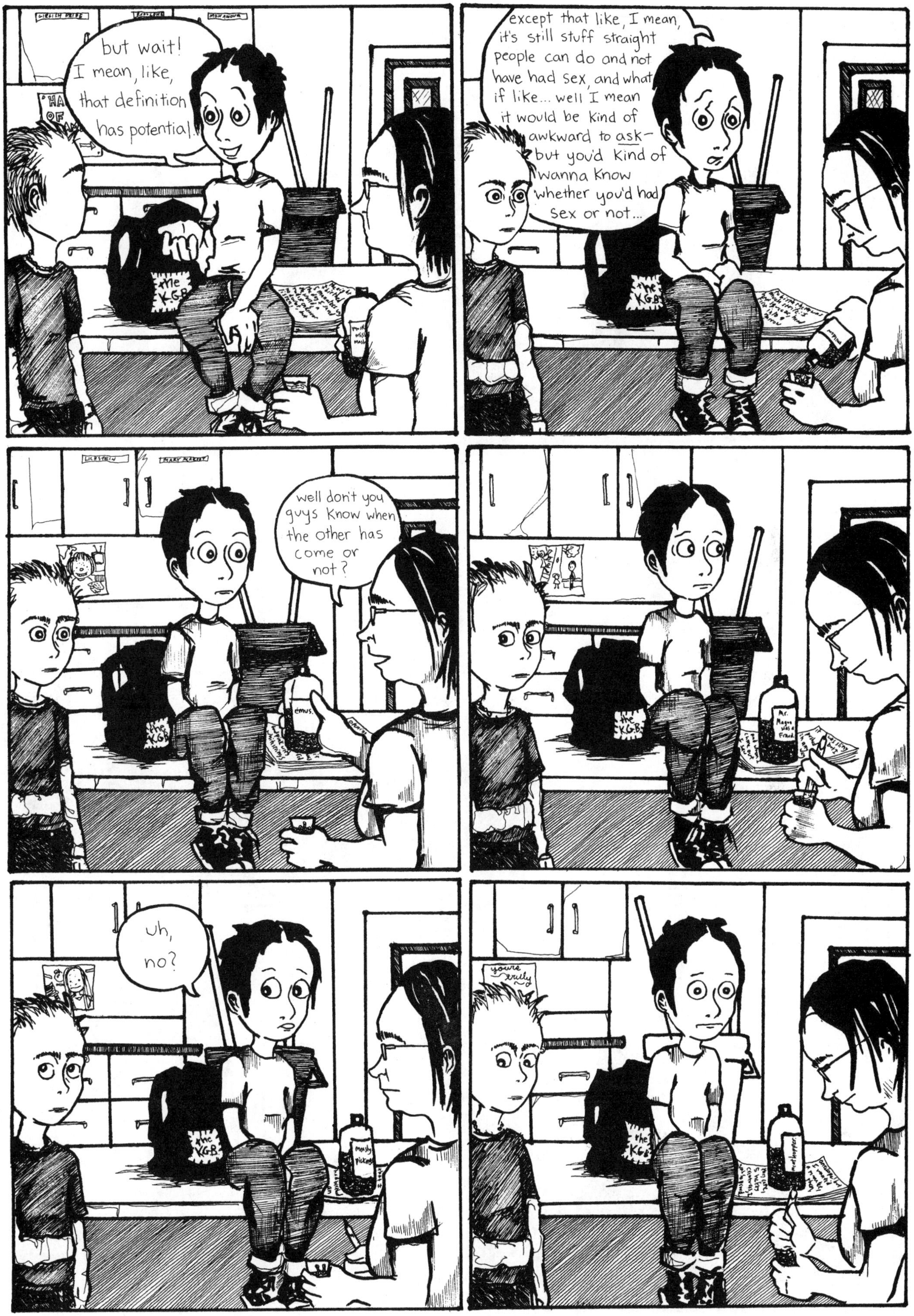
but wait! I mean, like, that definition has potential!
except that like, I mean, it's still stuff straight people can do and not have had sex, and what if like... well I mean it would be kind of awkward to ask- but you'd kind of wanna know whether you'd had sex or not...
well don't you guys know when the other has come or not?
uh, no?
the KGB
you're truly

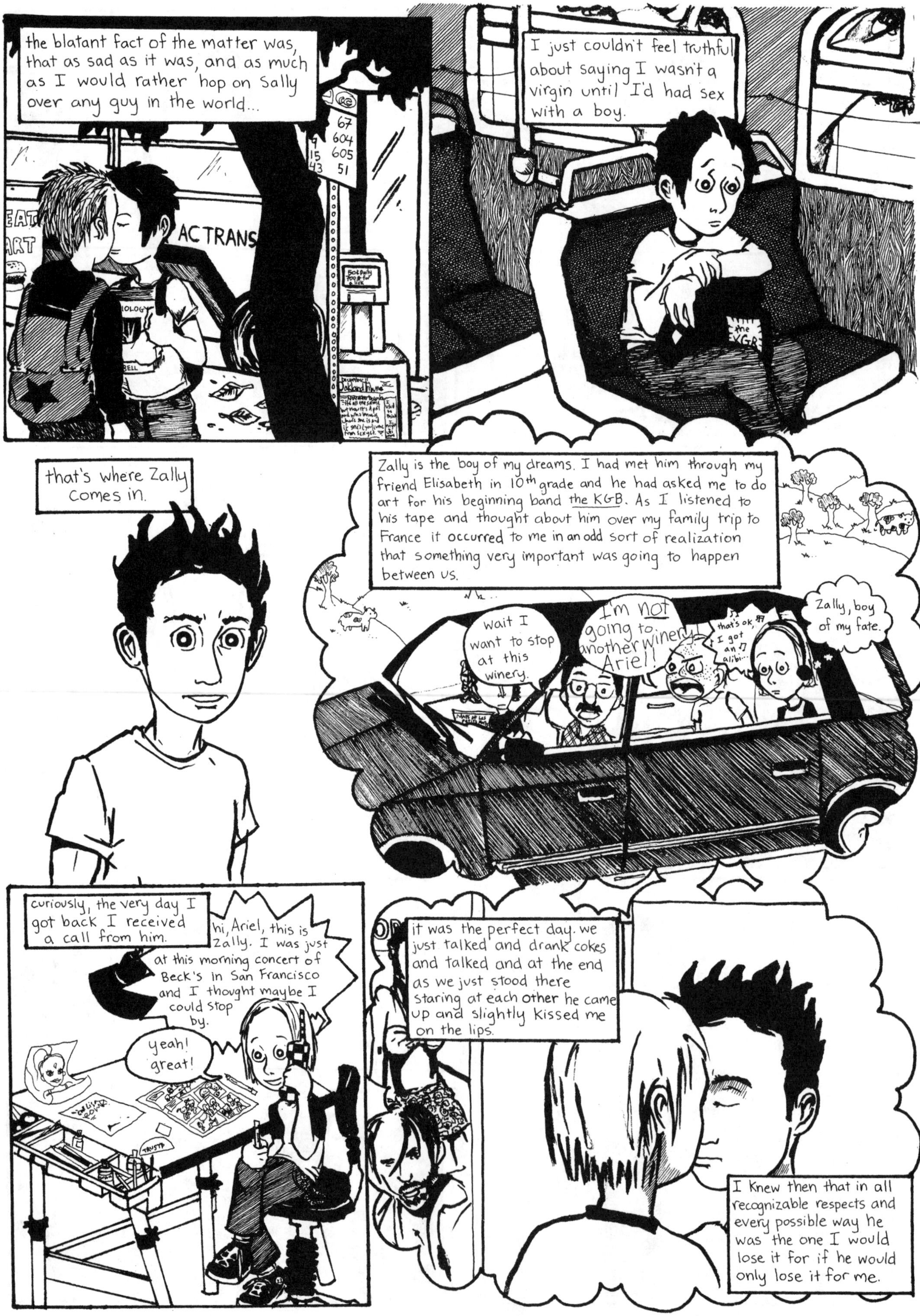
the blatant fact of the matter was, that as sad as it was, and as much as I would rather hop on Sally over any guy in the world...
ACTRANS
I just couldn't feel truthful about saying I wasn't a virgin until I'd had sex with a boy.
that's where Zally comes in.
Zally is the boy of my dreams. I had met him through my friend Elisabeth in 10th grade and he had asked me to do art for his beginning band the KGB. As I listened to his tape and thought about him over my family trip to France it occurred to me in an odd sort of realization that something very important was going to happen between us.
wait I want to stop at this winery.
I'm not going to another winery Ariel!
that's ok, I got an alibi...
Zally, boy of my fate.
curiously, the very day I got back I received a call from him.
hi, Ariel, this is Zally. I was just at this morning concert of Beck's in San Francisco and I thought maybe I could stop by.
yeah! great!
it was the perfect day. we just talked and drank cokes and talked and at the end as we just stood there staring at each other he came up and slightly kissed me on the lips.
I knew then that in all recognizable respects and every possible way he was the one I would lose it for if he would only lose it for me.

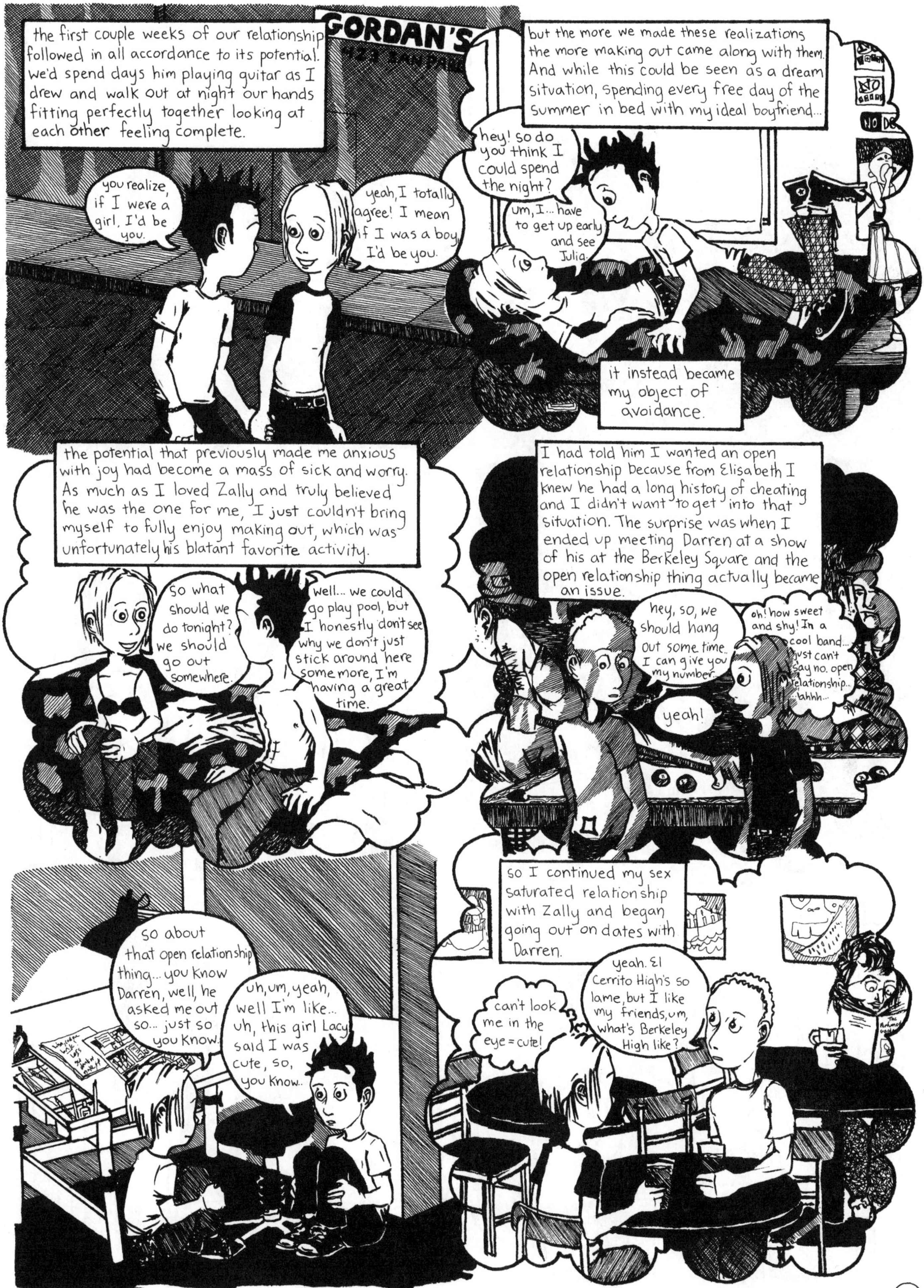
the first couple weeks of our relationship followed in all accordance to its potential. we'd spend days him playing guitar as I drew and walk out at night our hands fitting perfectly together looking at each other feeling complete.
GORDAN'S
you realize, if I were a girl, I'd be you.
yeah, I totally agree! I mean if I was a boy, I'd be you.
but the more we made these realizations the more making out came along with them. And while this could be seen as a dream situation, spending every free day of the summer in bed with my ideal boyfriend...
hey! so do you think I could spend the night?
um, I... have to get up early and see Julia.
it instead became my object of avoidance.
the potential that previously made me anxious with joy had become a mass of sick and worry. As much as I loved Zally and truly believed he was the one for me, I just couldn't bring myself to fully enjoy making out, which was unfortunately his blatant favorite activity.
So what should we do tonight? we should go out somewhere.
well... we could go play pool, but I honestly don't see why we don't just stick around here some more, I'm having a great time.
I had told him I wanted an open relationship because from Elisabeth I knew he had a long history of cheating and I didn't want to get into that situation. The surprise was when I ended up meeting Darren at a show of his at the Berkeley Square and the open relationship thing actually became an issue.
hey, so, we should hang out some time.. I can give you my number..
oh! how sweet and shy! In a cool band... just can't say no. open relationship.. ahhh...
yeah!
so about that open relationship thing... you know Darren, well, he asked me out so... just so you know.
uh, um, yeah, well I'm like... uh, this girl Lacy said I was cute, so, you know..
so I continued my sex saturated relationship with Zally and began going out on dates with Darren.
can't look me in the eye = cute!
yeah. El Cerrito High's so lame, but I like my friends, um, what's Berkeley High like?

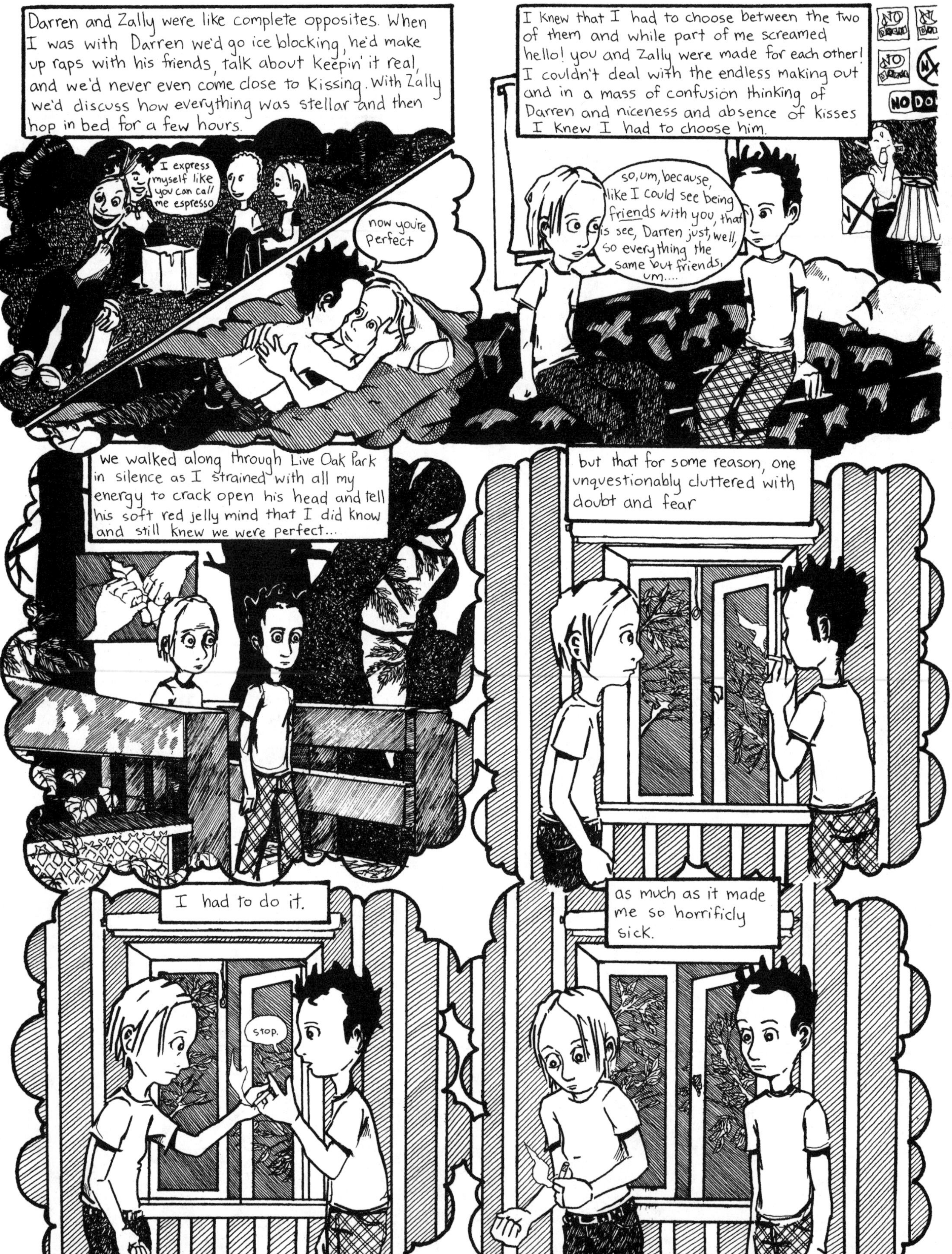

Darren and Zally were like complete opposites. When I was with Darren we'd go ice blocking, he'd make up raps with his friends, talk about keepin' it real, and we'd never even come close to kissing. With Zally we'd discuss how everything was stellar and then hop in bed for a few hours.
I express myself like you can call me espresso
now you're perfect
I knew that I had to choose between the two of them and while part of me screamed hello! you and Zally were made for each other! I couldn't deal with the endless making out and in a mass of confusion thinking of Darren and niceness and absence of kisses I knew I had to choose him.
so, um, because, like I could see being friends with you, that is see, Darren just, well, so everything the same but friends, um....
NO
NO DO
we walked along through Live Oak Park in silence as I strained with all my energy to crack open his head and tell his soft red jelly mind that I did know and still knew we were perfect...
but that for some reason, one unquestionably cluttered with doubt and fear
I had to do it.
stop.
as much as it made me so horrificly sick.

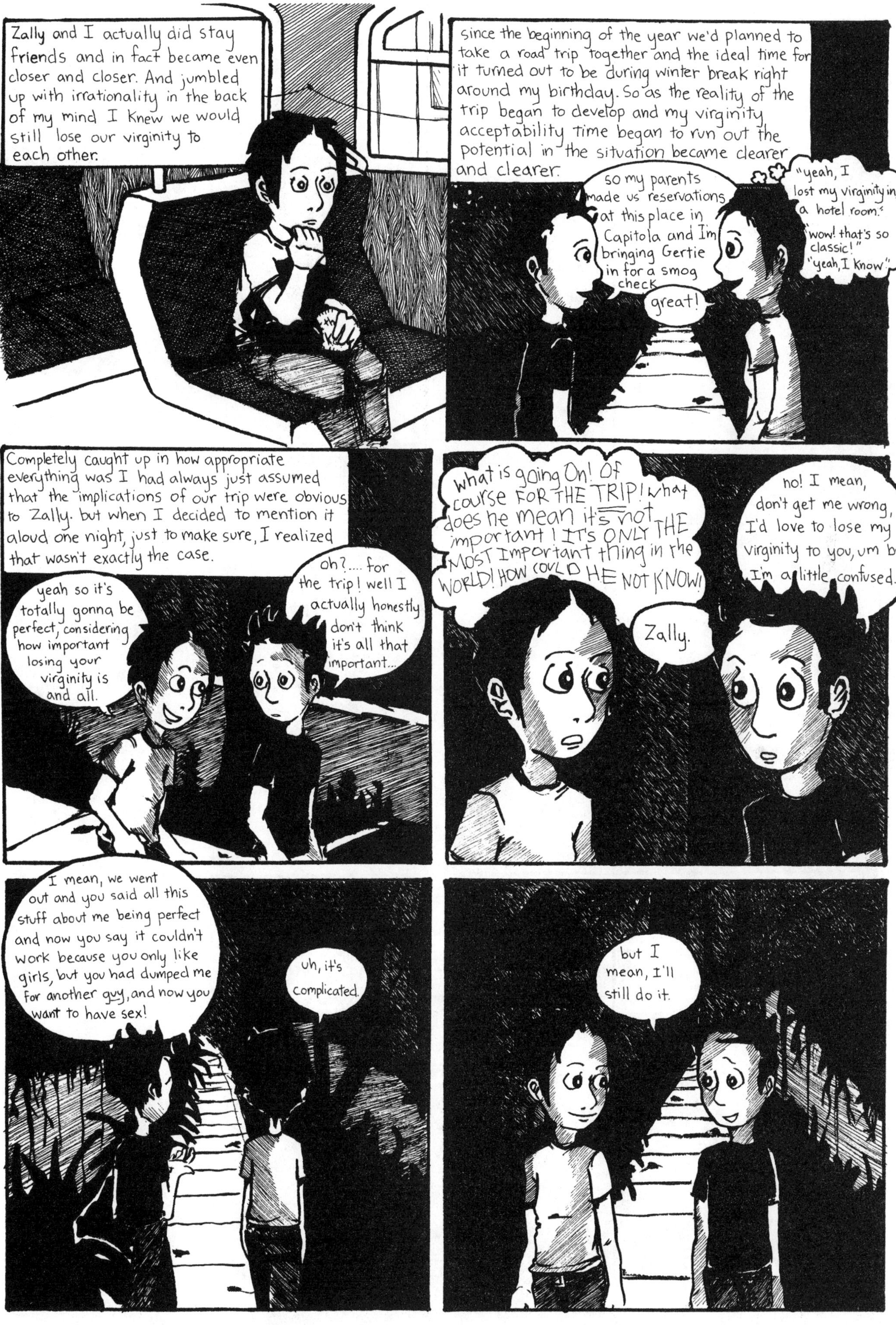
Zally and I actually did stay friends and in fact became even closer and closer. And jumbled up with irrationality in the back of my mind I Knew we would still lose our virginity to each other.
since the beginning of the year we'd planned to take a road trip together and the ideal time for it turned out to be during winter break right around my birthday. So as the reality of the trip began to develop and my virginity acceptability time began to run out the potential in the situation became clearer and clearer.
so my parents made us reservations at this place in Capitola and I'm bringing Gertie in for a smog check
"yeah, I lost my virginity in a hotel room." "wow! that's so classic!" "yeah, I Know"
great!
Completely caught up in how appropriate everything was I had always just assumed that the implications of our trip were obvious to Zally. but when I decided to mention it aloud one night, just to make sure, I realized that wasn't exactly the case.
yeah so it's totally gonna be perfect, considering how important losing your virginity is and all.
oh?.... for the trip! well I actually honestly don't think it's all that important...
what is going On! Of course FOR THE TRIP! what does he mean it's not important! IT'S ONLY THE MOST Important thing in the WORLD! HOW COULD HE NOT KNOW!
no! I mean, don't get me wrong, I'd love to lose my virginity to you, um but I'm a little confused...
Zally.
I mean, we went out and you said all this stuff about me being perfect and now you say it couldn't work because you only like girls, but you had dumped me for another guy, and now you want to have sex!
uh, it's complicated.
but I mean, I'll still do it.

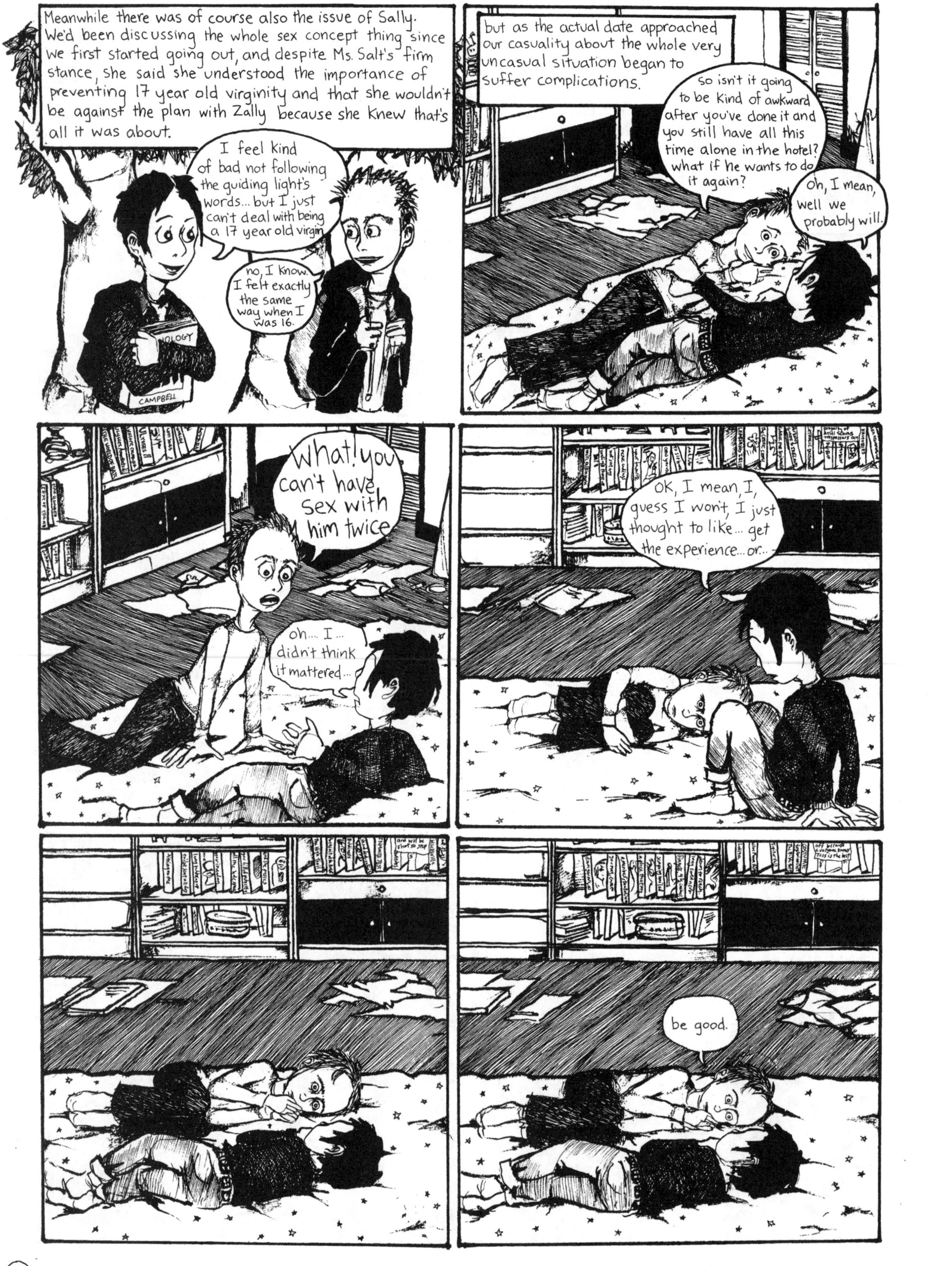
Meanwhile there was of course also the issue of Sally. We'd been discussing the whole sex concept thing since we first started going out, and despite Ms. Salt's firm stance, she said she understood the importance of preventing 17 year old virginity and that she wouldn't be against the plan with Zally because she knew that's all it was about.
I feel kind of bad not following the guiding light's words... but I just can't deal with being a 17 year old virgin
no, I know. I felt exactly the same way when I was 16.
NOLOGY
CAMPBELL
but as the actual date approached our casuality about the whole very uncasual situation began to suffer complications.
So isn't it going to be kind of awkward after you've done it and you still have all this time alone in the hotel? what if he wants to do it again?
Oh, I mean, well we probably will.
What! you can't have sex with him twice
oh... I... didn't think it mattered...
OK, I mean, I, guess I won't, I just thought to like... get the experience... or...
be good.

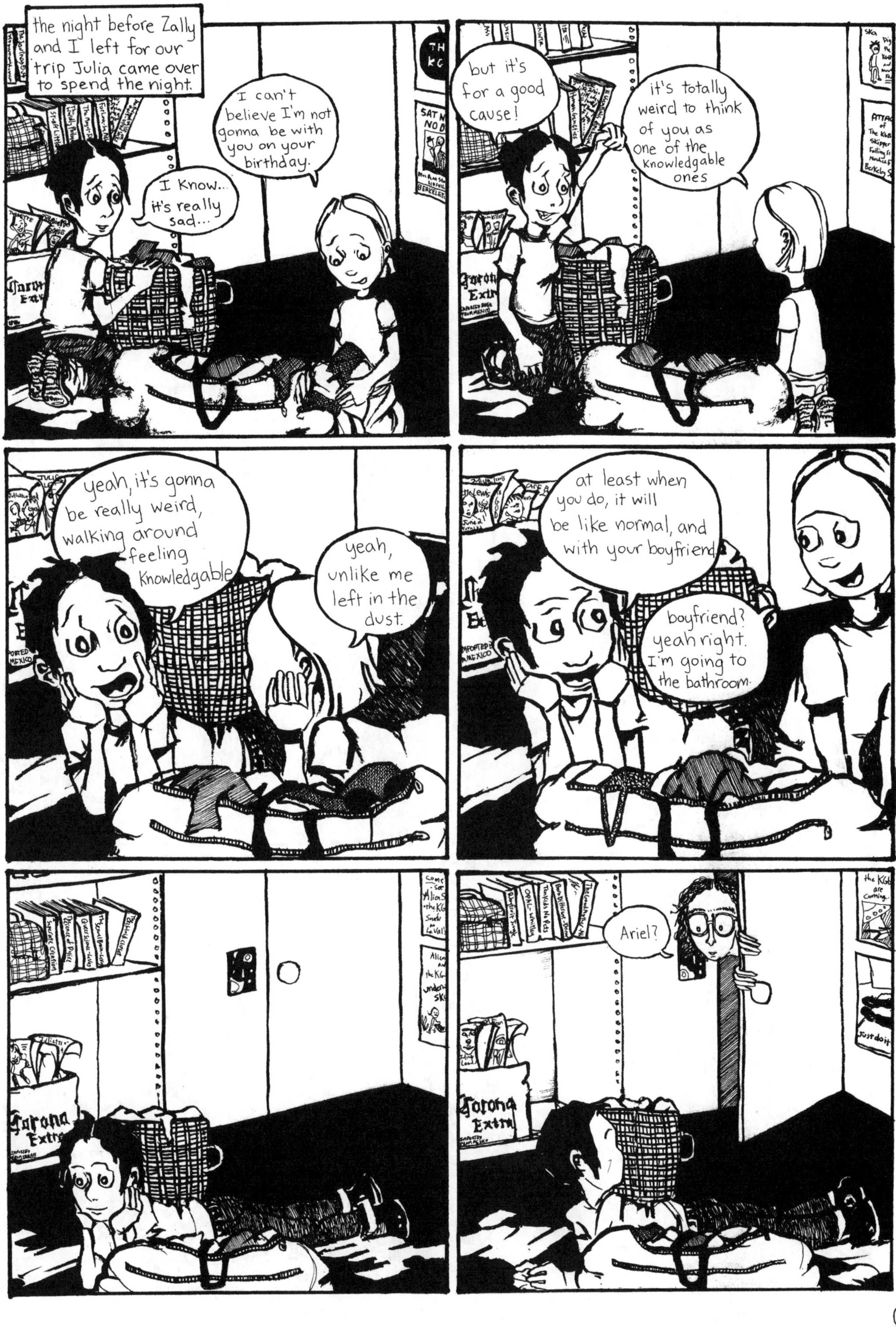
the night before Zally and I left for our trip Julia came over to spend the night.
I can't believe I'm not gonna be with you on your birthday.
I Know... it's really sad...
but it's for a good cause!
it's totally weird to think of you as one of the Knowledgable ones
yeah, it's gonna be really weird, walking around feeling Knowledgable
yeah, unlike me left in the dust.
at least when you do, it will be like normal, and with your boyfriend
boyfriend? yeah right. I'm going to the bathroom.
Ariel?

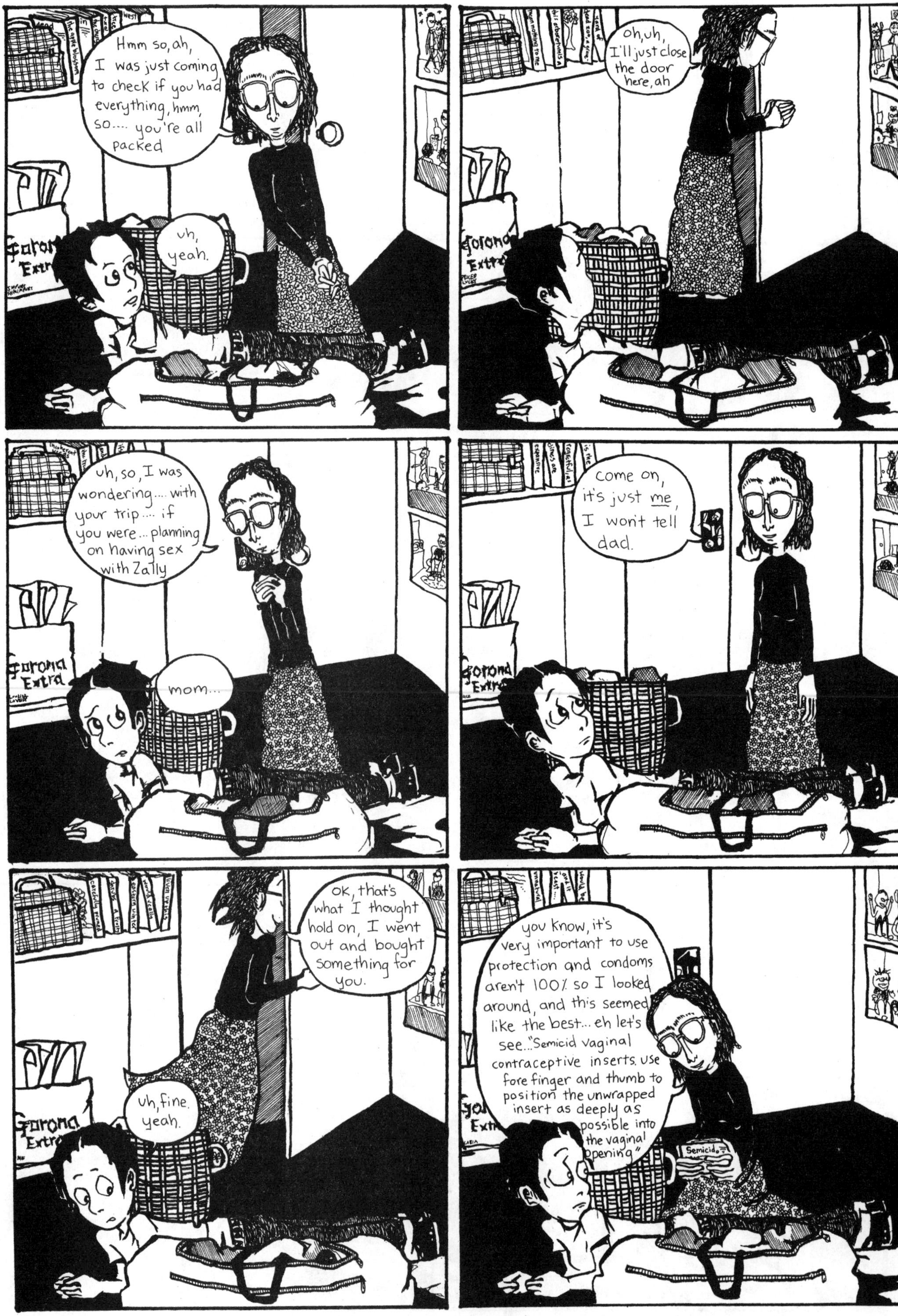
Hmm so, ah, I was just coming to check if you had everything, hmm, so.... you're all packed
uh, yeah.
oh, uh, I'll just close the door here, ah
uh, so, I was wondering.... with your trip.... if you were... planning on having sex with Zally
mom...
come on, it's just me, I won't tell dad.
ok, that's what I thought hold on, I went out and bought something for you.
uh, fine. yeah.
you know, it's very important to use protection and condoms aren't 100% so I looked around, and this seemed like the best... eh let's see..."Semicid vaginal contraceptive inserts. Use fore finger and thumb to position the unwrapped insert as deeply as possible into the vaginal opening."
Semicid

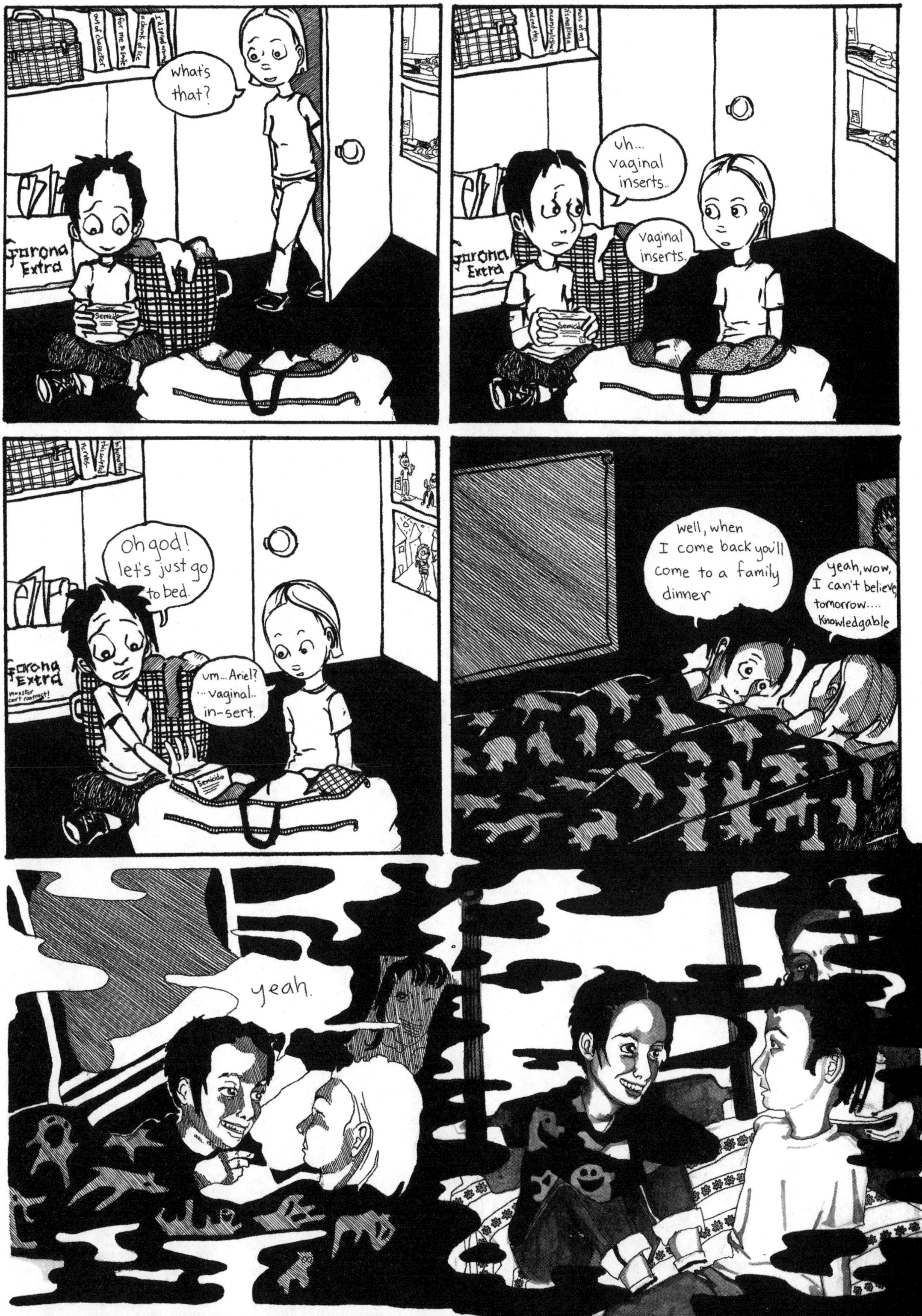
what's that?
uh... vaginal inserts..
vaginal inserts.
Oh god! let's just go to bed.
um...Ariel? ...vaginal.. in-sert.
well, when I come back you'll come to a family dinner
yeah, wow, I can't believe tomorrow.... Knowledgable
yeah.

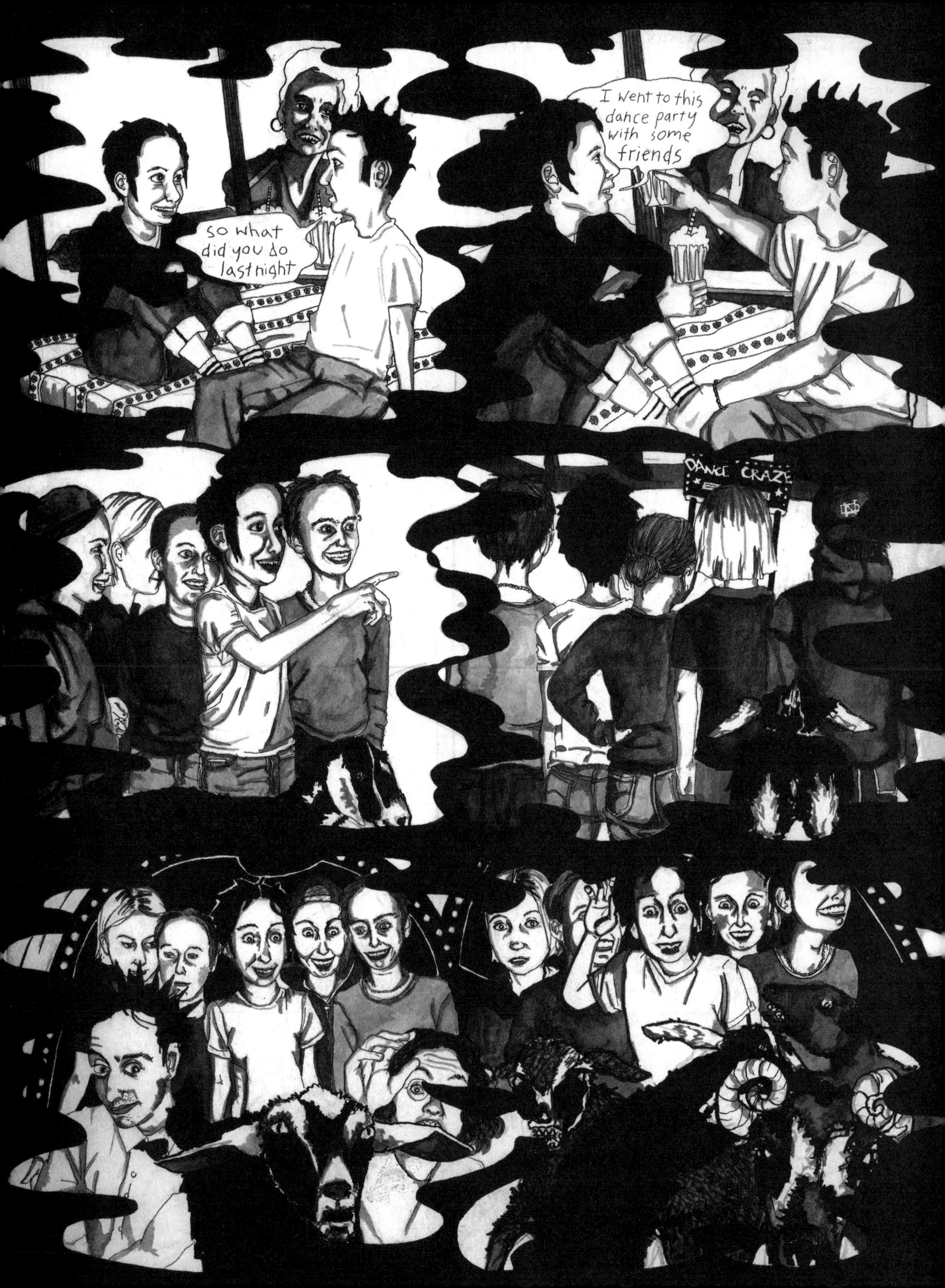
so what did you do last night
I went to this dance party with some friends
DANCE CRAZE

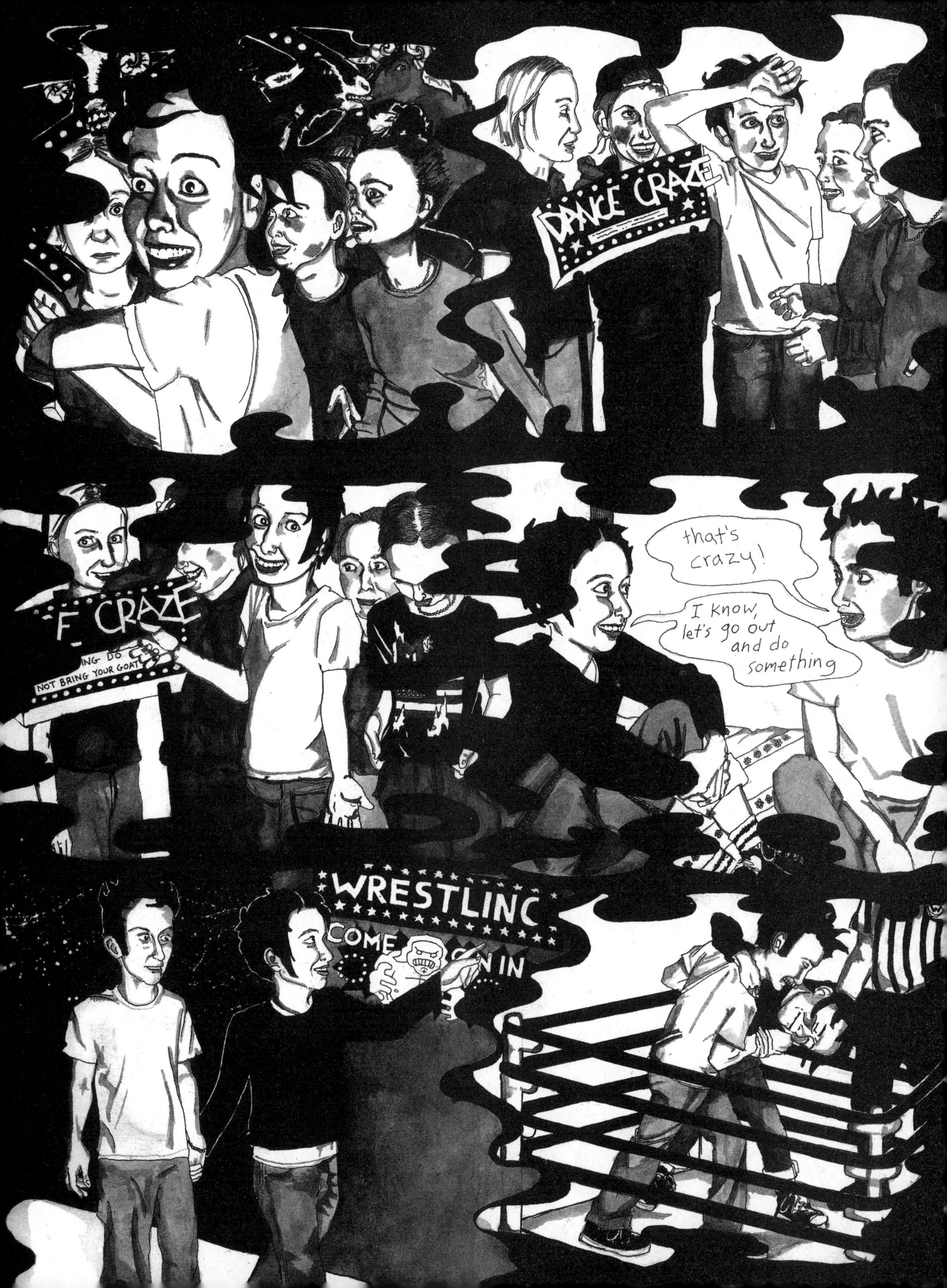
DANCE CRAZE
F CRAZE
ING DO
NOT BRING YOUR GOAT
that's crazy!
I know, let's go out and do something
WRESTLINC
COME
IN

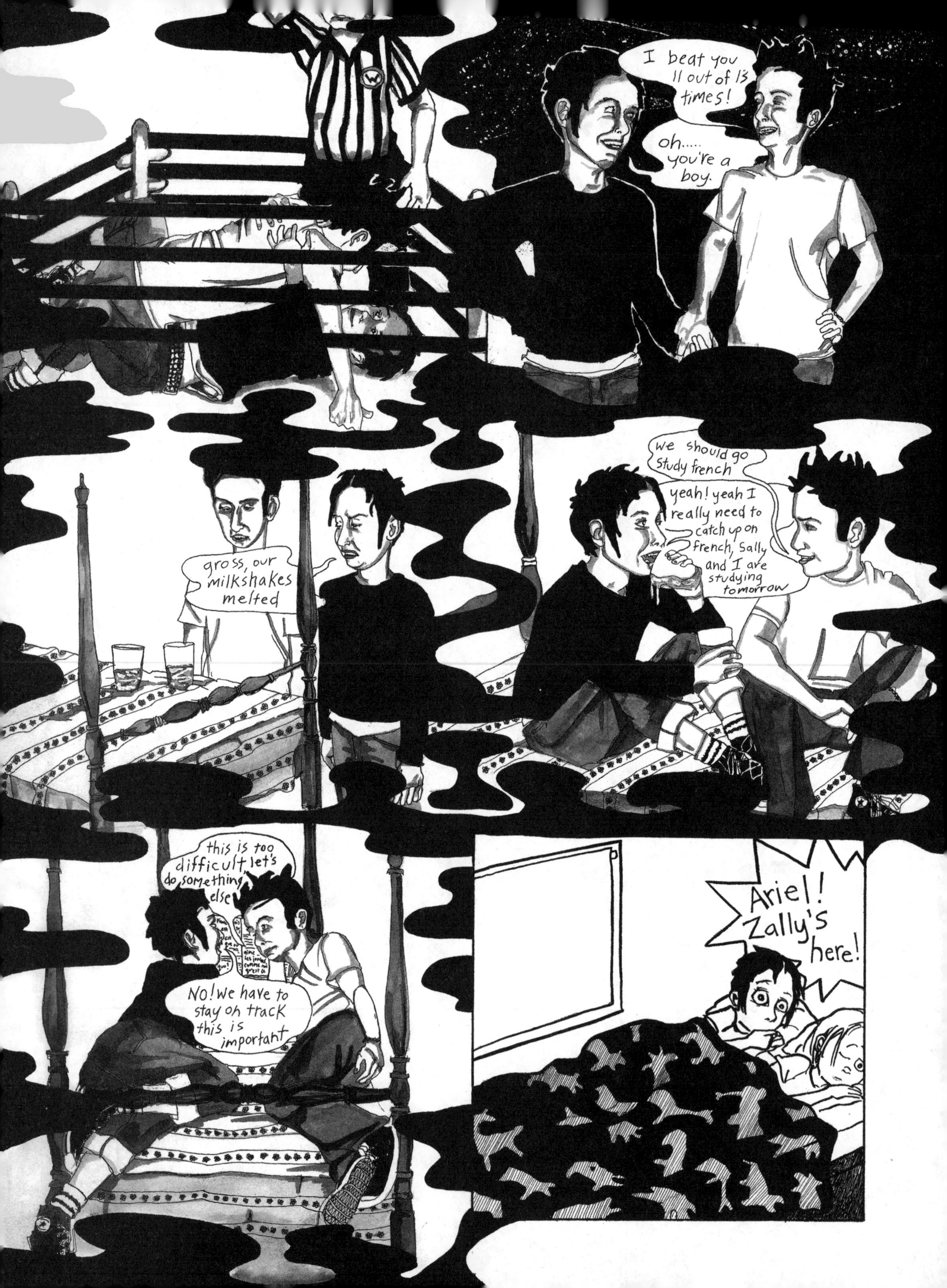

I beat you 11 out of 13 times!
oh..... you're a boy.
gross, our milkshakes melted
we should go study french
yeah! yeah I really need to catch up on french, Sally and I are studying tomorrow
this is too difficult, let's do something else
No! we have to stay on track this is important
Ariel! Zally's here!

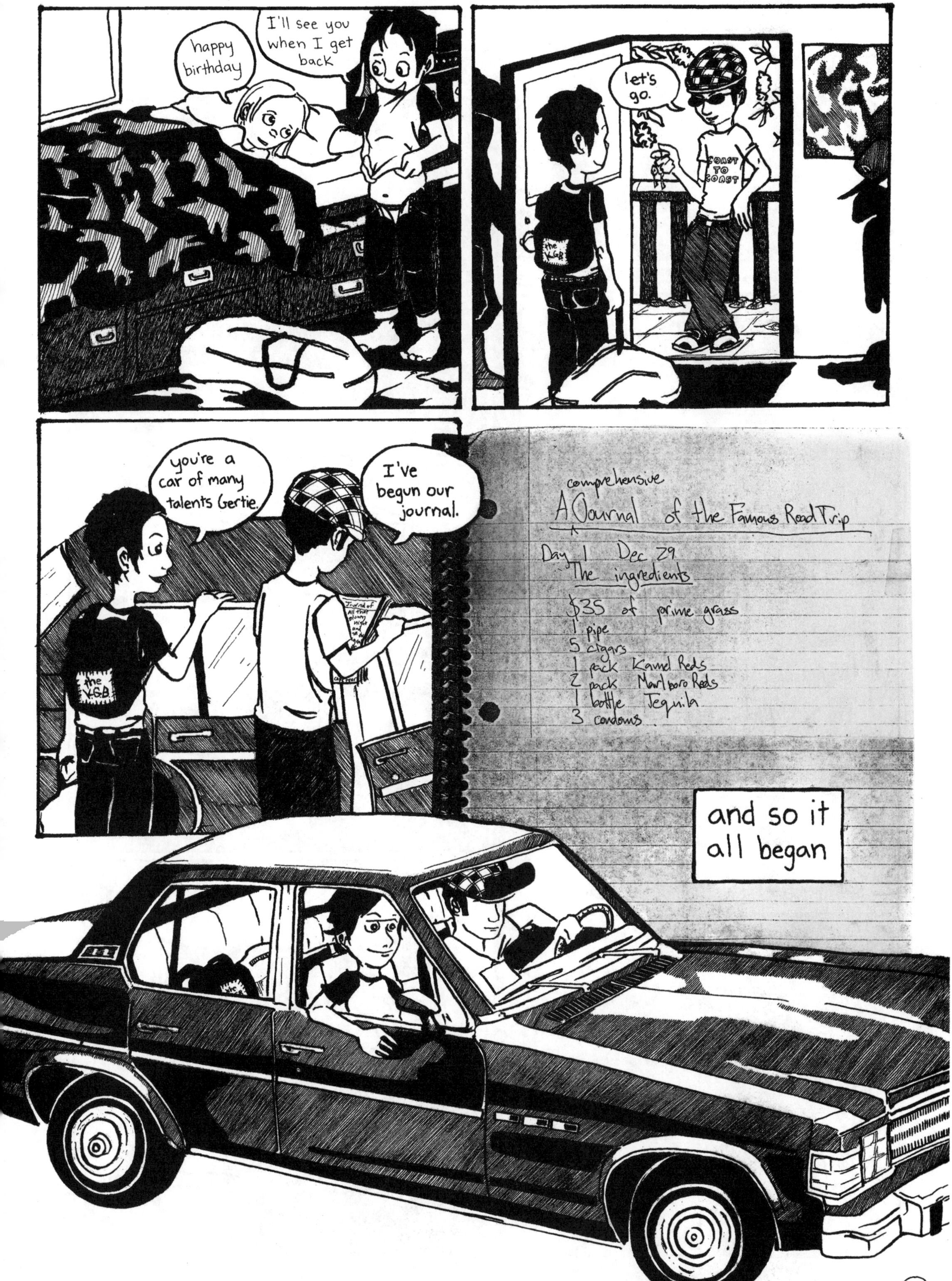
happy birthday
I'll see you when I get back
let's go.
COAST TO COAST
the VGB
you're a car of many talents Gertie.
I've begun our journal.
comprehensive
A Journal of the Famous Road Trip
Day 1 Dec 29
The ingredients
$35 of prime grass
1 pipe
5 cigars
1 pack Kamel Reds
2 pack Marlboro Reds
1 bottle Tequila
3 condoms
and so it all began

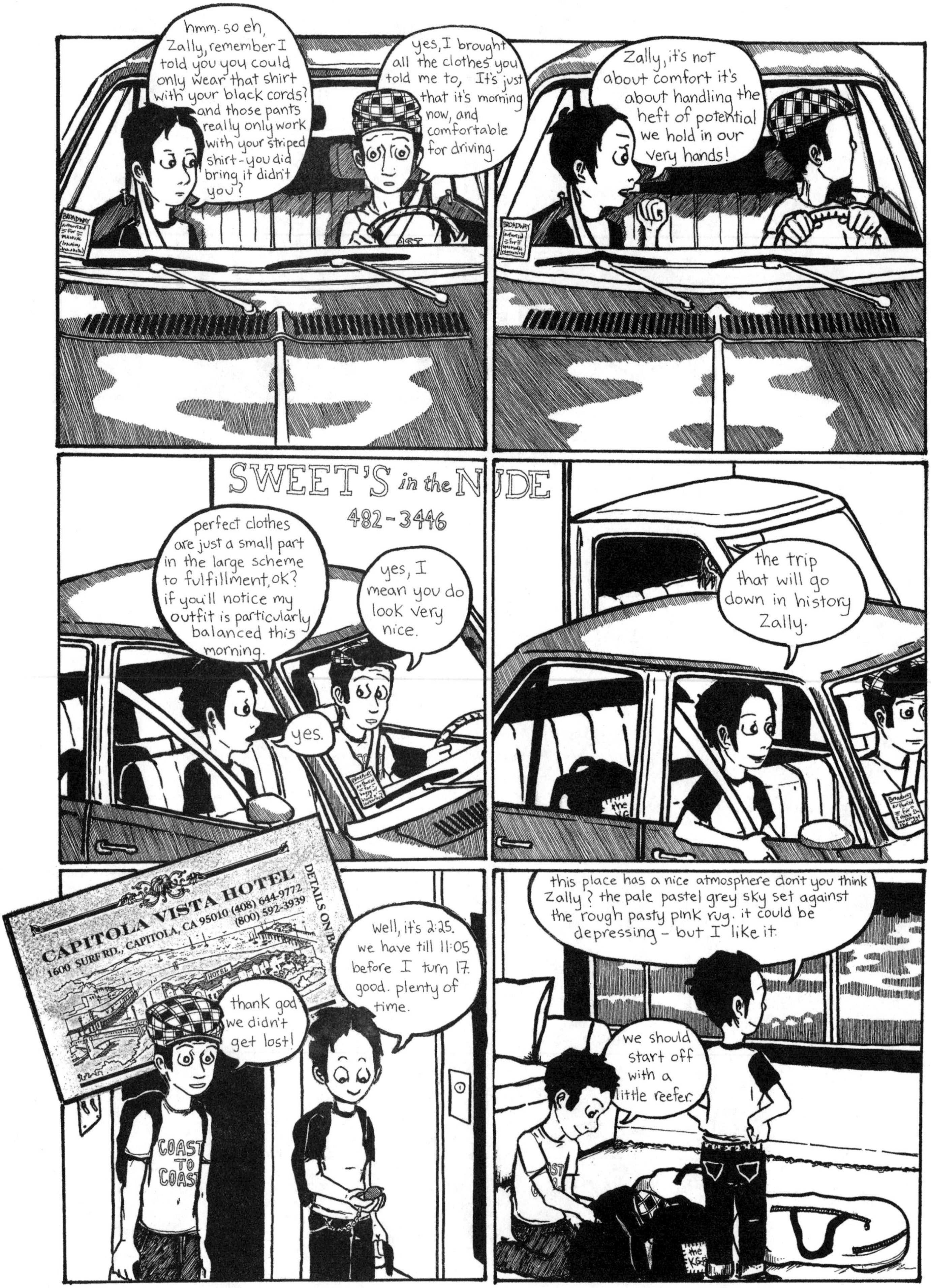

hmm. so eh, Zally, remember I told you you could only wear that shirt with your black cords? and those pants really only work with your striped shirt - you did bring it didn't you?
yes, I brought all the clothes you told me to, It's just that it's morning now, and comfortable for driving.
Zally, it's not about comfort it's about handling the heft of potential we hold in our very hands!
SWEET'S in the NUDE
482-3446
perfect clothes are just a small part in the large scheme to fulfillment, OK? if you'll notice my outfit is particularly balanced this morning.
yes, I mean you do look very nice.
yes.
the trip that will go down in history Zally.
CAPITOLA VISTA HOTEL
1600 SURF RD., CAPITOLA, CA 95010 (408) 644-9772
(800) 592-3939
thank god we didn't get lost!
well, it's 2:25. we have till 11:05 before I turn 17. good. plenty of time.
COAST TO COAST
this place has a nice atmosphere don't you think Zally? the pale pastel grey sky set against the rough pasty pink rug. it could be depressing - but I like it.
we should start off with a little reefer.

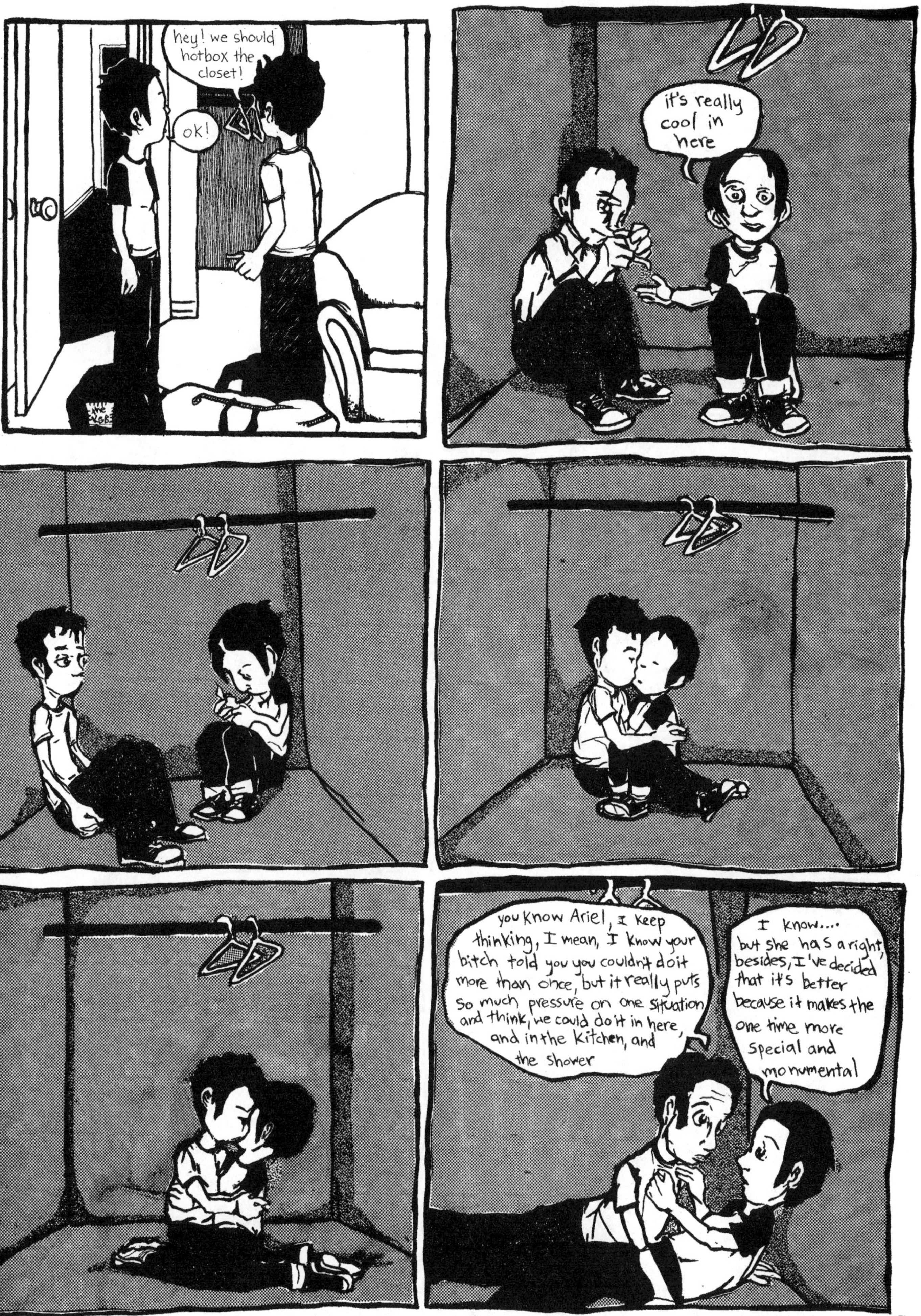
hey! we should hotbox the closet!
ok!
it's really cool in here
you know Ariel, I keep thinking, I mean, I know your bitch told you you couldn't do it more than once, but it really puts so much pressure on one situation and think, we could do it in here, and in the kitchen, and the shower
I know.... but she has a right, besides, I've decided that it's better because it makes the one time more special and monumental

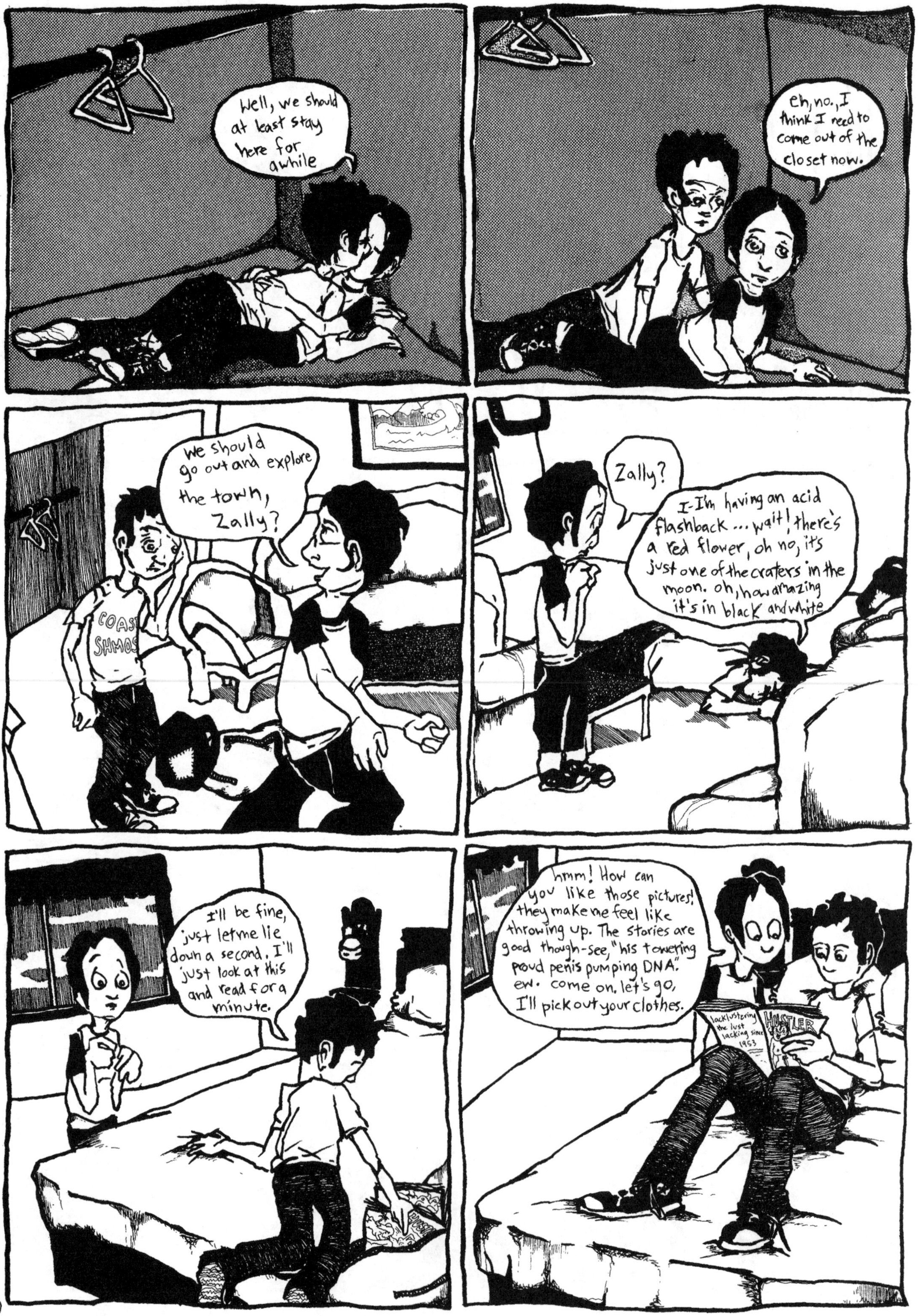
Well, we should at least stay here for awhile
eh, no., I think I need to come out of the closet now.
We should go out and explore the town, Zally?
Zally?
I-I'm having an acid flashback ... wait! there's a red flower, oh no, it's just one of the craters in the moon. oh, how amazing it's in black and white
I'll be fine, just let me lie down a second. I'll just look at this and read for a minute.
hmm! How can you like those pictures! they make me feel like throwing up. The stories are good though-see, "his towering proud penis pumping DNA." ew. come on. let's go, I'll pick out your clothes.
COAST SHMOS
HUSTLER
lackluster the lust lacking since 1953

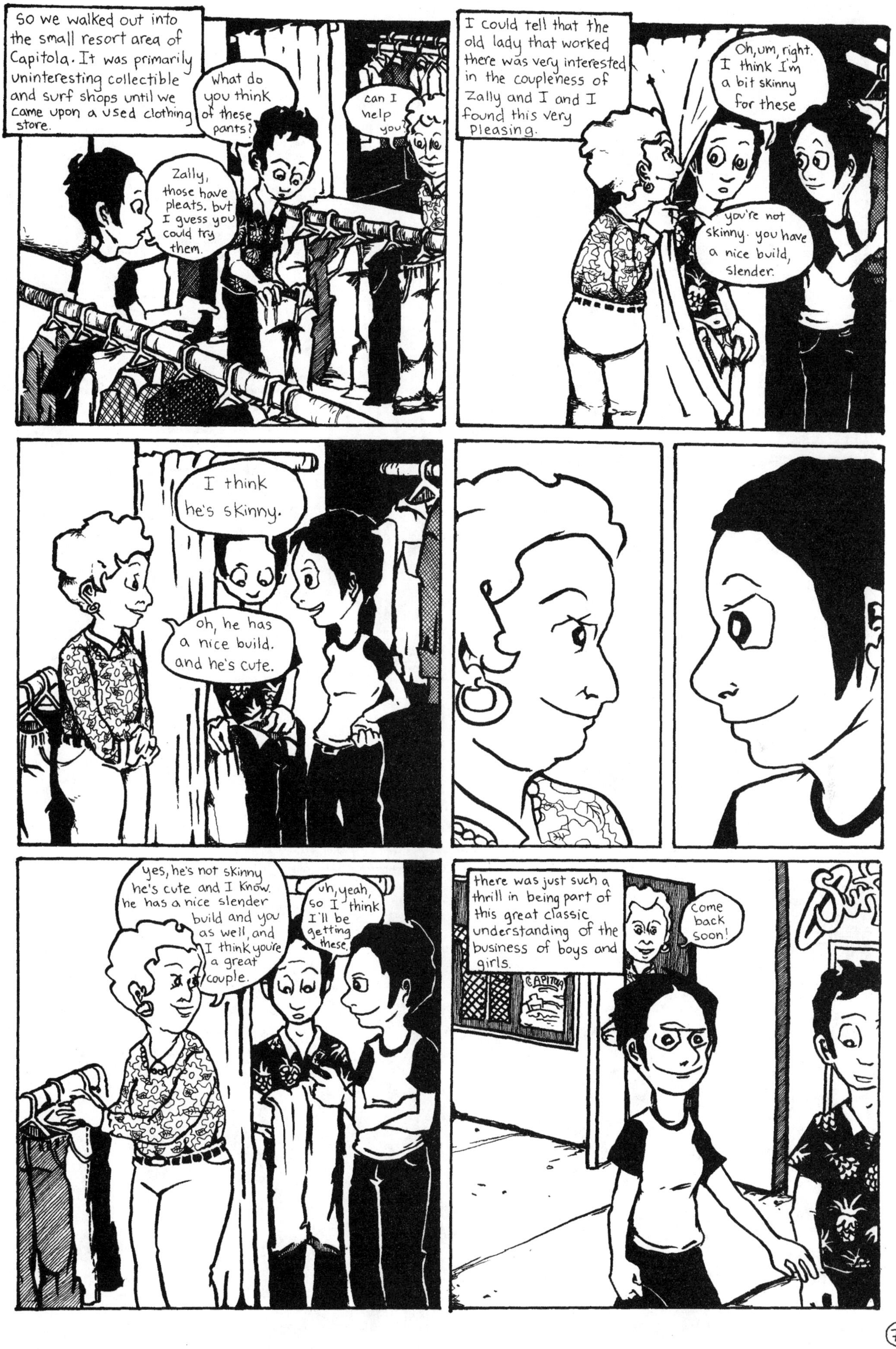
So we walked out into the small resort area of Capitola. It was primarily uninteresting collectible and surf shops until we came upon a used clothing store.
What do you think of these pants?
can I help you?
Zally, those have pleats. but I guess you could try them.
I could tell that the old lady that worked there was very interested in the coupleness of Zally and I and I found this very pleasing.
Oh, um, right. I think I'm a bit skinny for these
you're not skinny. you have a nice build, slender.
I think he's skinny.
oh, he has a nice build. and he's cute.
yes, he's not skinny he's cute and I know. he has a nice slender build and you as well, and I think you're a great couple.
uh, yeah, so I think I'll be getting these.
there was just such a thrill in being part of this great classic understanding of the business of boys and girls.
Come back soon!
CAPITOLA

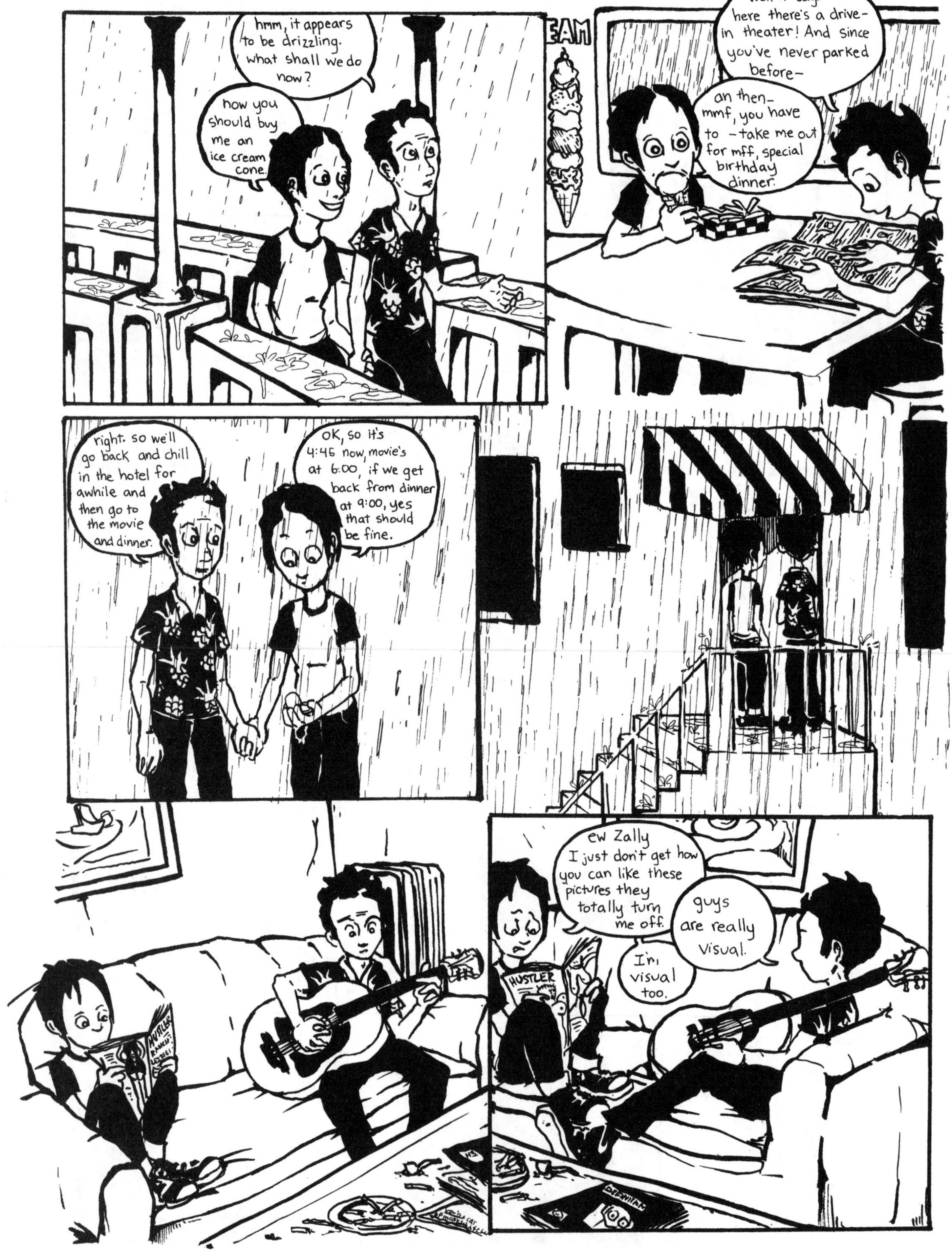
hmm, it appears to be drizzling. what shall we do now?
now you should buy me an ice cream cone.
EAM
well it says here there's a drive-in theater! And since you've never parked before—
an then— mmf, you have to —take me out for mff, special birthday dinner.
right. so we'll go back and chill in the hotel for awhile and then go to the movie and dinner.
OK, so it's 4:45 now, movie's at 6:00, if we get back from dinner at 9:00, yes that should be fine.
ew Zally I just don't get how you can like these pictures they totally turn me off.
guys are really visual.
I'm visual too.
HUSTLER

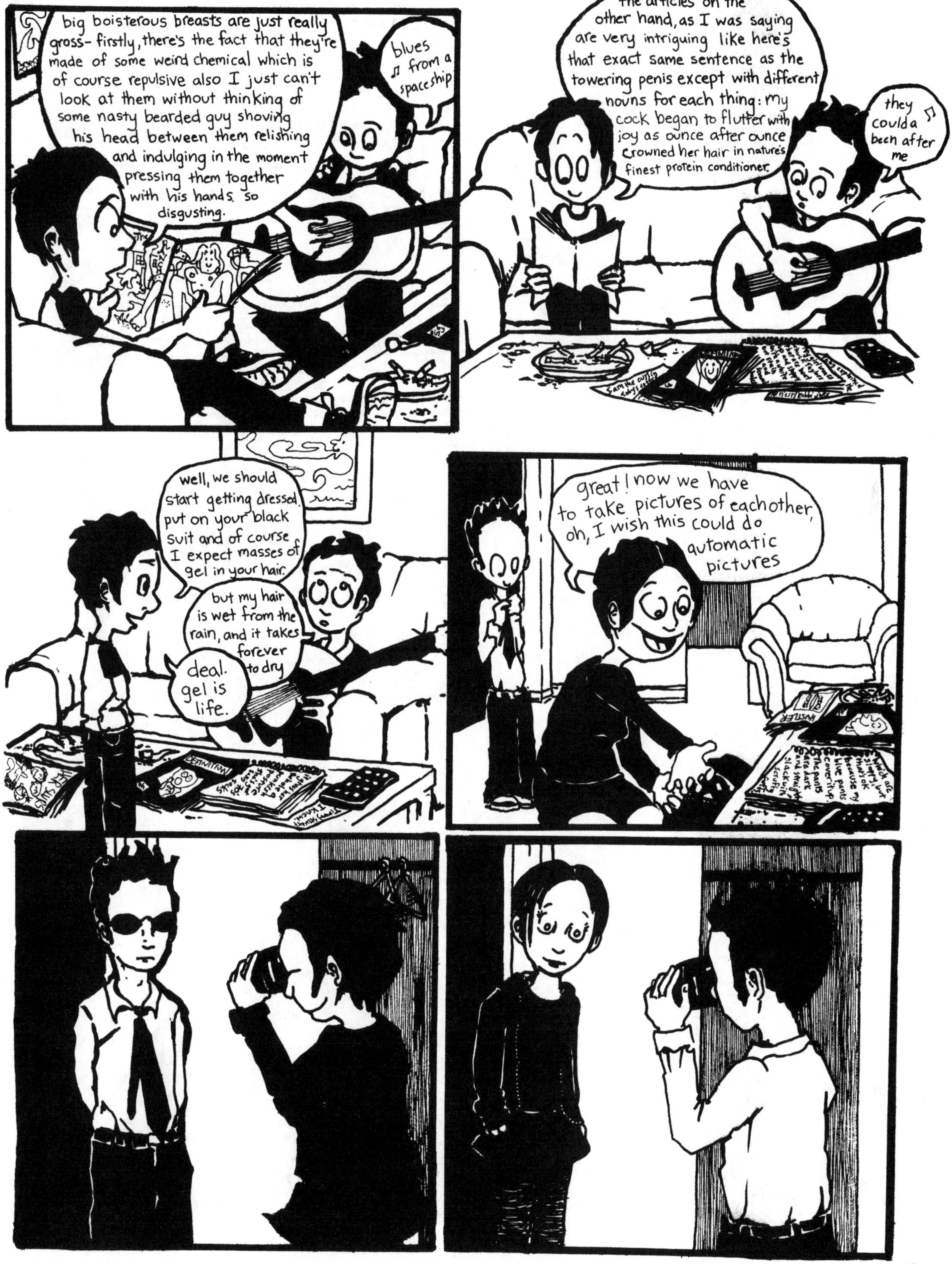
big boisterous breasts are just really gross- firstly, there's the fact that they're made of some weird chemical which is of course repulsive also I just can't look at them without thinking of some nasty bearded guy shoving his head between them relishing and indulging in the moment pressing them together with his hands. so disgusting.
blues ♫ from a spaceship
the articles on the other hand, as I was saying are very intriguing like here's that exact same sentence as the towering penis except with different nouns for each thing: my cock began to flutter with joy as ounce after ounce crowned her hair in nature's finest protein conditioner.
they coulda ♫ been after me
well, we should start getting dressed. put on your black suit and of course I expect masses of gel in your hair.
but my hair is wet from the rain, and it takes forever to dry
deal. gel is life.
great! now we have to take pictures of eachother, oh, I wish this could do automatic pictures

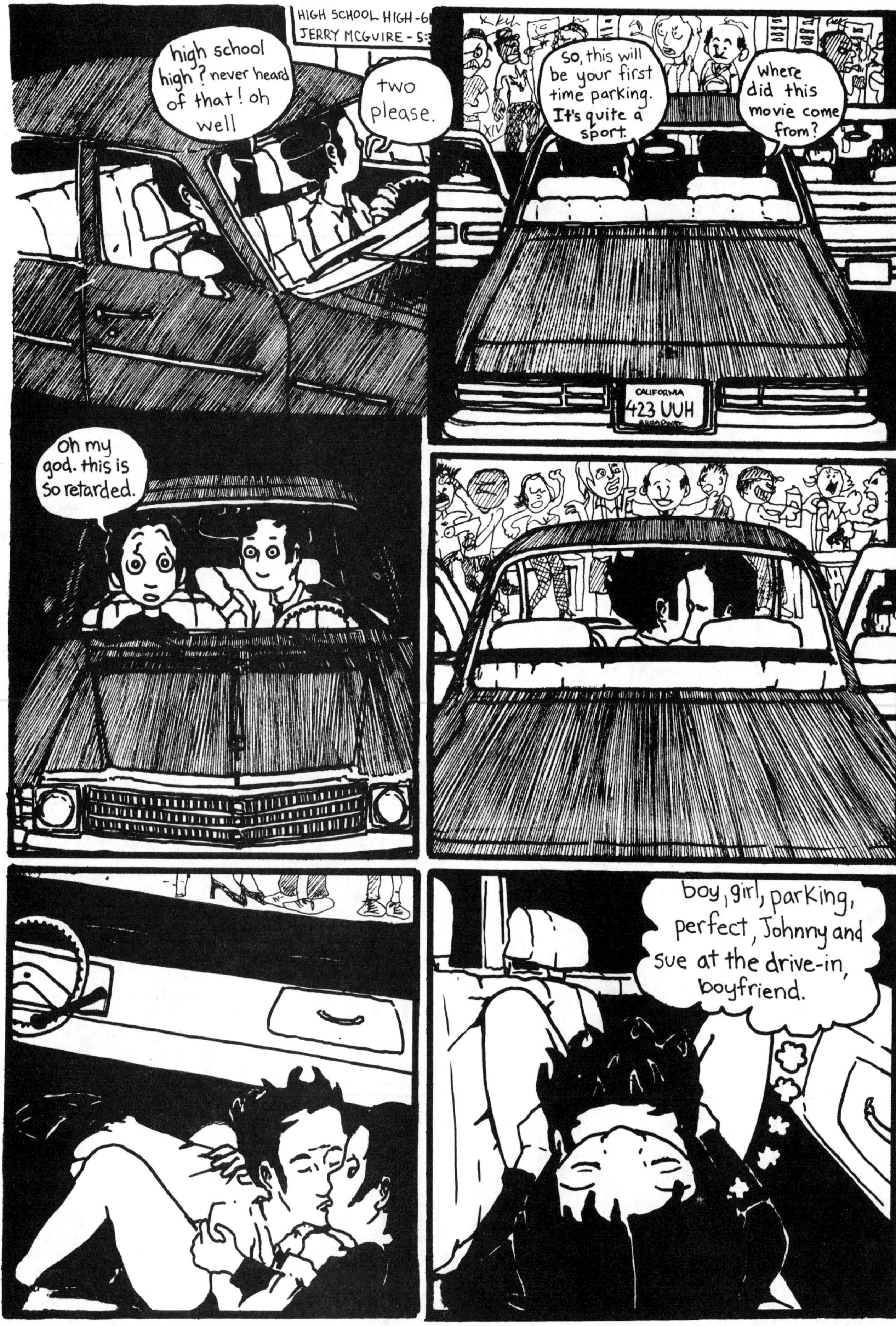
HIGH SCHOOL HIGH - 6
JERRY MCGUIRE - 5:3
high school high? never heard of that! oh well
two please.
So, this will be your first time parking. It's quite a sport.
Where did this movie come from?
CALIFORNIA
423 UUH
Oh my god. this is so retarded.
boy, girl, parking, perfect, Johnny and sue at the drive-in, boyfriend.

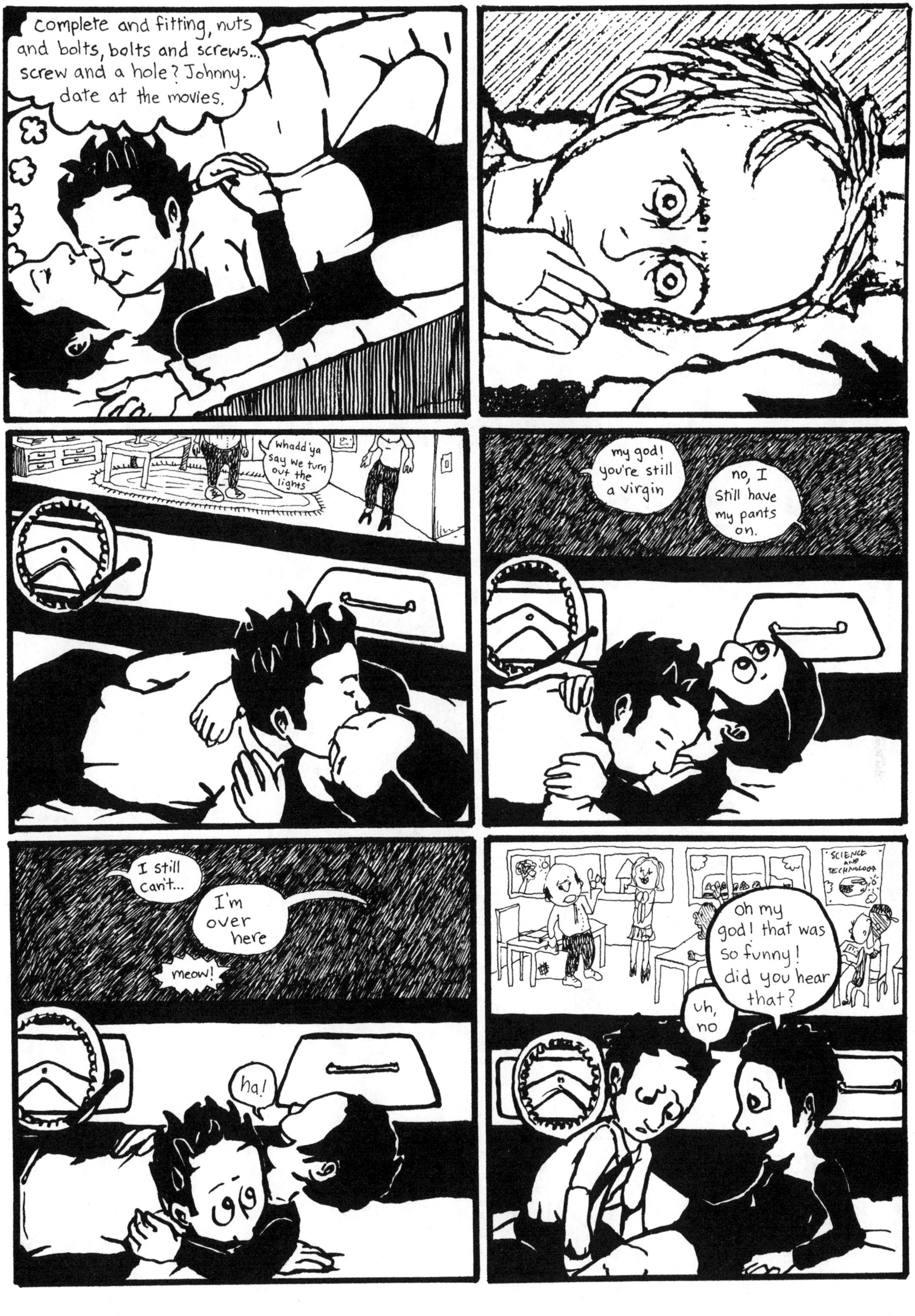
complete and fitting, nuts and bolts, bolts and screws... screw and a hole? Johnny. date at the movies.
Whadd'ya say we turn out the lights
my god! you're still a virgin
no, I still have my pants on.
I still can't...
I'm over here
meow!
ha!
SCIENCE AND TECHNOLOGA
oh my god! that was so funny! did you hear that?
uh, no

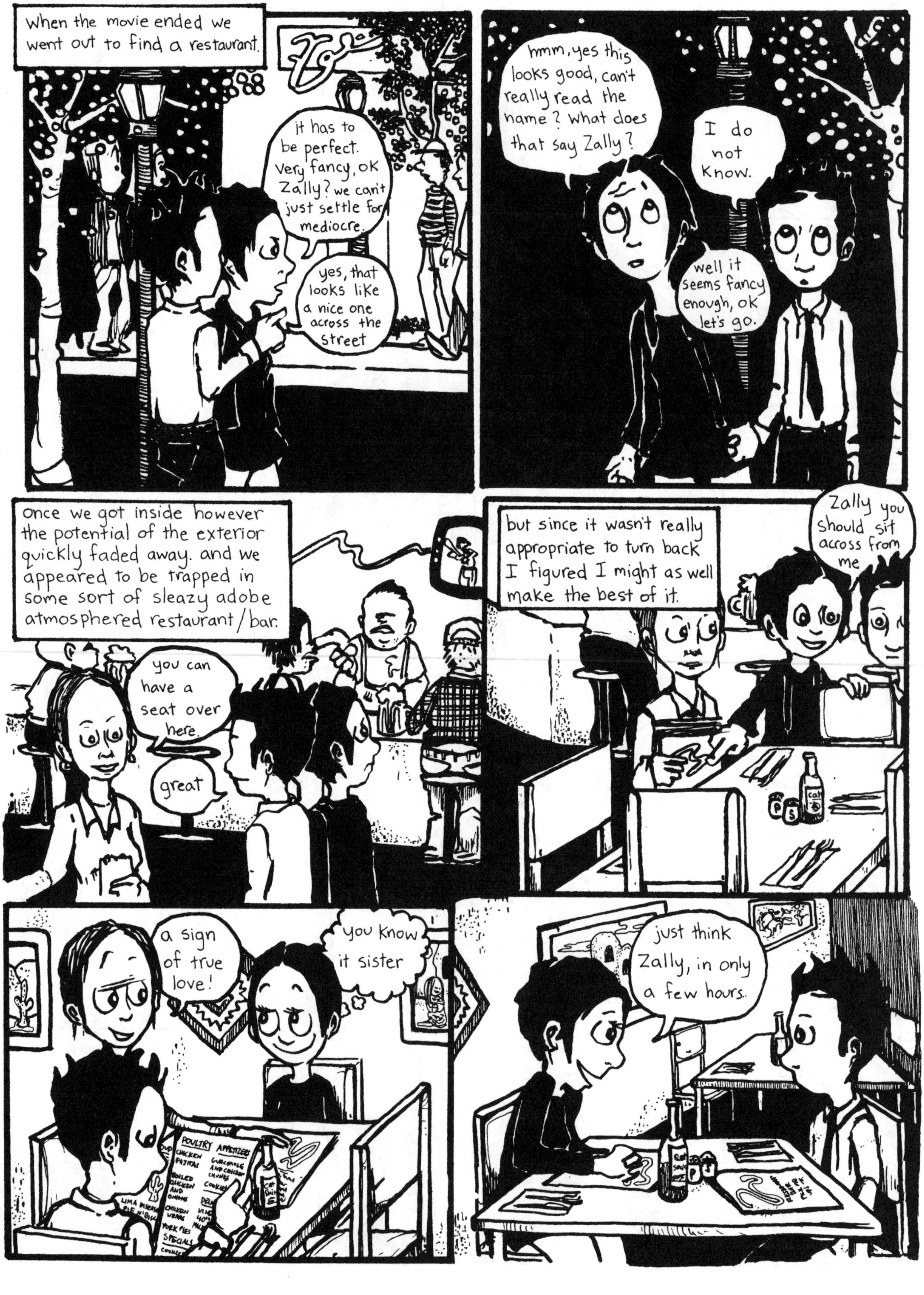

When the movie ended we went out to find a restaurant.
it has to be perfect. Very fancy, OK Zally? we can't just settle for mediocre.
yes, that looks like a nice one across the street
hmm, yes this looks good, can't really read the name? what does that say Zally?
I do not Know.
well it seems fancy enough, ok let's go.
once we got inside however the potential of the exterior quickly faded away. and we appeared to be trapped in some sort of sleazy adobe atmosphered restaurant/bar.
you can have a seat over here.
great
but since it wasn't really appropriate to turn back I figured I might as well make the best of it.
Zally you should sit across from me
a sign of true love!
you know it sister
just think Zally, in only a few hours..

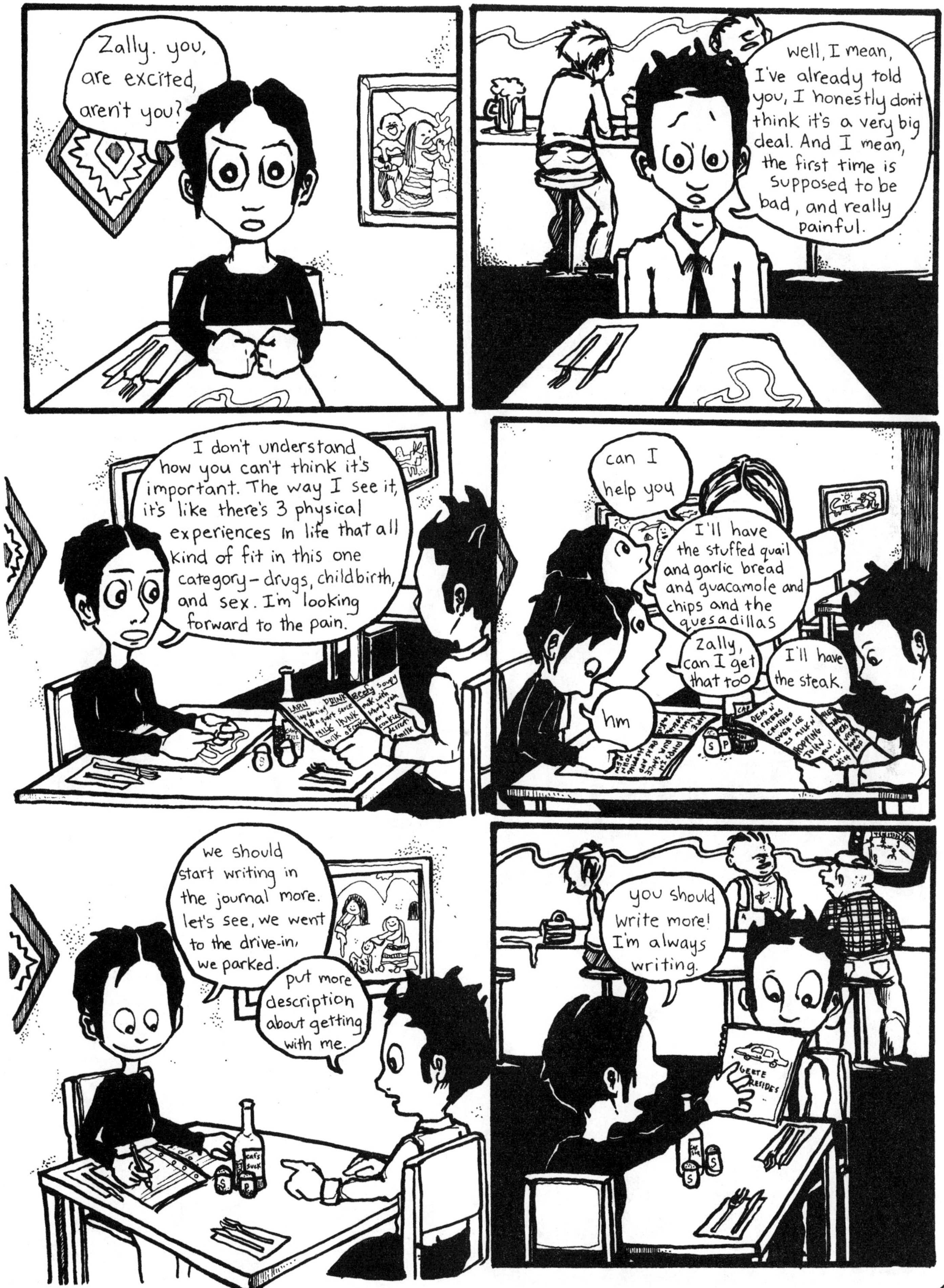
Zally. you, are excited, aren't you?
well, I mean, I've already told you, I honestly don't think it's a very big deal. And I mean, the first time is supposed to be bad, and really painful.
I don't understand how you can't think it's important. The way I see it, it's like there's 3 physical experiences in life that all kind of fit in this one category - drugs, childbirth, and sex. I'm looking forward to the pain.
can I help you
I'll have the stuffed quail and garlic bread and guacamole and chips and the quesadillas
Zally, can I get that too
I'll have the steak.
hm
we should start writing in the journal more. let's see, we went to the drive-in, we parked.
put more description about getting with me.
you should write more! I'm always writing.

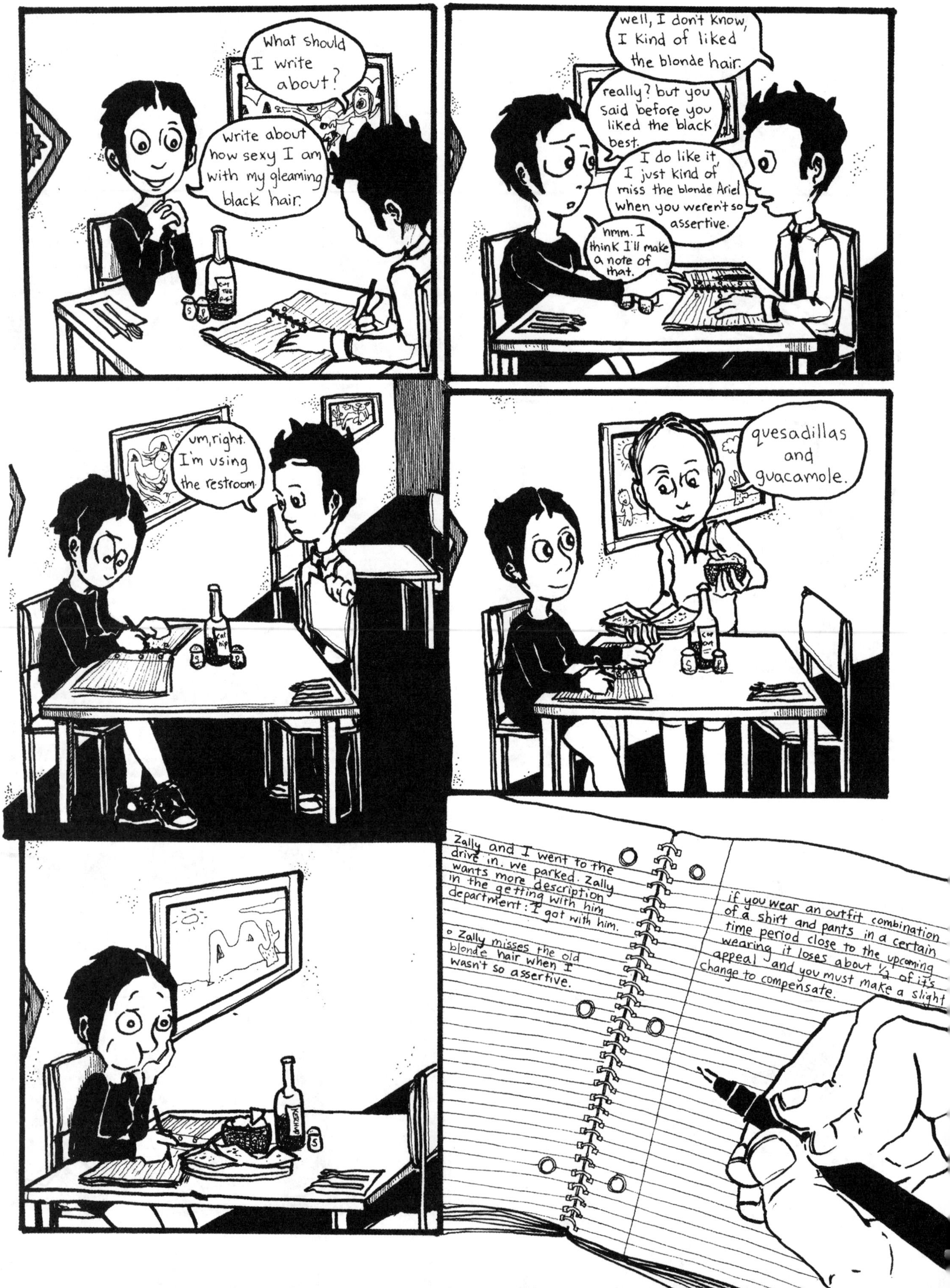
What should I write about?
Write about how sexy I am with my gleaming black hair.
well, I don't know, I kind of liked the blonde hair.
really? but you said before you liked the black best.
I do like it, I just kind of miss the blonde Ariel when you weren't so assertive.
hmm. I think I'll make a note of that.
um, right. I'm using the restroom.
quesadillas and guacamole.
Zally and I went to the drive in. we parked. Zally wants more description in the getting with him department: I got with him.
○ Zally misses the old blonde hair when I wasn't so assertive.
if you wear an outfit combination of a shirt and pants in a certain time period close to the upcoming wearing it loses about ½ of it's appeal and you must make a slight change to compensate.

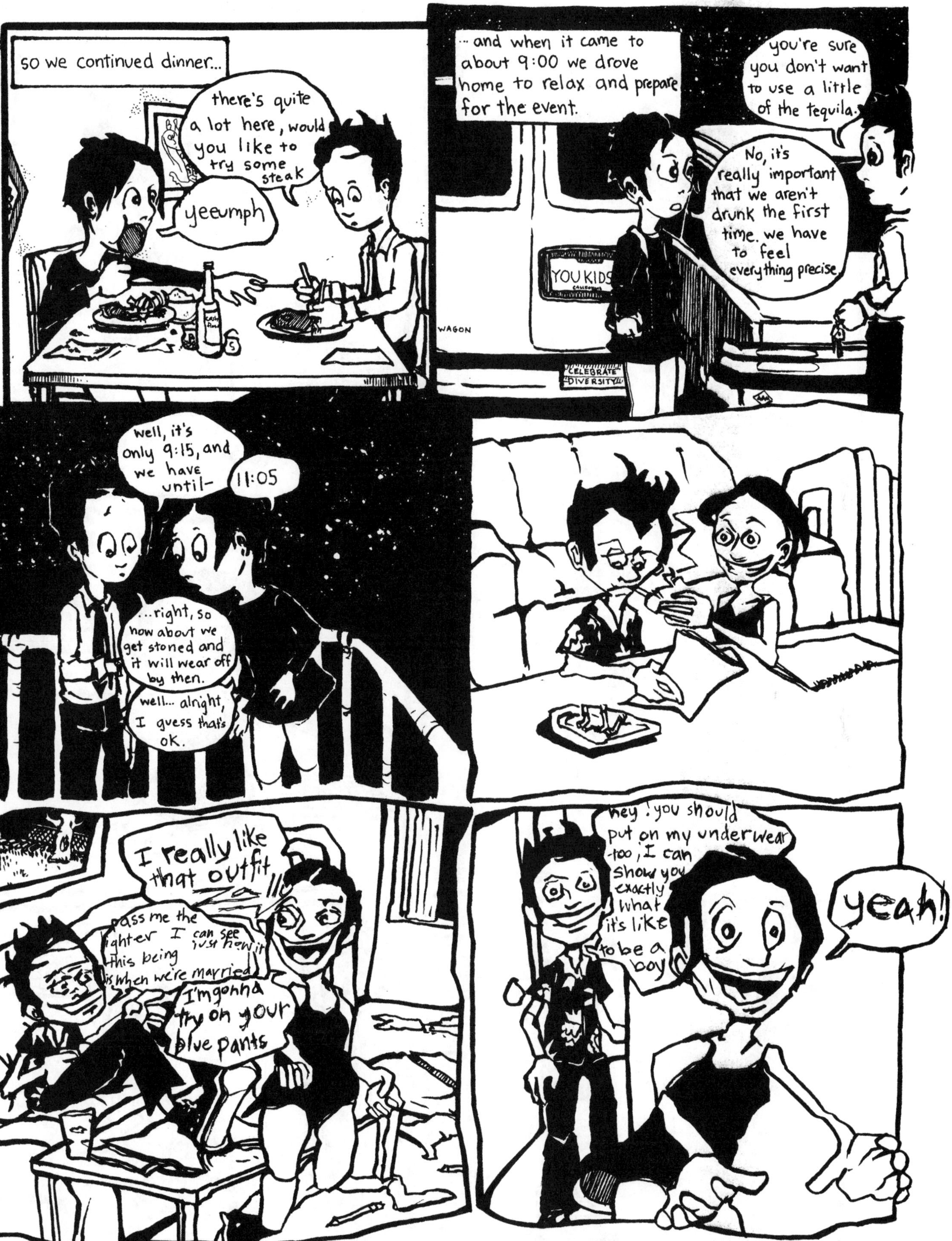
so we continued dinner...
there's quite a lot here, would you like to try some steak
yeeumph
... and when it came to about 9:00 we drove home to relax and prepare for the event.
you're sure you don't want to use a little of the tequila.
No, it's really important that we aren't drunk the first time. we have to feel everything precise.
YOU KIDS
CELEBRATE DIVERSITY
WAGON
well, it's only 9:15, and we have until-
11:05
...right, so how about we get stoned and it will wear off by then.
well... alright, I guess that's ok.
I really like that outfit
pass me the lighter I can see just how it this being is when we're married
I'm gonna try on your blue pants
hey! you should put on my underwear too, I can show you exactly what it's like to be a boy
yeah!

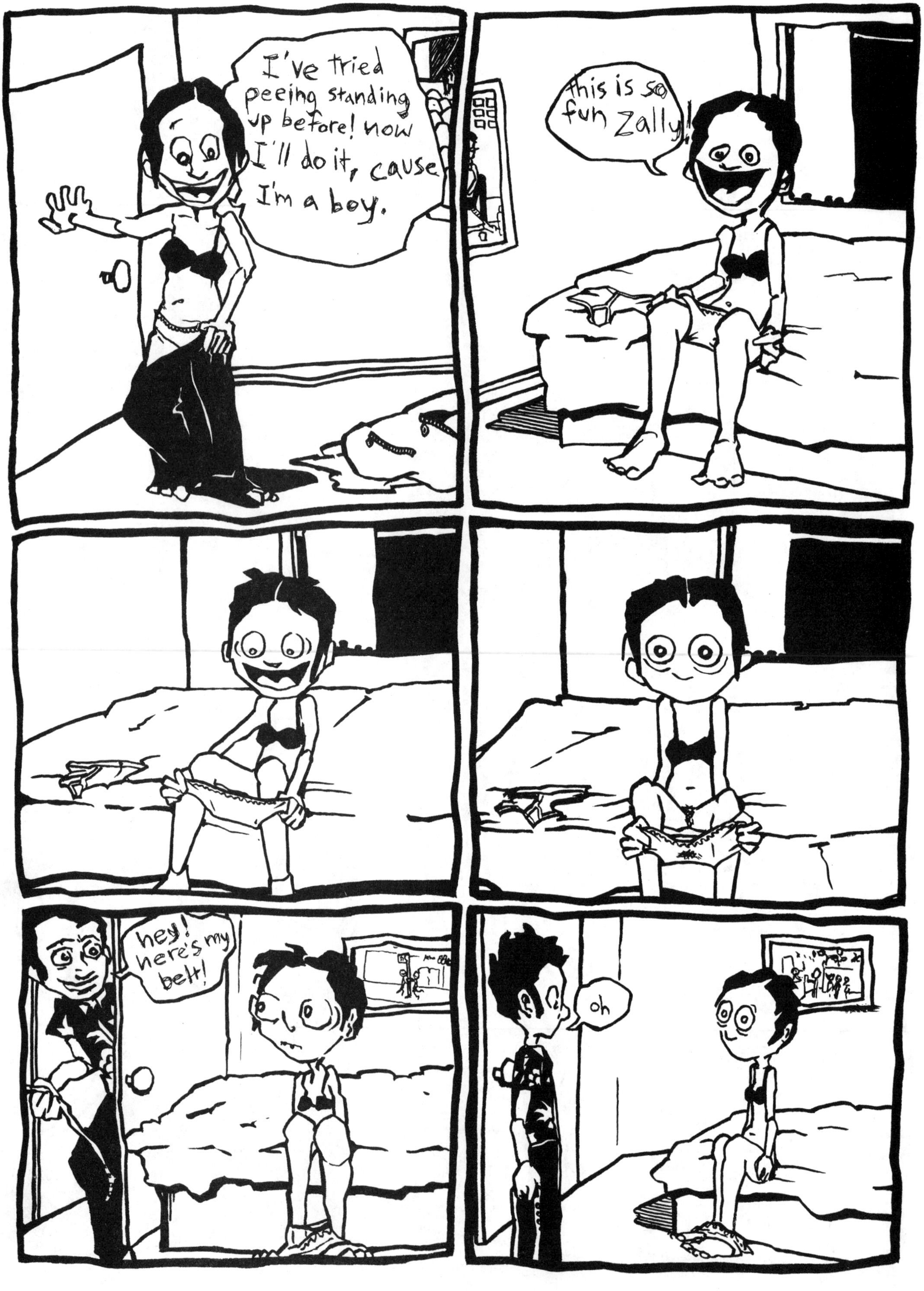
I've tried peeing standing up before! now I'll do it, cause I'm a boy.
this is so fun Zally!
hey! here's my belt!
oh

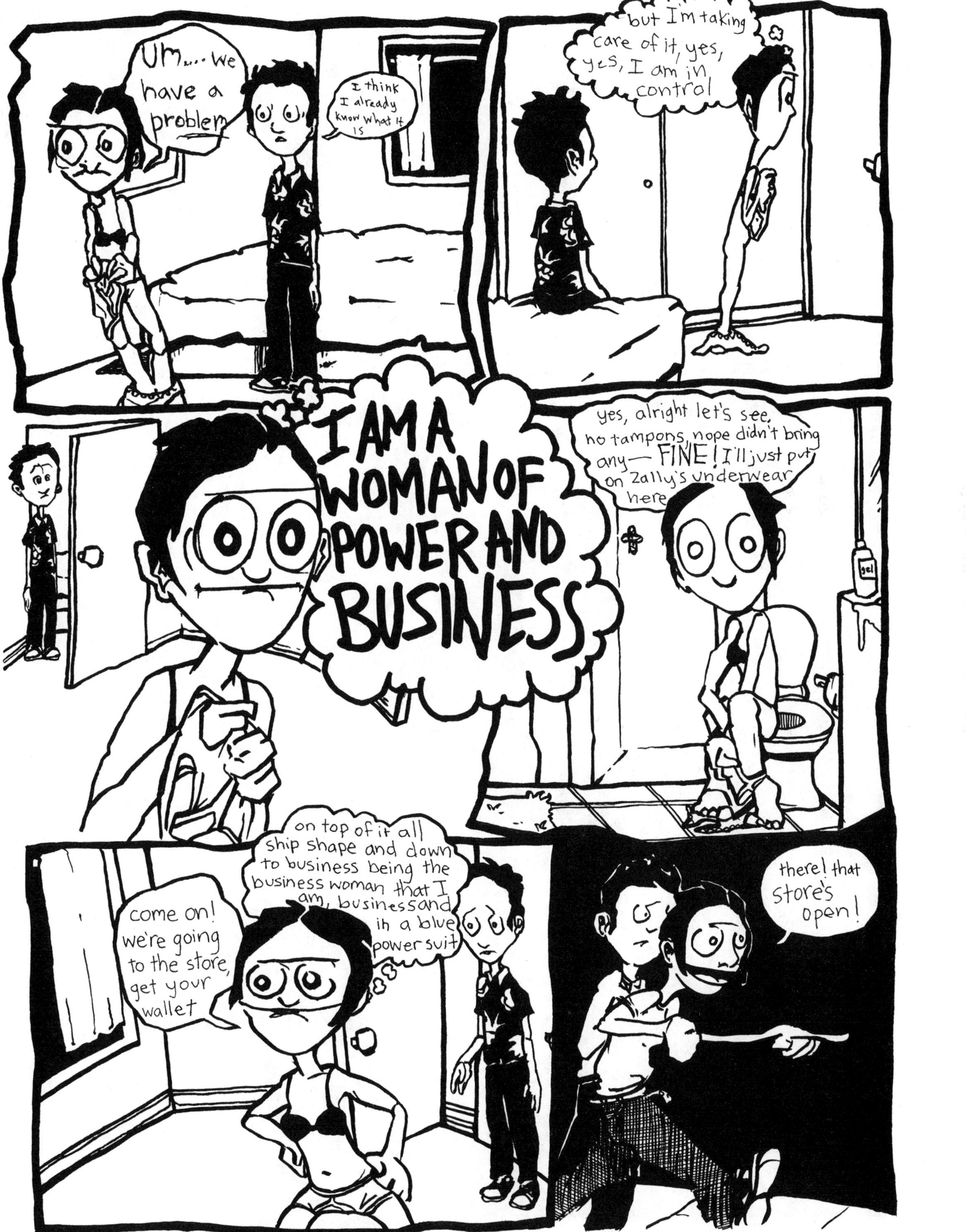
Um... we have a problem
I think I already know what it is
but I'm taking care of it, yes, yes, I am in control
I AM A WOMAN OF POWER AND BUSINESS
yes, alright let's see, no tampons, nope didn't bring any— FINE! I'll just put on Zally's underwear here
gel
come on! we're going to the store, get your wallet
on top of it all ship shape and down to business being the business woman that I am, business and in a blue power suit
there! that store's open!

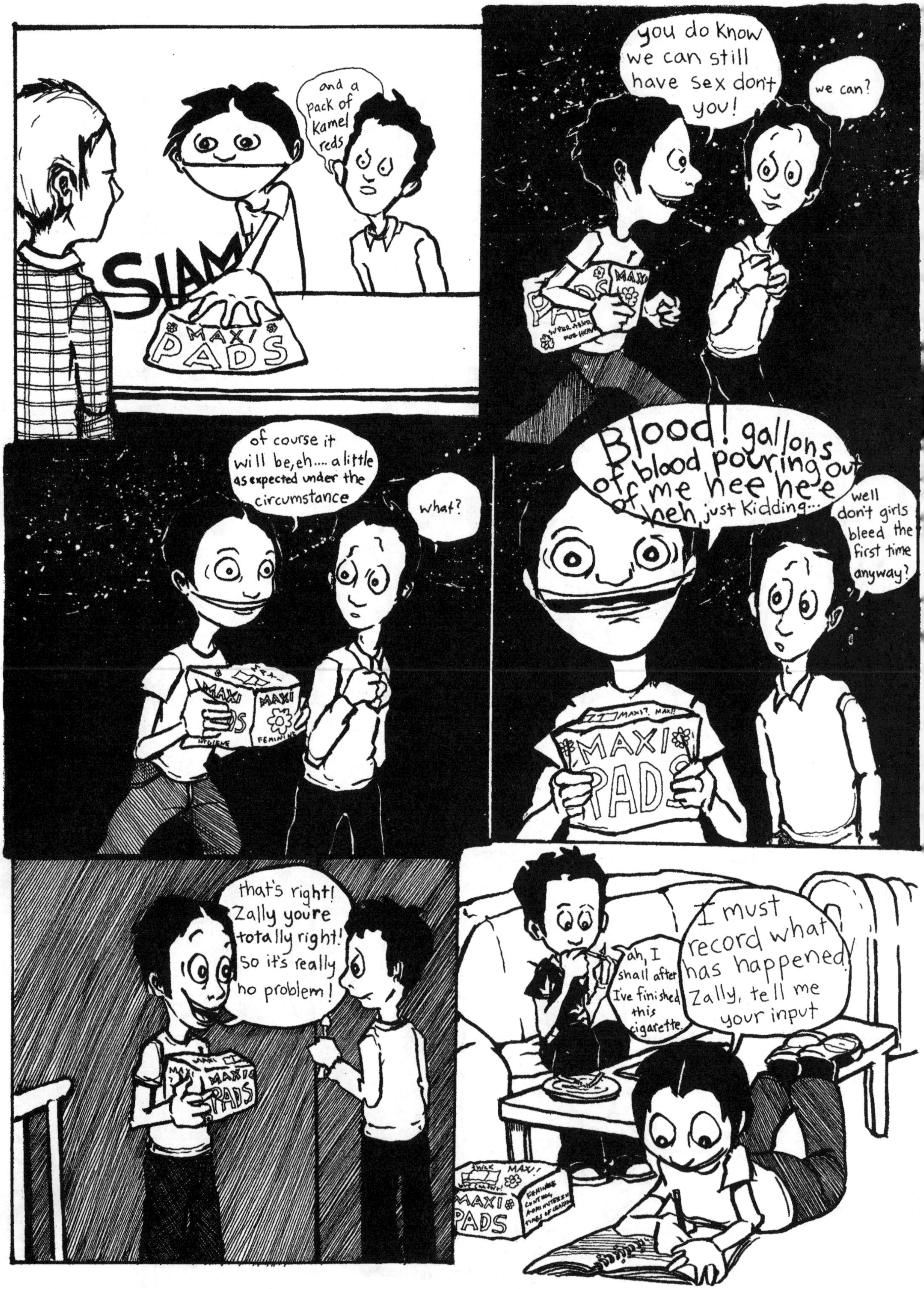
and a pack of Kamel reds
SLAM
MAXI PADS
you do know we can still have sex don't you!
we can?
of course it will be, eh.... a little as expected under the circumstance
what?
Blood! gallons of blood pouring out of me hee hee heh, just kidding...
well don't girls bleed the first time anyway?
that's right! Zally you're totally right! So it's really no problem!
I must record what has happened! Zally, tell me your input
ah, I shall after I've finished this cigarette.
MAXI PADS

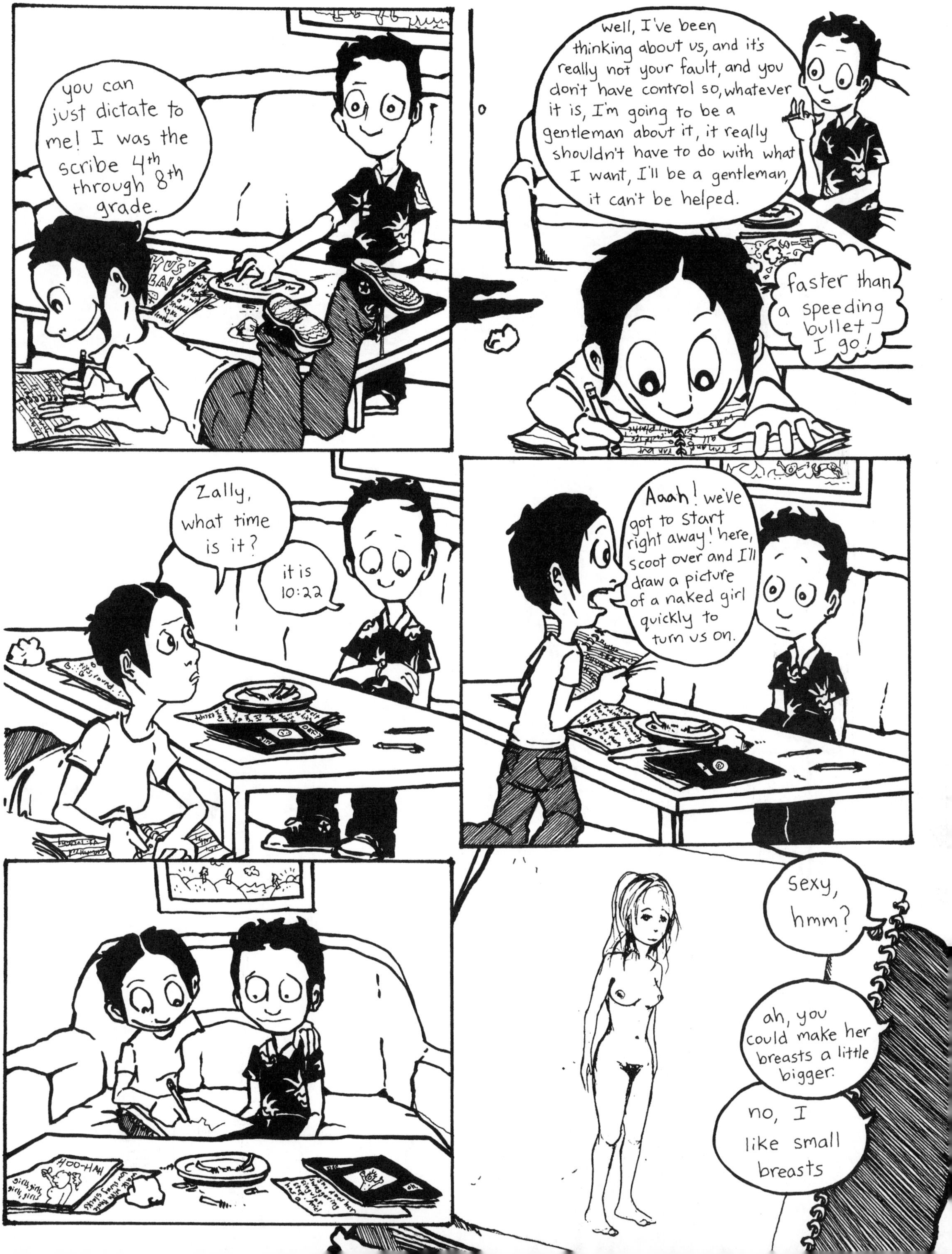

you can just dictate to me! I was the scribe 4th through 8th grade.
well, I've been thinking about us, and it's really not your fault, and you don't have control so, whatever it is, I'm going to be a gentleman about it, it really shouldn't have to do with what I want, I'll be a gentleman, it can't be helped.
faster than a speeding bullet I go!
Zally, what time is it?
it is 10:22
Aaah! we've got to start right away! here, scoot over and I'll draw a picture of a naked girl quickly to turn us on.
Sexy, hmm?
ah, you could make her breasts a little bigger.
no, I like small breasts

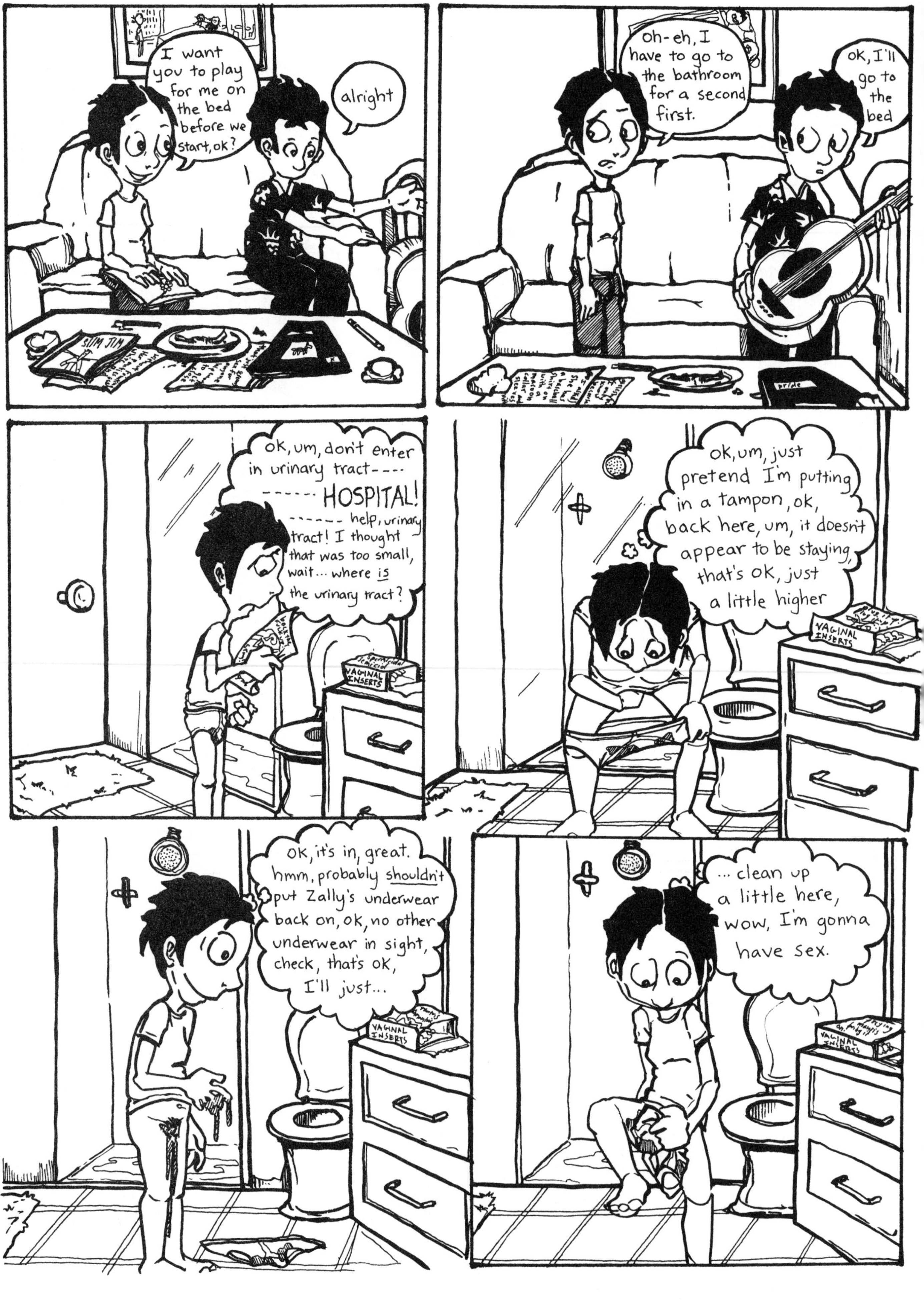
I want you to play for me on the bed before we start, ok?
alright
Oh-eh, I have to go to the bathroom for a second first.
ok, I'll go to the bed
ok, um, don't enter in urinary tract----
-----HOSPITAL!
------help, urinary tract! I thought that was too small, wait... where is the urinary tract?
VAGINAL INSERTS
ok, um, just pretend I'm putting in a tampon, ok, back here, um, it doesn't appear to be staying, that's ok, just a little higher
VAGINAL INSERTS
ok, it's in, great. hmm, probably shouldn't put Zally's underwear back on, ok, no other underwear in sight, check, that's ok, I'll just...
VAGINAL INSERTS
... clean up a little here, wow, I'm gonna have sex.

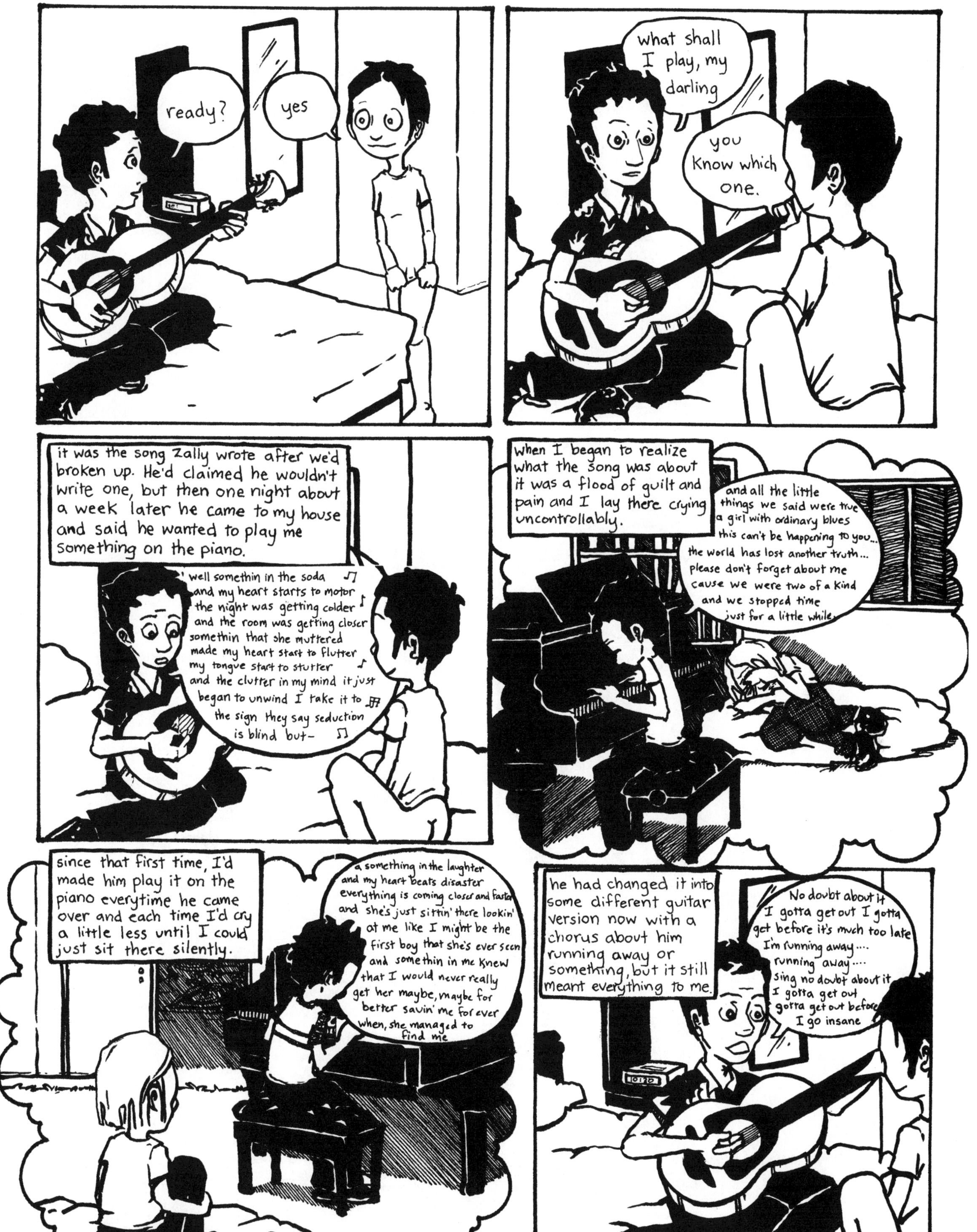
ready?
yes
what shall I play, my darling
you know which one.
it was the song Zally wrote after we'd broken up. He'd claimed he wouldn't write one, but then one night about a week later he came to my house and said he wanted to play me something on the piano.
well somethin in the soda and my heart starts to motor the night was getting colder and the room was getting closer somethin that she muttered made my heart start to flutter my tongue start to stutter and the clutter in my mind it just began to unwind I take it to the sign they say seduction is blind but-
when I began to realize what the song was about it was a flood of guilt and pain and I lay there crying uncontrollably.
and all the little things we said were true a girl with ordinary blues this can't be happening to you... the world has lost another truth... please don't forget about me cause we were two of a kind and we stopped time just for a little while.
since that first time, I'd made him play it on the piano everytime he came over and each time I'd cry a little less until I could just sit there silently.
a something in the laughter and my heart beats disaster everything is coming closer and faster and she's just sittin' there lookin' at me like I might be the first boy that she's ever seen and somethin in me knew that I would never really get her maybe, maybe for better savin' me forever when, she managed to find me
he had changed it into some different guitar version now with a chorus about him running away or something, but it still meant everything to me.
No doubt about it I gotta get out I gotta get before it's much too late I'm running away.... running away.... sing no doubt about it I gotta get out gotta get out before I go insane

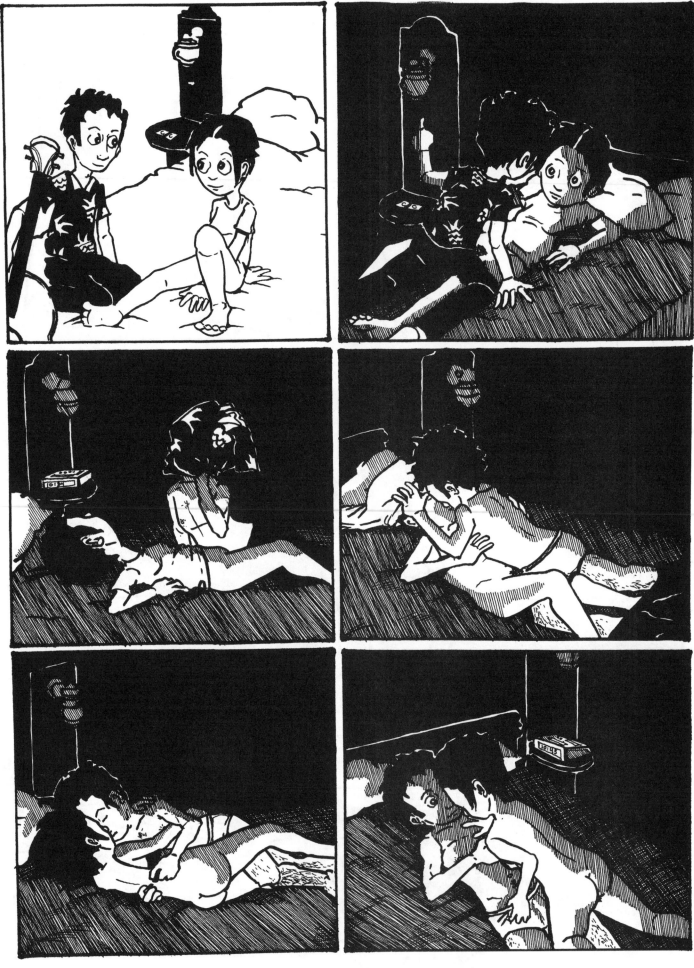

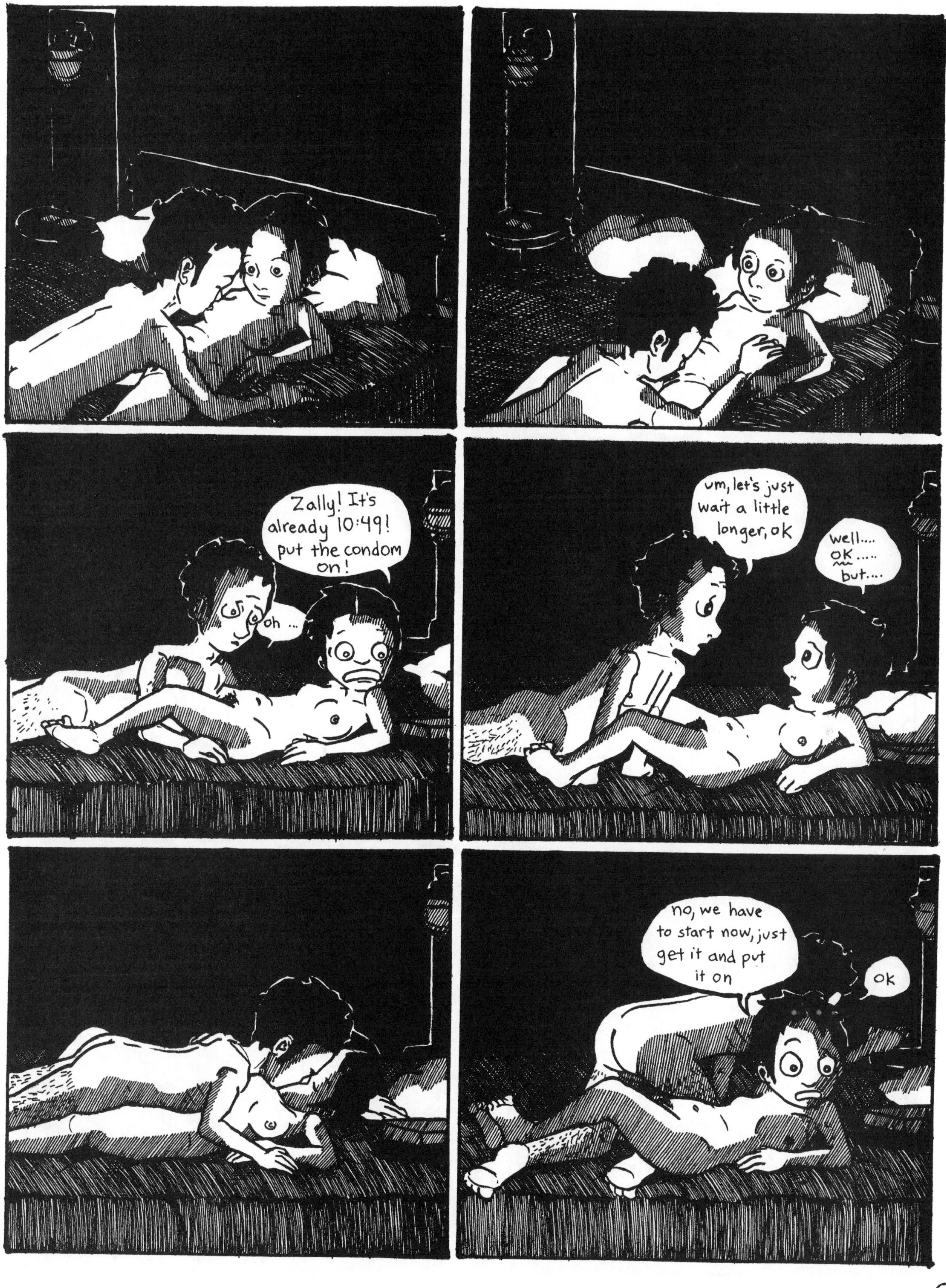
Zally! It's already 10:49! put the condom on!
oh ...
um, let's just wait a little longer, ok
well.... OK..... but....
no, we have to start now, just get it and put it on
ok

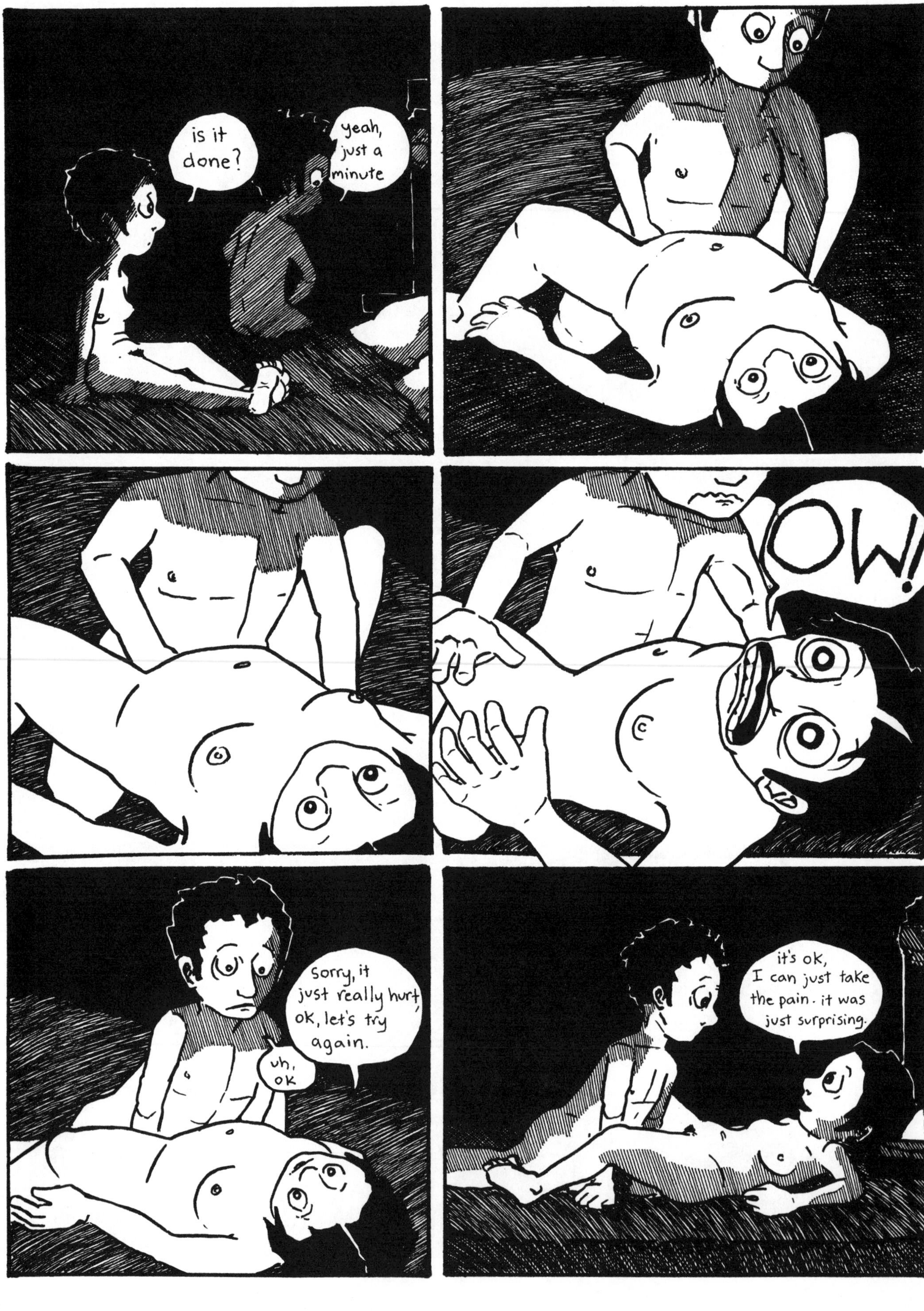
is it done?
yeah, just a minute
OW!
Sorry, it just really hurt ok, let's try again.
uh, ok
it's ok, I can just take the pain. it was just surprising.

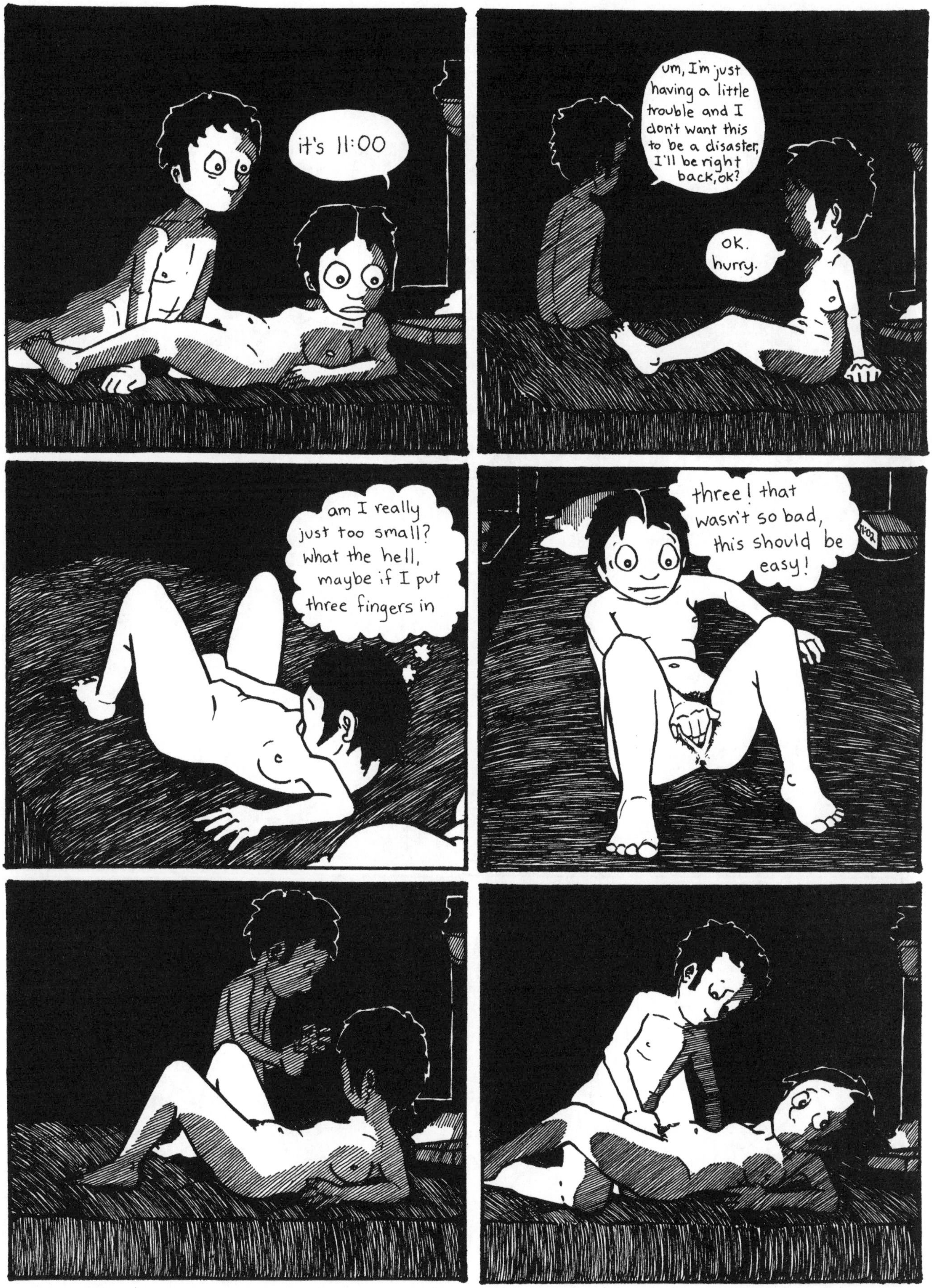
it's 11:00
um, I'm just having a little trouble and I don't want this to be a disaster, I'll be right back, ok?
ok. hurry.
am I really just too small? what the hell, maybe if I put three fingers in
three! that wasn't so bad, this should be easy!

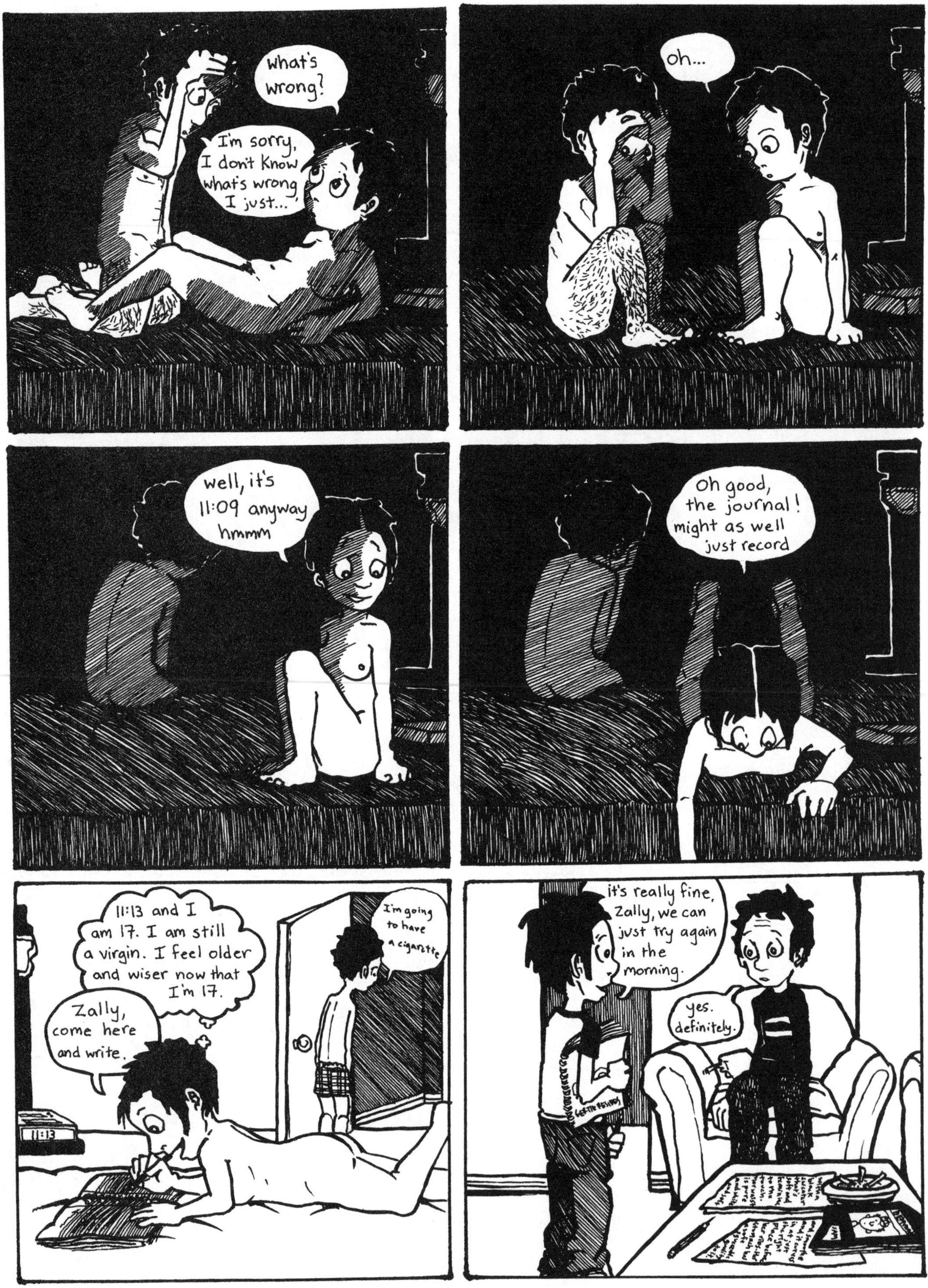
what's wrong?
I'm sorry, I don't Know what's wrong I just...
oh...
well, it's 11:09 anyway hmmm
Oh good, the journal! might as well just record
11:13 and I am 17. I am still a virgin. I feel older and wiser now that I'm 17.
Zally, come here and write.
I'm going to have a cigarette
11:13
it's really fine, Zally, we can just try again in the morning.
yes. definitely.

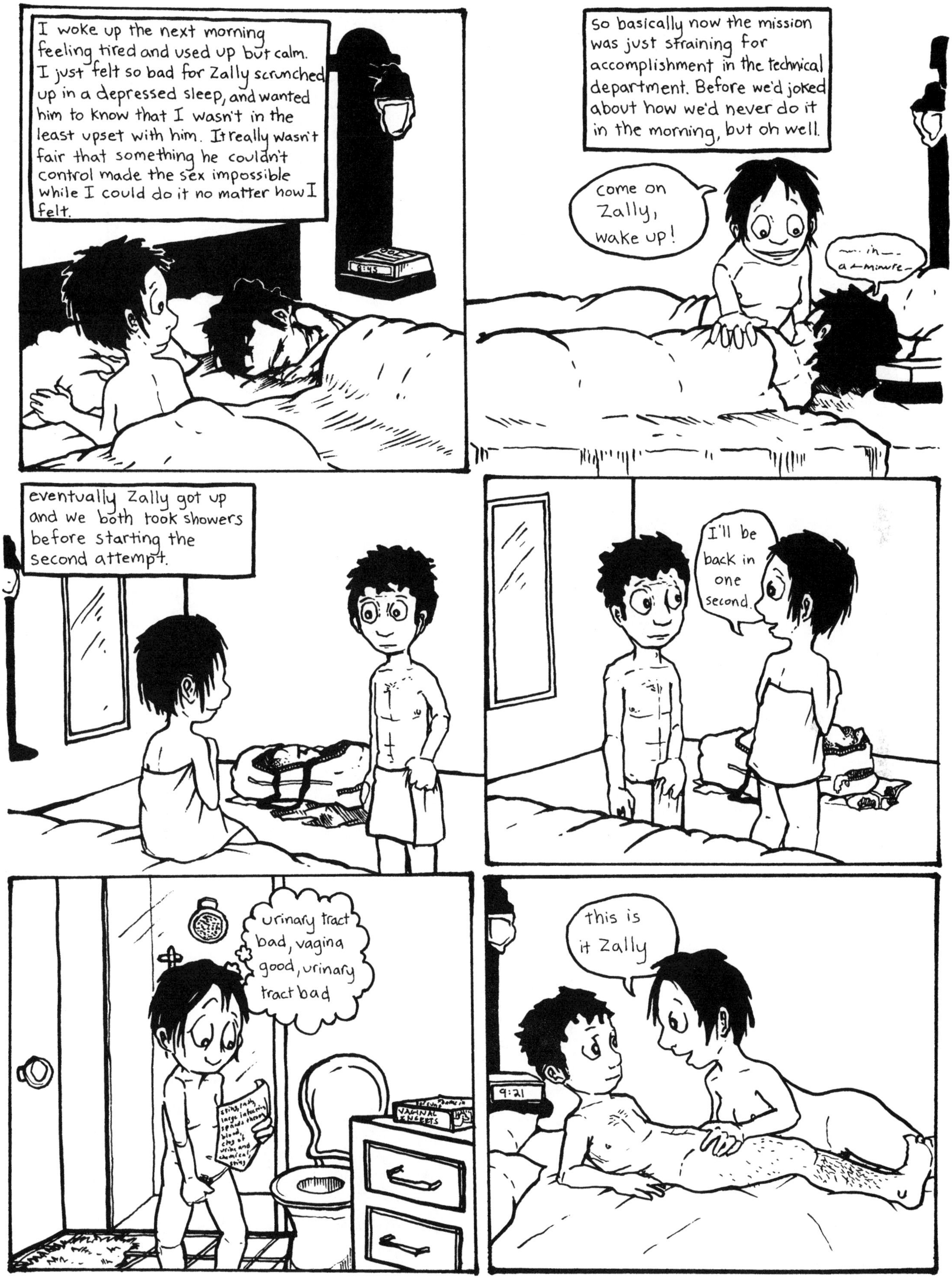
I woke up the next morning feeling tired and used up but calm. I just felt so bad for Zally scrunched up in a depressed sleep, and wanted him to know that I wasn't in the least upset with him. It really wasn't fair that something he couldn't control made the sex impossible while I could do it no matter how I felt.
So basically now the mission was just straining for accomplishment in the technical department. Before we'd joked about how we'd never do it in the morning, but oh well.
come on Zally, wake up!
... in ... a minute ...
eventually Zally got up and we both took showers before starting the second attempt.
I'll be back in one second.
urinary tract bad, vagina good, urinary tract bad
VAGINAL INSERTS
this is it Zally
9:21

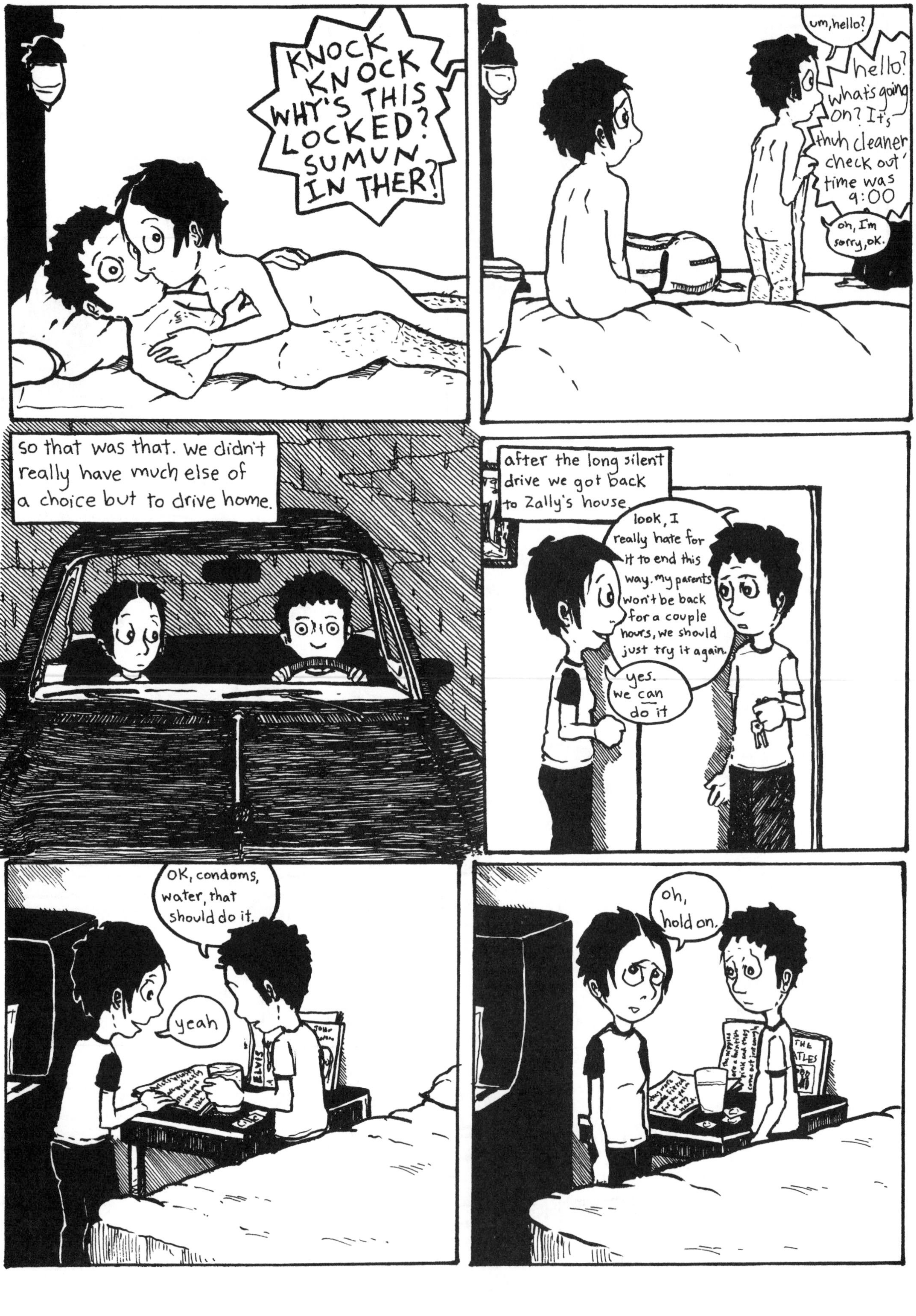
KNOCK KNOCK WHY'S THIS LOCKED? SUMUN IN THER?
um, hello?
hello? what's going on? It's thuh cleaner check out time was 9:00
oh, I'm sorry, OK.
so that was that. we didn't really have much else of a choice but to drive home.
after the long silent drive we got back to Zally's house
look, I really hate for it to end this way. my parents won't be back for a couple hours, we should just try it again.
yes. we can do it
OK, condoms, water, that should do it.
yeah
oh, hold on.

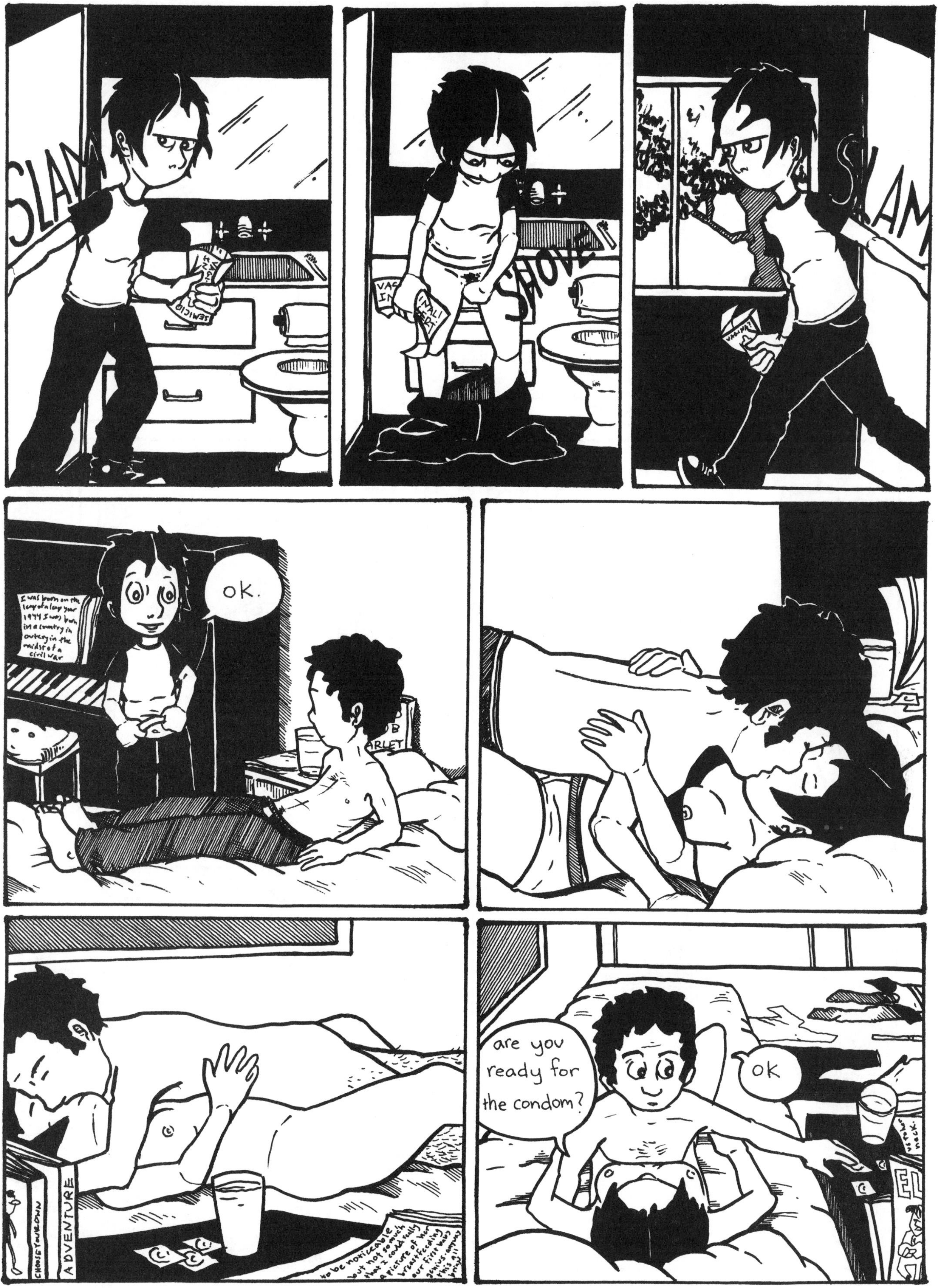
SLAM
SHOVE
SLAM
ok.
are you ready for the condom?
ok

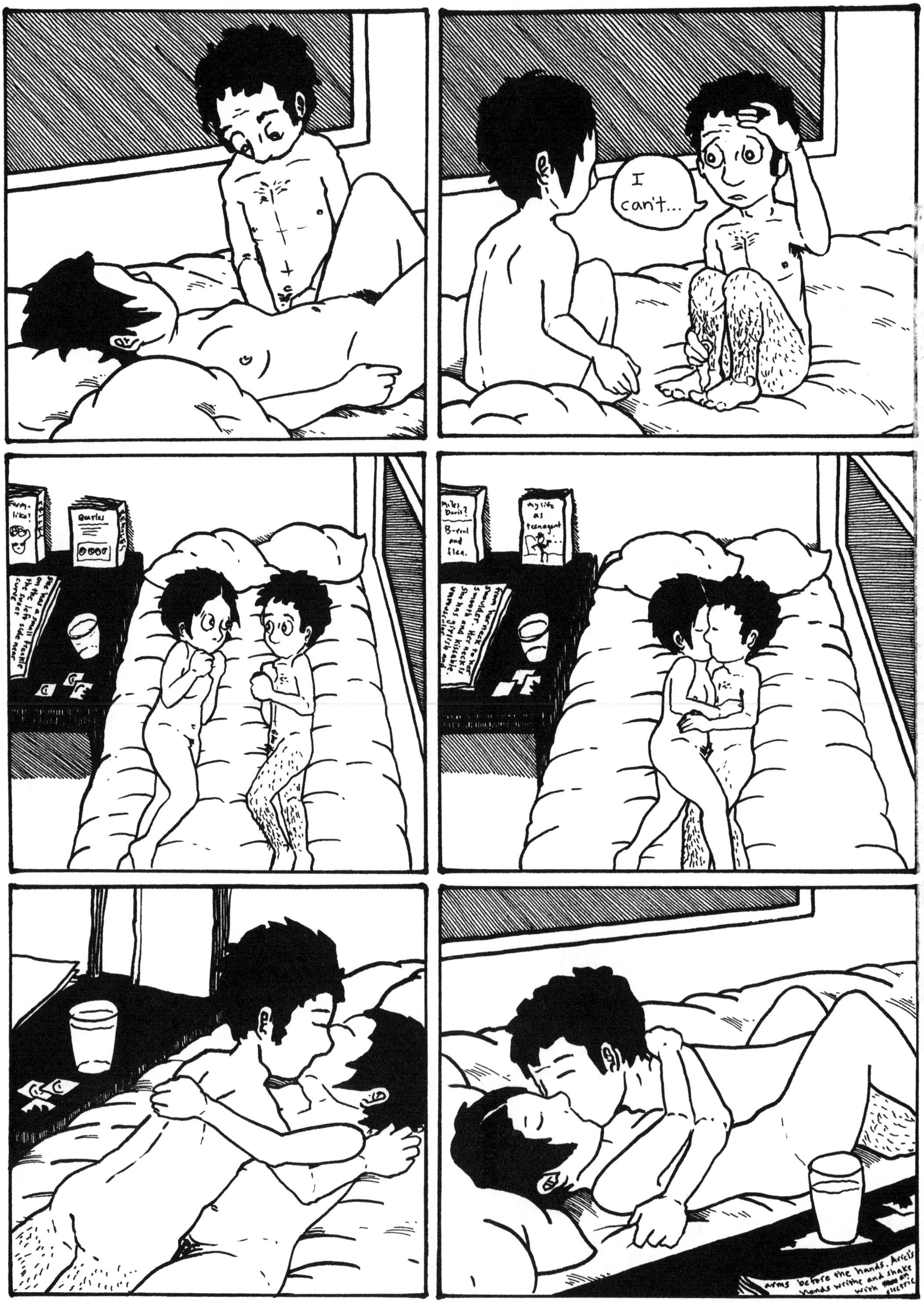
I can't...
Farm-like!
Quarles
She has a small freckle on the left side near the sweet curve
Miles Davis?
B-real and flea.
My life as teenagent
from her neck to her shoulder. Her neck is smooth and kissable. She has girlish and unmuscular and
arms before the hands. Ariel's hands writhe and shake with an electric

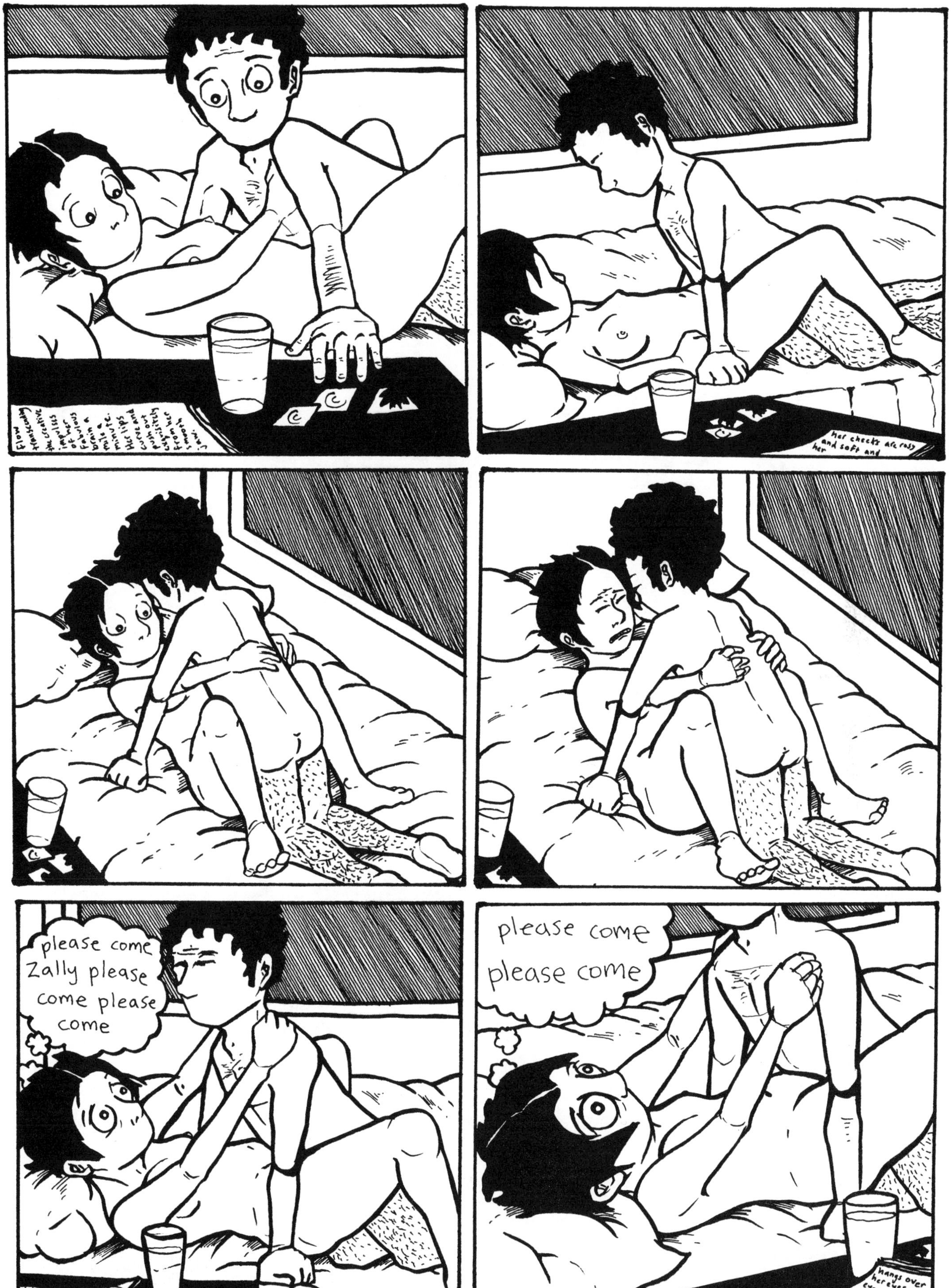
Flow frantically the creative impulses of her fabulous brain a mile a minute. Her lips curve and push out expressively from her smooth jaw.
her cheeks are rosy and soft and her
please come Zally please come please come
black cropped hair
please come please come
hangs over her eyes. Anil's eyes have a quality to

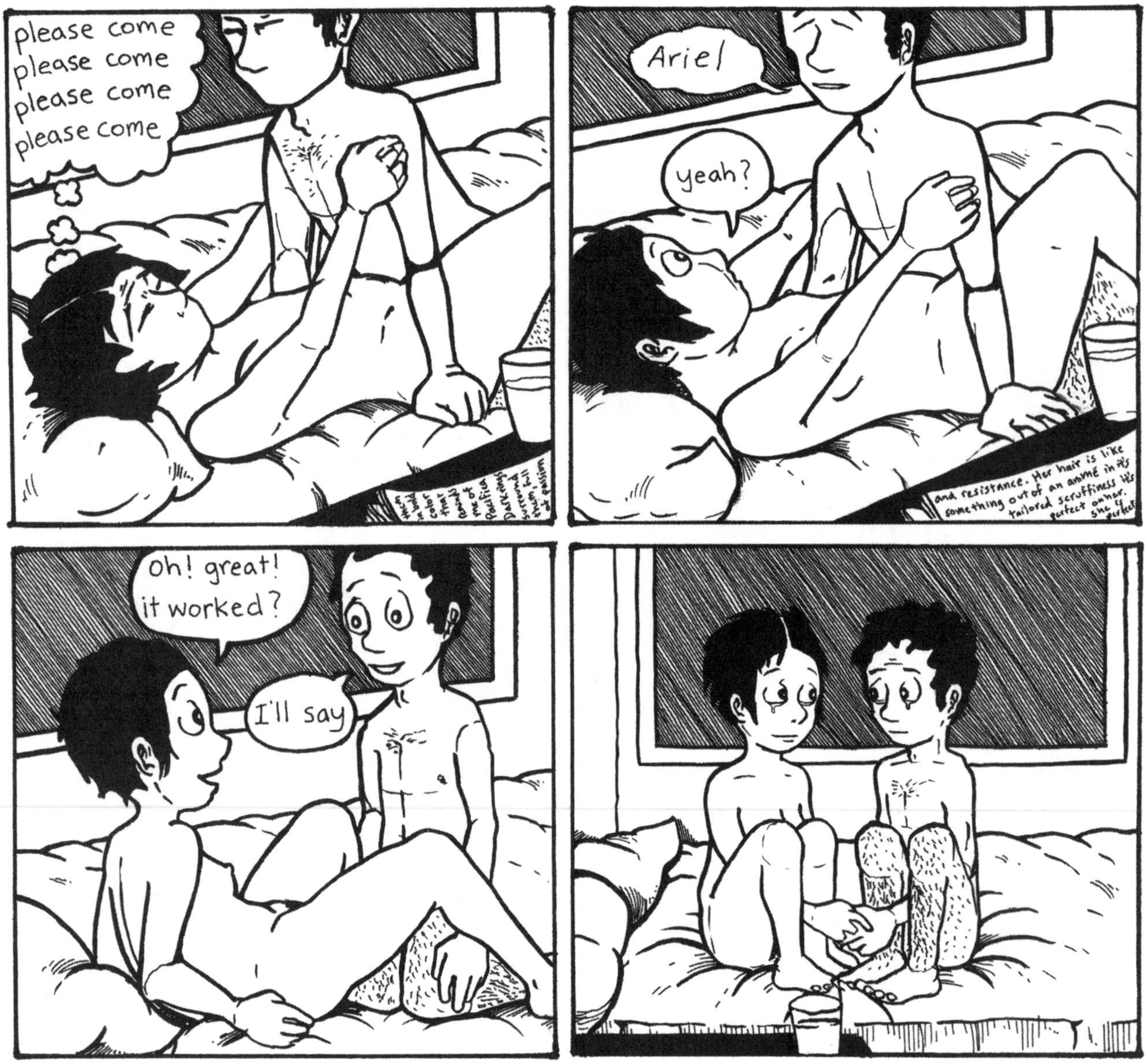
please come
please come
please come
please come
Ariel
yeah?
and resistance. Her hair is like something out of an anime in its tailored scruffiness. It's perfect on her. She is perfect.
Oh! great! it worked?
I'll say

Zally:

[redacted] Tears and blood
suds and stains
Ariel remains
intact

Sometime well I'm sure that when I'm older I'll realize that the whole thing was totally comical and pathetic but for now I'm happy. I'm sure it was very painful for her and unenjoyable, but that kind of thing is to be expected the first time. I mean, for a guy any sex is the satisfact of getting off [redacted] and the subtleties of whether or not it was slow or fast or right side up or [redacted] upside down are mostly irrelevant. In any case...

I thoroughly enjoyed screwing Ariel, however awkward it may have been. She's got a body like a sculpture. Both of our lips are bruised.

Ariel:

well, while Zally's lips may be bruised that is the understatement of a lifetime in concern of another part of my body. it was extremely painful. I don't know about the most painful thing in the world but definitely in the top 10. However, I was pleased to [redacted] be doing it and am glad it's done even if I did spend every second of it's course praying for Zally to come. It didn't feel like he was in that deep but he says ½ – ¾ most of the time so that's sufficient. I am sore and somewhat exhausted. It is pleasing not to be a virgin.

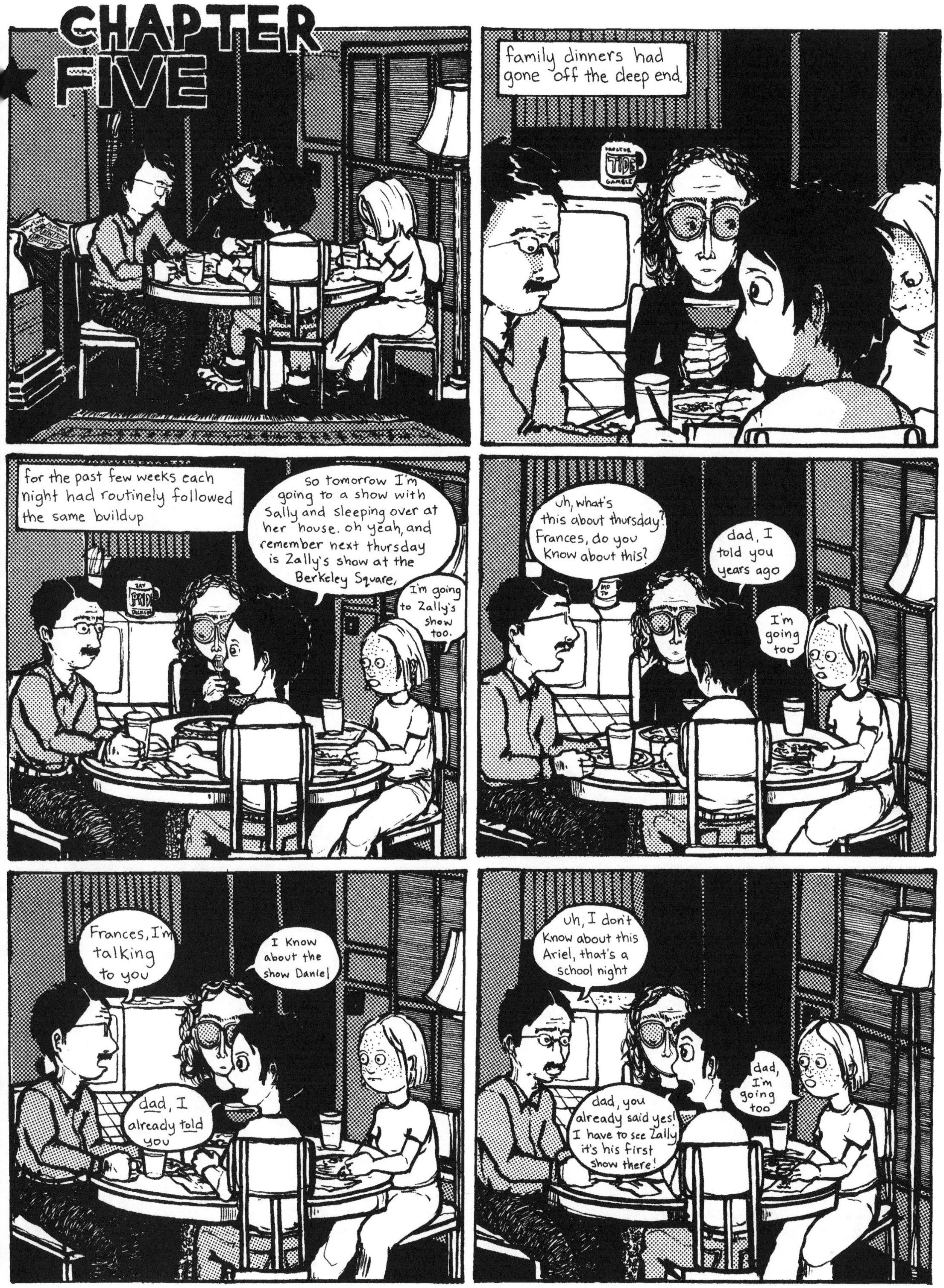

CHAPTER FIVE
family dinners had gone off the deep end.
TIDE
for the past few weeks each night had routinely followed the same buildup
so tomorrow I'm going to a show with Sally and sleeping over at her house. oh yeah, and remember next thursday is Zally's show at the Berkeley Square,
I'm going to Zally's show too.
uh, what's this about thursday? Frances, do you know about this?
dad, I told you years ago
I'm going too
Frances, I'm talking to you
I know about the show Daniel
dad, I already told you
uh, I don't know about this Ariel, that's a school night
dad, you already said yes! I have to see Zally it's his first show there!
dad, I'm going too

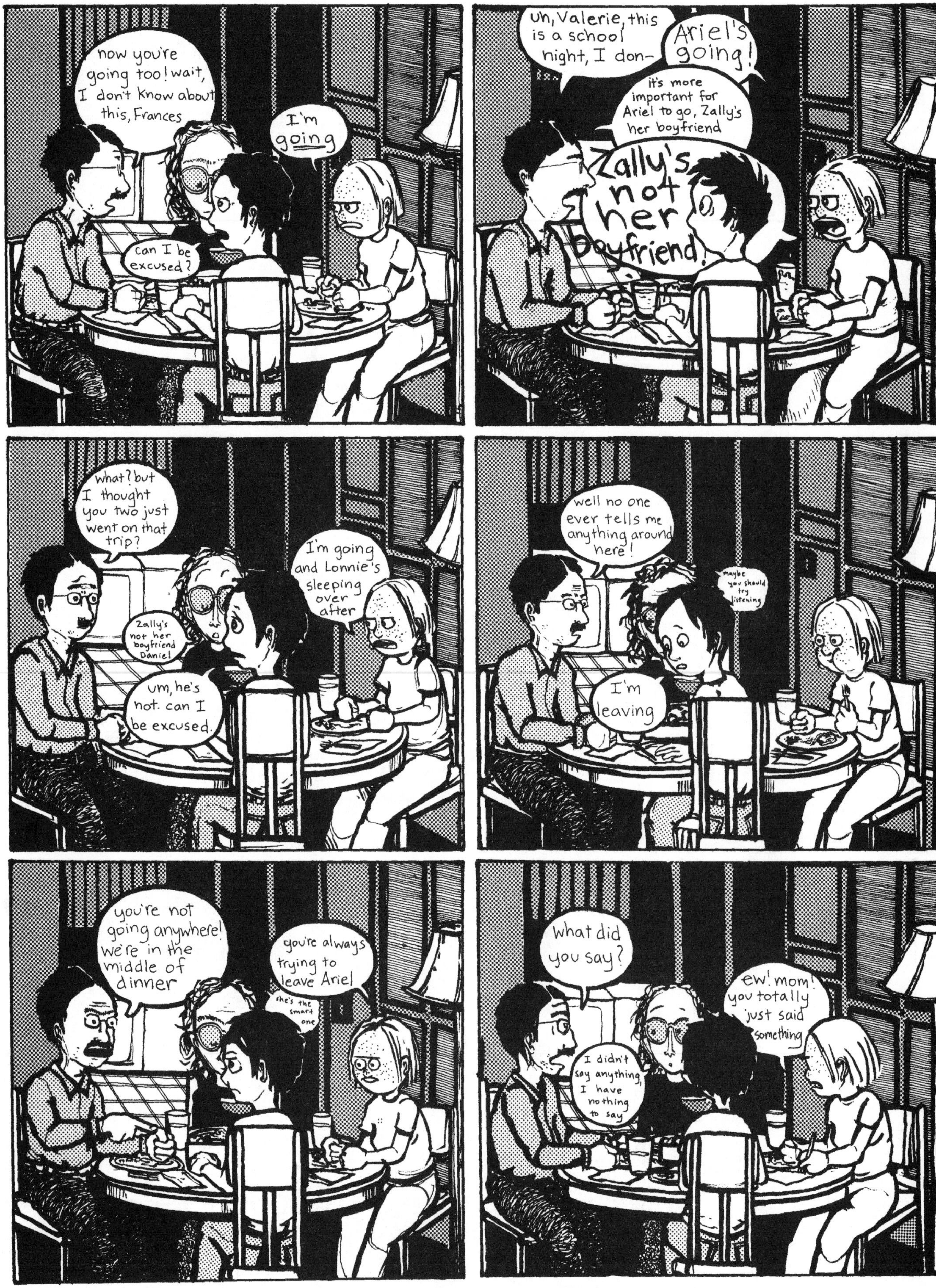
now you're going too! wait, I don't know about this, Frances
I'm going
can I be excused?
uh, Valerie, this is a school night, I don-
Ariel's going!
it's more important for Ariel to go, Zally's her boyfriend
Zally's not her boyfriend!
what? but I thought you two just went on that trip?
I'm going and Lonnie's sleeping over after
Zally's not her boyfriend Daniel!
um, he's not. can I be excused.
well no one ever tells me anything around here!
maybe you should try listening
I'm leaving
you're not going anywhere! we're in the middle of dinner
you're always trying to leave Ariel
she's the smart one
What did you say?
ew! mom! you totally just said something
I didn't say anything, I have nothing to say

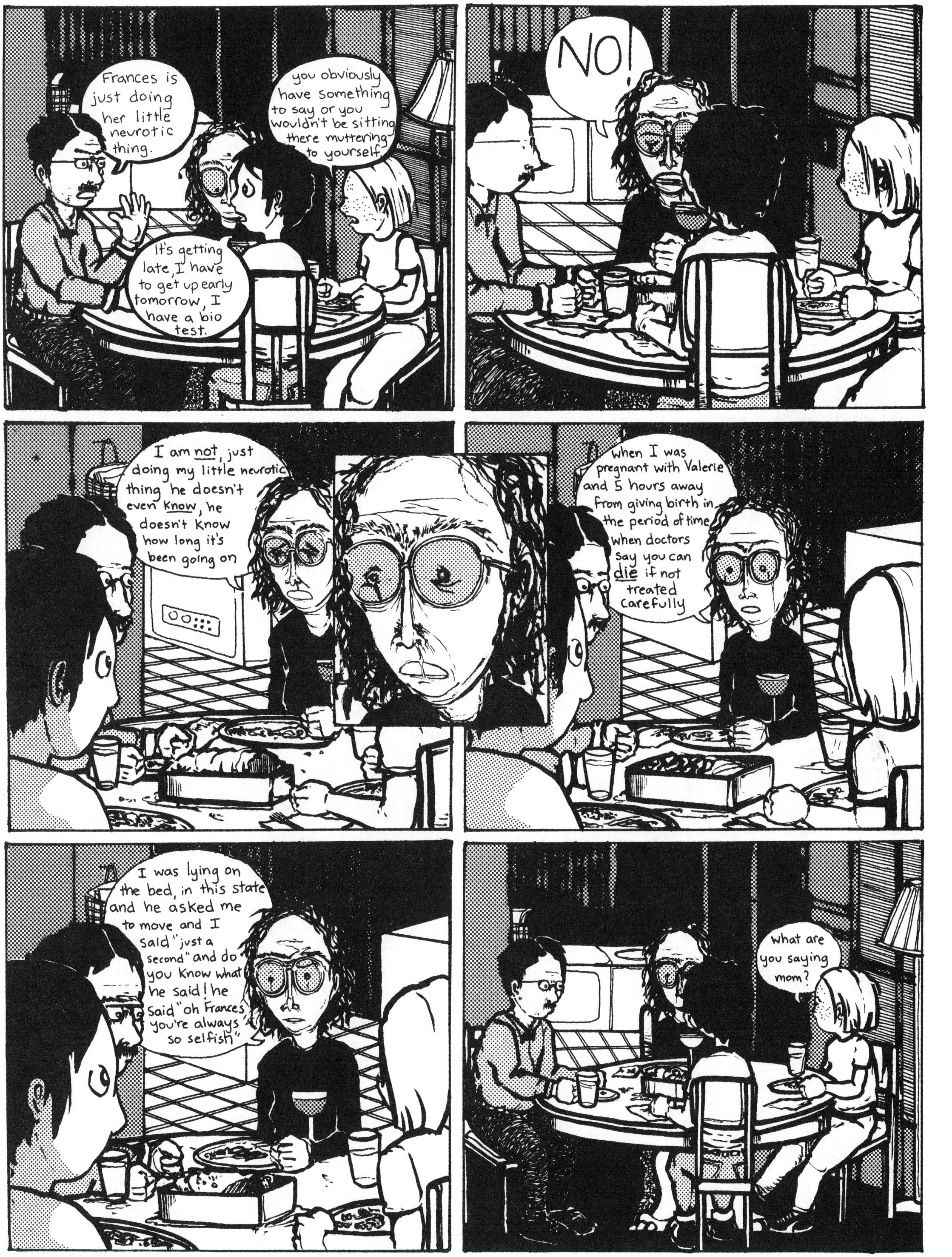
Frances is just doing her little neurotic thing.
you obviously have something to say or you wouldn't be sitting there muttering to yourself.
It's getting late, I have to get up early tomorrow, I have a bio test.
NO!
I am not, just doing my little neurotic thing he doesn't even know, he doesn't know how long it's been going on
when I was pregnant with Valerie and 5 hours away from giving birth in the period of time when doctors say you can die if not treated carefully
I was lying on the bed, in this state and he asked me to move and I said "just a second" and do you know what he said! he said "oh Frances you're always so selfish"
what are you saying mom?

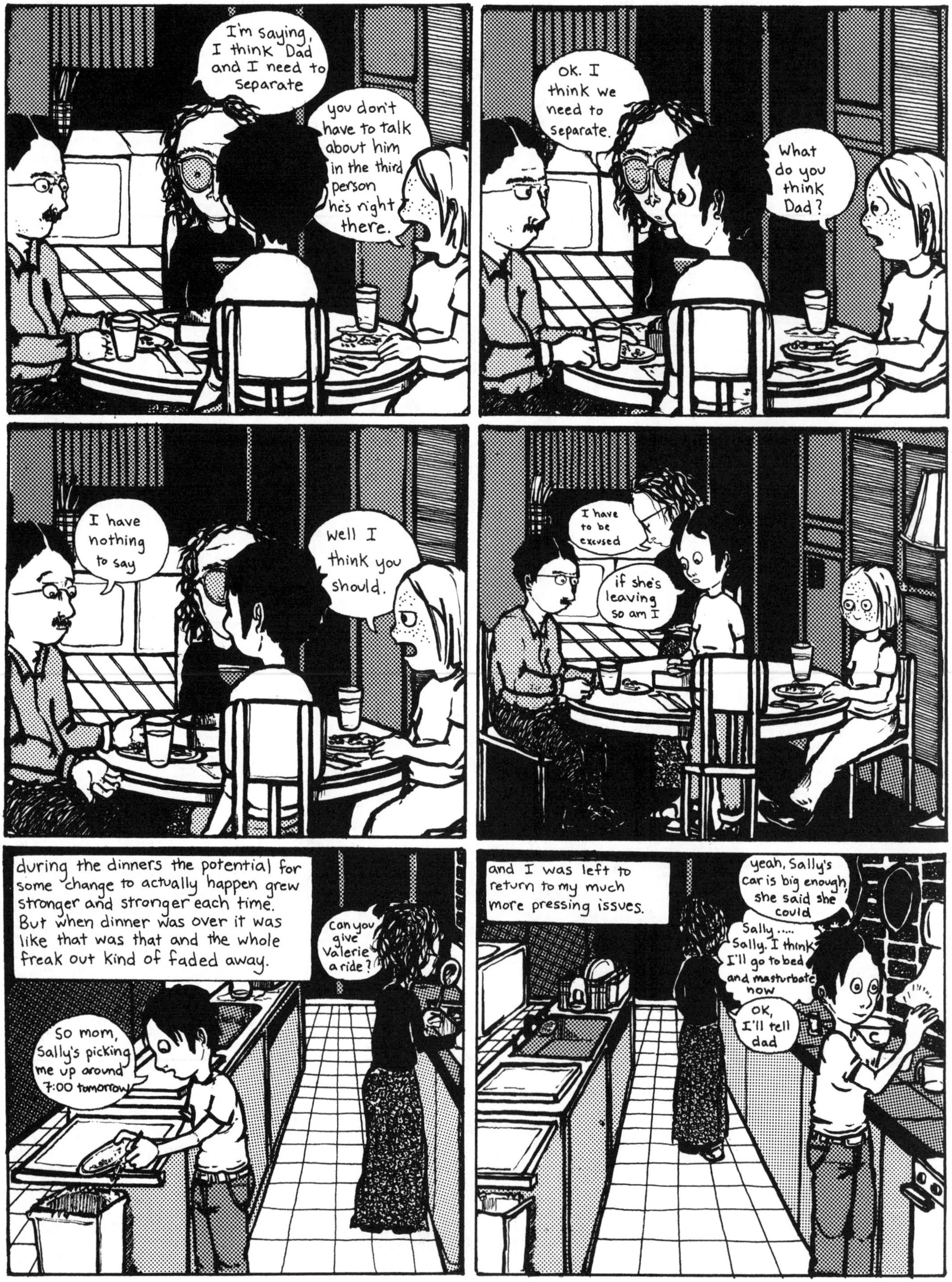
I'm saying, I think Dad and I need to separate
you don't have to talk about him in the third person he's right there.
OK. I think we need to separate.
What do you think Dad?
I have nothing to say
Well I think you should.
I have to be excused
if she's leaving so am I
during the dinners the potential for some change to actually happen grew stronger and stronger each time. But when dinner was over it was like that was that and the whole freak out kind of faded away.
Can you give Valerie a ride?
So mom, Sally's picking me up around 7:00 tomorrow
and I was left to return to my much more pressing issues.
yeah, Sally's car is big enough, she said she could
Sally.... Sally. I think I'll go to bed and masturbate now
OK, I'll tell dad

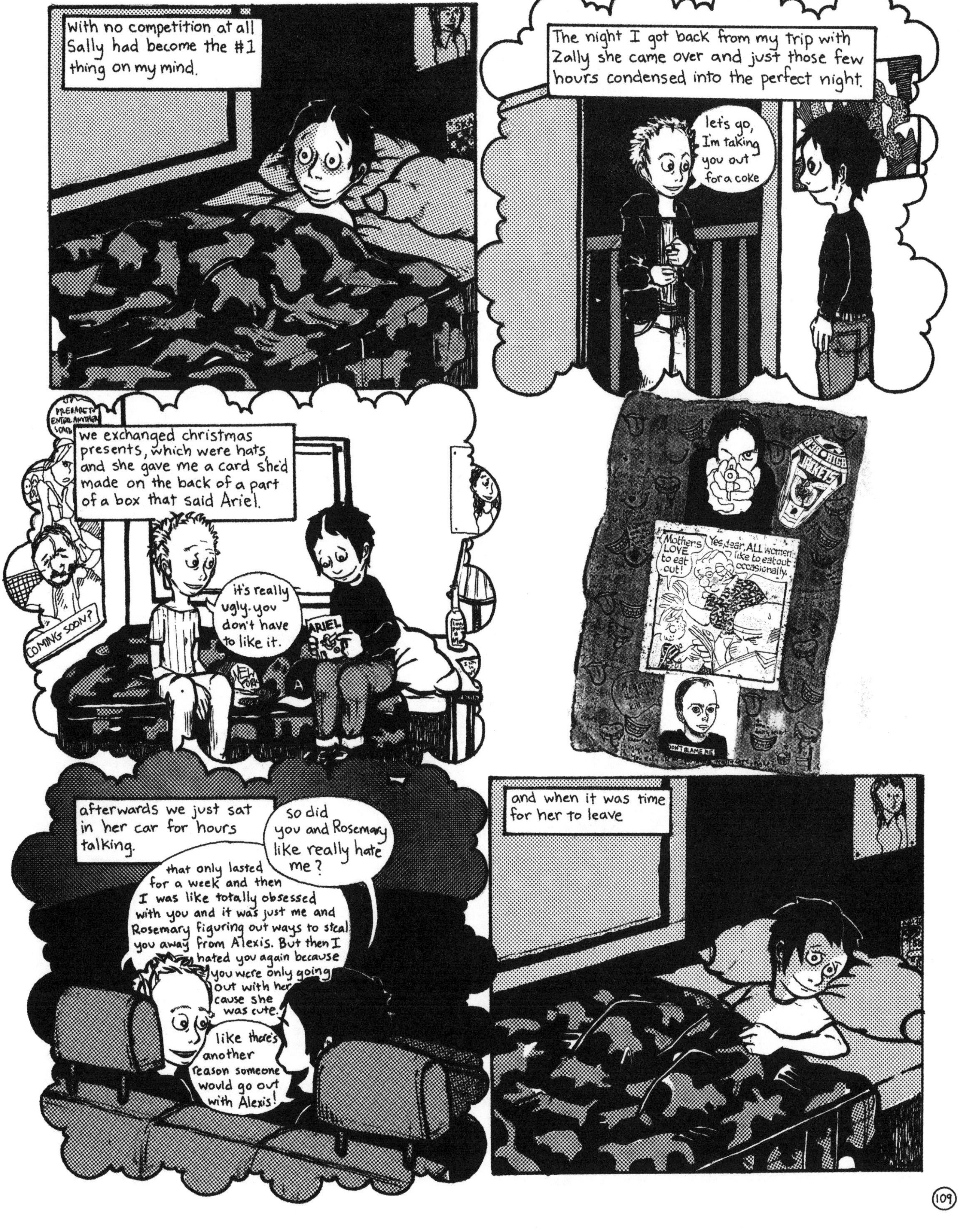
With no competition at all Sally had become the #1 thing on my mind.
The night I got back from my trip with Zally she came over and just those few hours condensed into the perfect night.
let's go, I'm taking you out for a coke
we exchanged christmas presents, which were hats and she gave me a card she'd made on the back of a part of a box that said Ariel.
COMING SOON?
it's really ugly. you don't have to like it.
ARIEL
Mothers LOVE to eat out!
Yes, dear, ALL women like to eat out occasionally.
DON'T BLAME ME
afterwards we just sat in her car for hours talking.
so did you and Rosemary like really hate me?
that only lasted for a week and then I was like totally obsessed with you and it was just me and Rosemary figuring out ways to steal you away from Alexis. But then I hated you again because you were only going out with her cause she was cute.
like there's another reason someone would go out with Alexis!
and when it was time for her to leave

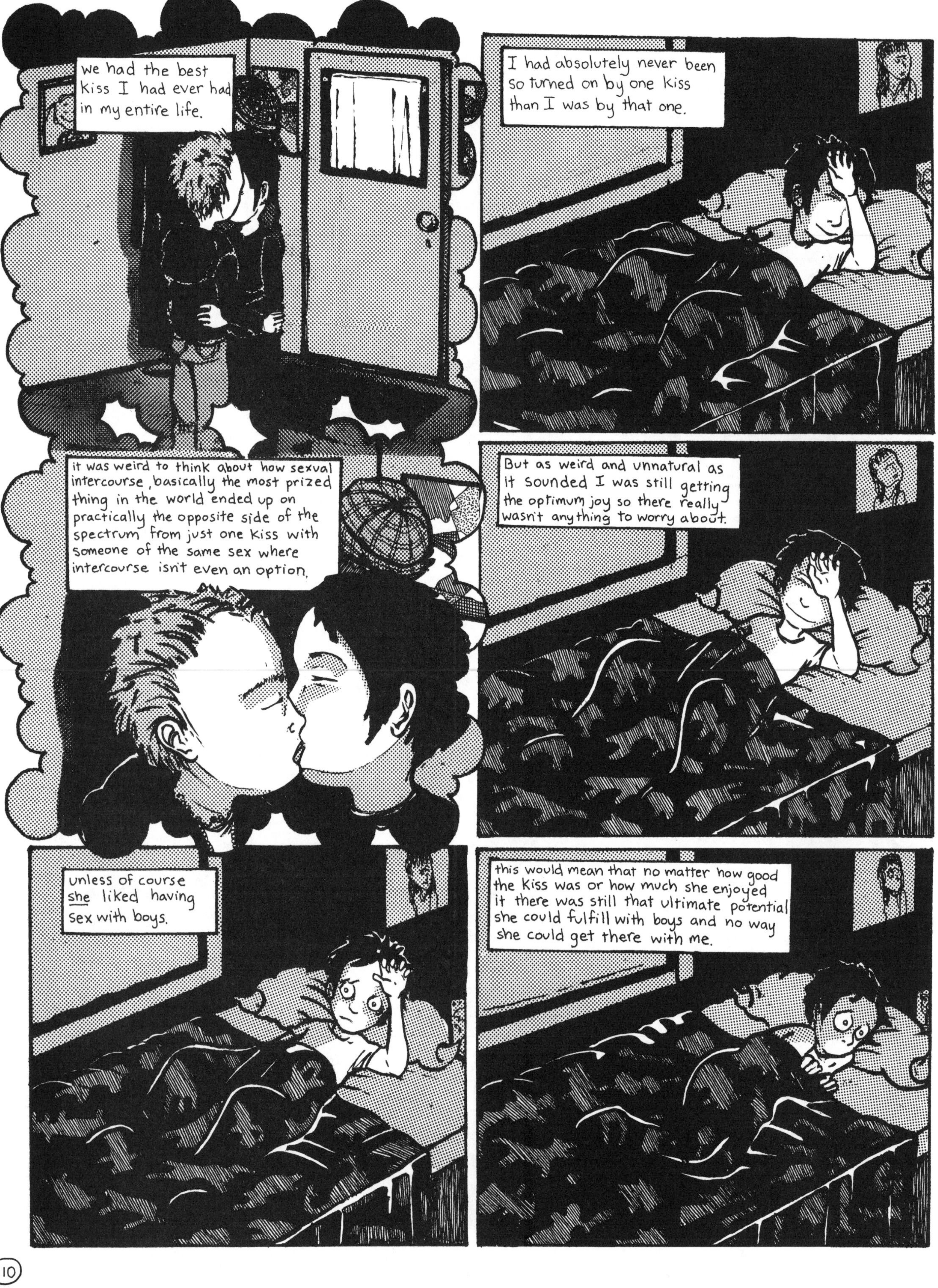
we had the best kiss I had ever had in my entire life.
I had absolutely never been so turned on by one kiss than I was by that one.
it was weird to think about how sexual intercourse, basically the most prized thing in the world ended up on practically the opposite side of the spectrum from just one kiss with someone of the same sex where intercourse isn't even an option.
But as weird and unnatural as it sounded I was still getting the optimum joy so there really wasn't anything to worry about.
unless of course she liked having sex with boys.
this would mean that no matter how good the kiss was or how much she enjoyed it there was still that ultimate potential she could fulfill with boys and no way she could get there with me.

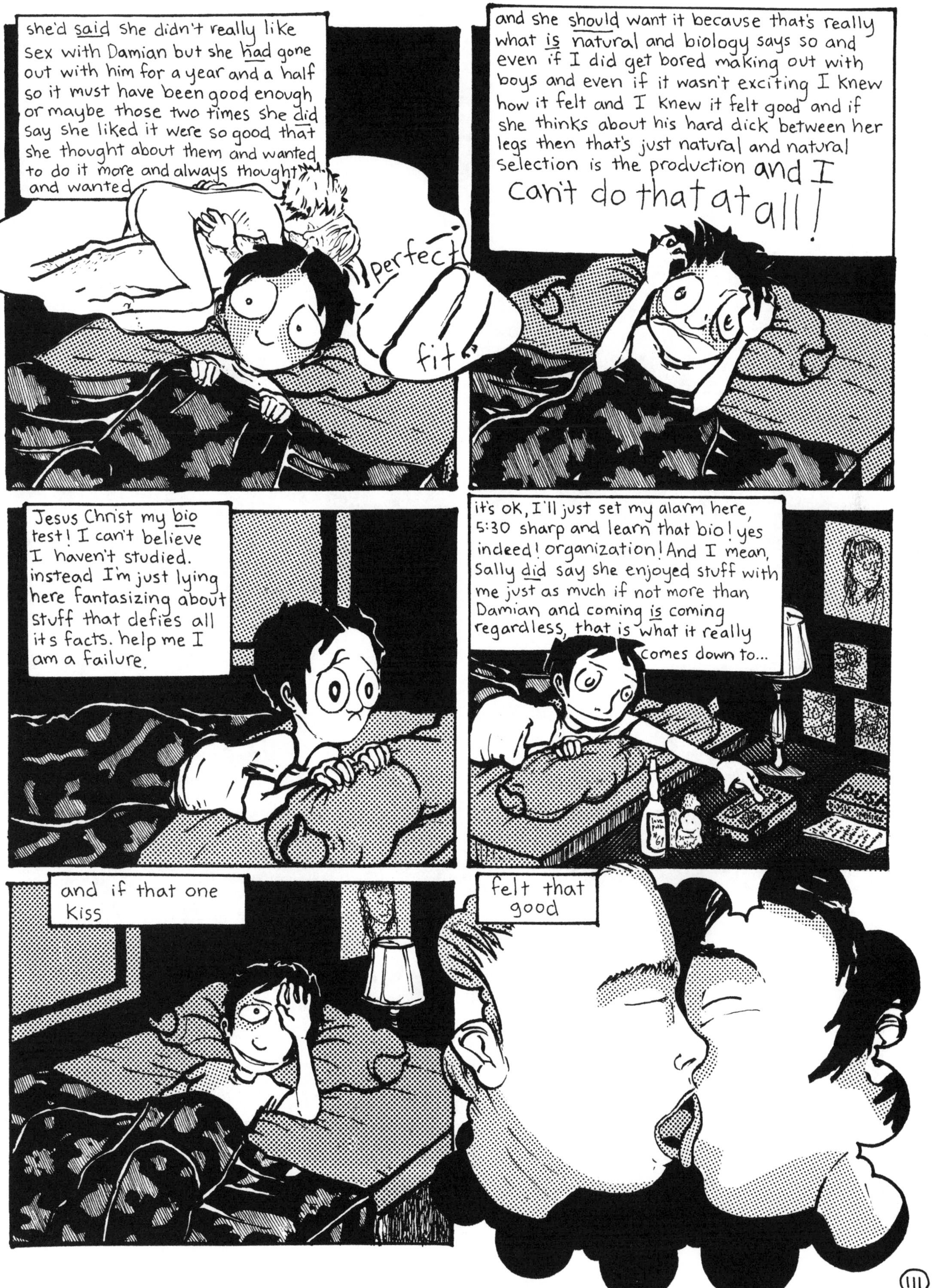
she'd said she didn't really like sex with Damian but she had gone out with him for a year and a half so it must have been good enough or maybe those two times she did say she liked it were so good that she thought about them and wanted to do it more and always thought and wanted
perfect
fit
and she should want it because that's really what is natural and biology says so and even if I did get bored making out with boys and even if it wasn't exciting I knew how it felt and I knew it felt good and if she thinks about his hard dick between her legs then that's just natural and natural selection is the production and I can't do that at all!
Jesus Christ my bio test! I can't believe I haven't studied. instead I'm just lying here fantasizing about stuff that defies all its facts. help me I am a failure.
it's OK, I'll just set my alarm here, 5:30 sharp and learn that bio! yes indeed! organization! And I mean, Sally did say she enjoyed stuff with me just as much if not more than Damian and coming is coming regardless, that is what it really comes down to...
and if that one kiss
felt that good

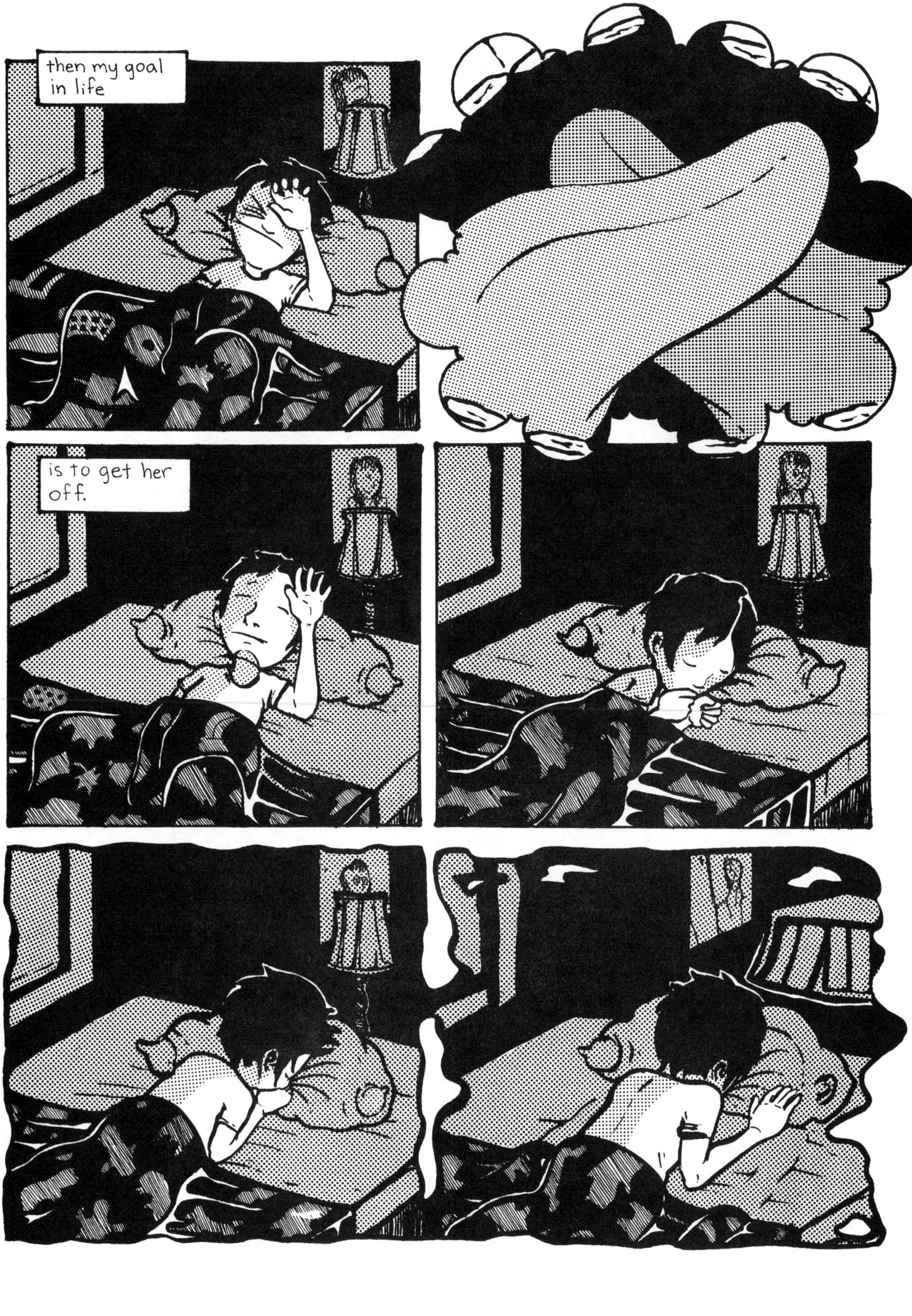
then my goal in life
is to get her off.

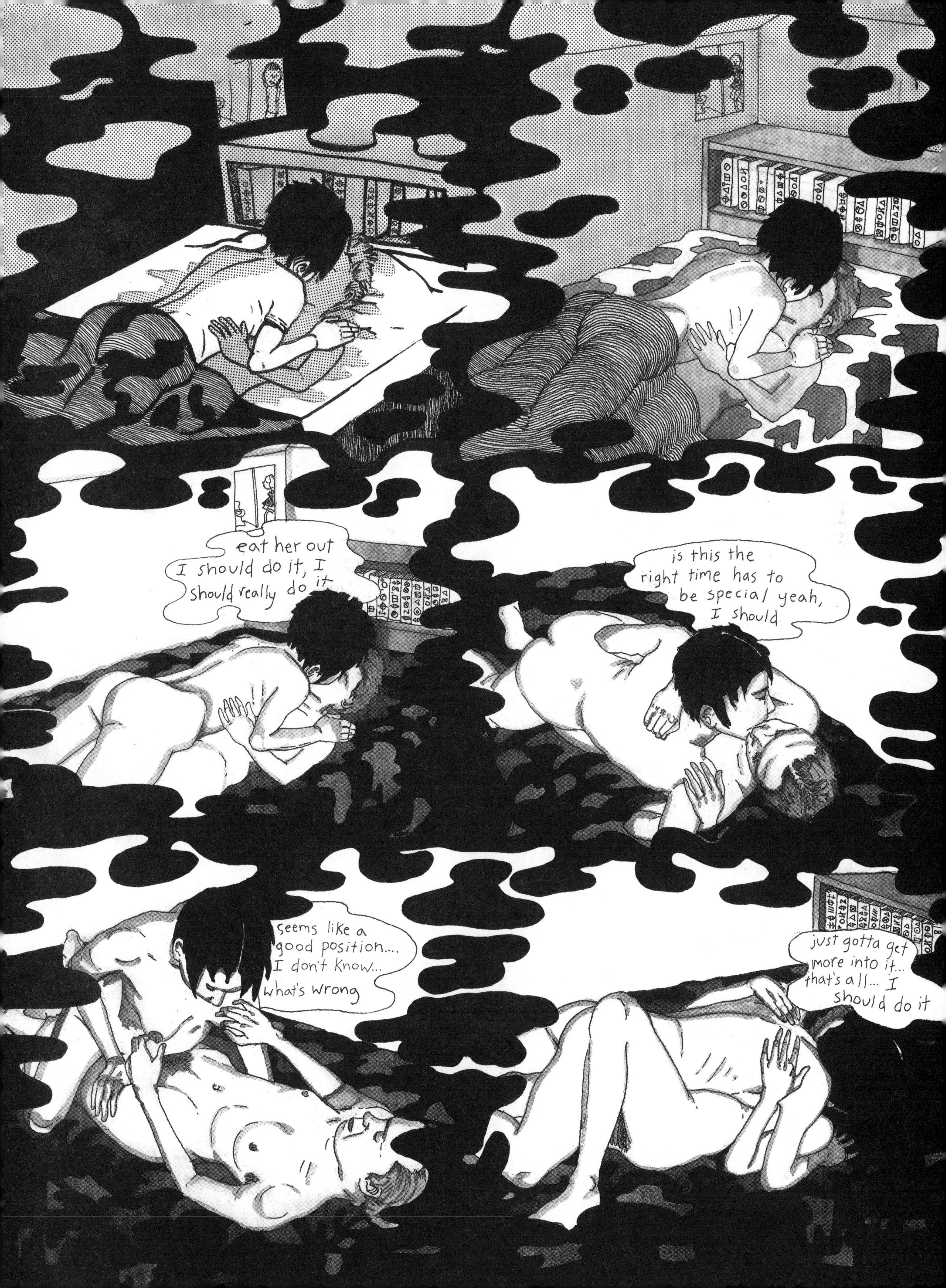
eat her out I should do it, I should really do it
is this the right time has to be special yeah, I should
seems like a good position.... I don't know... what's wrong
just gotta get more into it... that's all... I should do it

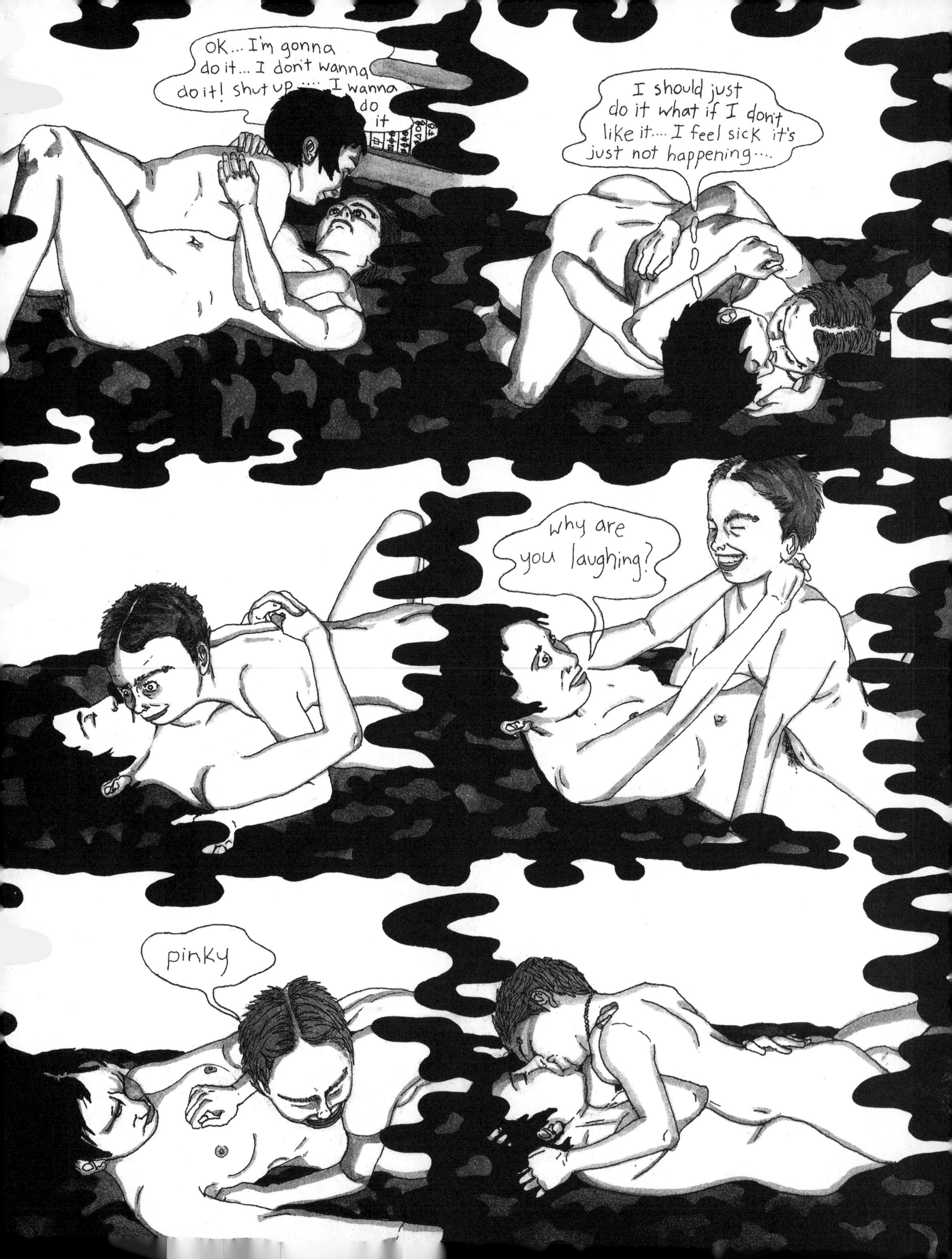
OK... I'm gonna do it... I don't wanna do it! shut up.... I wanna do it
I should just do it what if I don't like it.... I feel sick it's just not happening....
why are you laughing?
pinky

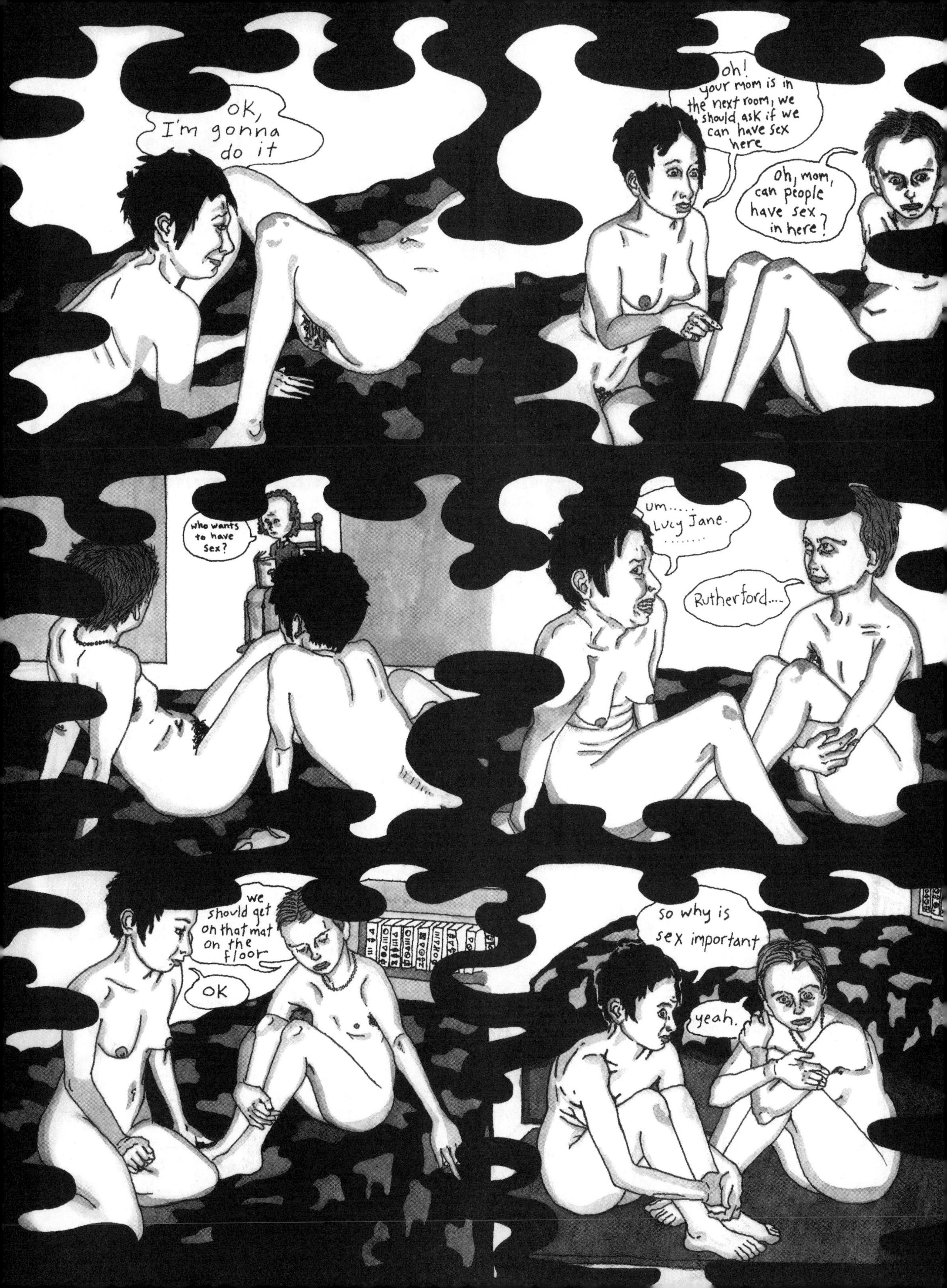
ok, I'm gonna do it
oh! your mom is in the next room, we should ask if we can have sex here
oh, mom, can people have sex in here?
who wants to have sex?
um..... Lucy Jane. ....
Rutherford.....
we should get on that mat on the floor
OK
so why is sex important
yeah.

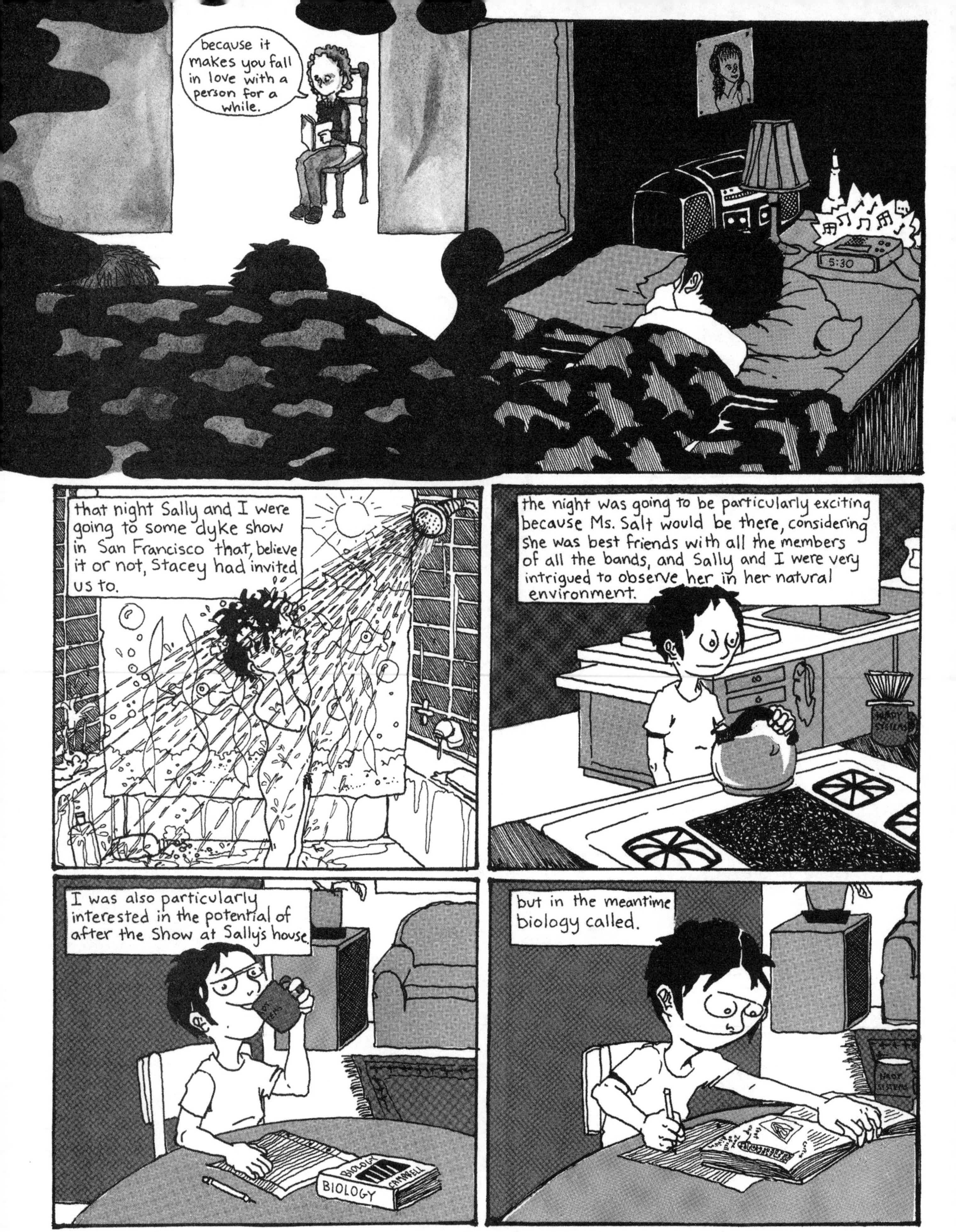
because it makes you fall in love with a person for a while.
5:30
that night Sally and I were going to some dyke show in San Francisco that, believe it or not, Stacey had invited us to.
the night was going to be particularly exciting because Ms. Salt would be there, considering she was best friends with all the members of all the bands, and Sally and I were very intrigued to observe her in her natural environment.
I was also particularly interested in the potential of after the show at Sally's house.
BIOLOGY
BIOLOGY
CAMPBELL
but in the meantime biology called.

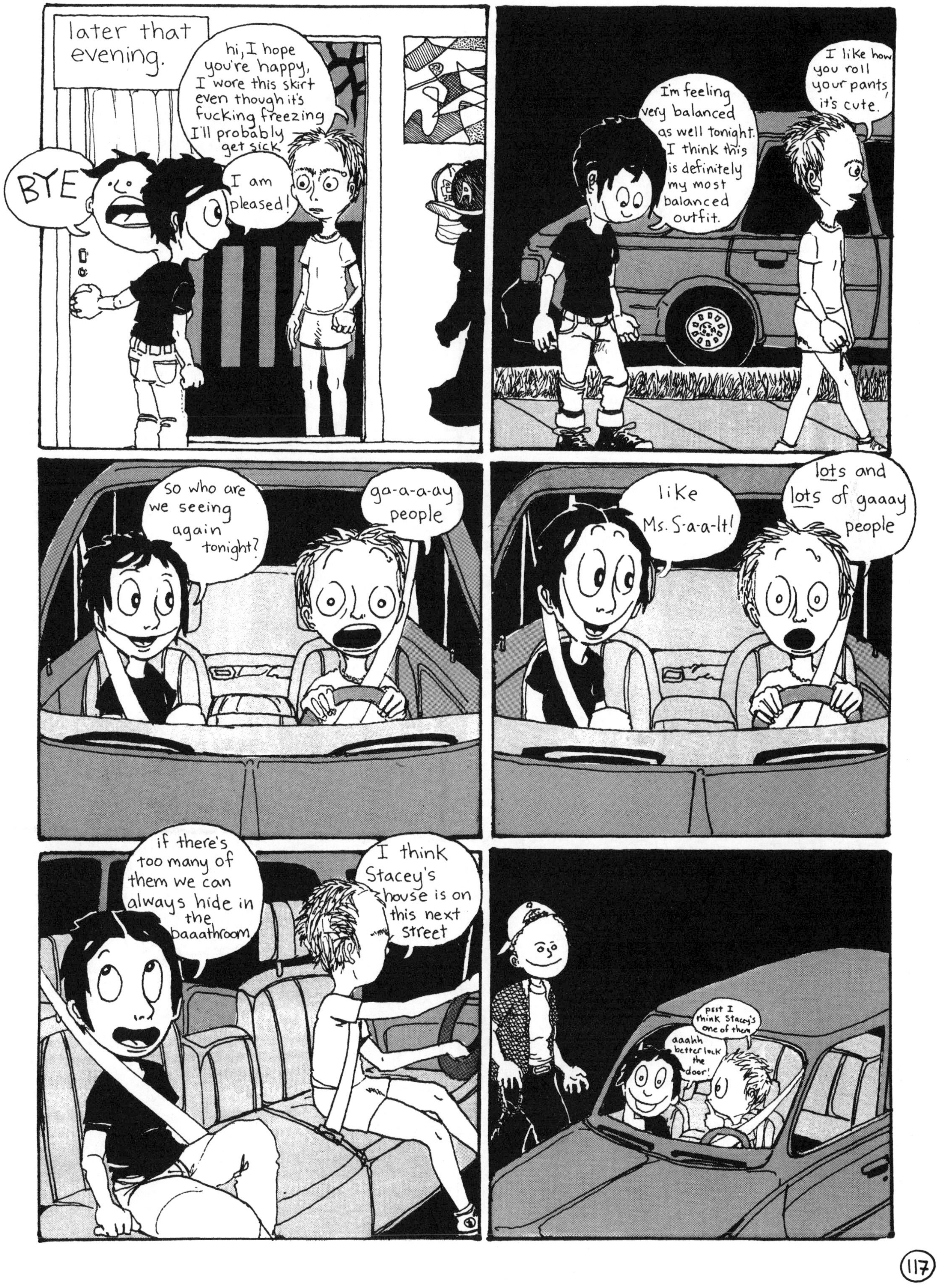
later that evening.
BYE
hi, I hope you're happy, I wore this skirt even though it's fucking freezing I'll probably get sick
I am pleased!
I'm feeling very balanced as well tonight. I think this is definitely my most balanced outfit.
I like how you roll your pants, it's cute.
so who are we seeing again tonight?
ga-a-a-ay people
like Ms. S-a-a-lt!
lots and lots of gaaay people
if there's too many of them we can always hide in the baaathroom
I think Stacey's house is on this next street
psst I think Stacey's one of them
aaahh better lock the door!

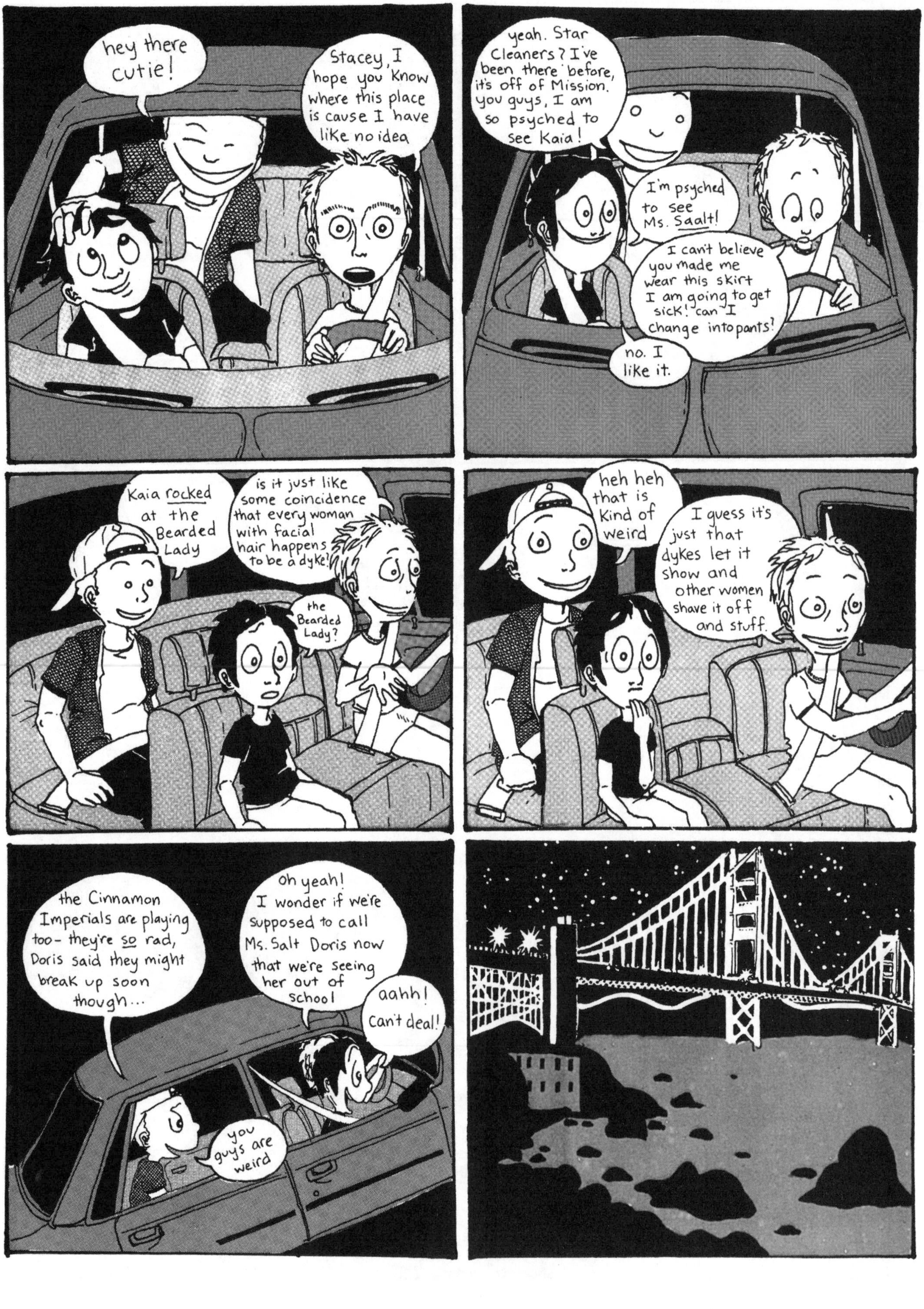
hey there cutie!
Stacey, I hope you know where this place is cause I have like no idea
yeah. Star Cleaners? I've been there before, it's off of Mission. you guys, I am so psyched to see Kaia!
I'm psyched to see Ms. Saalt!
I can't believe you made me wear this skirt I am going to get sick! can I change into pants?
no. I like it.
Kaia rocked at the Bearded Lady
is it just like some coincidence that every woman with facial hair happens to be a dyke?
the Bearded Lady?
heh heh that is kind of weird
I guess it's just that dykes let it show and other women shave it off and stuff.
the Cinnamon Imperials are playing too- they're so rad, Doris said they might break up soon though...
oh yeah! I wonder if we're supposed to call Ms. Salt Doris now that we're seeing her out of school!
aahh! Can't deal!
you guys are weird

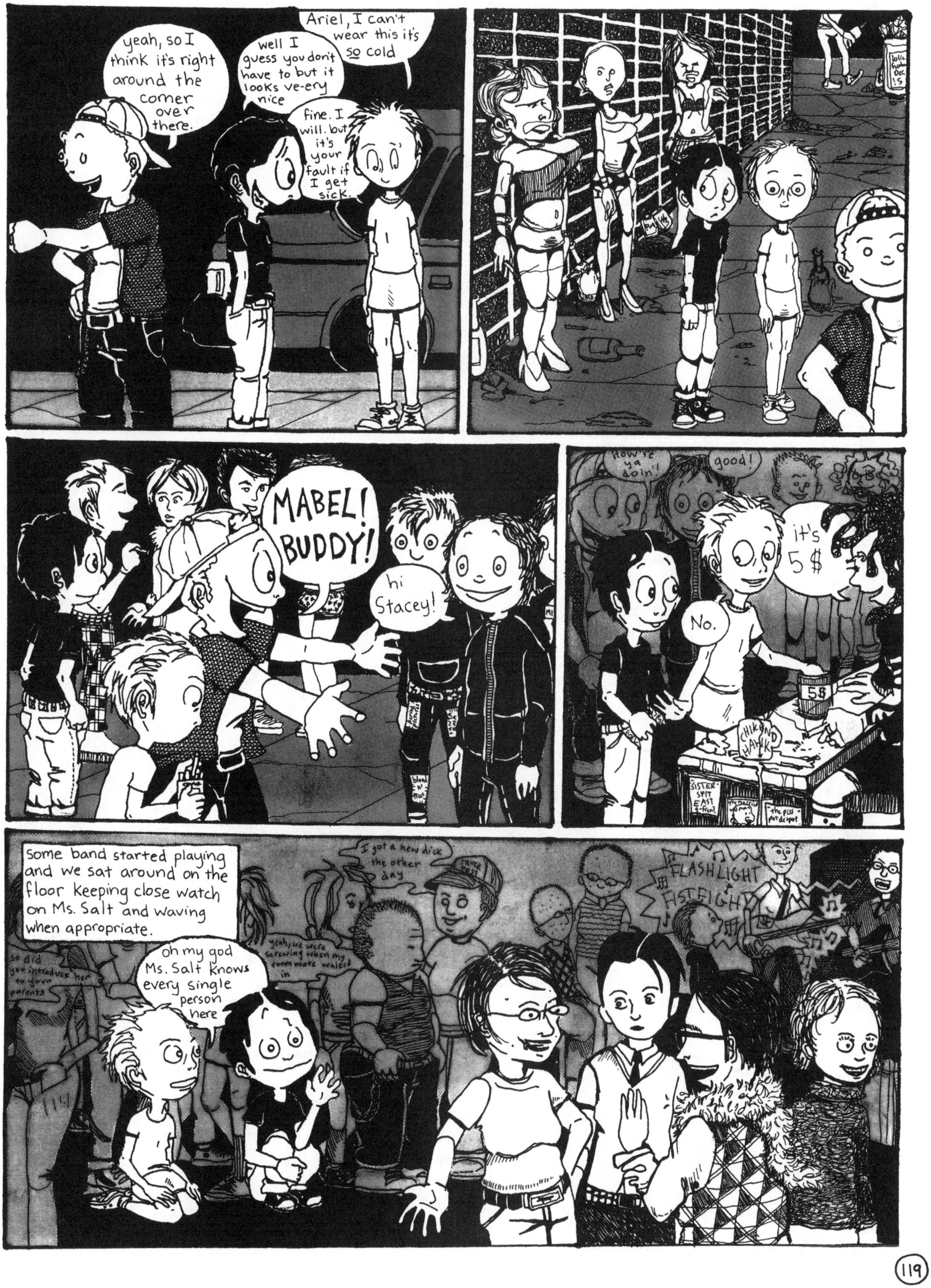
yeah, so I think it's right around the corner over there.
well I guess you don't have to but it looks ve-ery nice
Ariel, I can't wear this it's so cold
fine. I will. but it's your fault if I get sick.
MABEL! BUDDY!
hi Stacey!
blood n' trust
How're ya doin'!
good!
it's 5$
No.
5$
SISTER SPIT EAST
the piss pot despot
Some band started playing and we sat around on the floor keeping close watch on Ms. Salt and waving when appropriate.
I got a new dick the other day
FLASHLIGHT FISTFIGHT
so did you introduce her to your parents
oh my god Ms. Salt knows every single person here
yeah, we were screwing when my roommate walked in

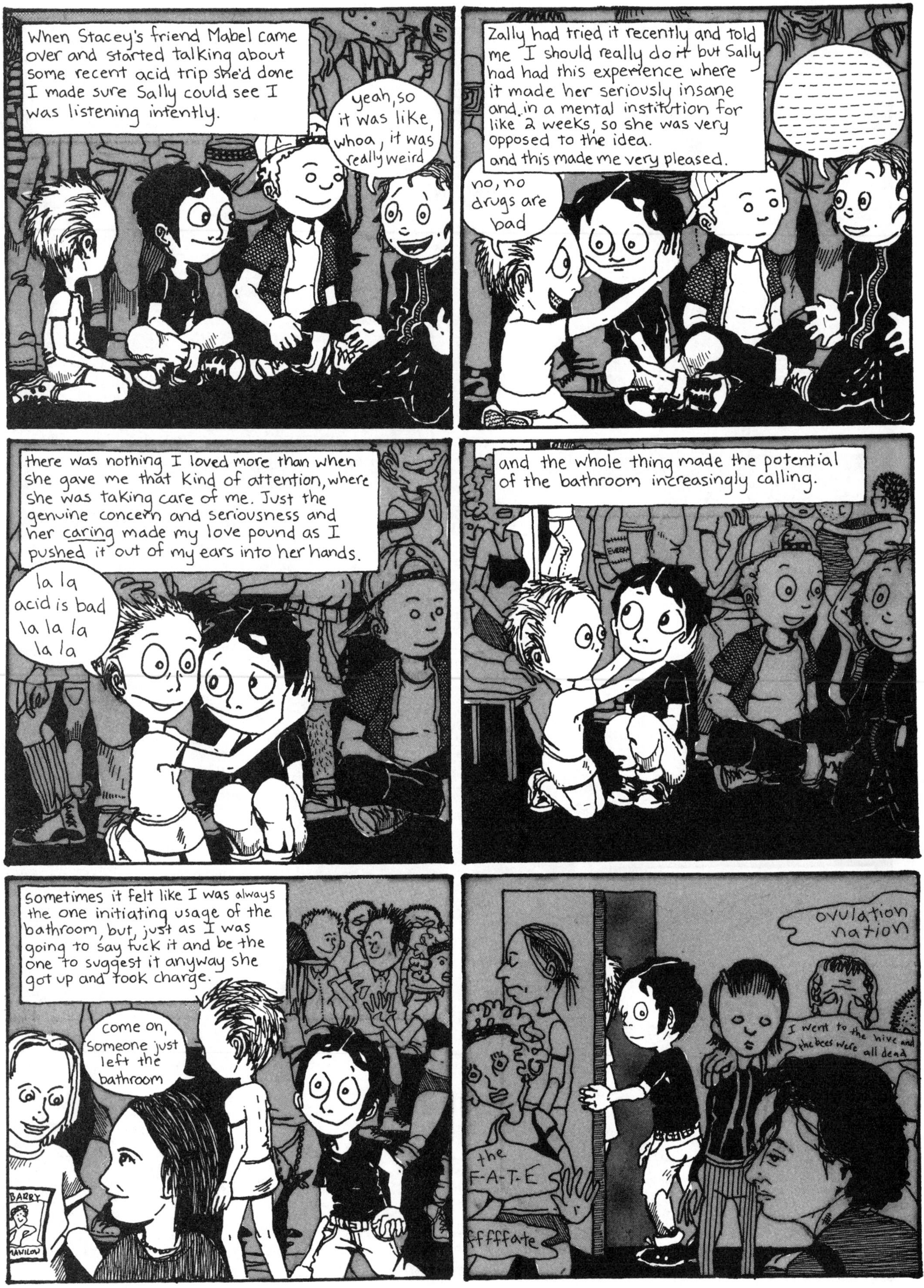
When Stacey's friend Mabel came over and started talking about some recent acid trip she'd done I made sure Sally could see I was listening intently.
yeah, so it was like, whoa, it was really weird
Zally had tried it recently and told me I should really do it but Sally had had this experience where it made her seriously insane and in a mental institution for like 2 weeks, so she was very opposed to the idea.
and this made me very pleased.
no, no drugs are bad
there was nothing I loved more than when she gave me that kind of attention, where she was taking care of me. Just the genuine concern and seriousness and her caring made my love pound as I pushed it out of my ears into her hands.
la la acid is bad la la la la la
and the whole thing made the potential of the bathroom increasingly calling.
Sometimes it felt like I was always the one initiating usage of the bathroom, but, just as I was going to say fuck it and be the one to suggest it anyway she got up and took charge.
come on, someone just left the bathroom
BARRY MANILOW
ovulation nation
I went to the hive and the bees were all dead
the F-A-T-E
ffffate

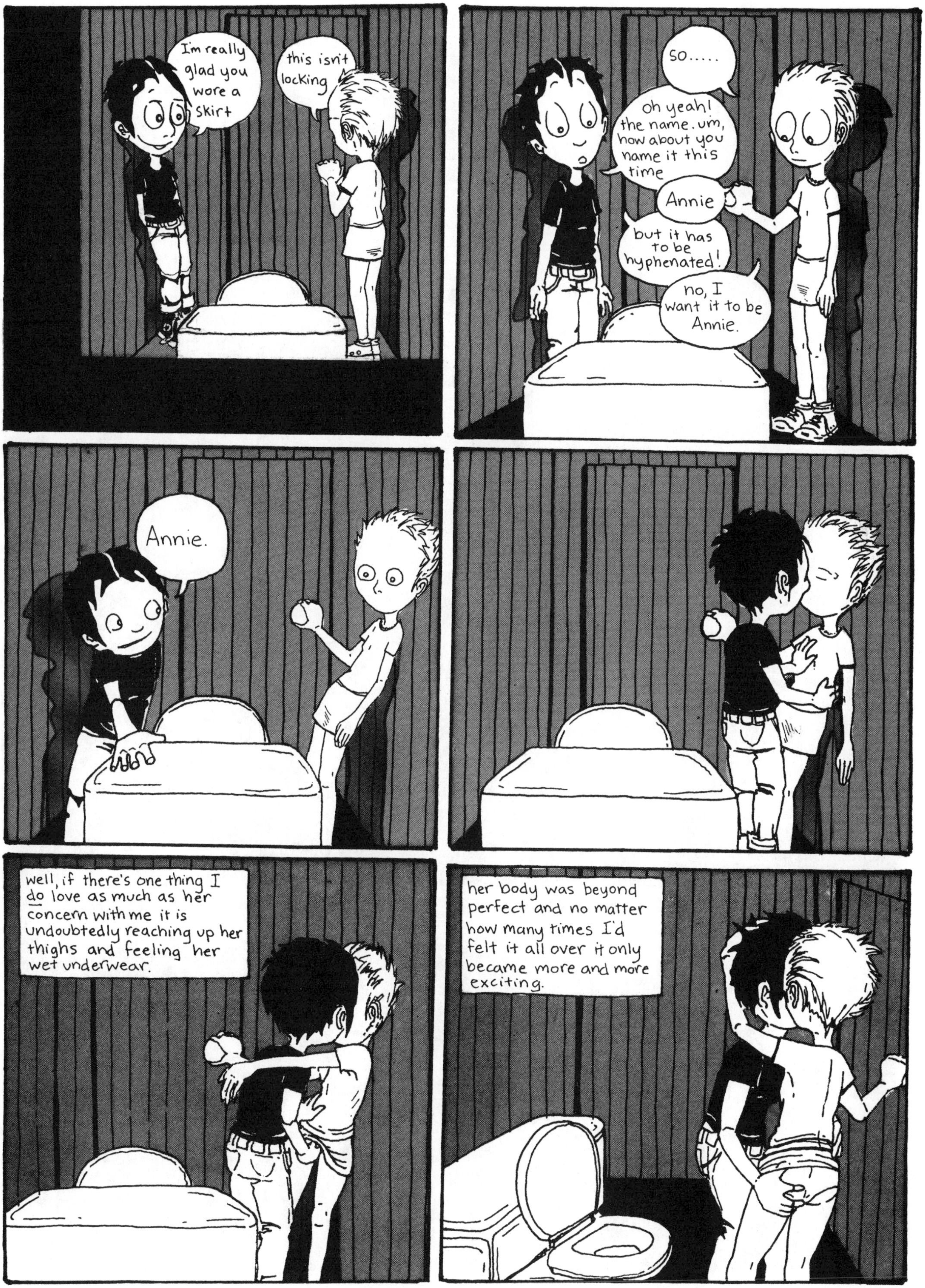
I'm really glad you wore a skirt
this isn't locking
so.....
oh yeah! the name. um, how about you name it this time
Annie
but it has to be hyphenated!
no, I want it to be Annie.
Annie.
well, if there's one thing I do love as much as her concern with me it is undoubtedly reaching up her thighs and feeling her wet underwear.
her body was beyond perfect and no matter how many times I'd felt it all over it only became more and more exciting.

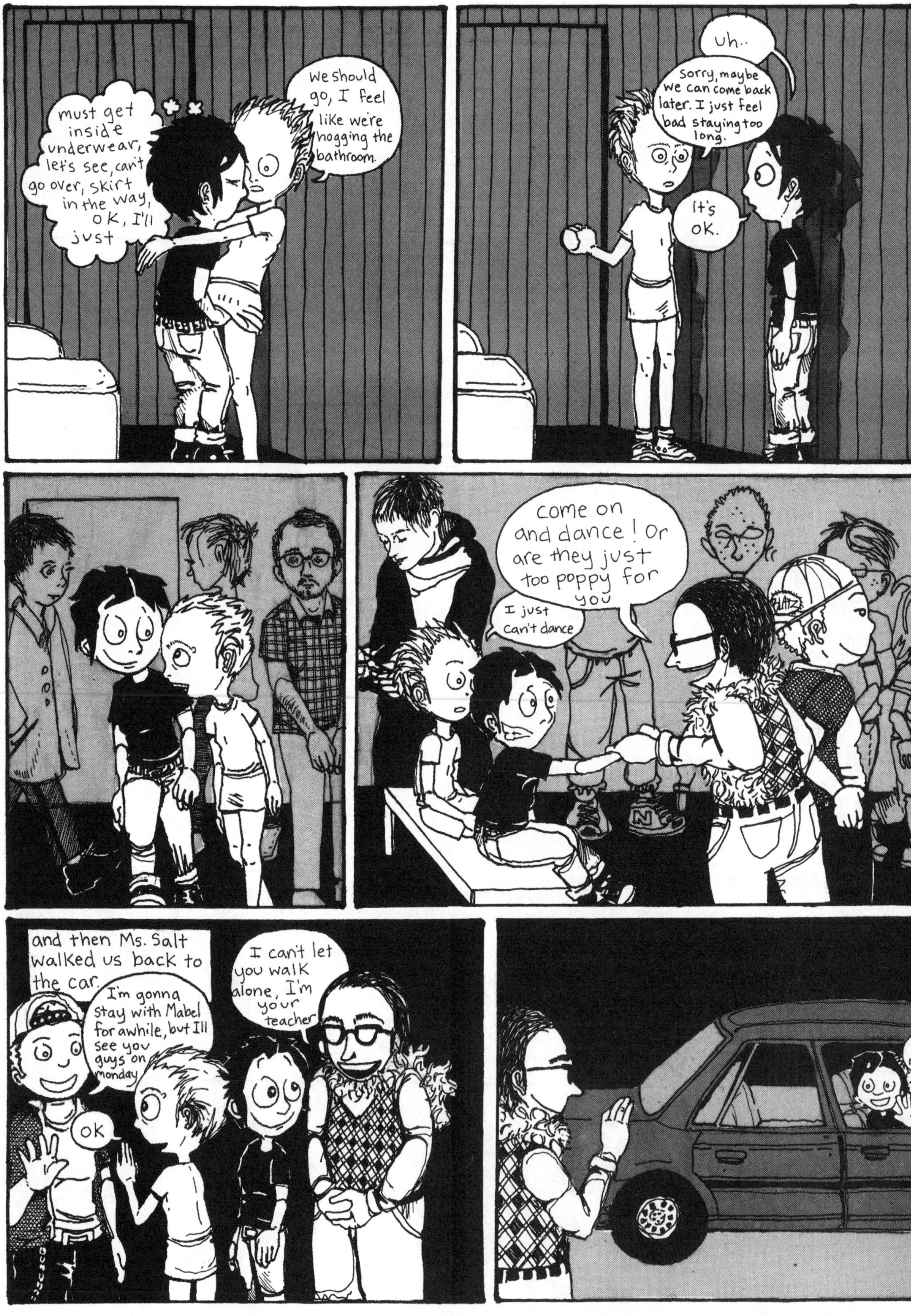
must get inside underwear, let's see, can't go over, skirt in the way, OK, I'll just
We should go, I feel like we're hogging the bathroom.
Uh..
Sorry, maybe we can come back later. I just feel bad staying too long.
It's ok.
come on and dance! Or are they just too poppy for you
I just can't dance
and then Ms. Salt walked us back to the car.
I'm gonna stay with Mabel for awhile, but I'll see you guys on monday
ok
I can't let you walk alone, I'm your teacher
I love Ms. Salt

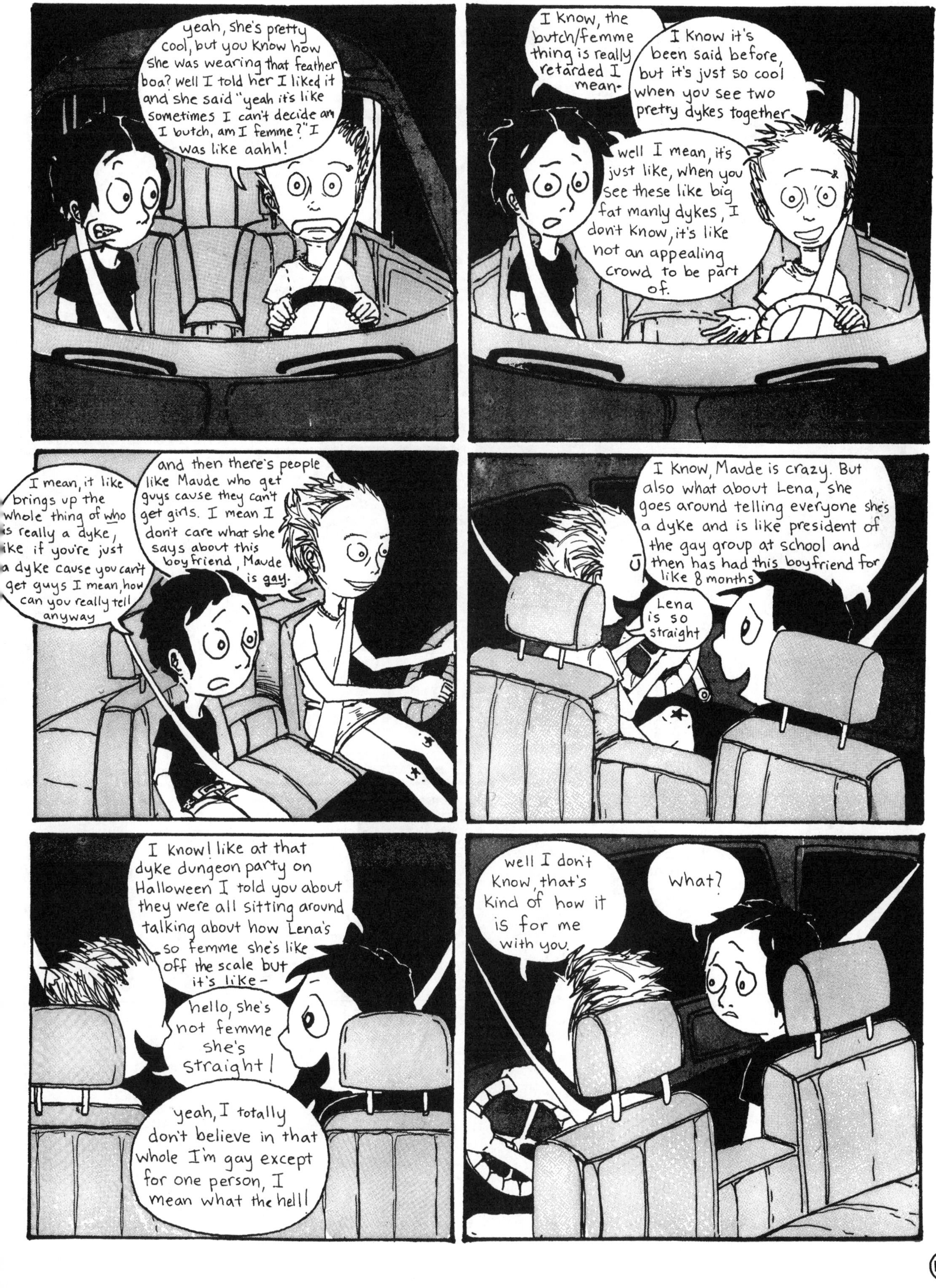

yeah, she's pretty cool, but you know how she was wearing that feather boa? well I told her I liked it and she said "yeah it's like sometimes I can't decide am I butch, am I femme?" I was like aahh!
I know, the butch/femme thing is really retarded I mean-
I know it's been said before, but it's just so cool when you see two pretty dykes together
well I mean, it's just like, when you see these like big fat manly dykes, I don't know, it's like not an appealing crowd to be part of.
I mean, it like brings up the whole thing of who is really a dyke, like if you're just a dyke cause you can't get guys I mean, how can you really tell anyway
and then there's people like Maude who get guys cause they can't get girls. I mean I don't care what she says about this boyfriend, Maude is gay.
I know, Maude is crazy. But also what about Lena, she goes around telling everyone she's a dyke and is like president of the gay group at school and then has had this boyfriend for like 8 months
Lena is so straight
I know! like at that dyke dungeon party on Halloween I told you about they were all sitting around talking about how Lena's so femme she's like off the scale but it's like-
hello, she's not femme she's straight!
yeah, I totally don't believe in that whole I'm gay except for one person, I mean what the hell!
well I don't know, that's kind of how it is for me with you.
What?

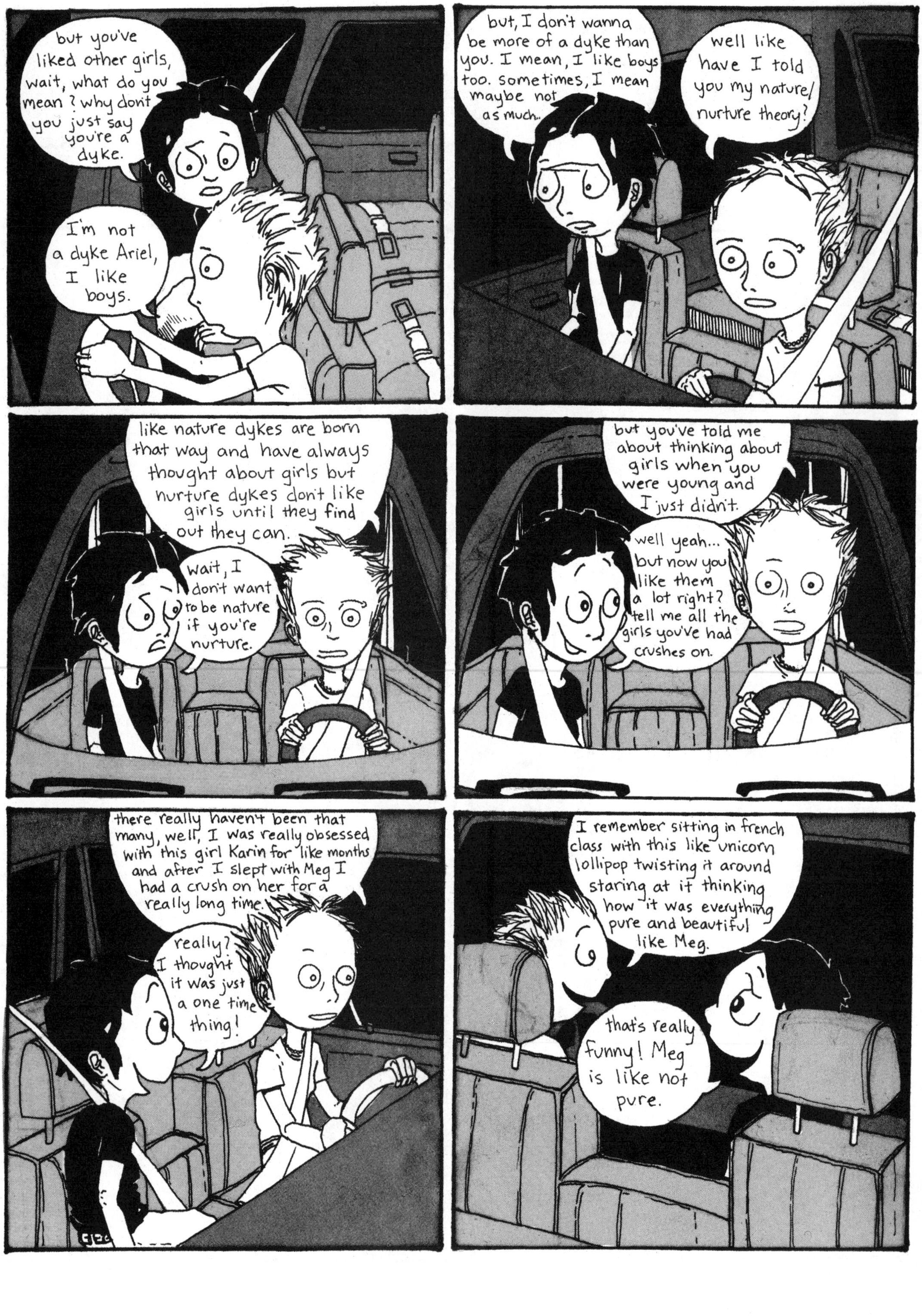

but you've liked other girls, wait, what do you mean? why don't you just say you're a dyke.
I'm not a dyke Ariel, I like boys.
but, I don't wanna be more of a dyke than you. I mean, I like boys too. sometimes, I mean maybe not as much..
well like have I told you my nature/nurture theory?
like nature dykes are born that way and have always thought about girls but nurture dykes don't like girls until they find out they can.
wait, I don't want to be nature if you're nurture.
but you've told me about thinking about girls when you were young and I just didn't.
well yeah... but now you like them a lot right? tell me all the girls you've had crushes on.
there really haven't been that many, well, I was really obsessed with this girl Karin for like months and after I slept with Meg I had a crush on her for a really long time.
really? I thought it was just a one time thing!
I remember sitting in french class with this like unicorn lollipop twisting it around staring at it thinking how it was everything pure and beautiful like Meg.
that's really funny! Meg is like not pure.

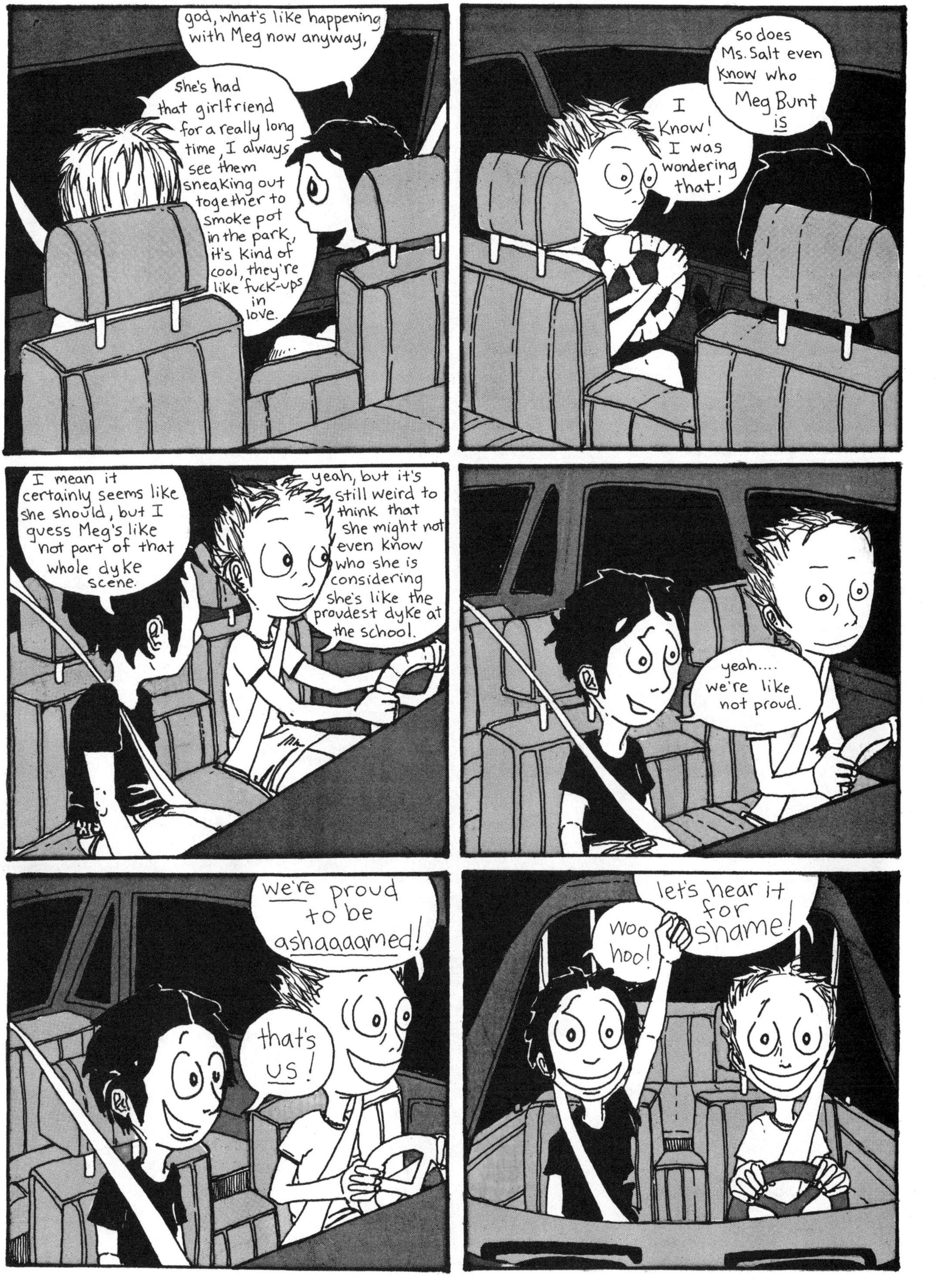
god, what's like happening with Meg now anyway,
she's had that girlfriend for a really long time, I always see them sneaking out together to smoke pot in the park, it's kind of cool, they're like fuck-ups in love.
so does Ms. Salt even know who Meg Bunt is
I know! I was wondering that!
I mean it certainly seems like she should, but I guess Meg's like not part of that whole dyke scene.
yeah, but it's still weird to think that she might not even know who she is considering she's like the proudest dyke at the school.
yeah.... we're like not proud.
we're proud to be ashaaaamed!
that's us!
let's hear it for shame!
woo hoo!

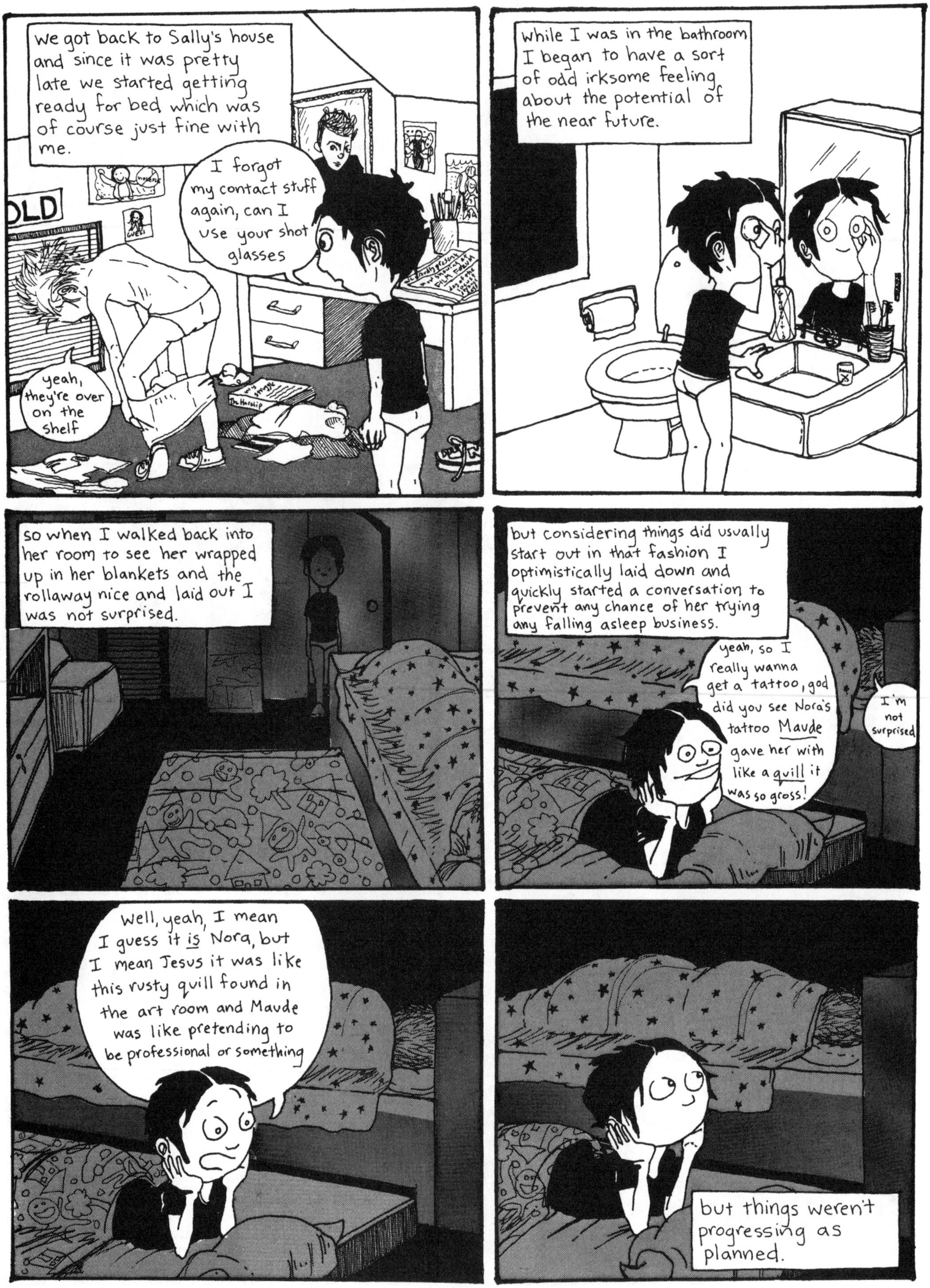
we got back to Sally's house and since it was pretty late we started getting ready for bed which was of course just fine with me.
I forgot my contact stuff again, can I use your shot glasses
yeah, they're over on the shelf
while I was in the bathroom I began to have a sort of odd irksome feeling about the potential of the near future.
so when I walked back into her room to see her wrapped up in her blankets and the rollaway nice and laid out I was not surprised.
but considering things did usually start out in that fashion I optimistically laid down and quickly started a conversation to prevent any chance of her trying any falling asleep business.
yeah, so I really wanna get a tattoo, god did you see Nora's tattoo Mavde gave her with like a quill it was so gross!
I'm not surprised
Well, yeah, I mean I guess it is Nora, but I mean Jesus it was like this rusty quill found in the art room and Mavde was like pretending to be professional or something
but things weren't progressing as planned.

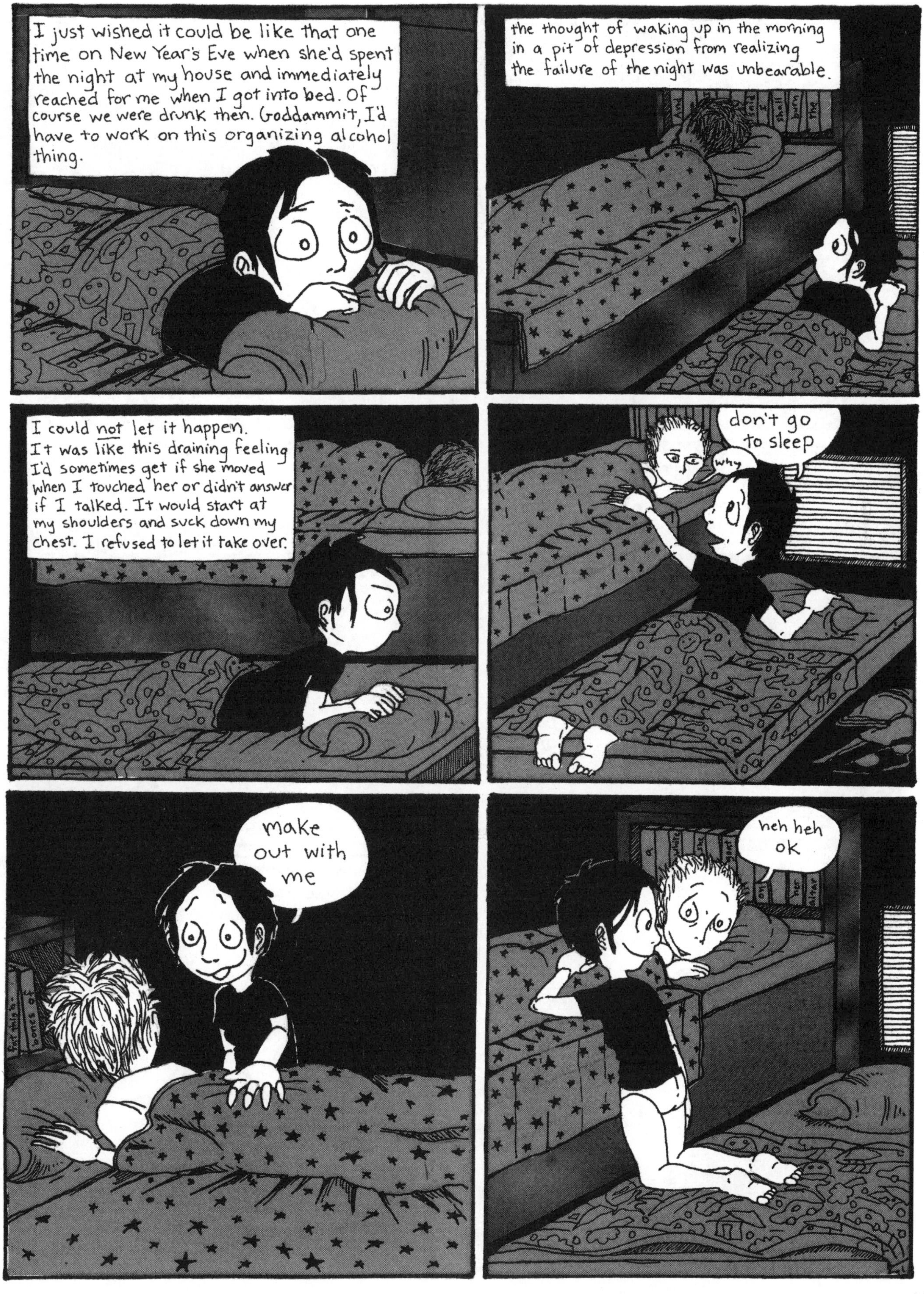
I just wished it could be like that one time on New Year's Eve when she'd spent the night at my house and immediately reached for me when I got into bed. Of course we were drunk then. Goddammit, I'd have to work on this organizing alcohol thing.
the thought of waking up in the morning in a pit of depression from realizing the failure of the night was unbearable.
I could not let it happen. It was like this draining feeling I'd sometimes get if she moved when I touched her or didn't answer if I talked. It would start at my shoulders and suck down my chest. I refused to let it take over.
don't go to sleep
why
make out with me
heh heh ok

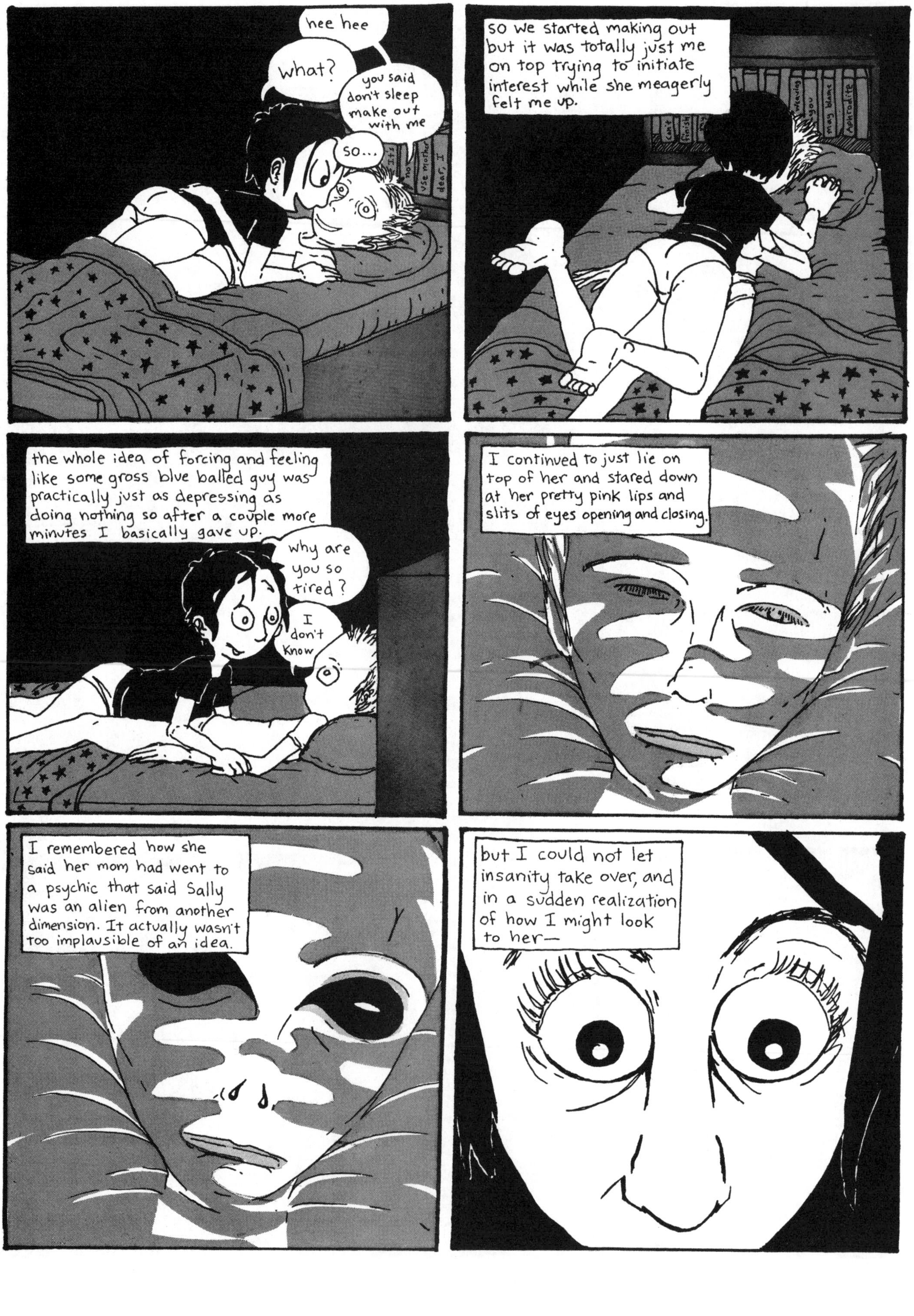
hee hee
what?
you said don't sleep make out with me
so...
so we started making out but it was totally just me on top trying to initiate interest while she meagerly felt me up.
the whole idea of forcing and feeling like some gross blue balled guy was practically just as depressing as doing nothing so after a couple more minutes I basically gave up.
why are you so tired?
I don't know
I continued to just lie on top of her and stared down at her pretty pink lips and slits of eyes opening and closing.
I remembered how she said her mom had went to a psychic that said Sally was an alien from another dimension. It actually wasn't too implausible of an idea.
but I could not let insanity take over, and in a sudden realization of how I might look to her—

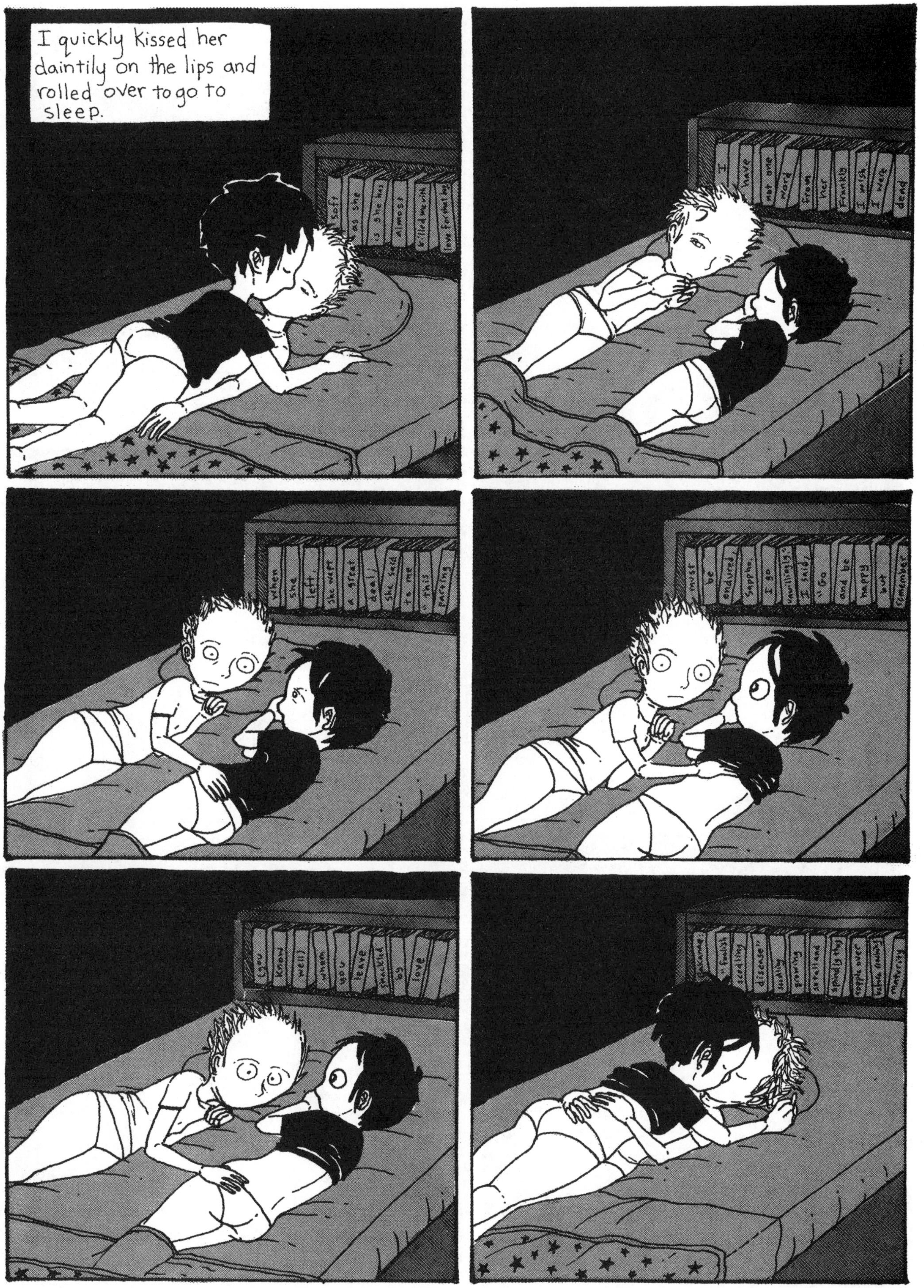
I quickly kissed her daintily on the lips and rolled over to go to sleep.
soft as she is she has almost killed me with love for that boy
I have not one word from her Frankly I wish I were dead
when she left, she wept a great deal; she said to me "this parting
must be endured, Sappho. I go unwillingly." I said, "Go and be happy but remember
(you know well) whom you leave shackled by love
"foolish scolding disease"
spindly thighs topple over

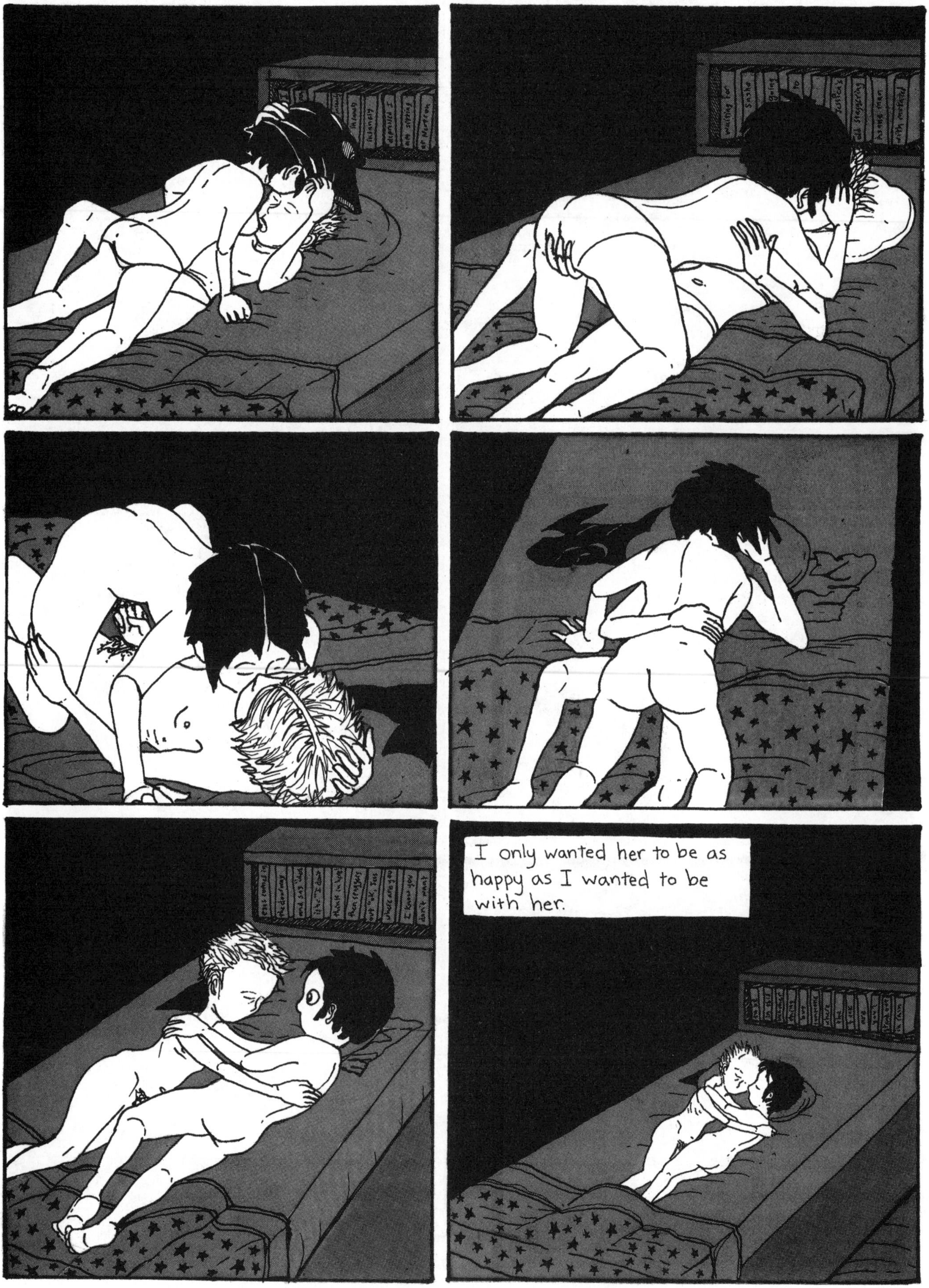
I only wanted her to be as happy as I wanted to be with her.

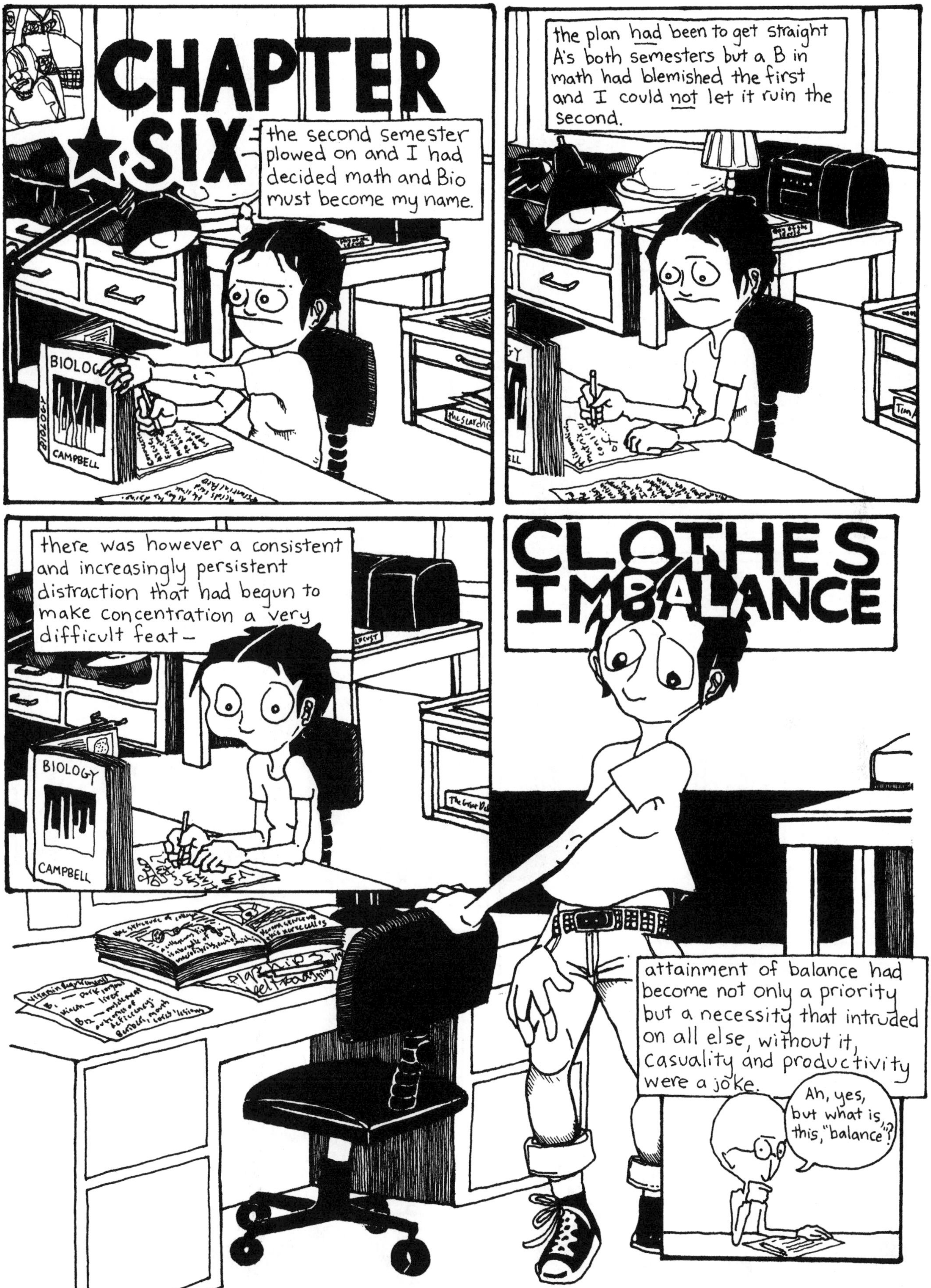
CHAPTER ★ SIX
the second semester plowed on and I had decided math and Bio must become my name.
BIOLOGY
CAMPBELL
the plan had been to get straight A's both semesters but a B in math had blemished the first and I could not let it ruin the second.
there was however a consistent and increasingly persistent distraction that had begun to make concentration a very difficult feat—
BIOLOGY
CAMPBELL
CLOTHES IMBALANCE
attainment of balance had become not only a priority but a necessity that intruded on all else, without it, casuality and productivity were a joke.
Ah, yes, but what is this, "balance"?

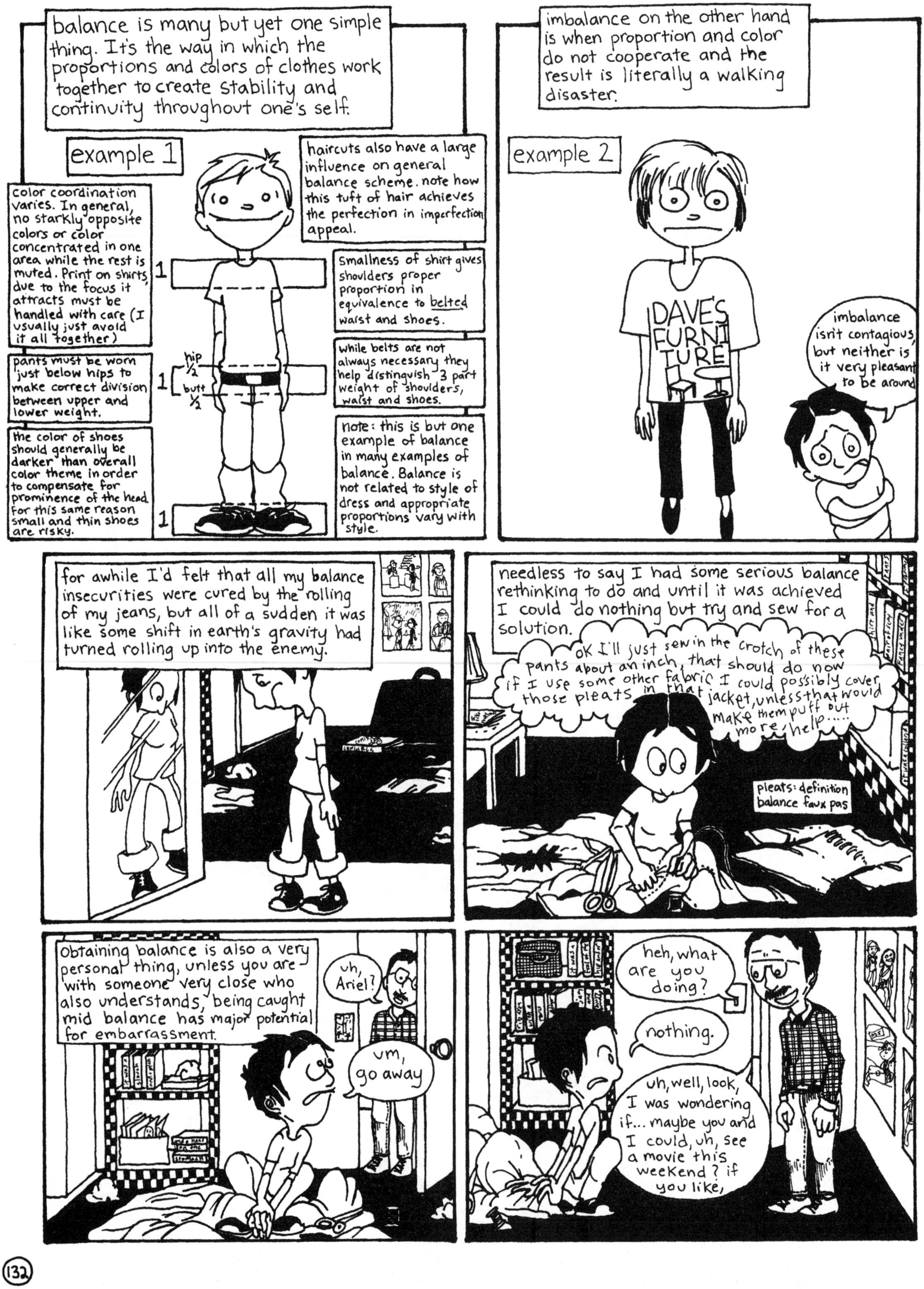
balance is many but yet one simple thing. It's the way in which the proportions and colors of clothes work together to create stability and continuity throughout one's self.
example 1
haircuts also have a large influence on general balance scheme. note how this tuft of hair achieves the perfection in imperfection appeal.
color coordination varies. In general, no starkly opposite colors or color concentrated in one area while the rest is muted. Print on shirts, due to the focus it attracts must be handled with care (I usually just avoid it all together)
1
smallness of shirt gives shoulders proper proportion in equivalence to belted waist and shoes.
pants must be worn just below hips to make correct division between upper and lower weight.
hip ½
1
butt ½
while belts are not always necessary they help distinguish 3 part weight of shoulders, waist and shoes.
the color of shoes should generally be darker than overall color theme in order to compensate for prominence of the head. For this same reason small and thin shoes are risky.
1
note: this is but one example of balance in many examples of balance. Balance is not related to style of dress and appropriate proportions vary with style.
imbalance on the other hand is when proportion and color do not cooperate and the result is literally a walking disaster.
example 2
DAVE'S FURNITURE
imbalance isn't contagious, but neither is it very pleasant to be around
for awhile I'd felt that all my balance insecurities were cured by the rolling of my jeans, but all of a sudden it was like some shift in earth's gravity had turned rolling up into the enemy.
needless to say I had some serious balance rethinking to do and until it was achieved I could do nothing but try and sew for a solution.
ok I'll just sew in the crotch of these pants about an inch, that should do now if I use some other fabric I could possibly cover those pleats in that jacket, unless that would make them puff out more, help.....
pleats: definition balance faux pas
Obtaining balance is also a very personal thing, unless you are with someone very close who also understands, being caught mid balance has major potential for embarrassment.
uh, Ariel?
um, go away
heh, what are you doing?
nothing.
uh, well, look, I was wondering if... maybe you and I could, uh, see a movie this weekend? if you like,

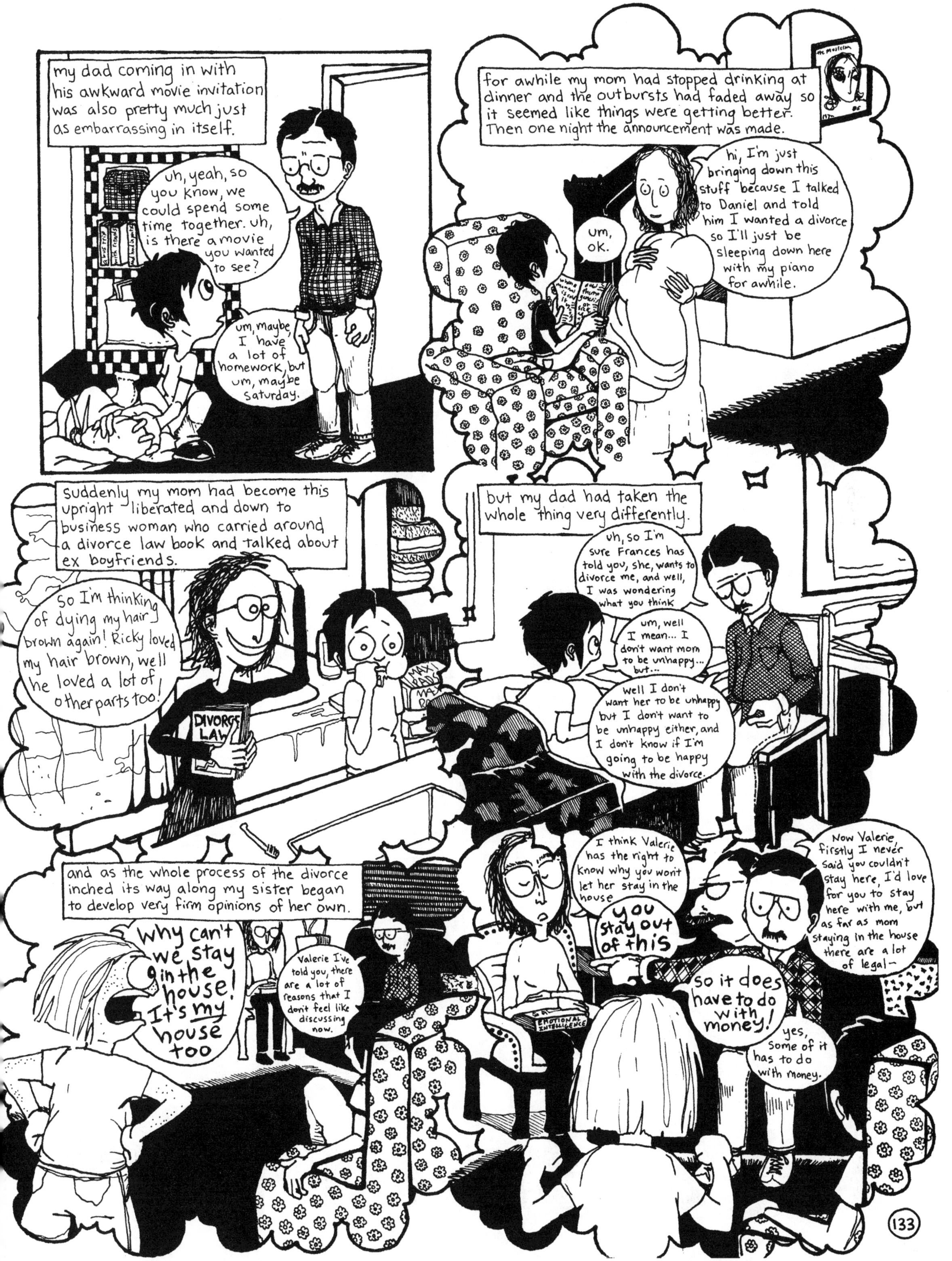

my dad coming in with his awkward movie invitation was also pretty much just as embarrassing in itself.
uh, yeah, so you know, we could spend some time together. uh, is there a movie you wanted to see?
um, maybe, I have a lot of homework, but um, maybe saturday.
for awhile my mom had stopped drinking at dinner and the outbursts had faded away so it seemed like things were getting better. Then one night the announcement was made.
hi, I'm just bringing down this stuff because I talked to Daniel and told him I wanted a divorce so I'll just be sleeping down here with my piano for awhile.
um, ok.
suddenly my mom had become this upright liberated and down to business woman who carried around a divorce law book and talked about ex boyfriends.
So I'm thinking of dying my hair brown again! Ricky loved my hair brown, well he loved a lot of other parts too!
DIVORCE LAW
MAXI PADS
but my dad had taken the whole thing very differently.
uh, so I'm sure Frances has told you, she, wants to divorce me, and well, I was wondering what you think
um, well I mean... I don't want mom to be unhappy... but...
well I don't want her to be unhappy but I don't want to be unhappy either, and I don't know if I'm going to be happy with the divorce.
and as the whole process of the divorce inched its way along my sister began to develop very firm opinions of her own.
why can't we stay in the house! It's my house too
Valerie I've told you, there are a lot of reasons that I don't feel like discussing now.
I think Valerie has the right to know why you won't let her stay in the house
you stay out of this
Now Valerie, firstly I never said you couldn't stay here, I'd love for you to stay here with me, but as far as mom staying in the house there are a lot of legal—
so it does have to do with money!
yes, some of it has to do with money.
EMOTIONAL INTELLIGENCE

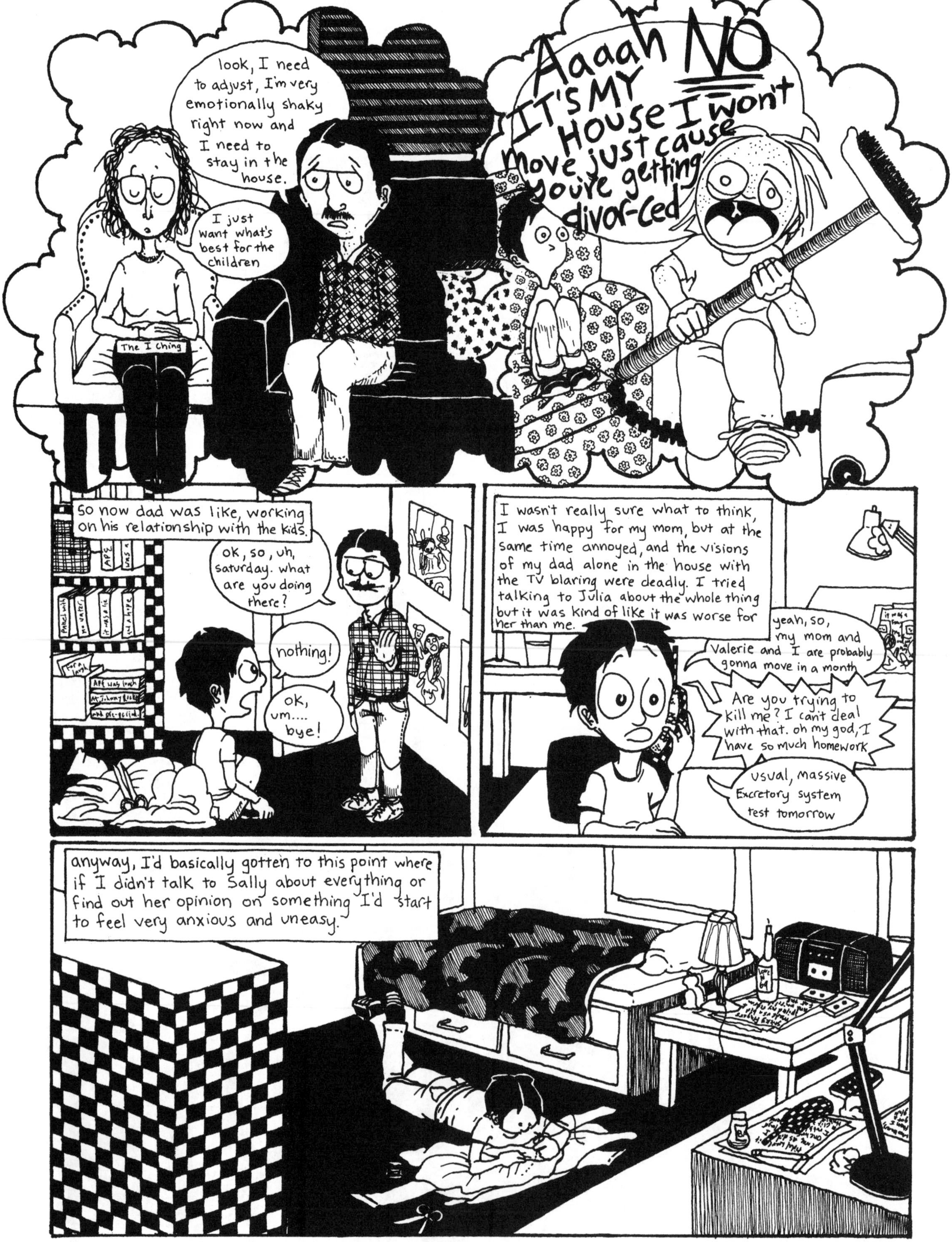
look, I need to adjust, I'm very emotionally shaky right now and I need to stay in the house.
I just want what's best for the children
The I Ching
Aaaah NO IT'S MY HOUSE I won't move just cause you're getting divor-ced
So now dad was like, working on his relationship with the kids.
ok, so, uh, saturday. what are you doing there?
nothing!
ok, um.... bye!
I wasn't really sure what to think, I was happy for my mom, but at the same time annoyed, and the visions of my dad alone in the house with the TV blaring were deadly. I tried talking to Julia about the whole thing but it was kind of like it was worse for her than me.
yeah, so, my mom and Valerie and I are probably gonna move in a month
Are you trying to kill me? I can't deal with that. oh my god, I have so much homework
usual, massive Excretory system test tomorrow
anyway, I'd basically gotten to this point where if I didn't talk to Sally about everything or find out her opinion on something I'd start to feel very anxious and uneasy.

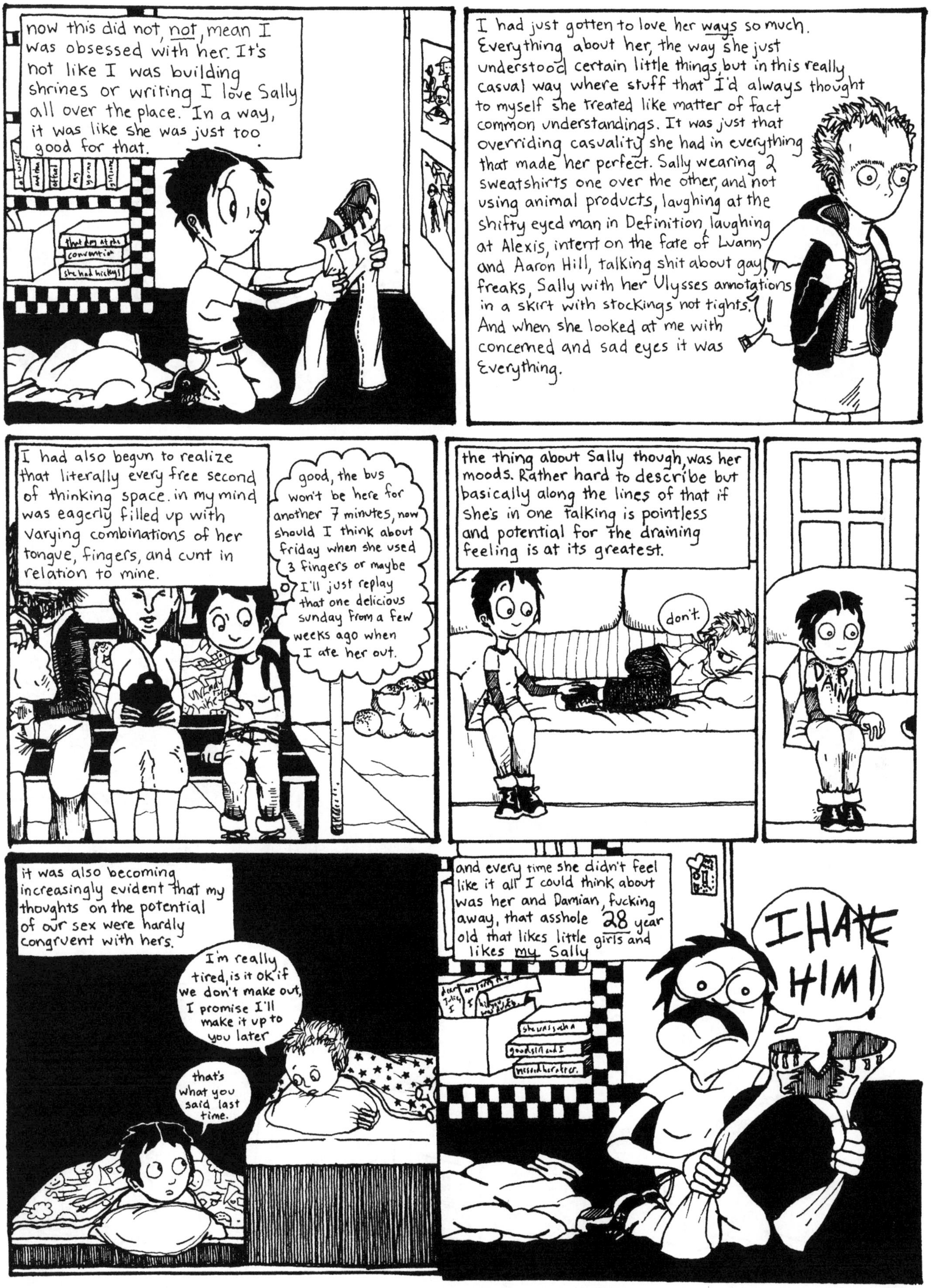
now this did not, not, mean I was obsessed with her. It's not like I was building shrines or writing I love Sally all over the place. In a way, it was like she was just too good for that.
I had just gotten to love her ways so much. Everything about her, the way she just understood certain little things, but in this really casual way where stuff that I'd always thought to myself she treated like matter of fact common understandings. It was just that overriding casuality she had in everything that made her perfect. Sally wearing 2 sweatshirts one over the other, and not using animal products, laughing at the shifty eyed man in Definition, laughing at Alexis, intent on the fate of Luann and Aaron Hill, talking shit about gay freaks, Sally with her Ulysses annotations in a skirt with stockings not tights. And when she looked at me with concerned and sad eyes it was Everything.
I had also begun to realize that literally every free second of thinking space in my mind was eagerly filled up with varying combinations of her tongue, fingers, and cunt in relation to mine.
good, the bus won't be here for another 7 minutes, now should I think about friday when she used 3 fingers or maybe I'll just replay that one delicious sunday from a few weeks ago when I ate her out.
the thing about Sally though, was her moods. Rather hard to describe but basically along the lines of that if she's in one talking is pointless and potential for the draining feeling is at its greatest.
don't.
it was also becoming increasingly evident that my thoughts on the potential of our sex were hardly congruent with hers.
I'm really tired, is it ok if we don't make out, I promise I'll make it up to you later
that's what you said last time.
and every time she didn't feel like it all I could think about was her and Damian, fucking away, that asshole 28 year old that likes little girls and likes my Sally
I HATE HIM!

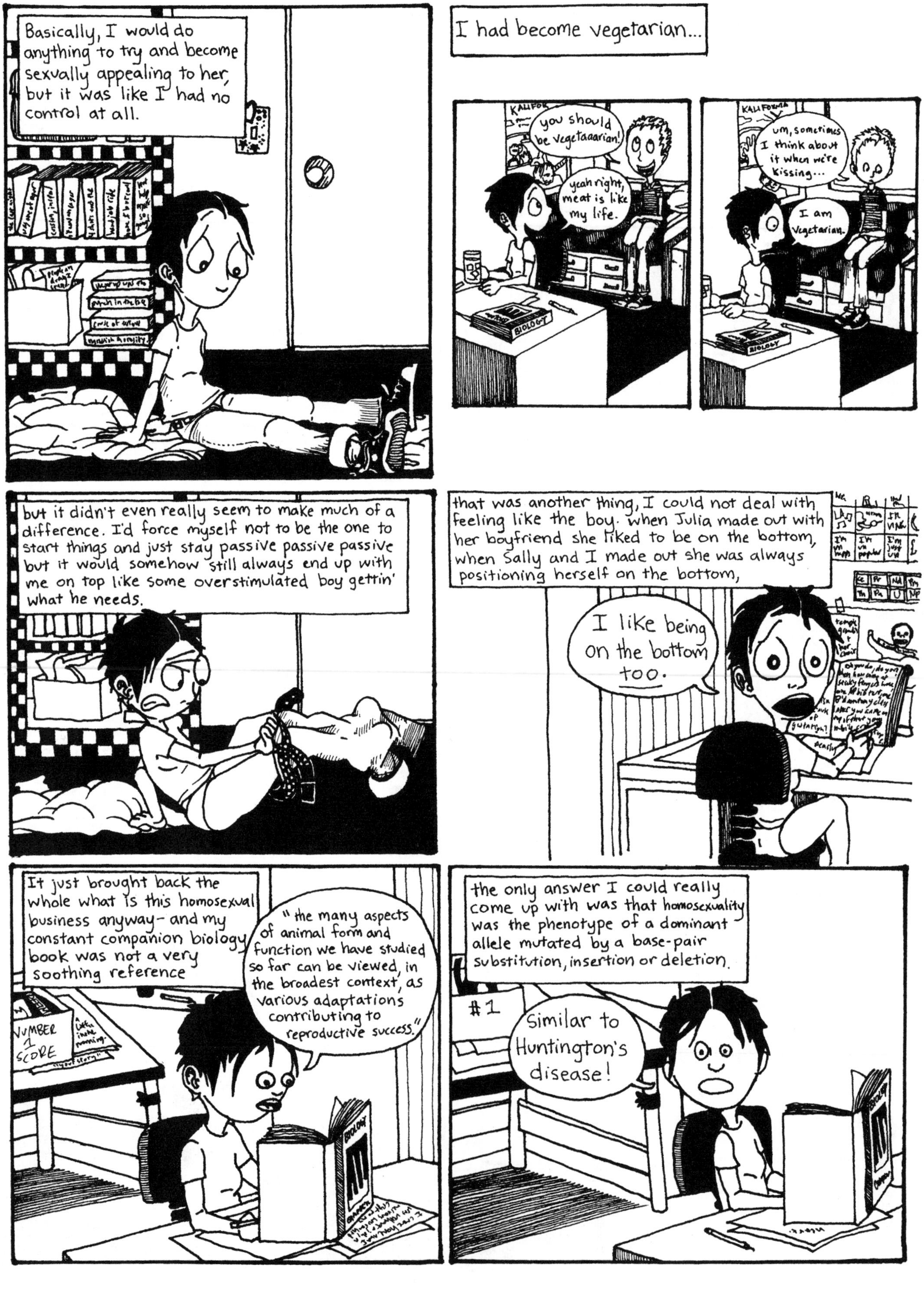
Basically, I would do anything to try and become sexually appealing to her, but it was like I had no control at all.
I had become vegetarian...
you should be vegetaaarian!
yeah right, meat is like my life.
um, sometimes I think about it when we're kissing...
I am vegetarian.
but it didn't even really seem to make much of a difference. I'd force myself not to be the one to start things and just stay passive passive passive but it would somehow still always end up with me on top like some overstimulated boy gettin' what he needs.
that was another thing, I could not deal with feeling like the boy. when Julia made out with her boyfriend she liked to be on the bottom, when Sally and I made out she was always positioning herself on the bottom,
I like being on the bottom too.
It just brought back the whole what is this homosexual business anyway- and my constant companion biology book was not a very soothing reference
"the many aspects of animal form and function we have studied so far can be viewed, in the broadest context, as various adaptations contributing to reproductive success."
the only answer I could really come up with was that homosexuality was the phenotype of a dominant allele mutated by a base-pair substitution, insertion or deletion.
Similar to Huntington's disease!
NUMBER 1 SCORE
#1
BIOLOGY

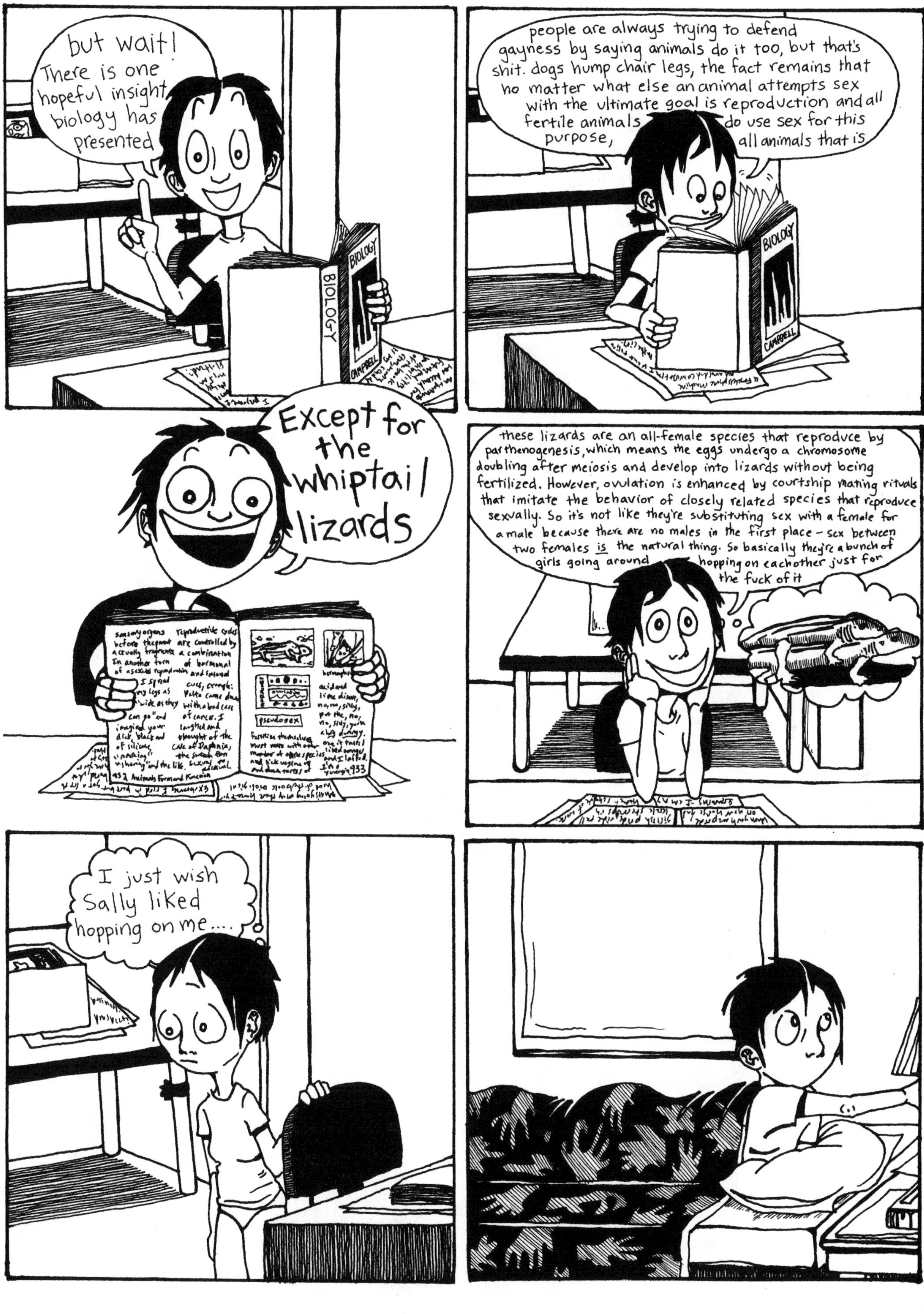

but wait! There is one hopeful insight biology has presented
people are always trying to defend gayness by saying animals do it too, but that's shit. dogs hump chair legs, the fact remains that no matter what else an animal attempts sex with the ultimate goal is reproduction and all fertile animals do use sex for this purpose, all animals that is
BIOLOGY
CAMPBELL
Except for the whiptail lizards
pseudosex
these lizards are an all-female species that reproduce by parthenogenesis, which means the eggs undergo a chromosome doubling after meiosis and develop into lizards without being fertilized. However, ovulation is enhanced by courtship mating rituals that imitate the behavior of closely related species that reproduce sexually. So it's not like they're substituting sex with a female for a male because there are no males in the first place - sex between two females is the natural thing. So basically they're a bunch of girls going around hopping on eachother just for the fuck of it
I just wish Sally liked hopping on me....

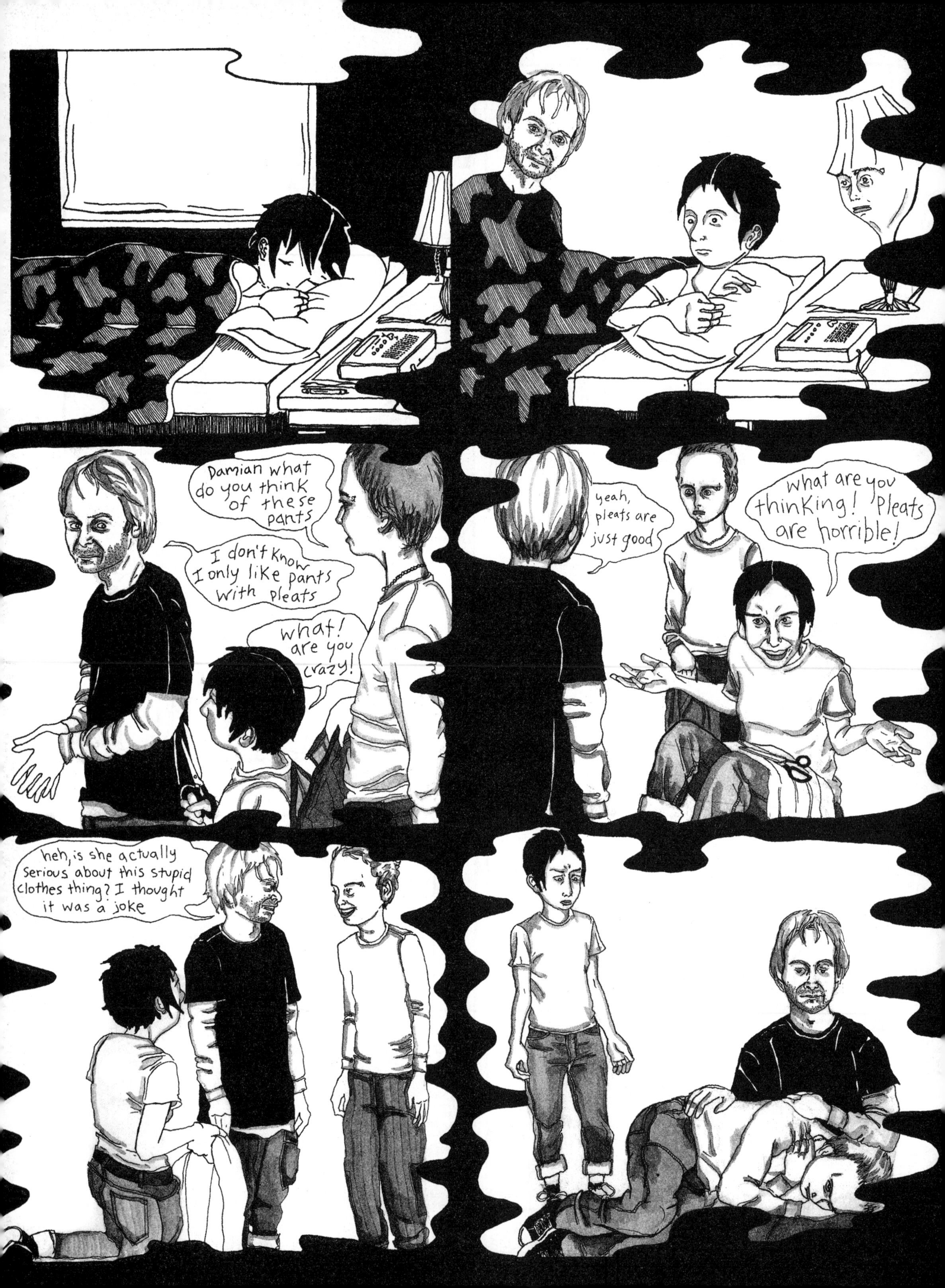
Damian what do you think of these pants
I don't know I only like pants with pleats
what! are you crazy!
yeah, pleats are just good
what are you thinking! Pleats are horrible!
heh, is she actually serious about this stupid clothes thing? I thought it was a joke

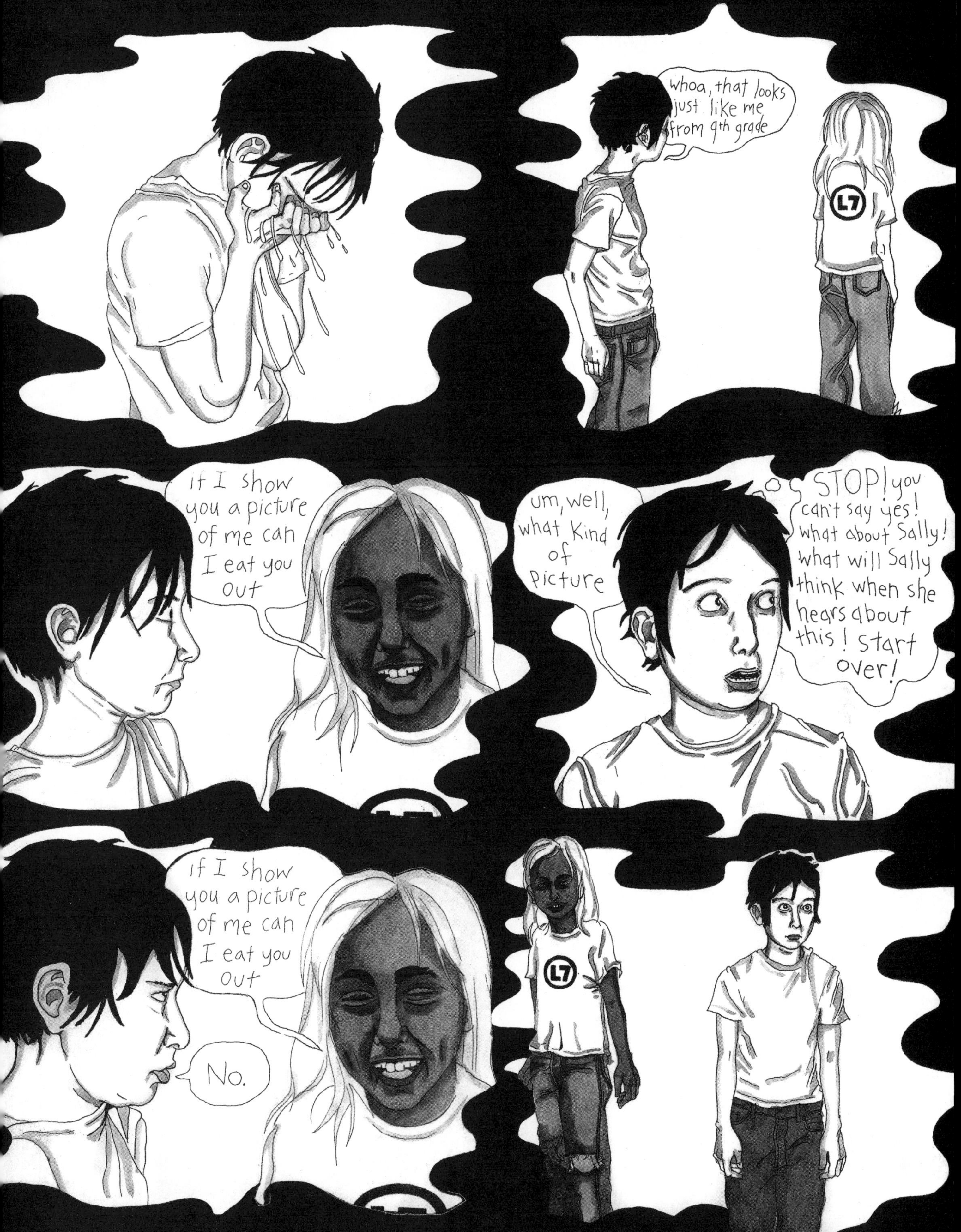
whoa, that looks just like me from 9th grade
L7
If I show you a picture of me can I eat you out
um, well, what Kind of picture
STOP! you can't say yes! what about Sally! what will Sally think when she hears about this! start over!
If I show you a picture of me can I eat you out
No.
L7

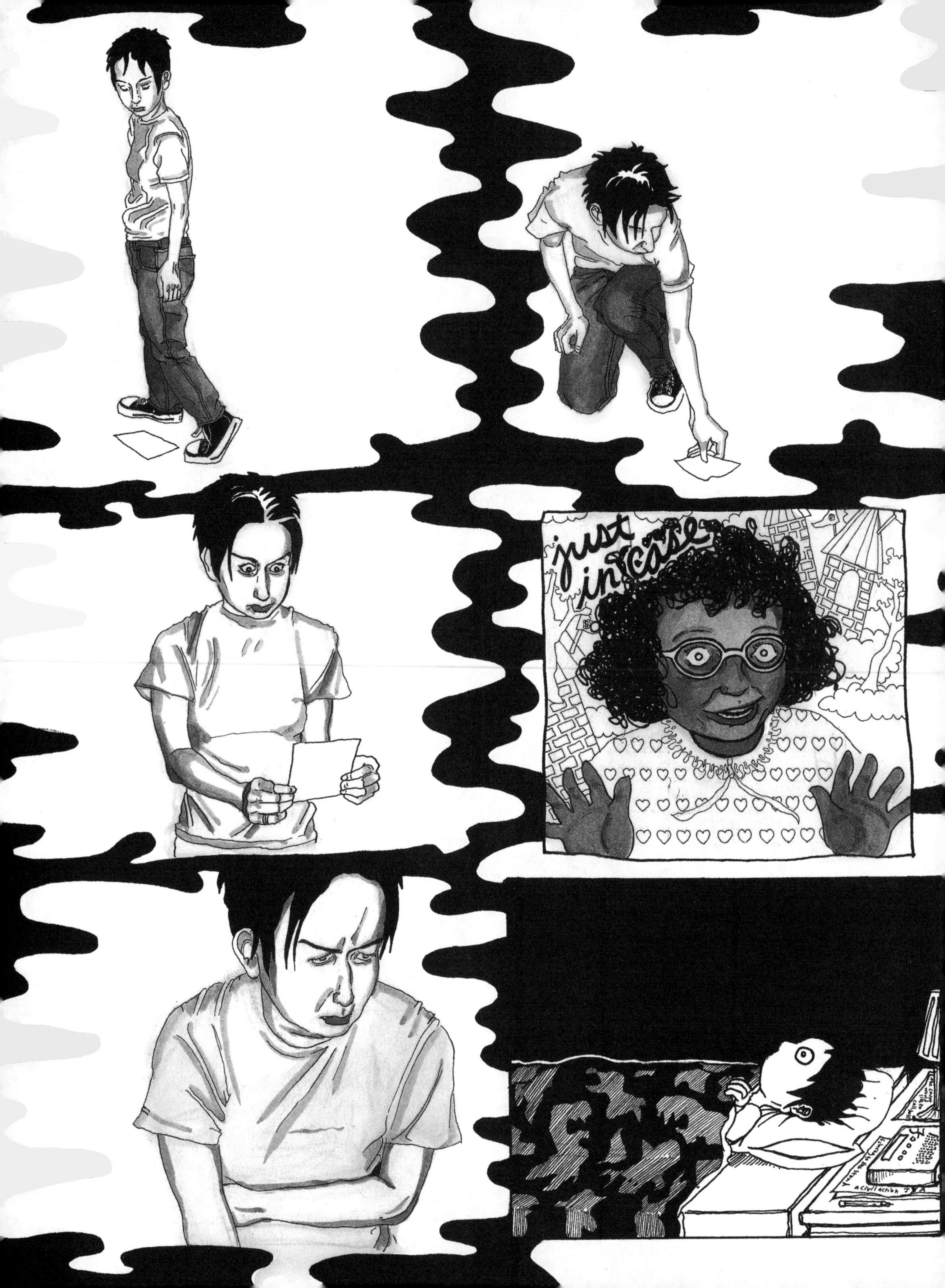
just in case
a civil action

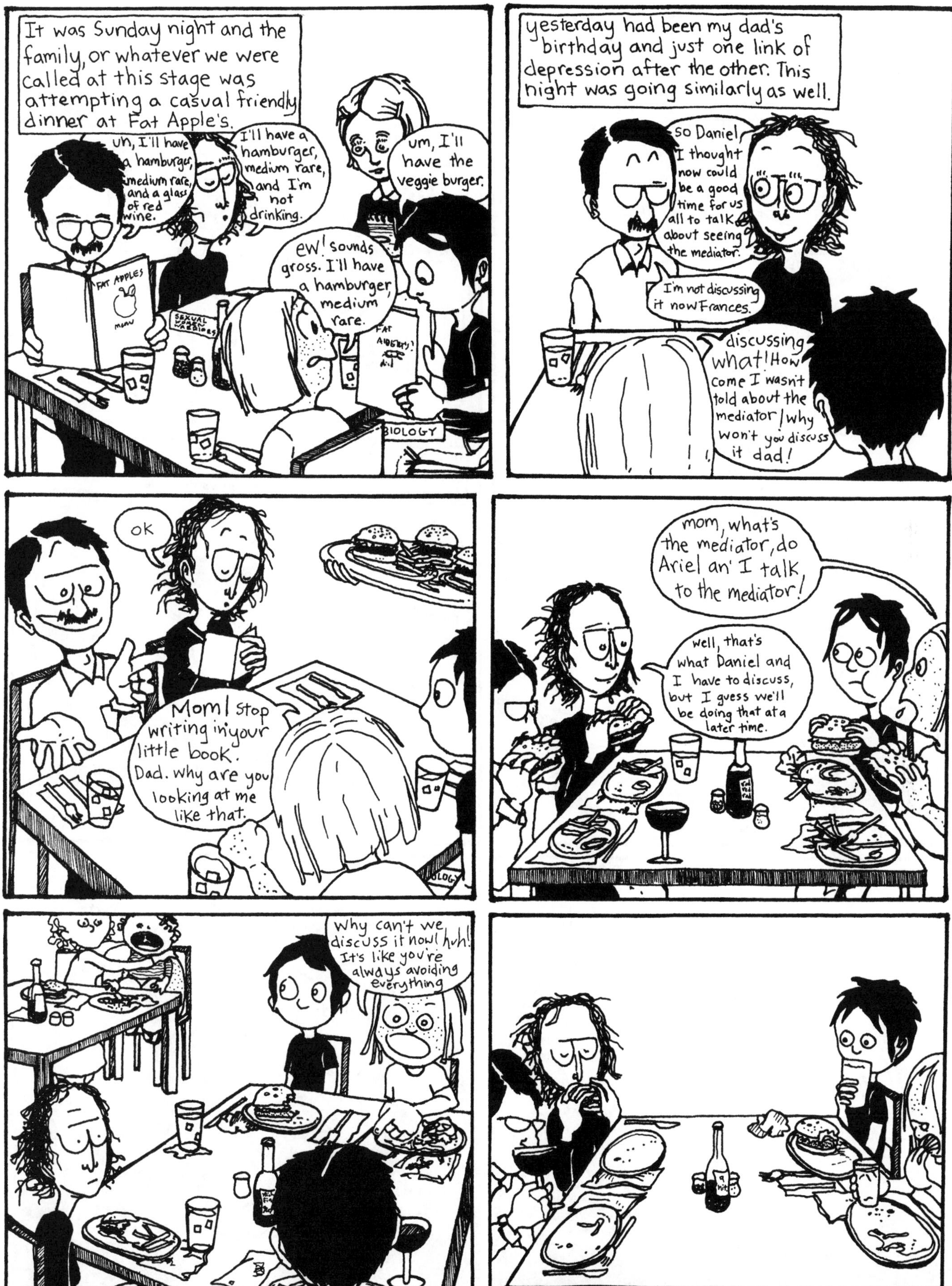
It was Sunday night and the family, or whatever we were called at this stage was attempting a casual friendly dinner at Fat Apple's.
un, I'll have a hamburger, medium rare, and a glass of red wine.
I'll have a hamburger, medium rare, and I'm not drinking.
um, I'll have the veggie burger.
ew! sounds gross. I'll have a hamburger, medium rare.
FAT APPLES
BIOLOGY
yesterday had been my dad's birthday and just one link of depression after the other. This night was going similarly as well.
so Daniel I thought now could be a good time for us all to talk about seeing the mediator.
I'm not discussing it now Frances.
discussing what! How come I wasn't told about the mediator! why won't you discuss it dad!
ok
Mom! stop writing in your little book. Dad. why are you looking at me like that.
mom, what's the mediator, do Ariel an' I talk to the mediator!
well, that's what Daniel and I have to discuss, but I guess we'll be doing that at a later time.
why can't we discuss it now! huh! It's like you're always avoiding everything

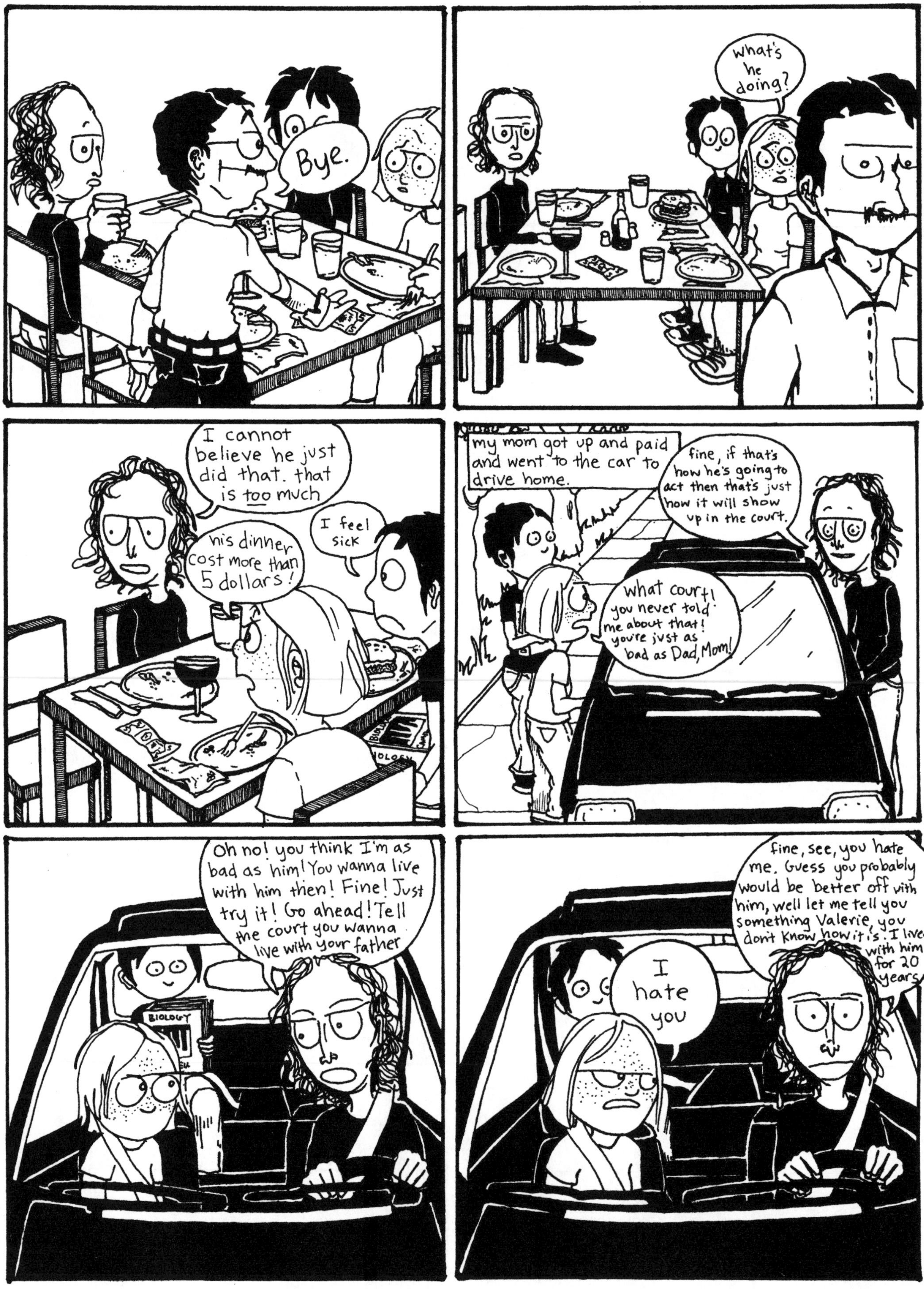
Bye.
what's he doing?
I cannot believe he just did that. that is too much
his dinner cost more than 5 dollars!
I feel sick
my mom got up and paid and went to the car to drive home.
fine, if that's how he's going to act then that's just how it will show up in the court.
what court! you never told me about that! you're just as bad as Dad, Mom!
Oh no! you think I'm as bad as him! You wanna live with him then! Fine! Just try it! Go ahead! Tell the court you wanna live with your father
BIOLOGY
I hate you
fine, see, you hate me. Guess you probably would be better off with him, well let me tell you something Valerie, you don't know how it is. I lived with him for 20 years

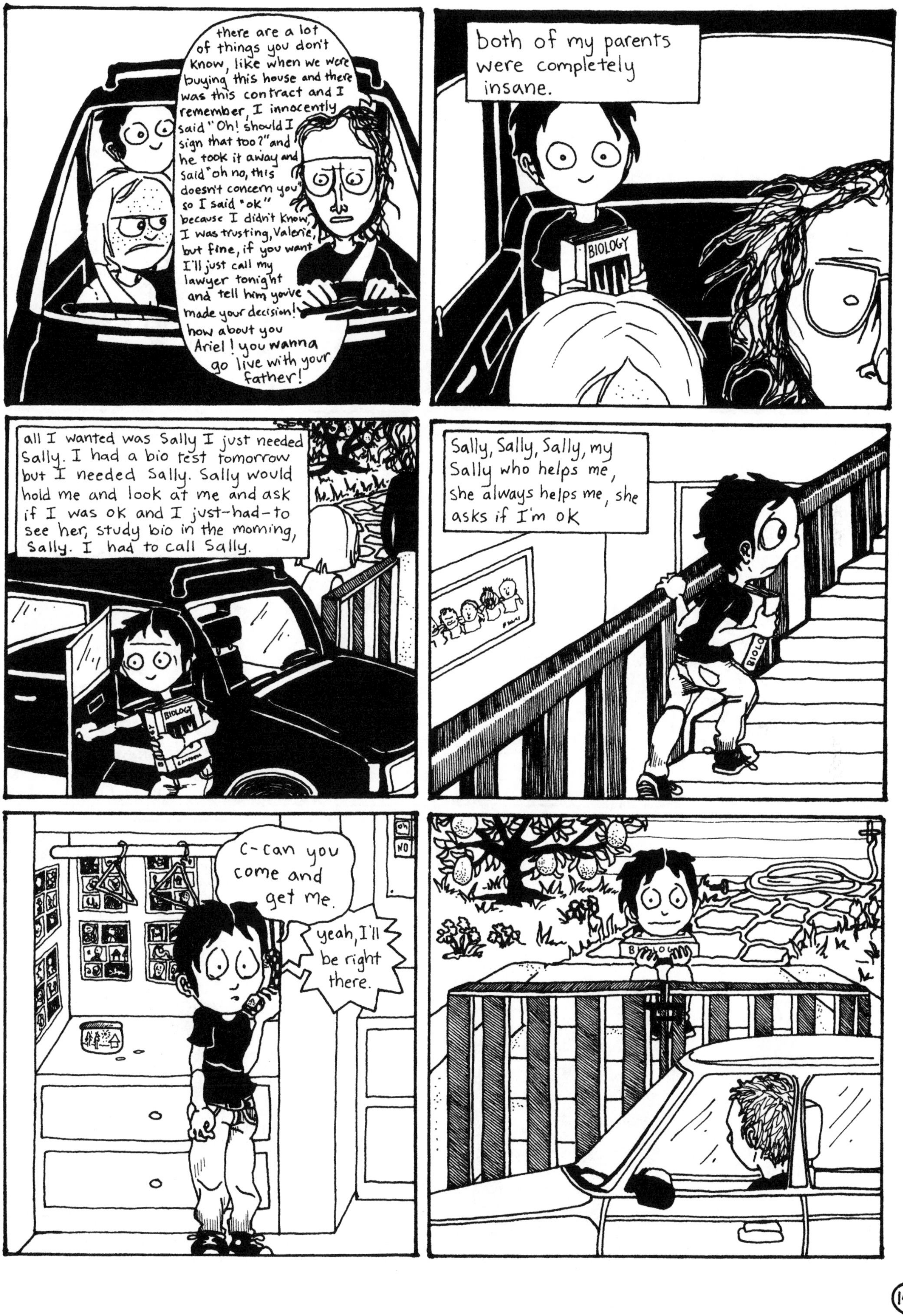
there are a lot of things you don't know, like when we were buying this house and there was this contract and I remember, I innocently said "Oh! should I sign that too?" and he took it away and said "oh no, this doesn't concern you" so I said "ok" because I didn't know, I was trusting, Valerie, but fine, if you want I'll just call my lawyer tonight and tell him you've made your decision! how about you Ariel! you wanna go live with your father!
both of my parents were completely insane.
BIOLOGY
all I wanted was Sally I just needed Sally. I had a bio test tomorrow but I needed Sally. Sally would hold me and look at me and ask if I was ok and I just-had-to see her, study bio in the morning, Sally. I had to call Sally.
BIOLOGY
Sally, Sally, Sally, my Sally who helps me, she always helps me, she asks if I'm ok
C-can you come and get me.
yeah, I'll be right there.

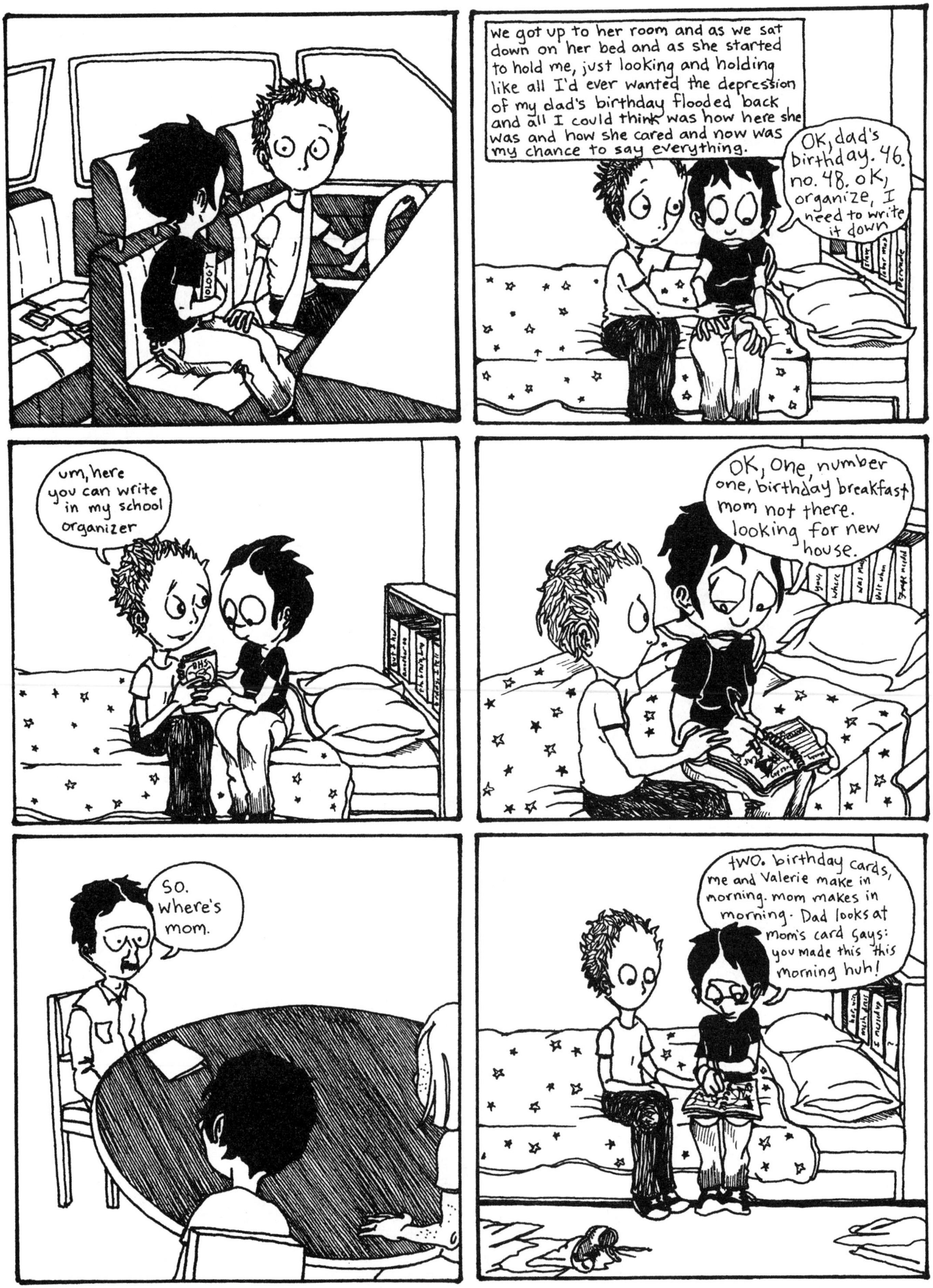
we got up to her room and as we sat down on her bed and as she started to hold me, just looking and holding like all I'd ever wanted the depression of my dad's birthday flooded back and all I could think was how here she was and how she cared and now was my chance to say everything.
OK, dad's birthday. 46. no. 48. OK, organize, I need to write it down
um, here you can write in my school organizer
OK, One, number one, birthday breakfast mom not there. looking for new house.
So. where's mom.
two. birthday cards, me and Valerie make in morning. mom makes in morning. Dad looks at mom's card says: you made this this morning huh!

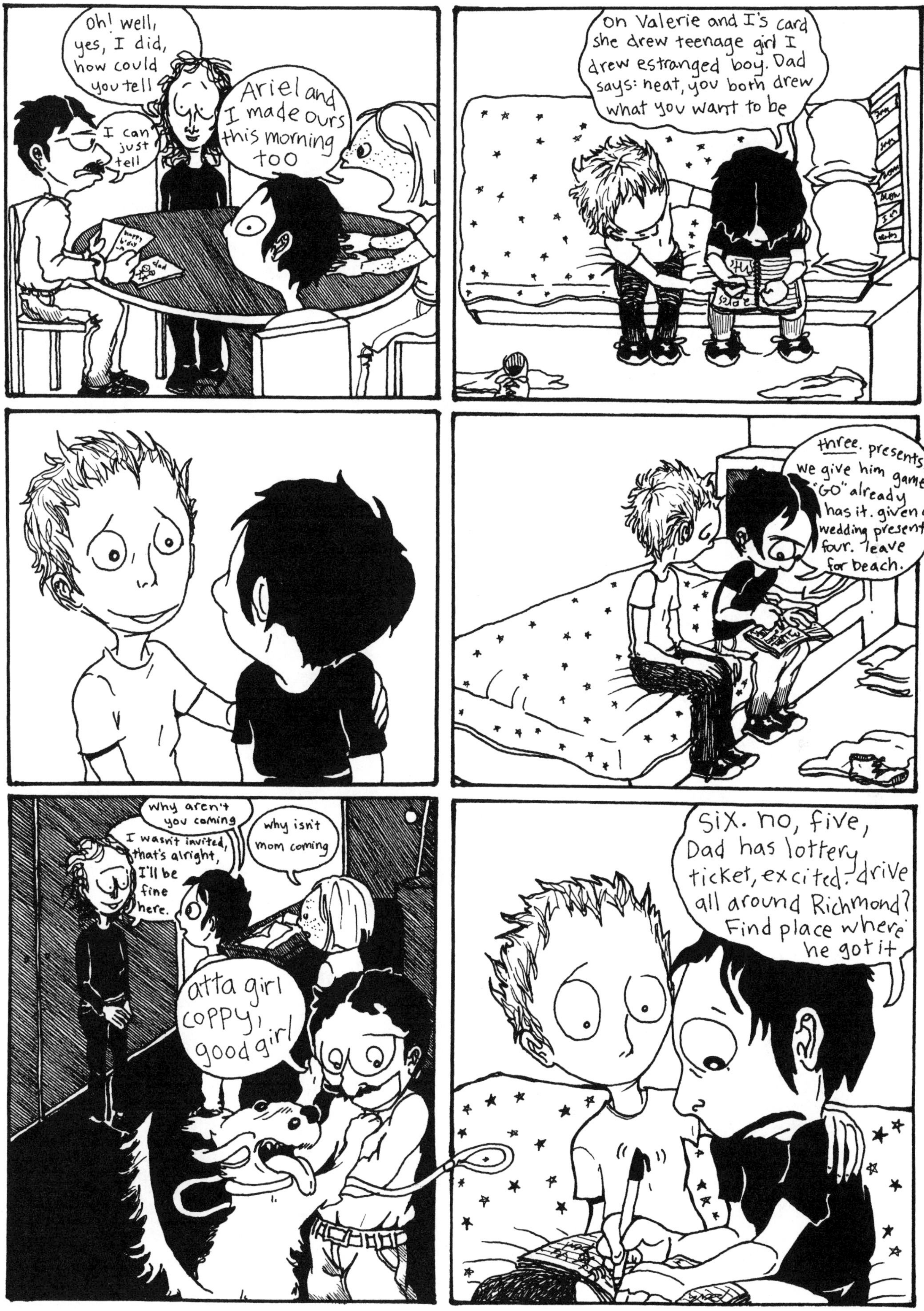

Oh! well, yes, I did, how could you tell
I can just tell
Ariel and I made ours this morning too
On Valerie and I's card she drew teenage girl I drew estranged boy. Dad says: neat, you both drew what you want to be
three. presents. we give him game "GO" already has it. given as wedding present. four. leave for beach.
why aren't you coming
I wasn't invited, that's alright, I'll be fine here.
why isn't mom coming
atta girl coppy, good girl
SIX. no, five, Dad has lottery ticket, excited. drive all around Richmond? Find place where he got it

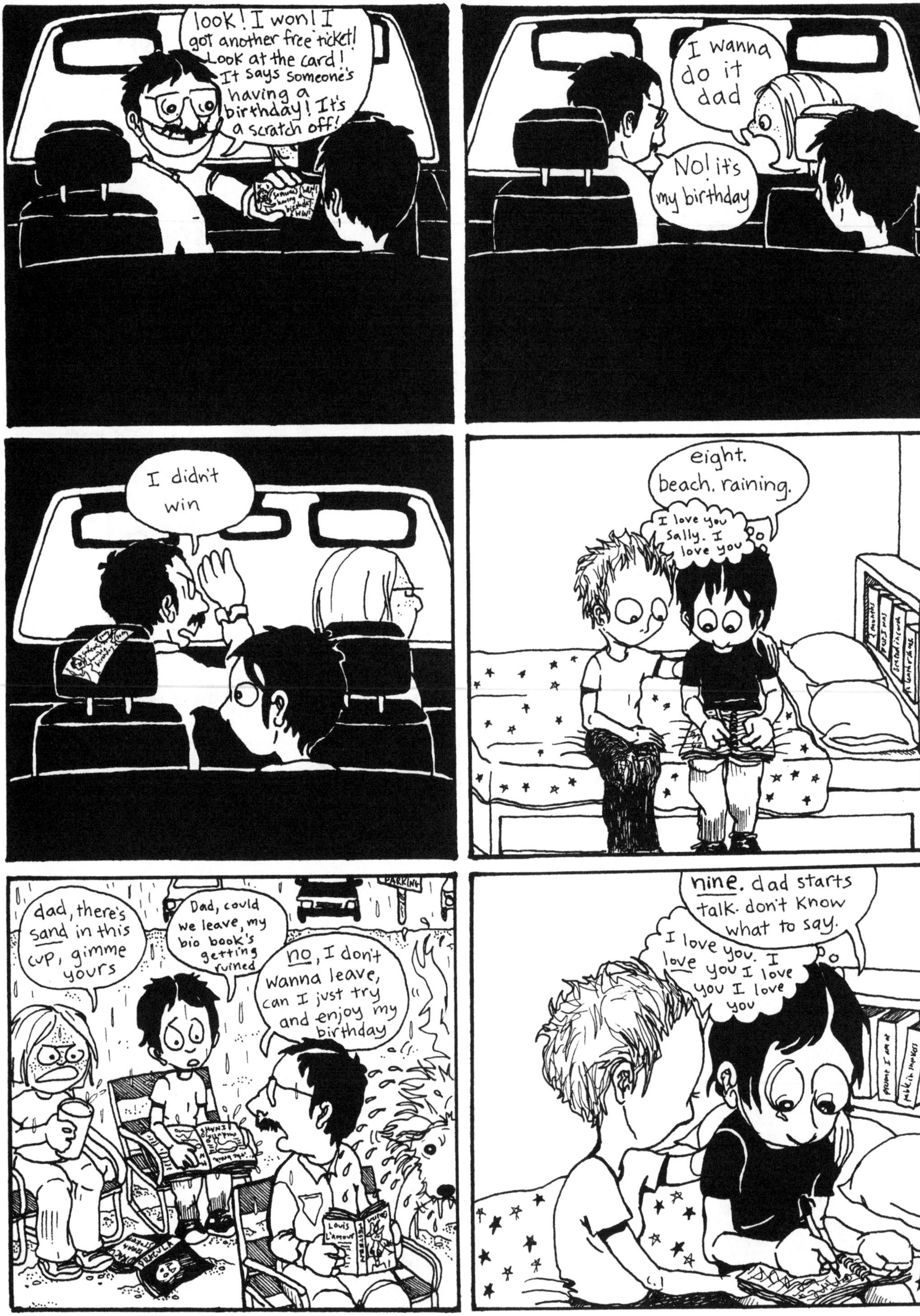
look! I won! I got another free ticket! Look at the card! It says someone's having a birthday! It's a scratch off!
I wanna do it dad
No! it's my birthday
I didn't win
eight. beach. raining.
I love you Sally. I love you
dad, there's sand in this cup, gimme yours
Dad, could we leave, my bio book's getting ruined
no, I don't wanna leave, can I just try and enjoy my birthday
PARKING
Louis L'Amour
DRACULA
nine. dad starts talk. don't know what to say.
I love you. I love you I love you I love you

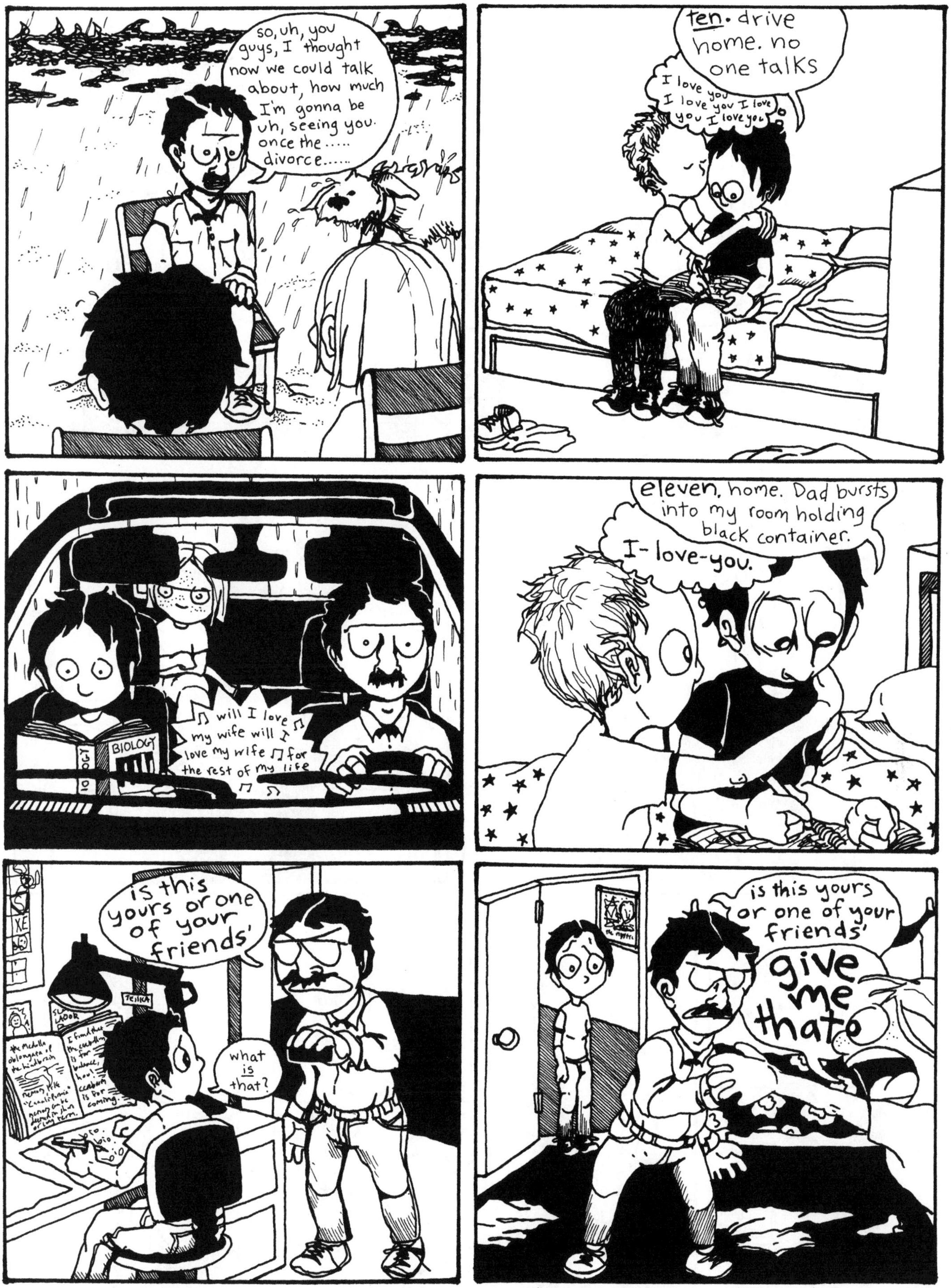
so, uh, you guys, I thought now we could talk about, how much I'm gonna be uh, seeing you. once the ..... divorce.....
ten. drive home. no one talks
I love you I love you I love you I love you
BIOLOGY
♫ will I love ♫ my wife will I love my wife ♫ for the rest of my life ♫ ♫
eleven. home. Dad bursts into my room holding black container.
I-love-you.
is this yours or one of your friends'
what is that?
is this yours or one of your friends'
give me that

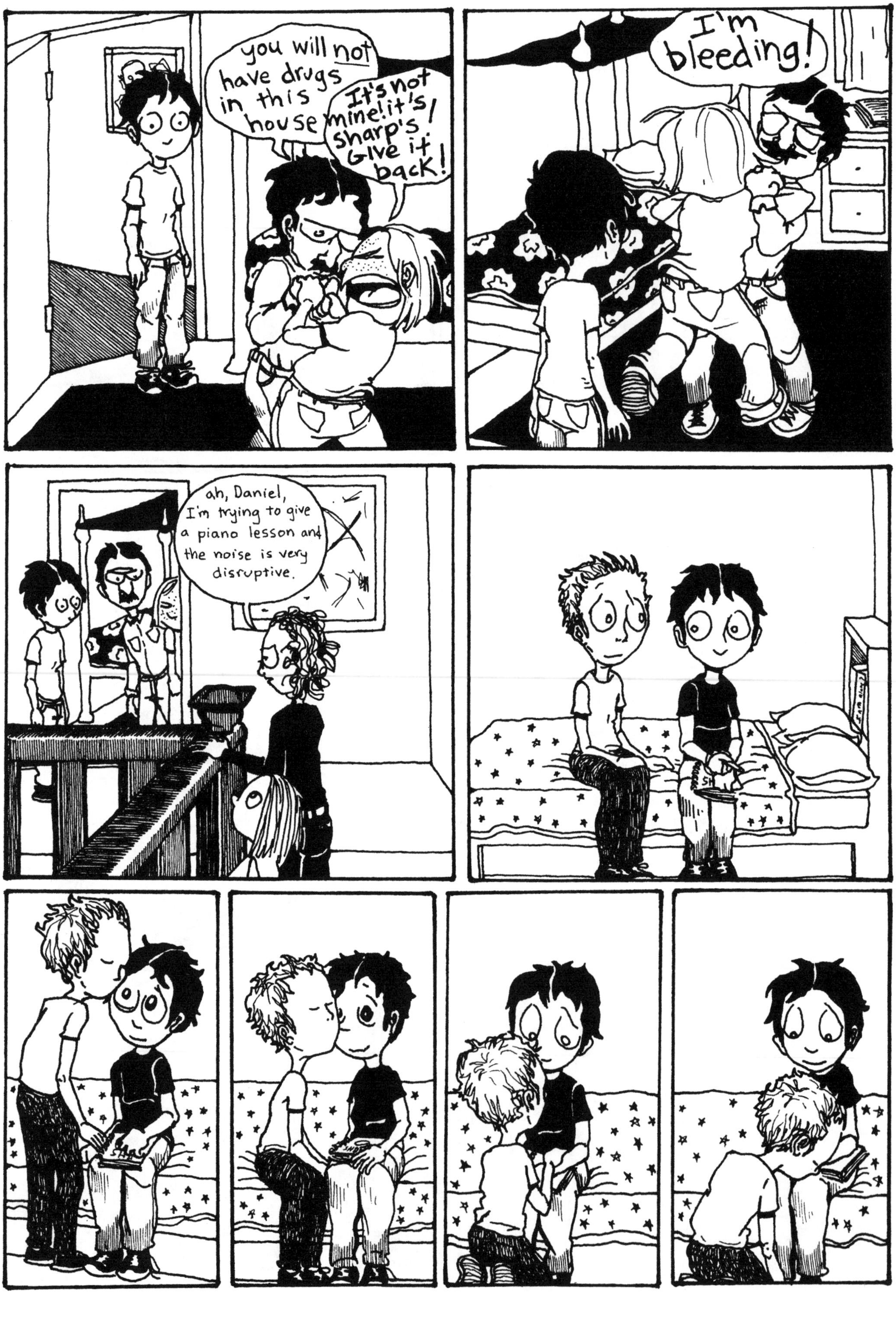
you will not have drugs in this house
It's not mine! it's sharp's! Give it back!
I'm bleeding!
ah, Daniel, I'm trying to give a piano lesson and the noise is very disruptive.

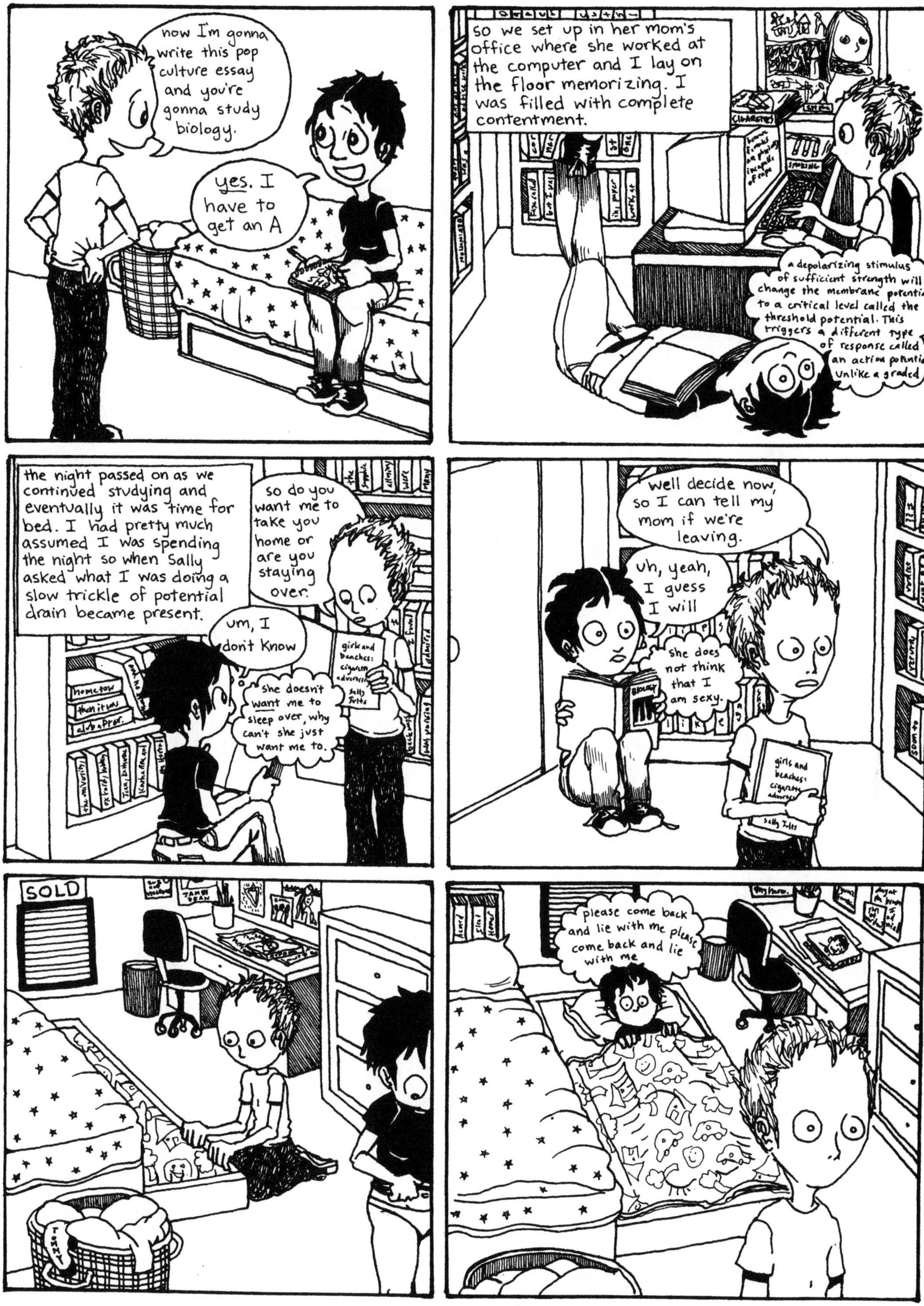
now I'm gonna write this pop culture essay and you're gonna study biology.
yes. I have to get an A
so we set up in her mom's office where she worked at the computer and I lay on the floor memorizing. I was filled with complete contentment.
a depolarizing stimulus of sufficient strength will change the membrane potential to a critical level called the threshold potential. This triggers a different type of response called an action potential. Unlike a graded
the night passed on as we continued studying and eventually it was time for bed. I had pretty much assumed I was spending the night so when Sally asked what I was doing a slow trickle of potential drain became present.
so do you want me to take you home or are you staying over.
um, I don't know
she doesn't want me to sleep over, why can't she just want me to.
well decide now, so I can tell my mom if we're leaving.
uh, yeah, I guess I will
she does not think that I am sexy.
SOLD
please come back and lie with me please come back and lie with me

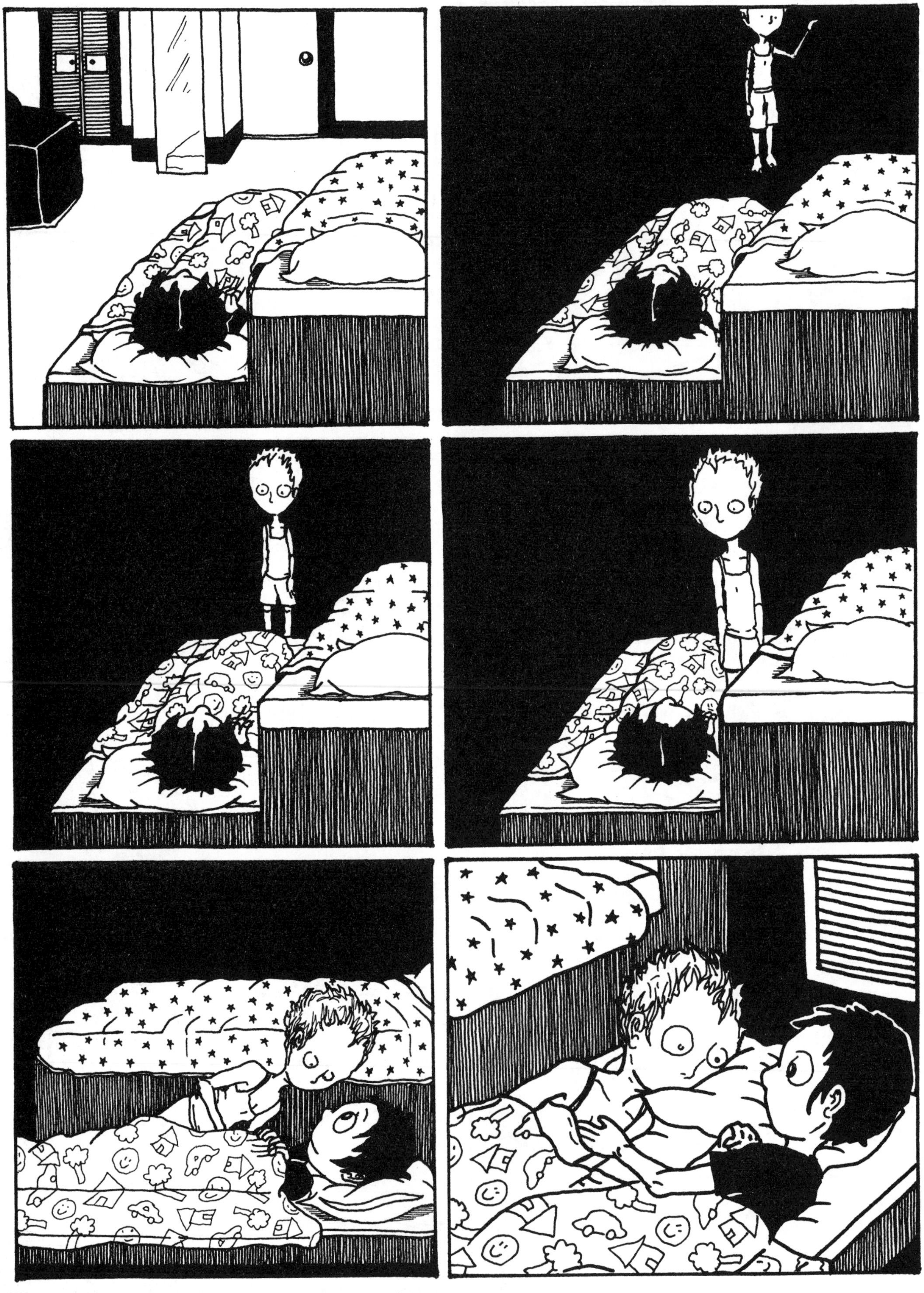

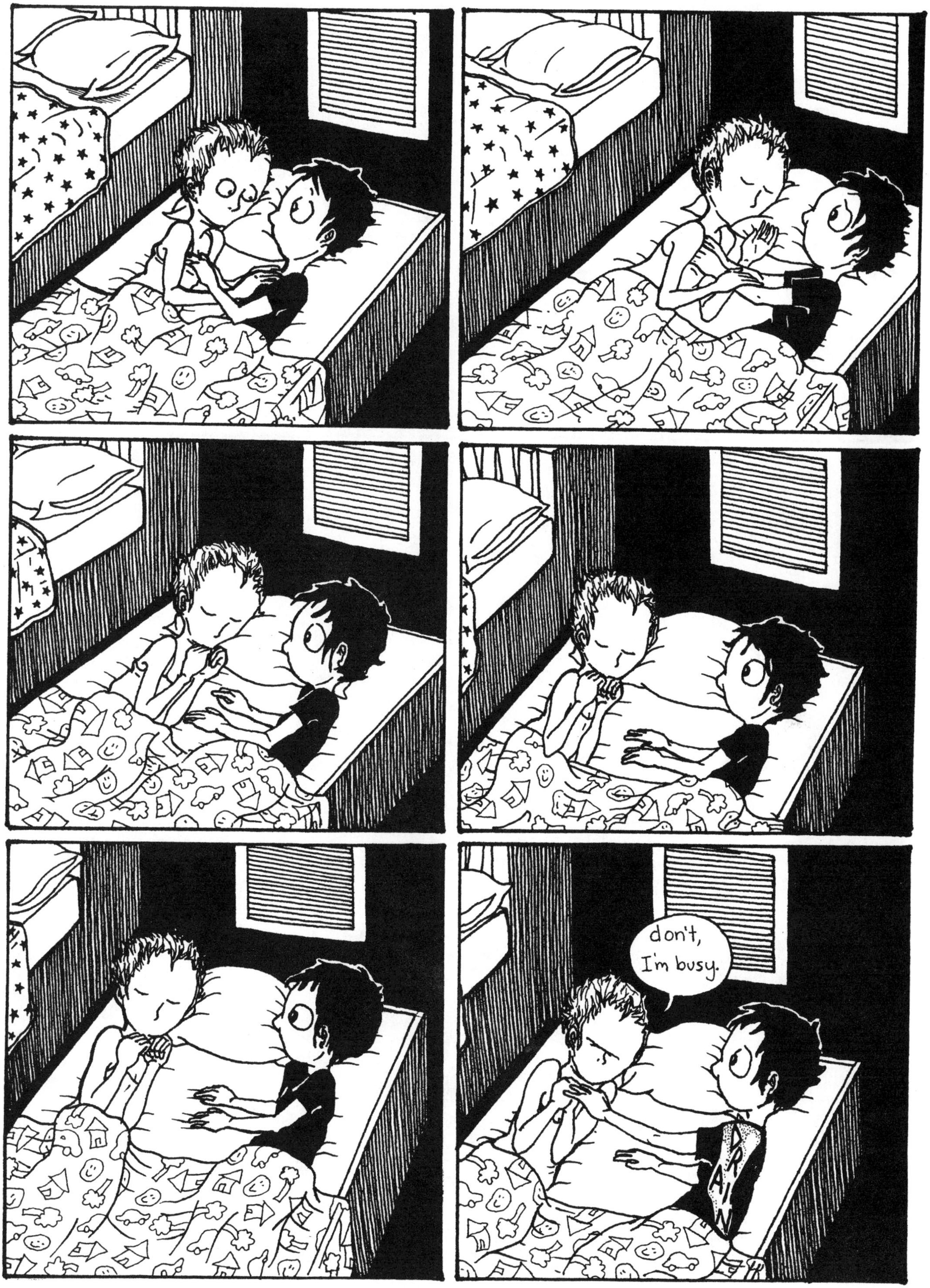
don't,
I'm busy.
BRAIN

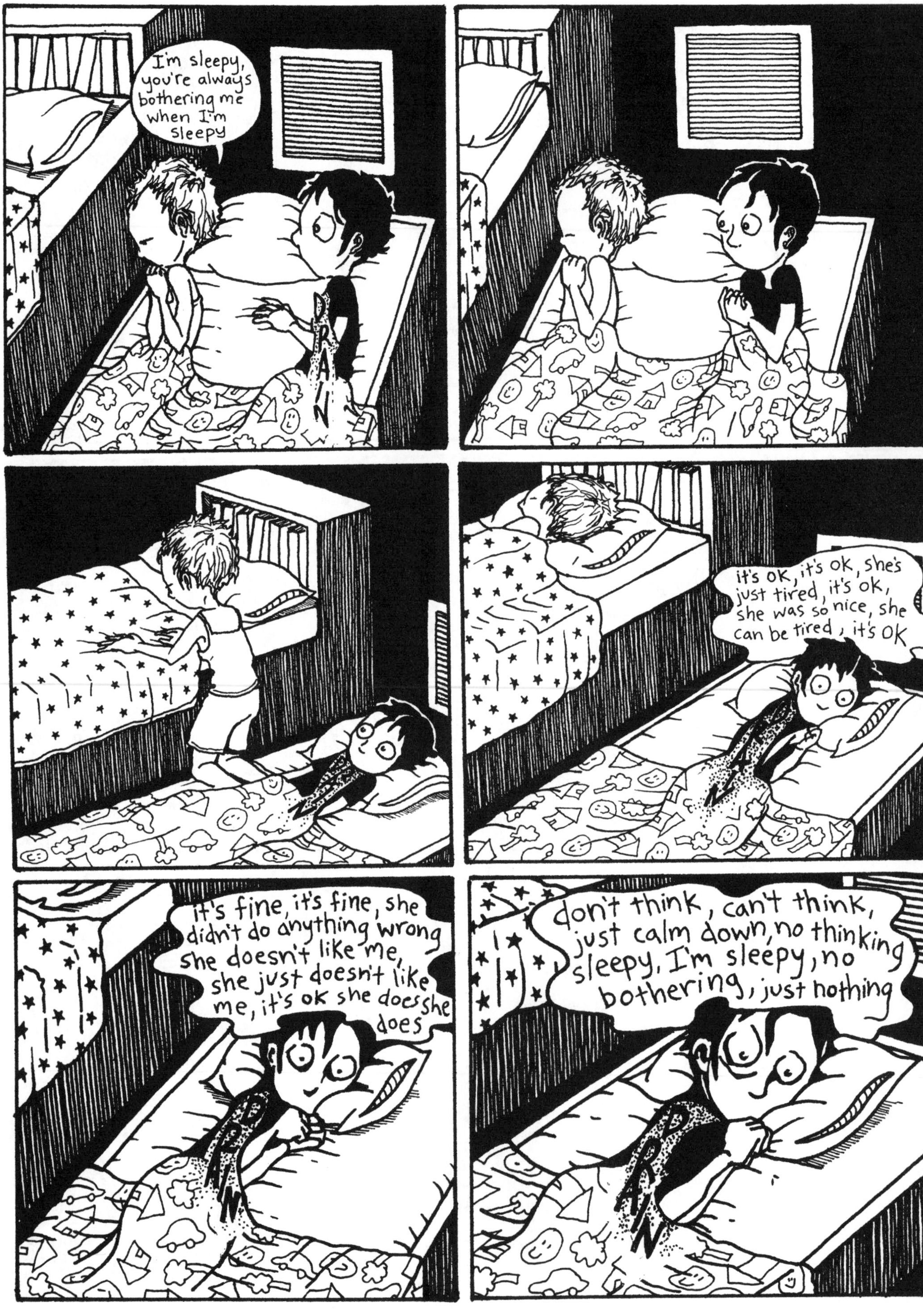

I'm sleepy, you're always bothering me when I'm sleepy
DRAIN
DRAIN
it's OK, it's OK, she's just tired, it's OK, she was so nice, she can be tired, it's OK
DRAIN
it's fine, it's fine, she didn't do anything wrong she doesn't like me, she just doesn't like me, it's ok she does she does
DRAIN
don't think, can't think, just calm down, no thinking sleepy, I'm sleepy, no bothering, just nothing
DRAIN

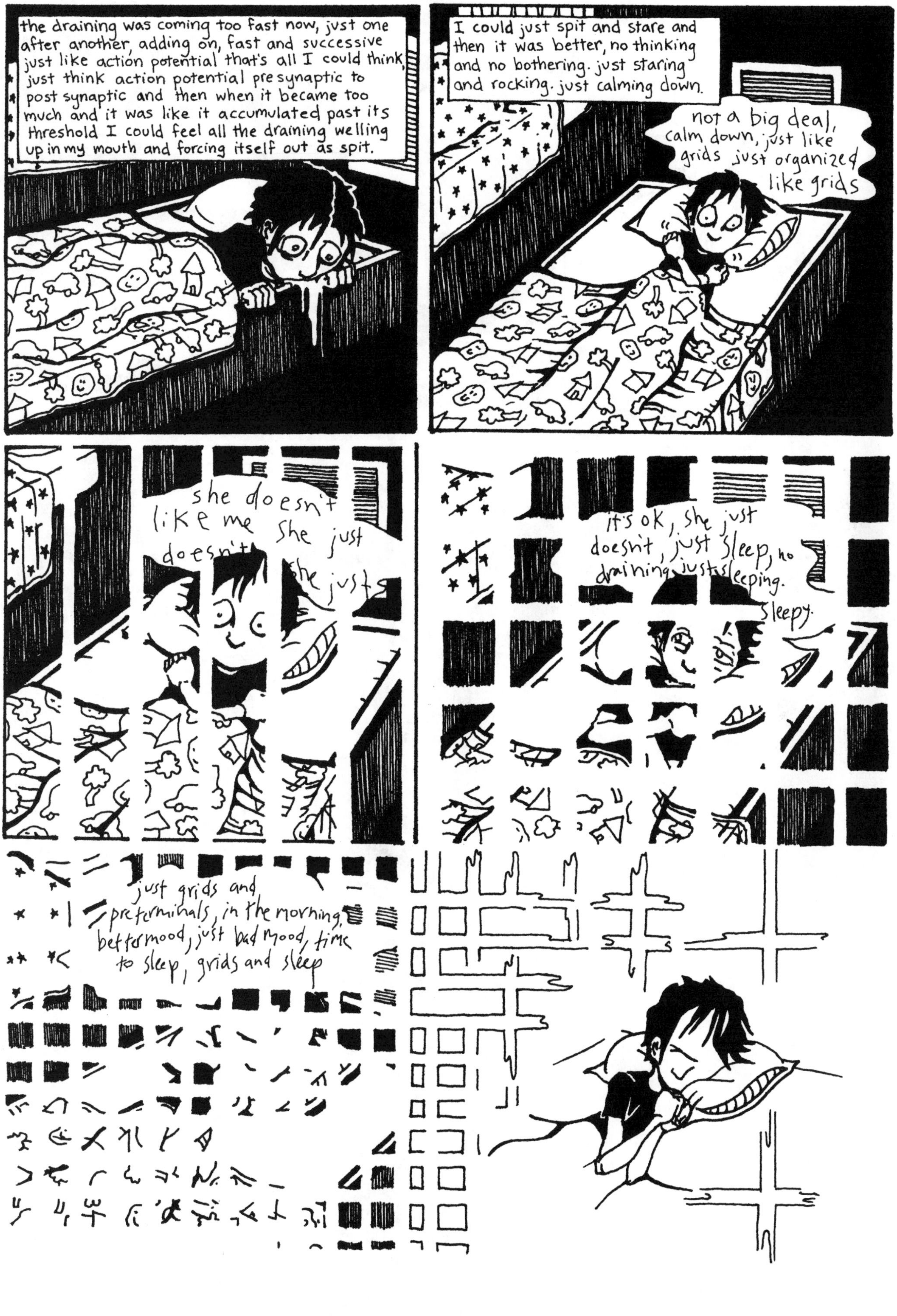
the draining was coming too fast now, just one after another, adding on, fast and successive just like action potential that's all I could think, just think action potential presynaptic to post synaptic and then when it became too much and it was like it accumulated past its threshold I could feel all the draining welling up in my mouth and forcing itself out as spit.
I could just spit and stare and then it was better, no thinking and no bothering. just staring and rocking. just calming down.
not a big deal, calm down, just like grids just organized like grids
she doesn't like me she just doesn't, she just
it's ok, she just doesn't, just sleep, no draining, just sleeping.
sleepy.
just grids and preterminals, in the morning, better mood, just bad mood, time to sleep, grids and sleep

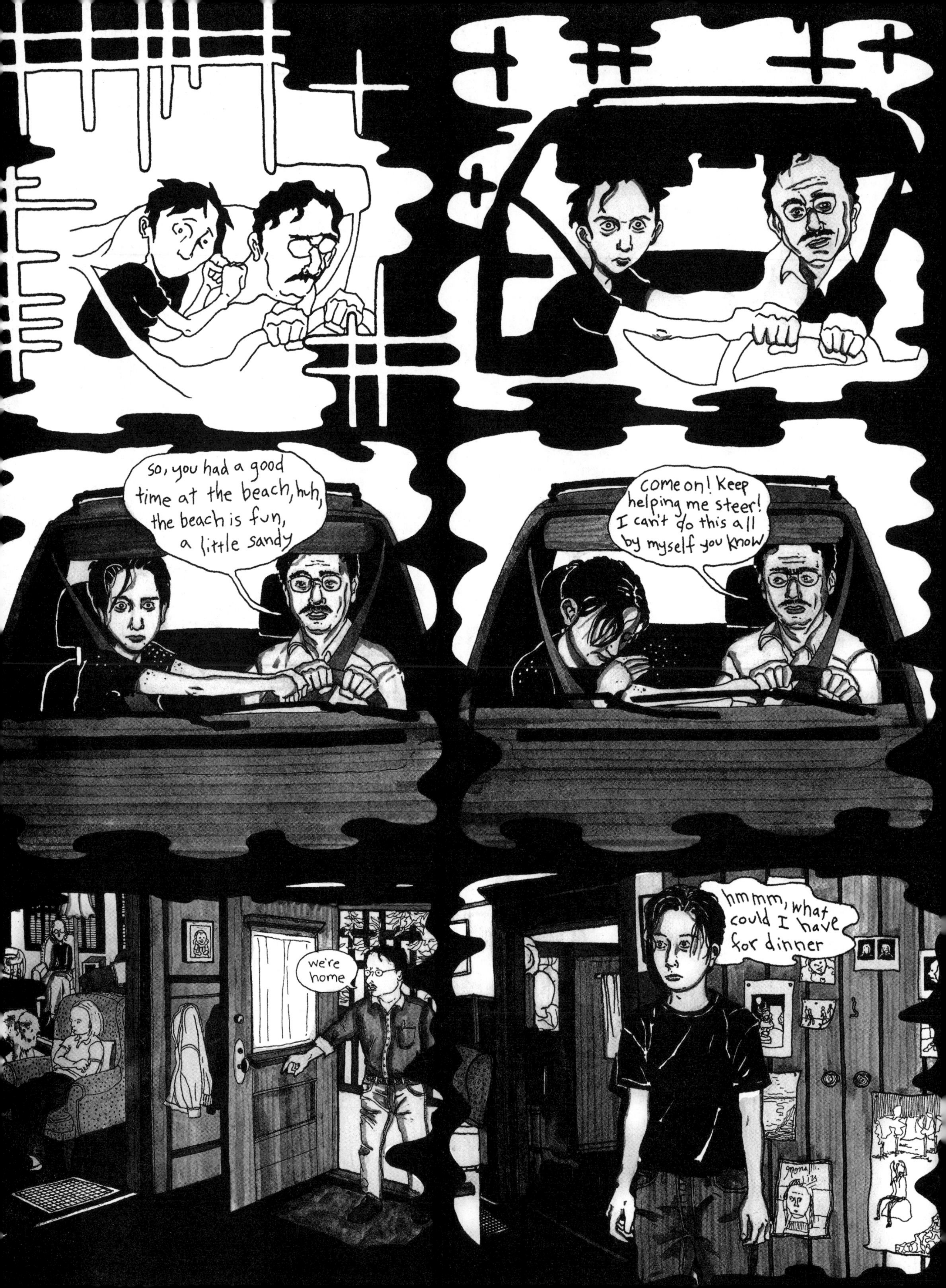
so, you had a good time at the beach, huh, the beach is fun, a little sandy
come on! Keep helping me steer! I can't do this all by myself you know
we're home
hmmm, what could I have for dinner

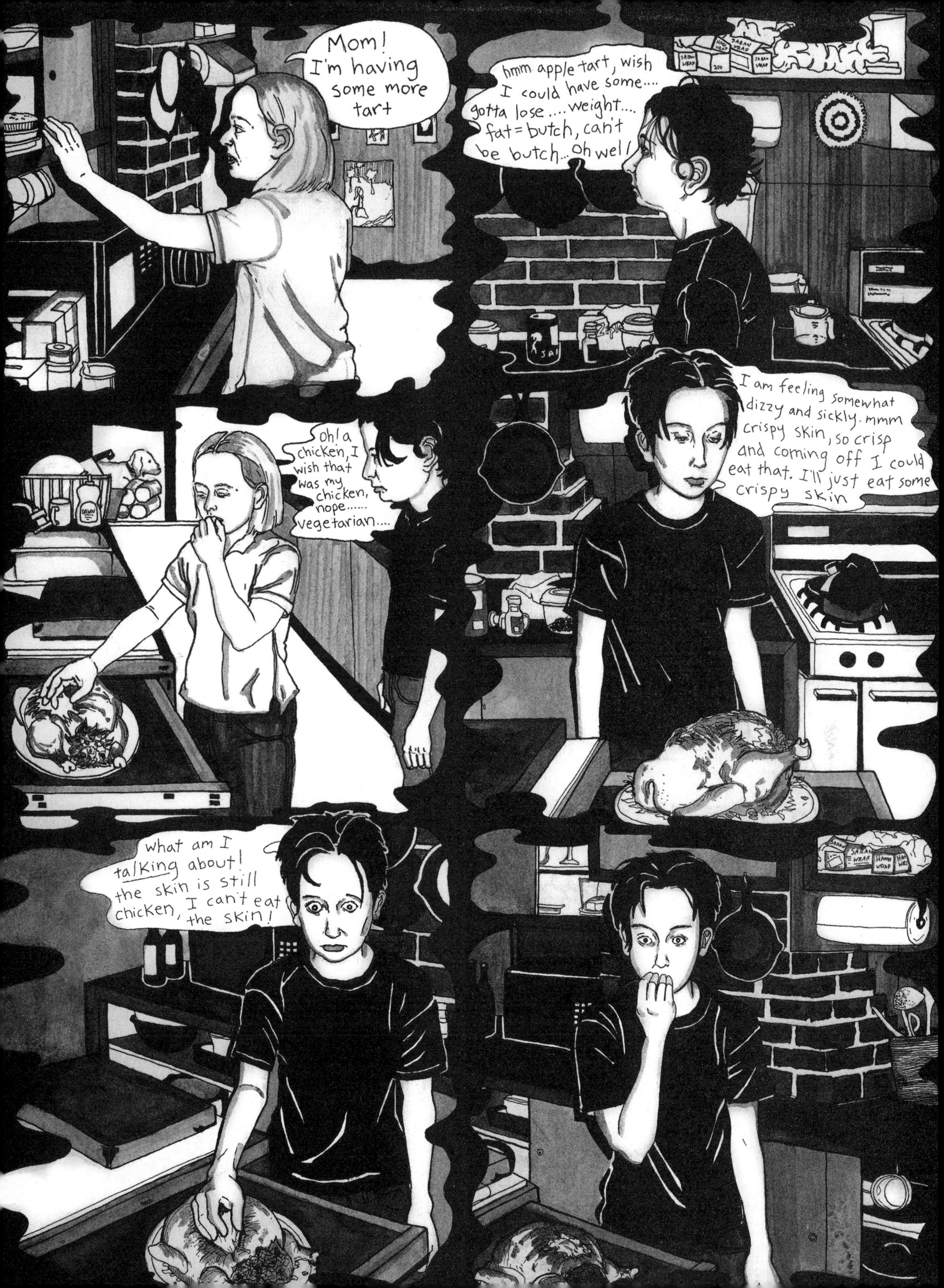
Mom! I'm having some more tart
hmm apple tart, wish I could have some.... gotta lose.... weight.... fat = butch, can't be butch... oh well
Oh! a chicken, I wish that was my chicken, nope...... vegetarian....
I am feeling somewhat dizzy and sickly. mmm crispy skin, so crisp and coming off I could eat that. I'll just eat some crispy skin
what am I talking about! the skin is still chicken, I can't eat the skin!

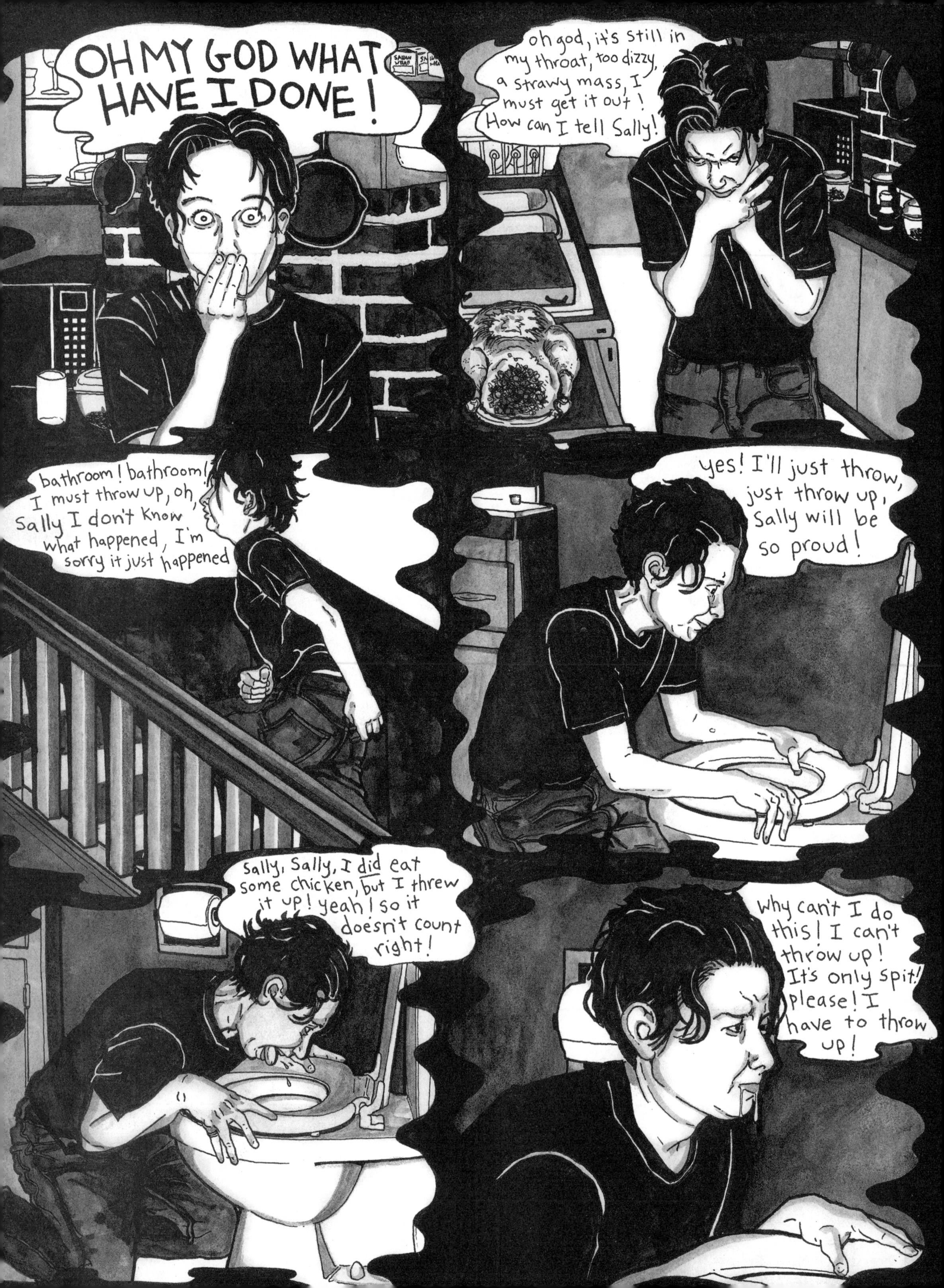
OH MY GOD WHAT HAVE I DONE!
oh god, it's still in my throat, too dizzy, a strawy mass, I must get it out! How can I tell Sally!
bathroom! bathroom! I must throw up, oh, Sally I don't know what happened, I'm sorry it just happened
yes! I'll just throw, just throw up, Sally will be so proud!
Sally, Sally, I did eat some chicken, but I threw it up! yeah! so it doesn't count right!
Why can't I do this! I can't throw up! It's only spit! please! I have to throw up!

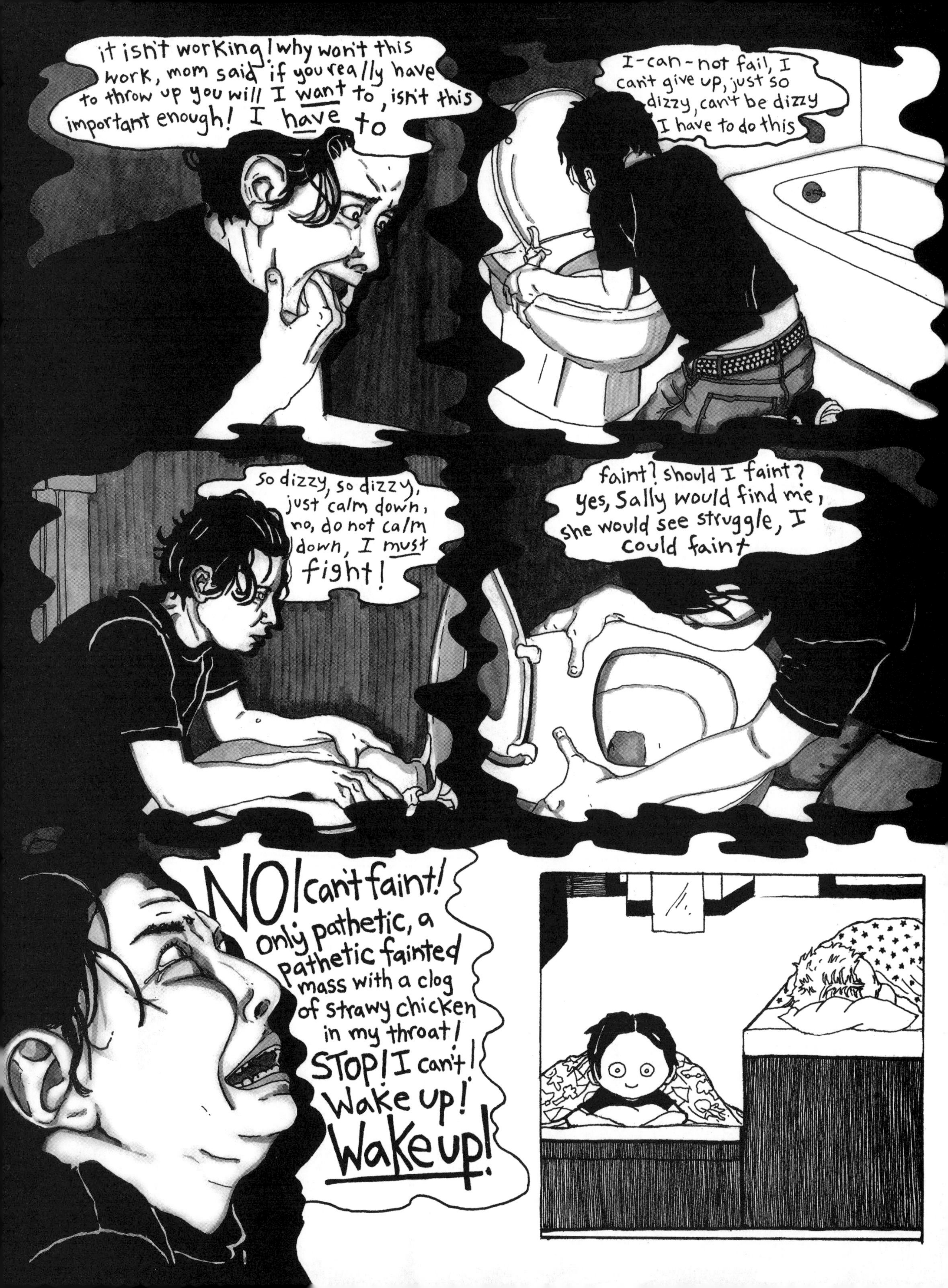

it isn't working! why won't this work, mom said if you really have to throw up you will I want to, isn't this important enough! I have to
I-can-not fail, I can't give up, just so dizzy, can't be dizzy I have to do this
so dizzy, so dizzy, just calm down, no, do not calm down, I must fight!
faint? should I faint? yes, Sally would find me, she would see struggle, I could faint
NO! can't faint! only pathetic, a pathetic fainted mass with a clog of strawy chicken in my throat! STOP! I can't! Wake up! Wake up!

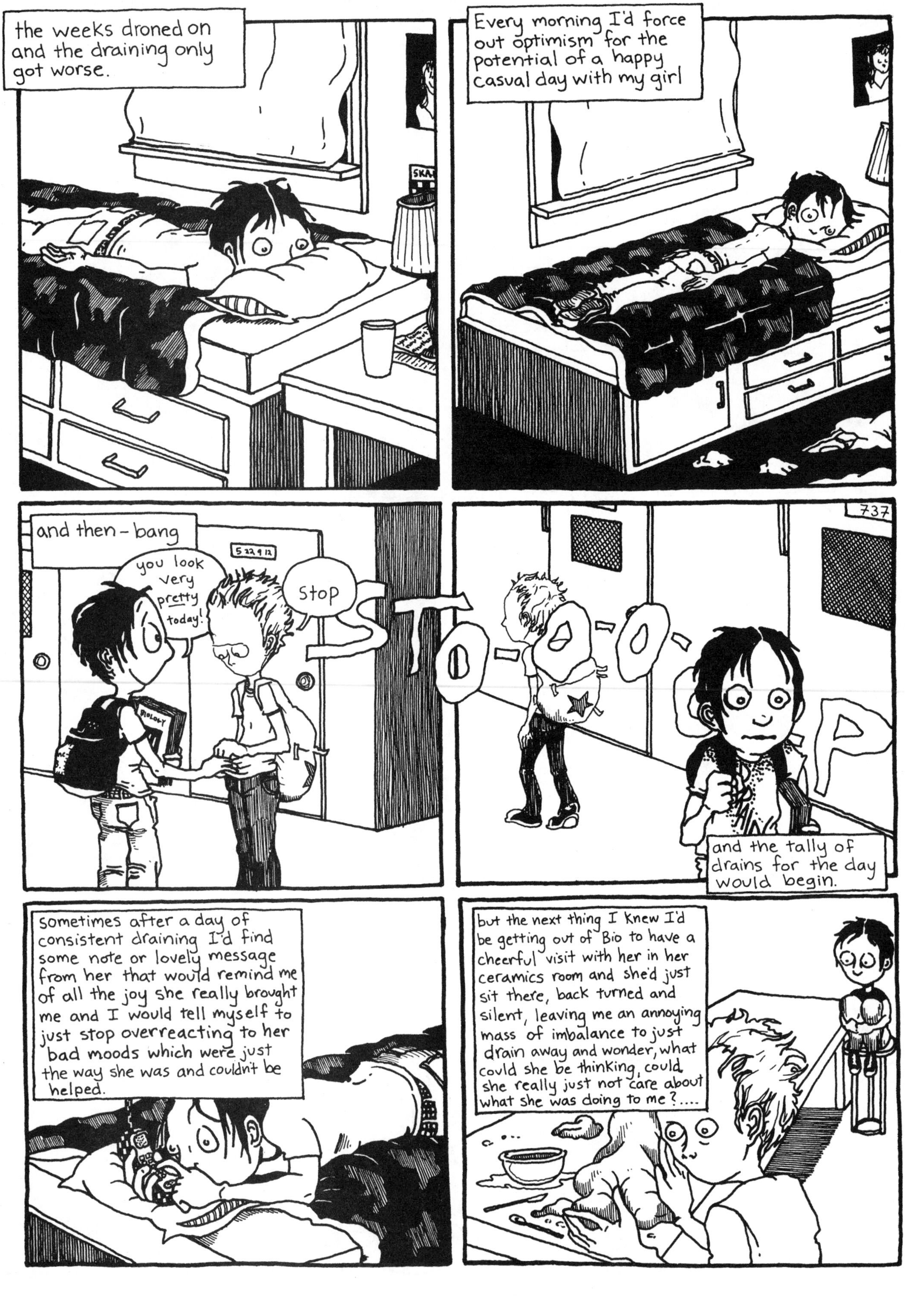
the weeks droned on and the draining only got worse.
Every morning I'd force out optimism for the potential of a happy casual day with my girl
and then - bang
you look very pretty today!
Stop
ST-O-O-O-OP
737
and the tally of drains for the day would begin.
Sometimes after a day of consistent draining I'd find some note or lovely message from her that would remind me of all the joy she really brought me and I would tell myself to just stop overreacting to her bad moods which were just the way she was and couldn't be helped.
but the next thing I knew I'd be getting out of Bio to have a cheerful visit with her in her ceramics room and she'd just sit there, back turned and silent, leaving me an annoying mass of imbalance to just drain away and wonder, what could she be thinking, could she really just not care about what she was doing to me?....

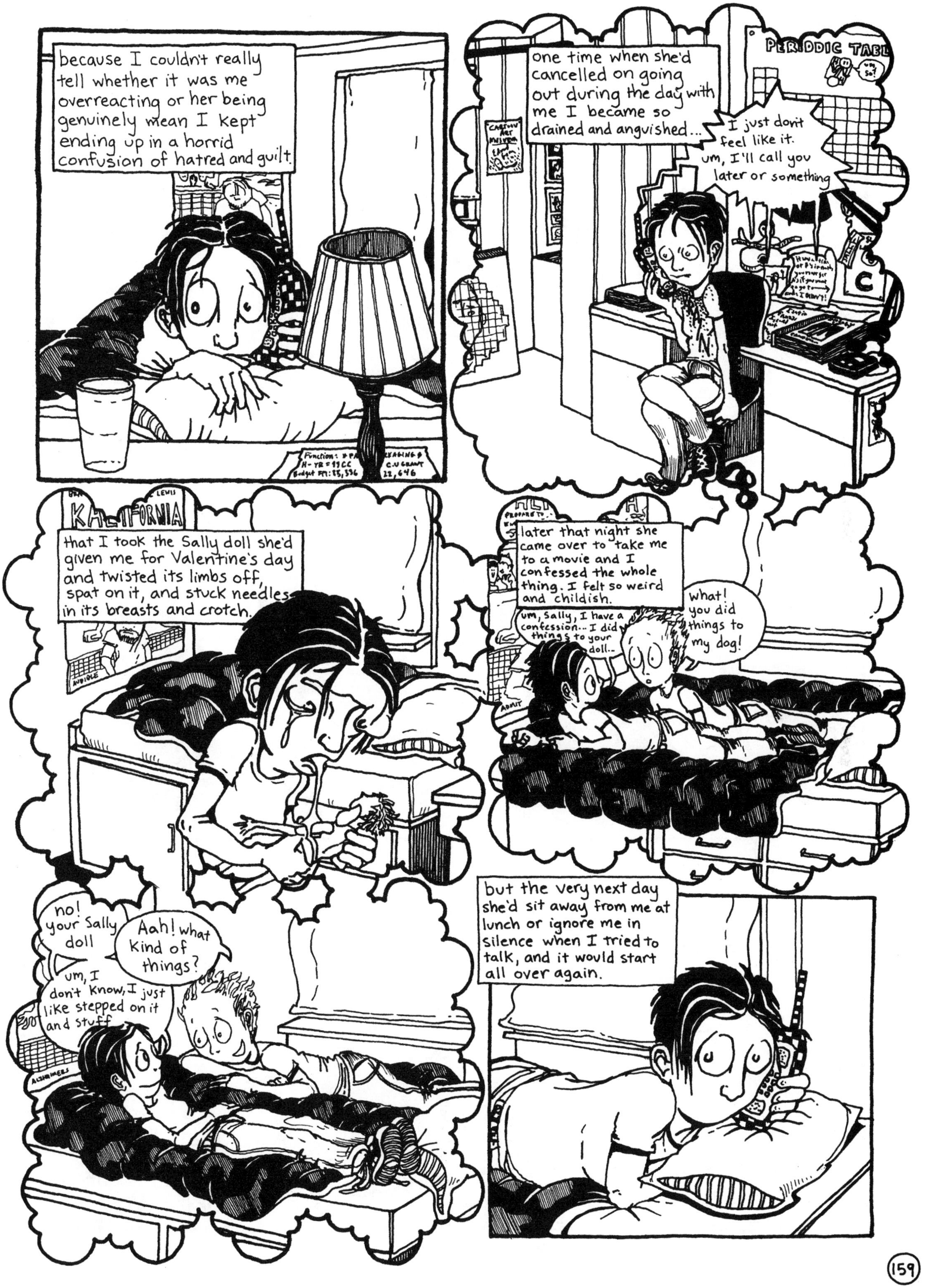
because I couldn't really tell whether it was me overreacting or her being genuinely mean I kept ending up in a horrid confusion of hatred and guilt.
one time when she'd cancelled on going out during the day with me I became so drained and anguished...
PERIODIC TABL
I just don't feel like it. um, I'll call you later or something
KALIFORNIA
that I took the Sally doll she'd given me for Valentine's day and twisted its limbs off, spat on it, and stuck needles in its breasts and crotch.
later that night she came over to take me to a movie and I confessed the whole thing. I felt so weird and childish.
um, Sally, I have a confession... I did things to your doll...
what! you did things to my dog!
no! your Sally doll
Aah! what kind of things?
um, I don't know, I just like stepped on it and stuff
but the very next day she'd sit away from me at lunch or ignore me in silence when I tried to talk, and it would start all over again.

all I wanted was just the Sally I knew she could be, the one who killed me I loved her so much, but no matter what, relentless as ever, the draining remained.

today was our 6 month anniversary, and I didn't know where she was.

due to my insisting we'd always made a notable event out of all our anniversaries, and I'd always seen the 6 month like the king they were all leading up to - 6 months, an actual half a year. plugged to the top in potential.

Hi Ariel! I'm coming over now and we're gonna go out to dinner, and I got us alcohol so we can get drunk and you can draw me n-a-aKed!

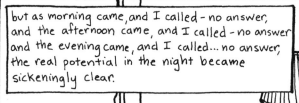

but as morning came, and I called - no answer, and the afternoon came, and I called - no answer and the evening came, and I called... no answer, the real potential in the night became sickeningly clear.

RING

160

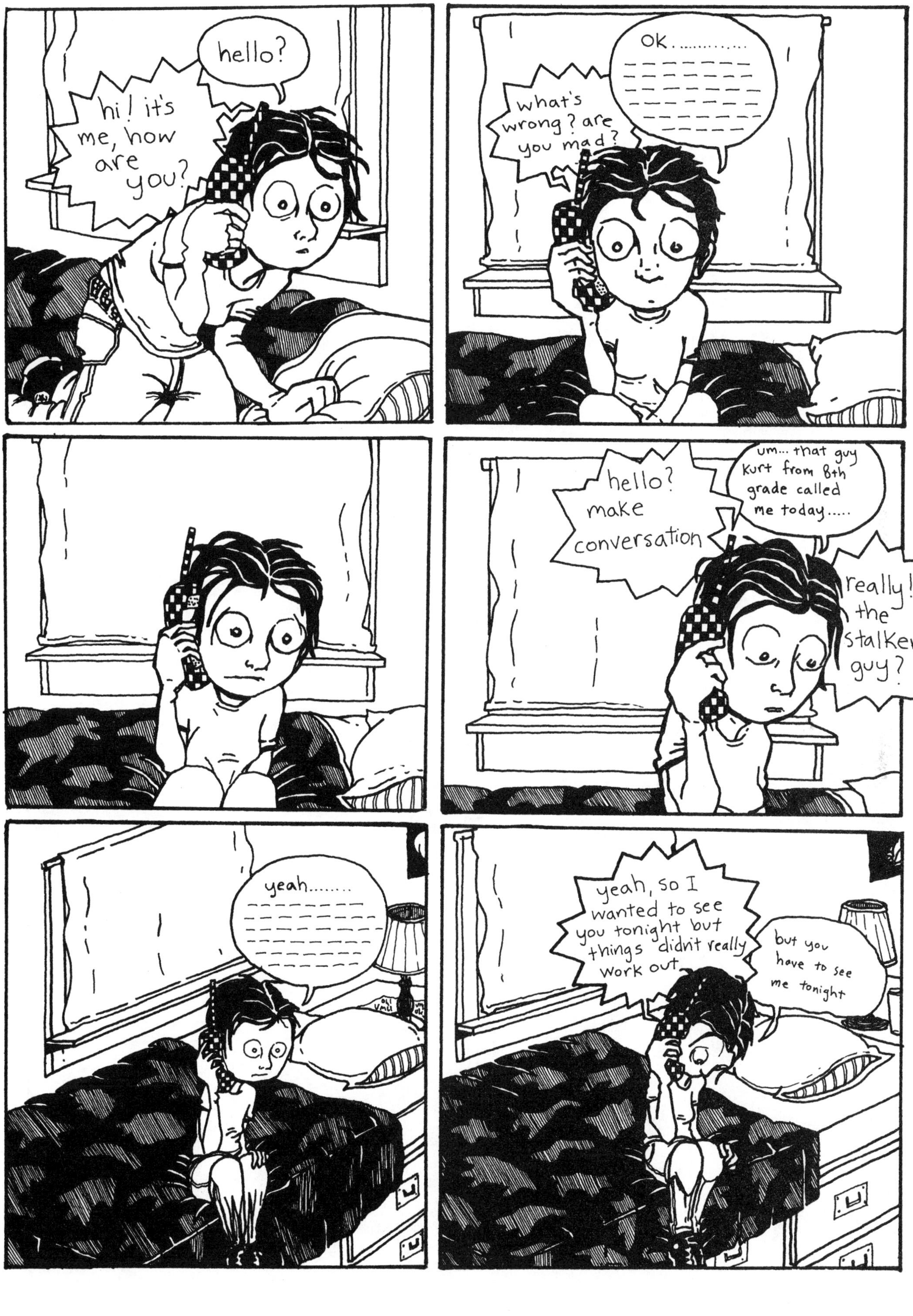
hello?
hi! it's me, how are you?
what's wrong? are you mad?
ok............
hello? make conversation
um... that guy Kurt from 8th grade called me today.....
really! the stalker guy?
yeah........
yeah, so I wanted to see you tonight but things didn't really work out
but you have to see me tonight

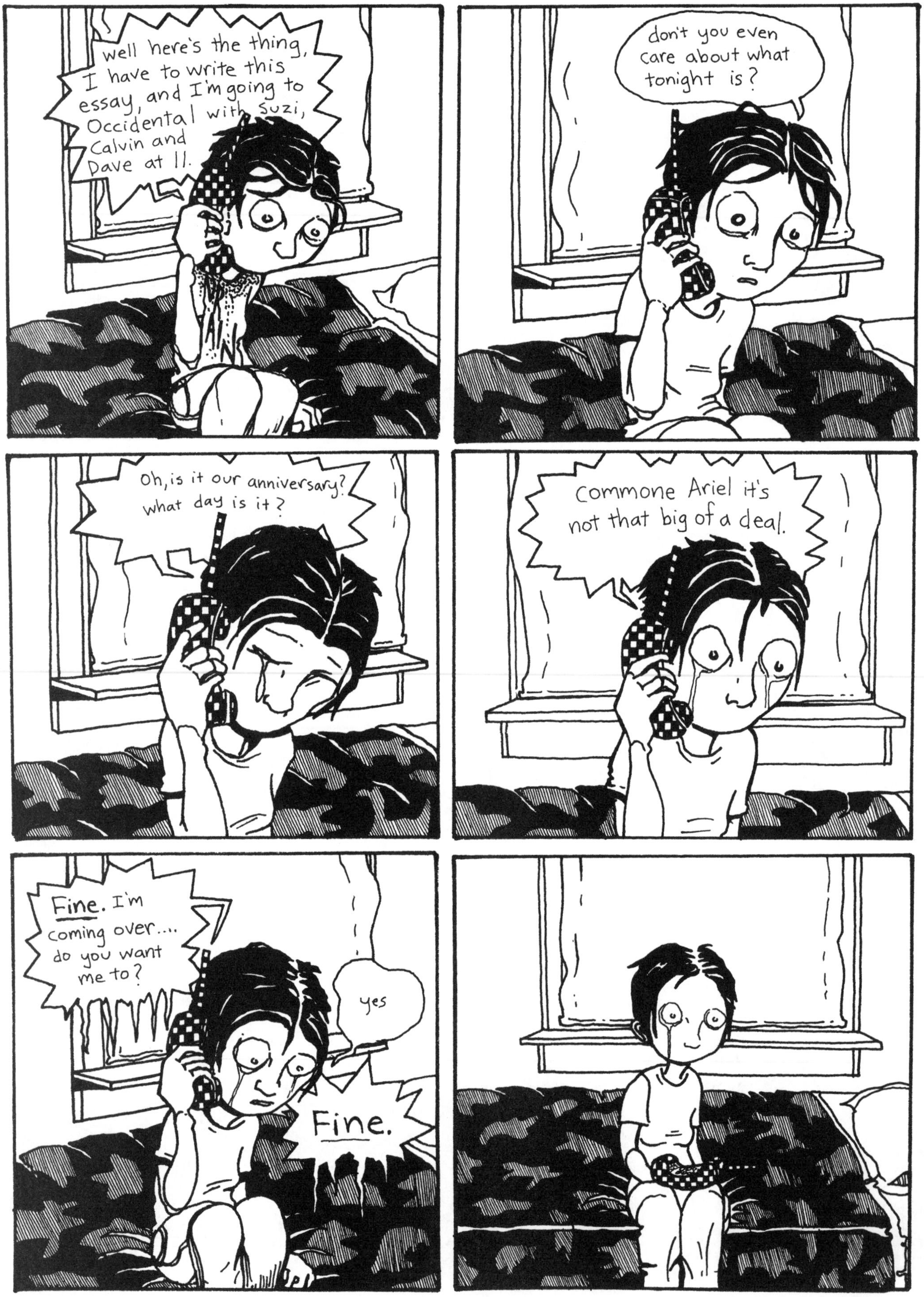
well here's the thing, I have to write this essay, and I'm going to Occidental with Suzi, Calvin and Dave at 11.
don't you even care about what tonight is?
Oh, is it our anniversary? what day is it?
Commone Ariel it's not that big of a deal.
Fine. I'm coming over.... do you want me to?
yes
Fine.

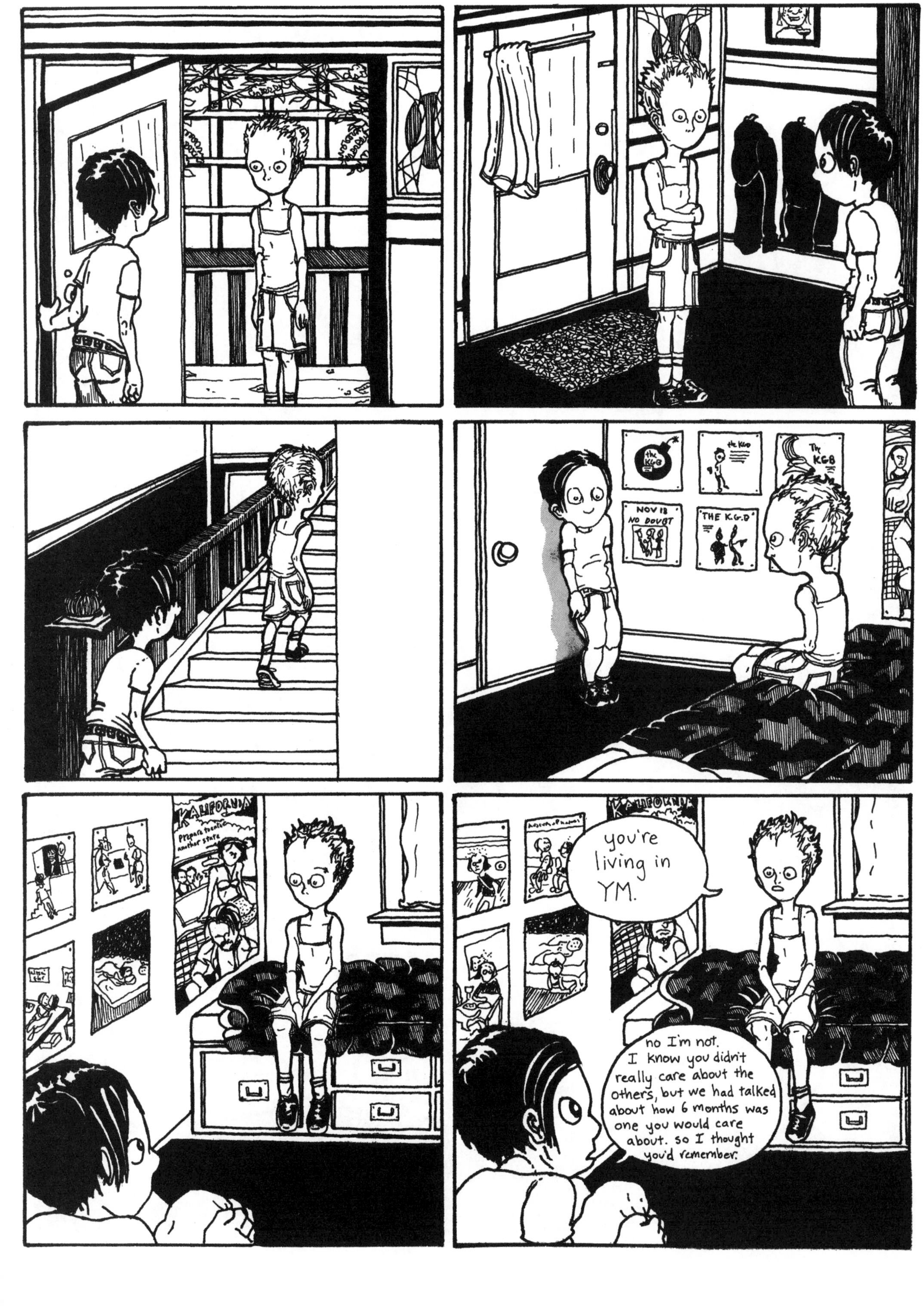
NOV 13
NO DOUBT
THE K.G.B
KALIFORNIA
you're living in YM.
no I'm not. I know you didn't really care about the others, but we had talked about how 6 months was one you would care about. so I thought you'd remember.

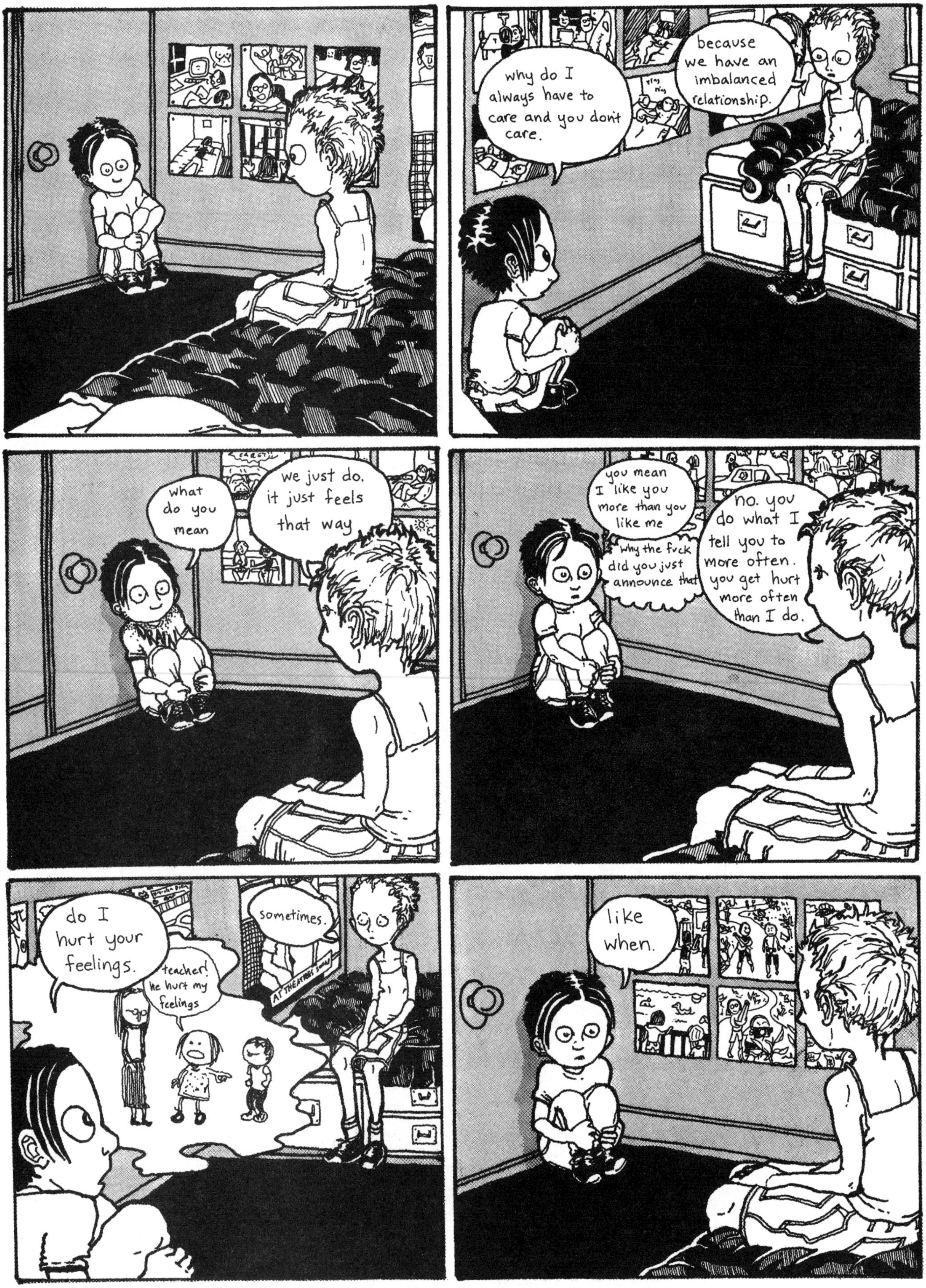
why do I always have to care and you don't care.
because we have an imbalanced relationship.
what do you mean
we just do. it just feels that way
you mean I like you more than you like me
why the fuck did you just announce that
no. you do what I tell you to more often. you get hurt more often than I do.
do I hurt your feelings.
sometimes.
teacher! he hurt my feelings
AT THEATRES SOON
like when.

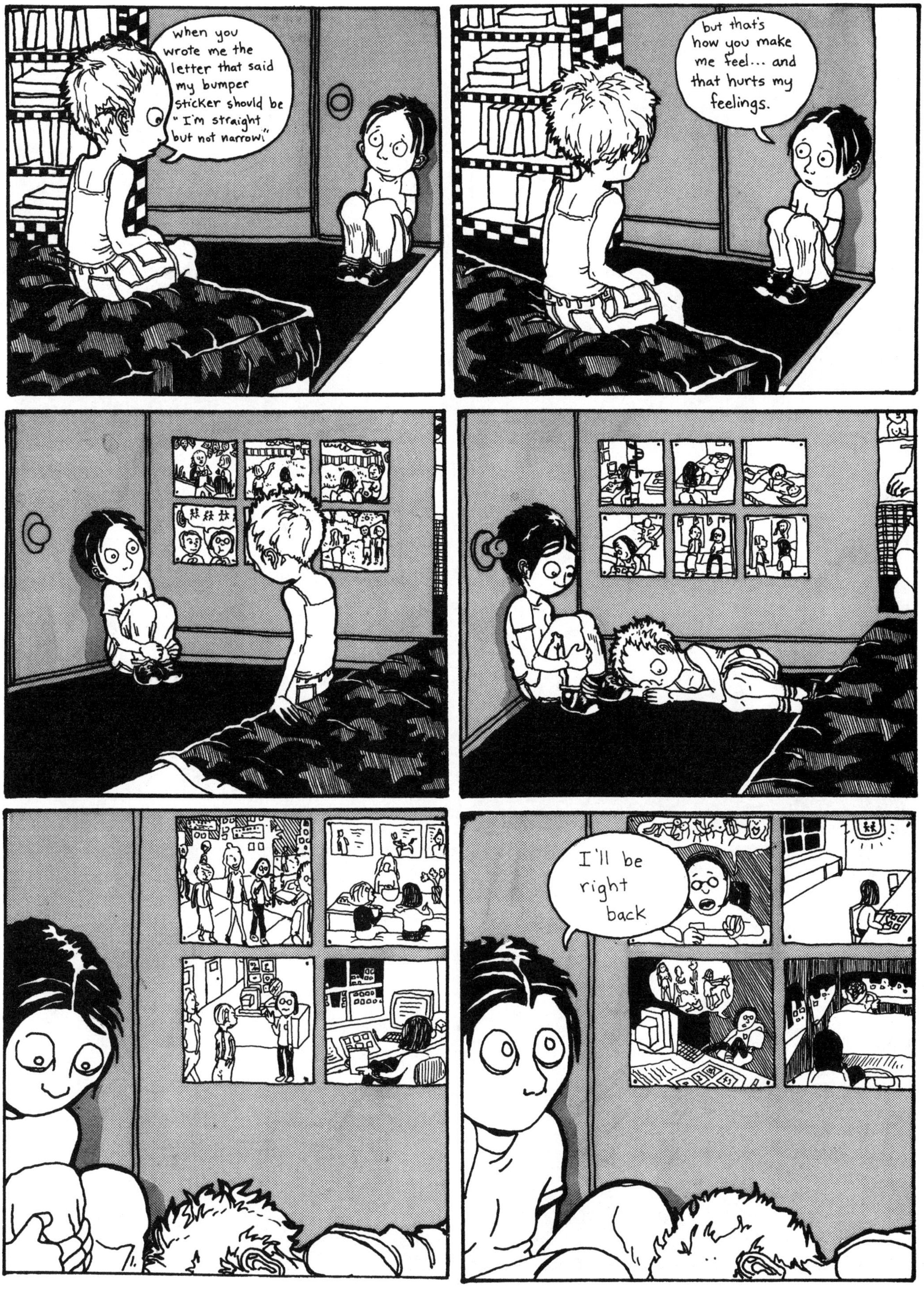
when you wrote me the letter that said my bumper sticker should be "I'm straight but not narrow!"
but that's how you make me feel... and that hurts my feelings.
I'll be right back

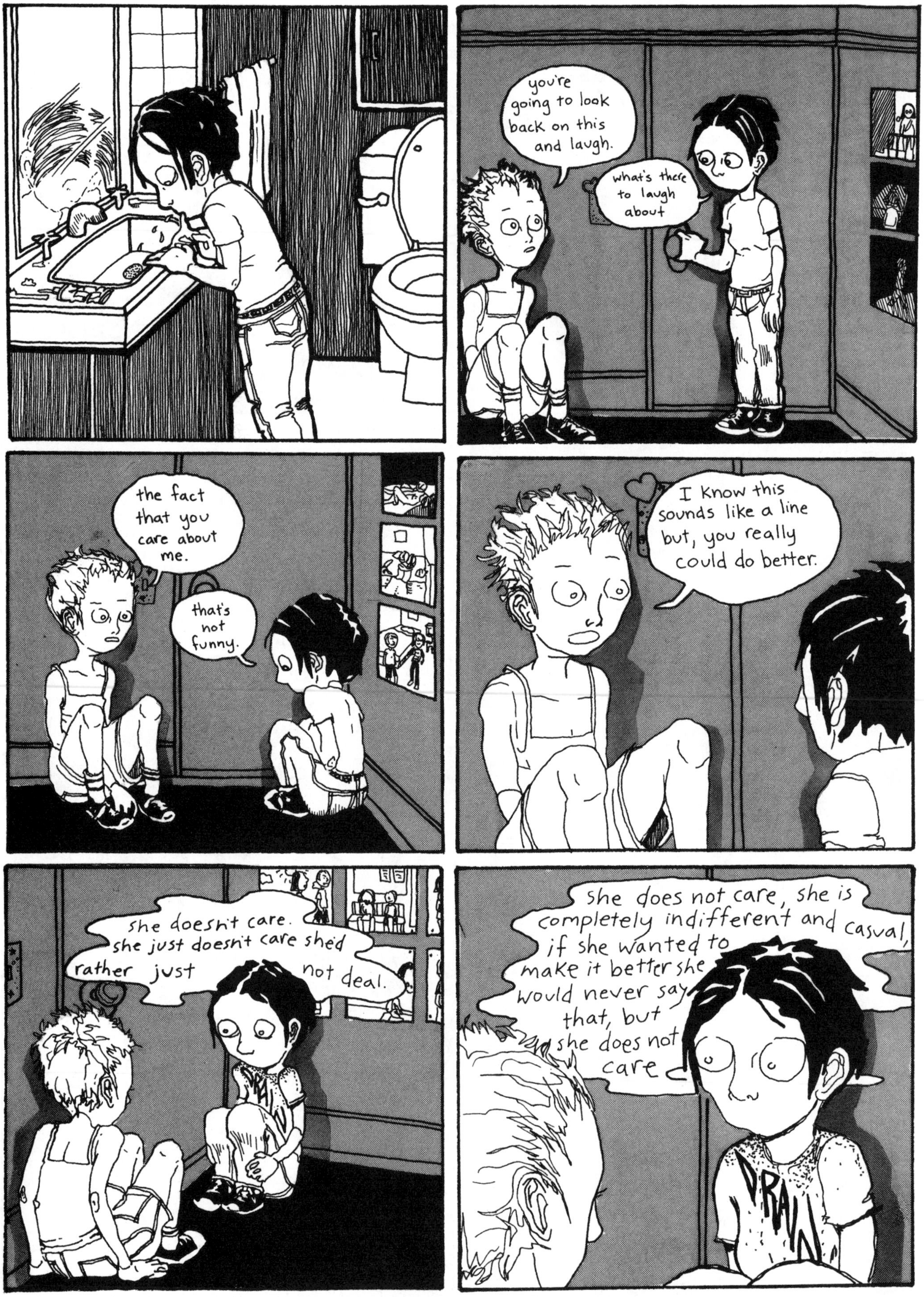
you're going to look back on this and laugh.
what's there to laugh about
the fact that you care about me.
that's not funny.
I know this sounds like a line but, you really could do better.
she doesn't care. she just doesn't care she'd rather just not deal.
she does not care, she is completely indifferent and casual, if she wanted to make it better she would never say that, but she does not care

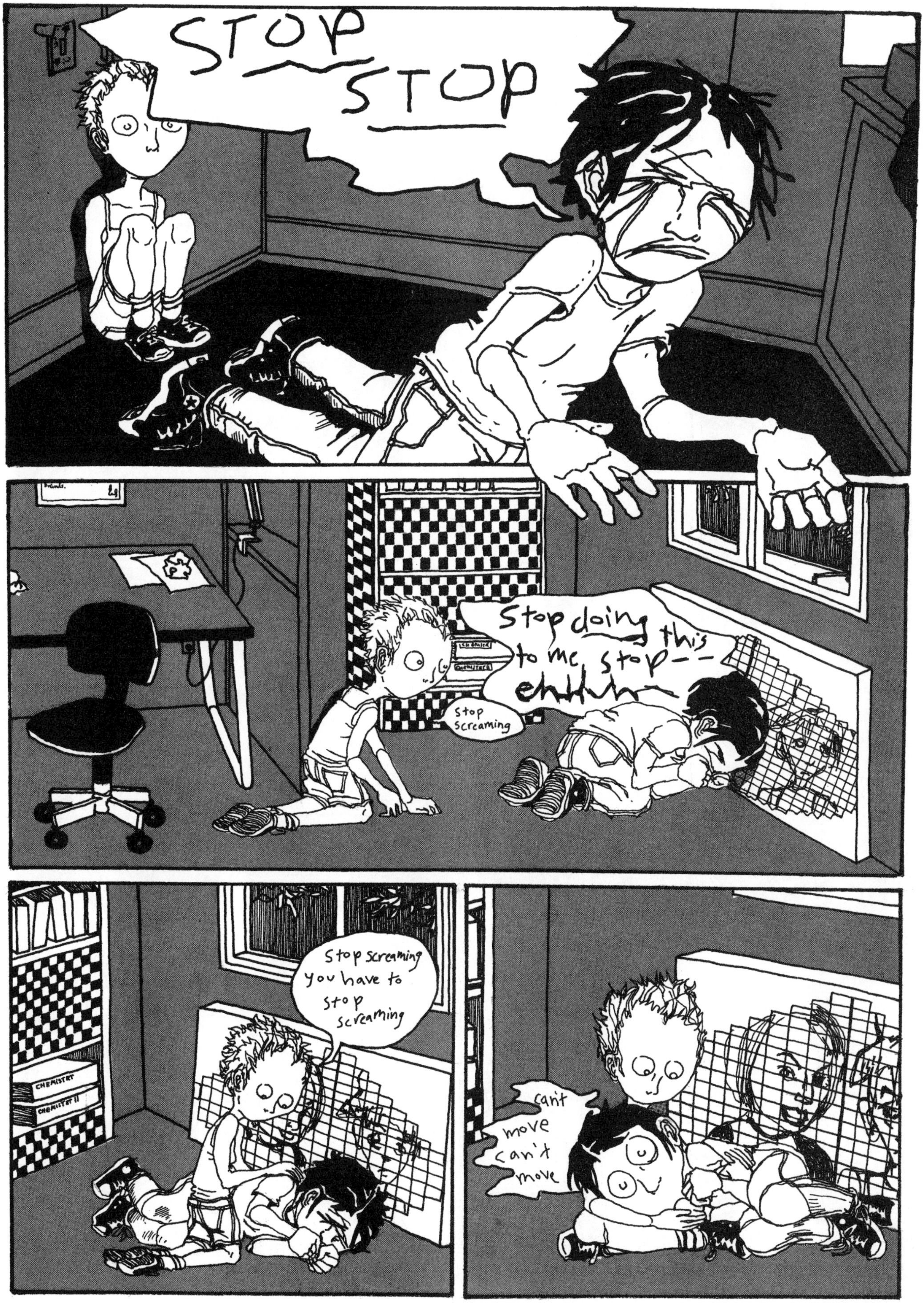
STOP STOP
Stop doing this to me stop---
ehhhh—
Stop screaming
Stop screaming you have to stop screaming
can't move can't move

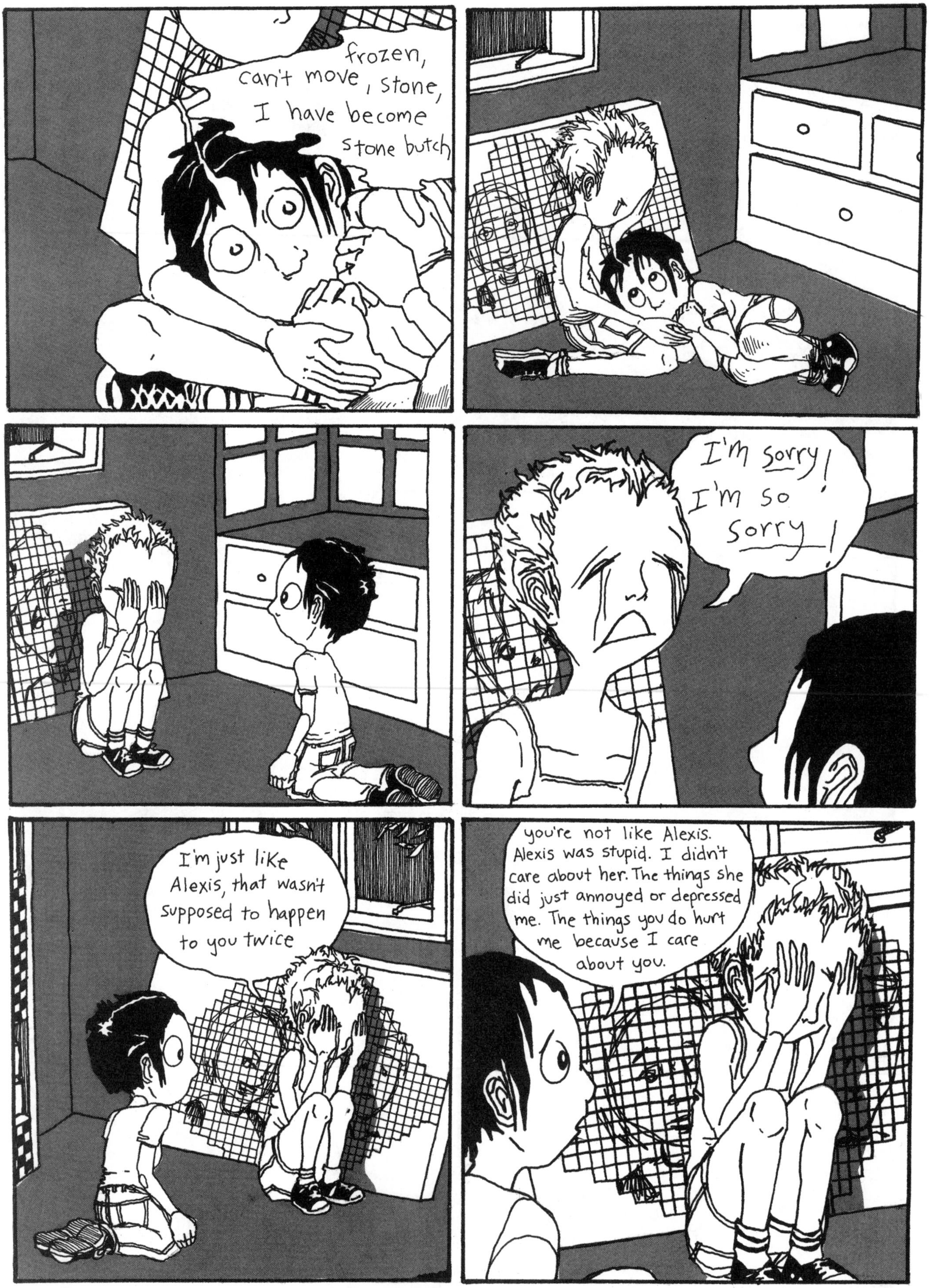
frozen, can't move, stone, I have become stone butch
I'm sorry! I'm so sorry!
I'm just like Alexis, that wasn't supposed to happen to you twice
you're not like Alexis. Alexis was stupid. I didn't care about her. The things she did just annoyed or depressed me. The things you do hurt me because I care about you.

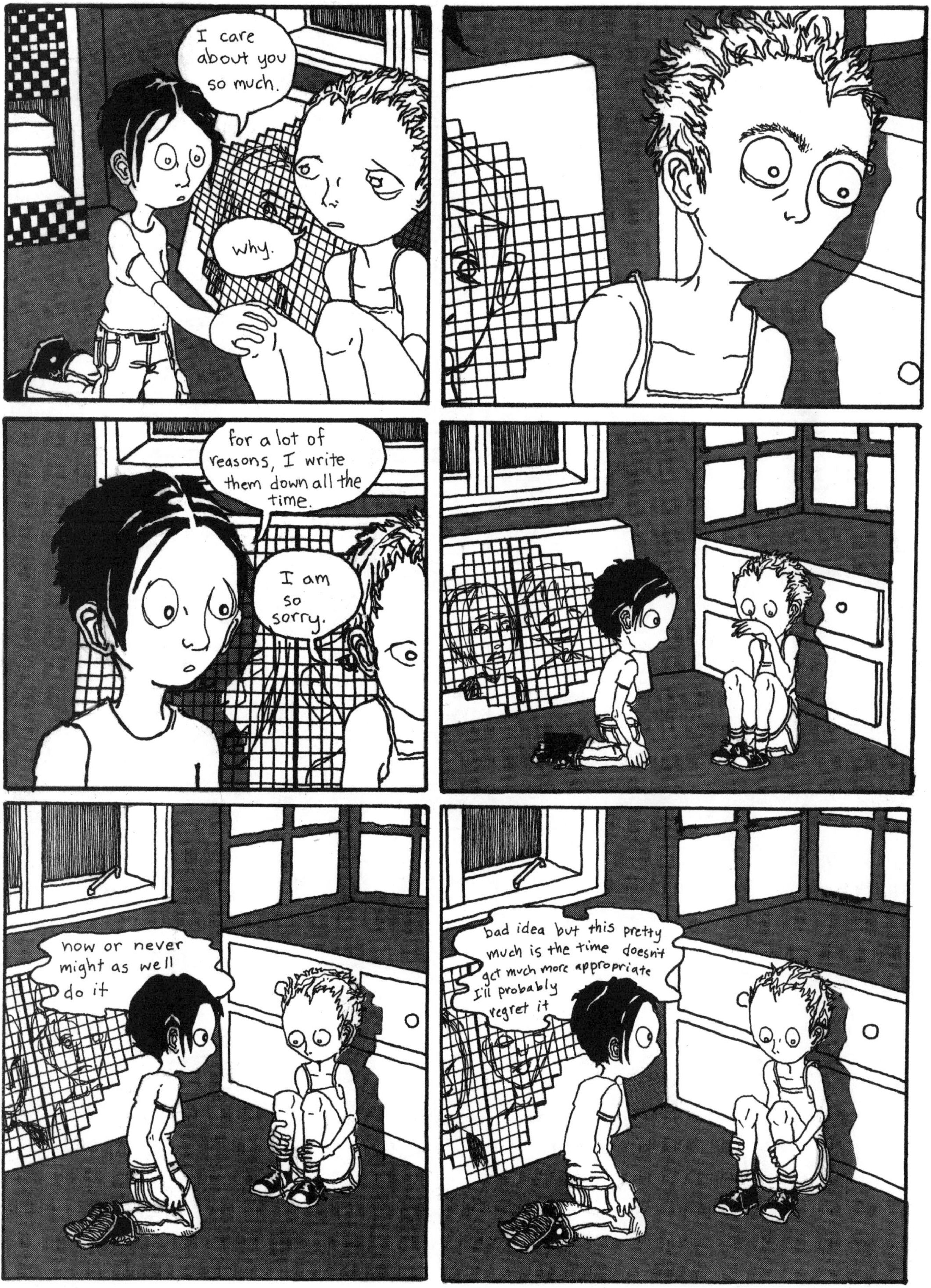
I care about you so much.
why.
for a lot of reasons, I write them down all the time.
I am so sorry.
now or never might as well do it
bad idea but this pretty much is the time doesn't get much more appropriate I'll probably regret it

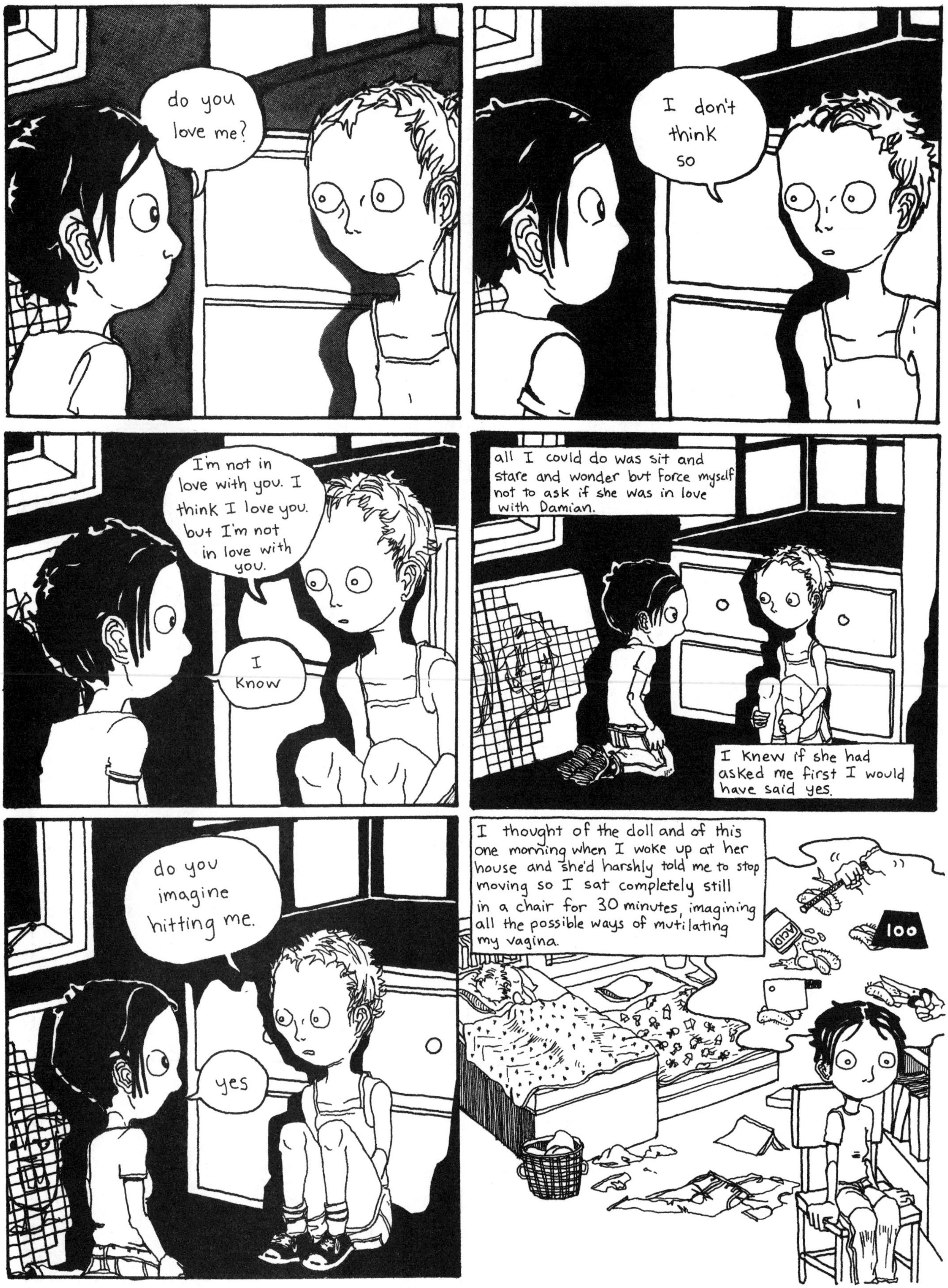
do you love me?
I don't think so
I'm not in love with you. I think I love you. but I'm not in love with you.
I know
all I could do was sit and stare and wonder but force myself not to ask if she was in love with Damian.
I knew if she had asked me first I would have said yes.
do you imagine hitting me.
yes
I thought of the doll and of this one morning when I woke up at her house and she'd harshly told me to stop moving so I sat completely still in a chair for 30 minutes, imagining all the possible ways of mutilating my vagina.
ACID
100

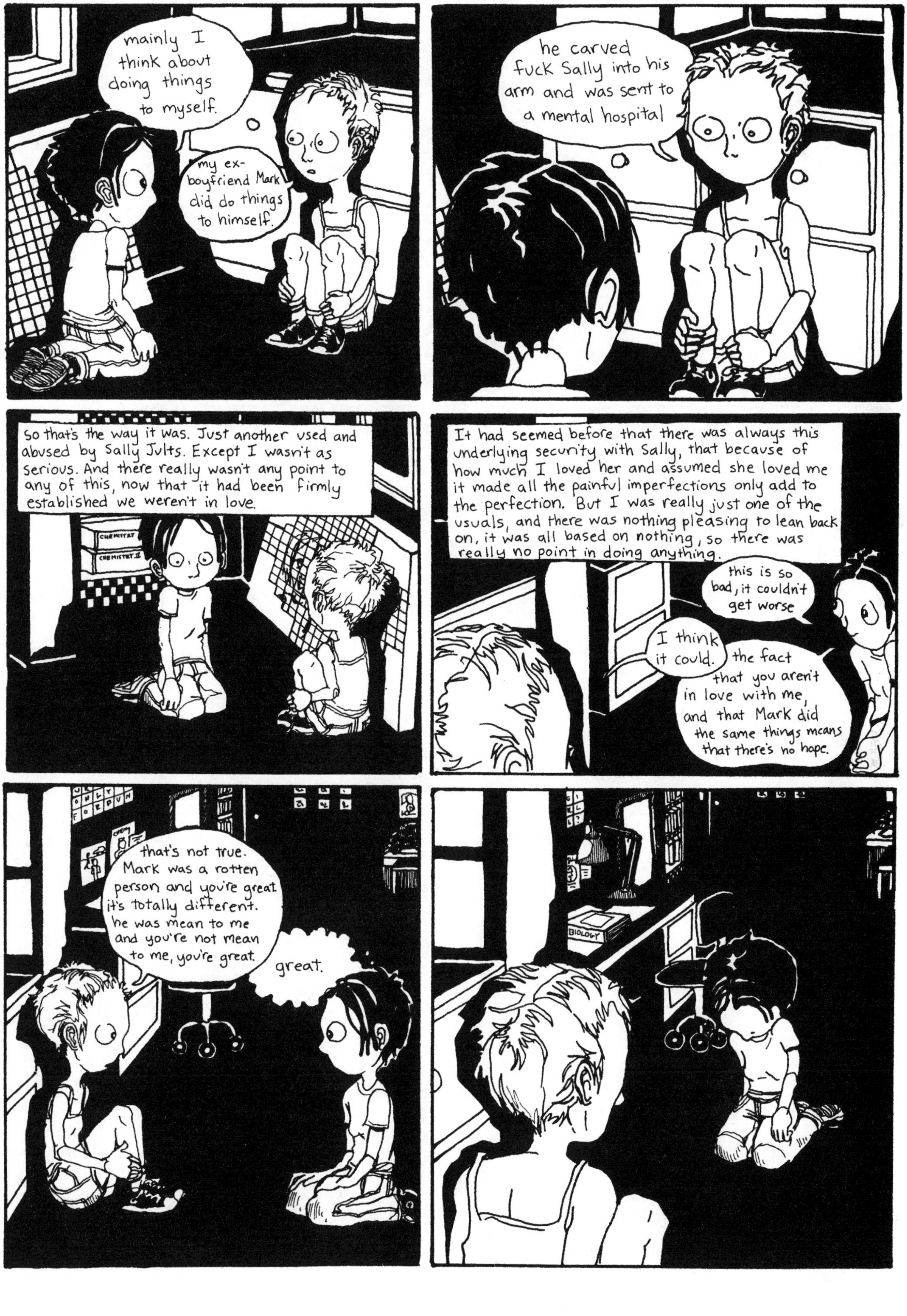
mainly I think about doing things to myself.
my ex-boyfriend Mark did do things to himself.
he carved fuck Sally into his arm and was sent to a mental hospital
So that's the way it was. Just another used and abused by Sally Jults. Except I wasn't as serious. And there really wasn't any point to any of this, now that it had been firmly established we weren't in love.
CHEMISTRY
CHEMISTRY II
It had seemed before that there was always this underlying security with Sally, that because of how much I loved her and assumed she loved me it made all the painful imperfections only add to the perfection. But I was really just one of the usuals, and there was nothing pleasing to lean back on, it was all based on nothing, so there was really no point in doing anything.
this is so bad, it couldn't get worse
I think it could.
the fact that you aren't in love with me, and that Mark did the same things means that there's no hope.
that's not true. Mark was a rotten person and you're great. it's totally different. he was mean to me and you're not mean to me, you're great.
great.
BIOLOGY

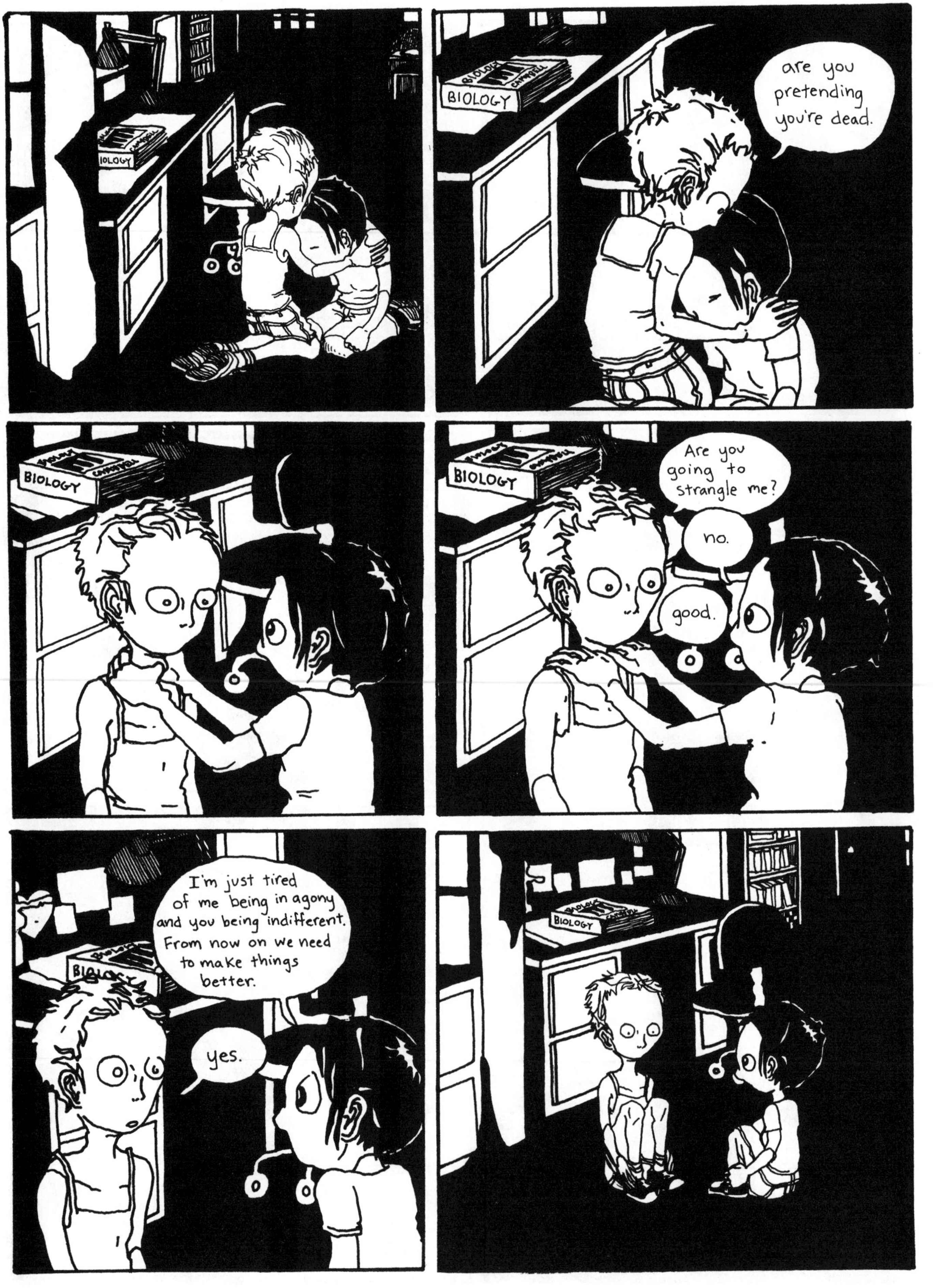
BIOLOGY
CAMPBELL
are you pretending you're dead.
Are you going to strangle me?
no.
good.
I'm just tired of me being in agony and you being indifferent. From now on we need to make things better.
yes.

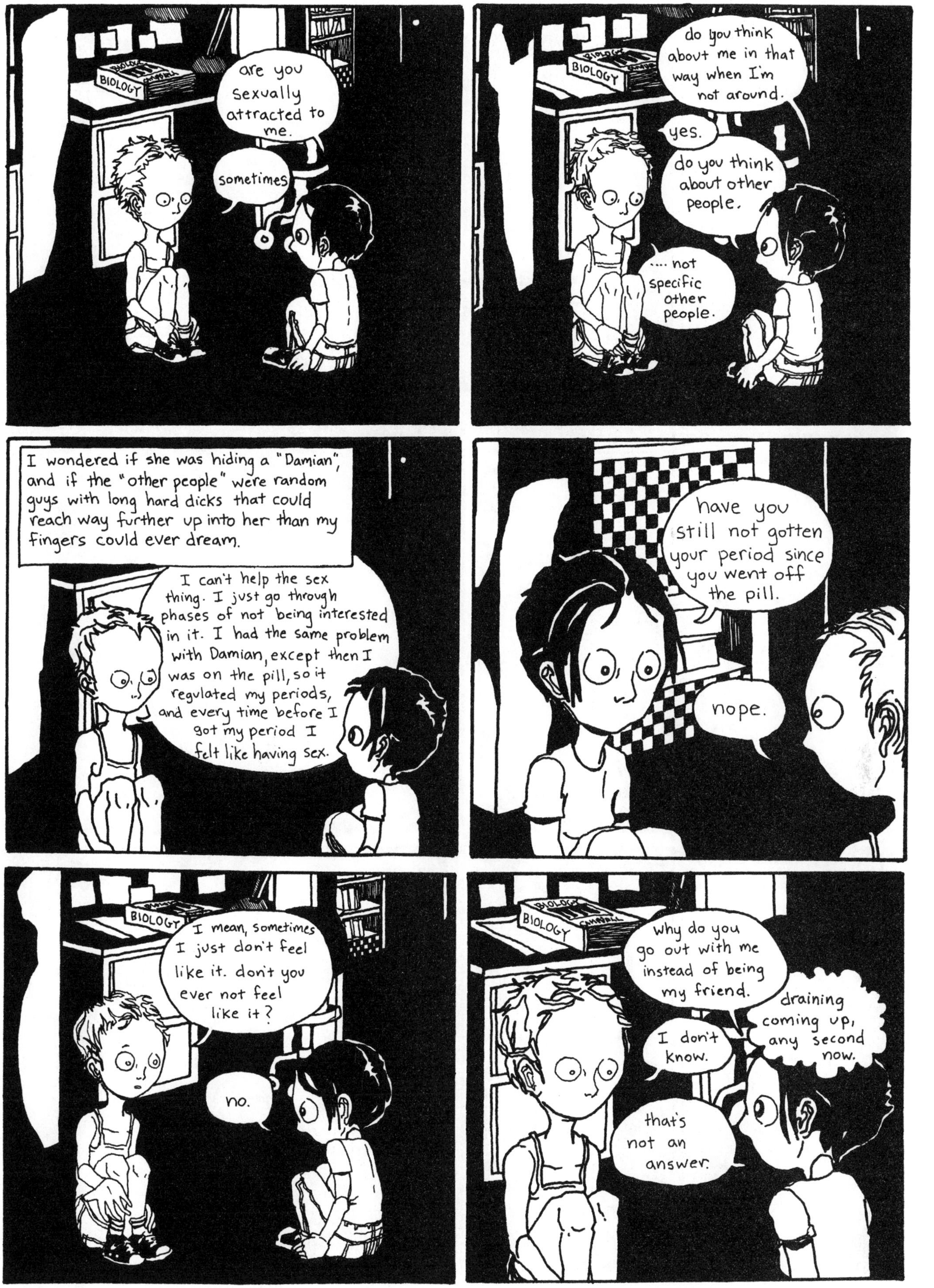
are you sexually attracted to me.
sometimes
do you think about me in that way when I'm not around.
yes.
do you think about other people.
.... not specific other people.
I wondered if she was hiding a "Damian", and if the "other people" were random guys with long hard dicks that could reach way further up into her than my fingers could ever dream.
I can't help the sex thing. I just go through phases of not being interested in it. I had the same problem with Damian, except then I was on the pill, so it regulated my periods, and every time before I got my period I felt like having sex.
have you still not gotten your period since you went off the pill.
nope.
I mean, sometimes I just don't feel like it. don't you ever not feel like it?
no.
why do you go out with me instead of being my friend.
draining coming up, any second now.
I don't know.
that's not an answer.

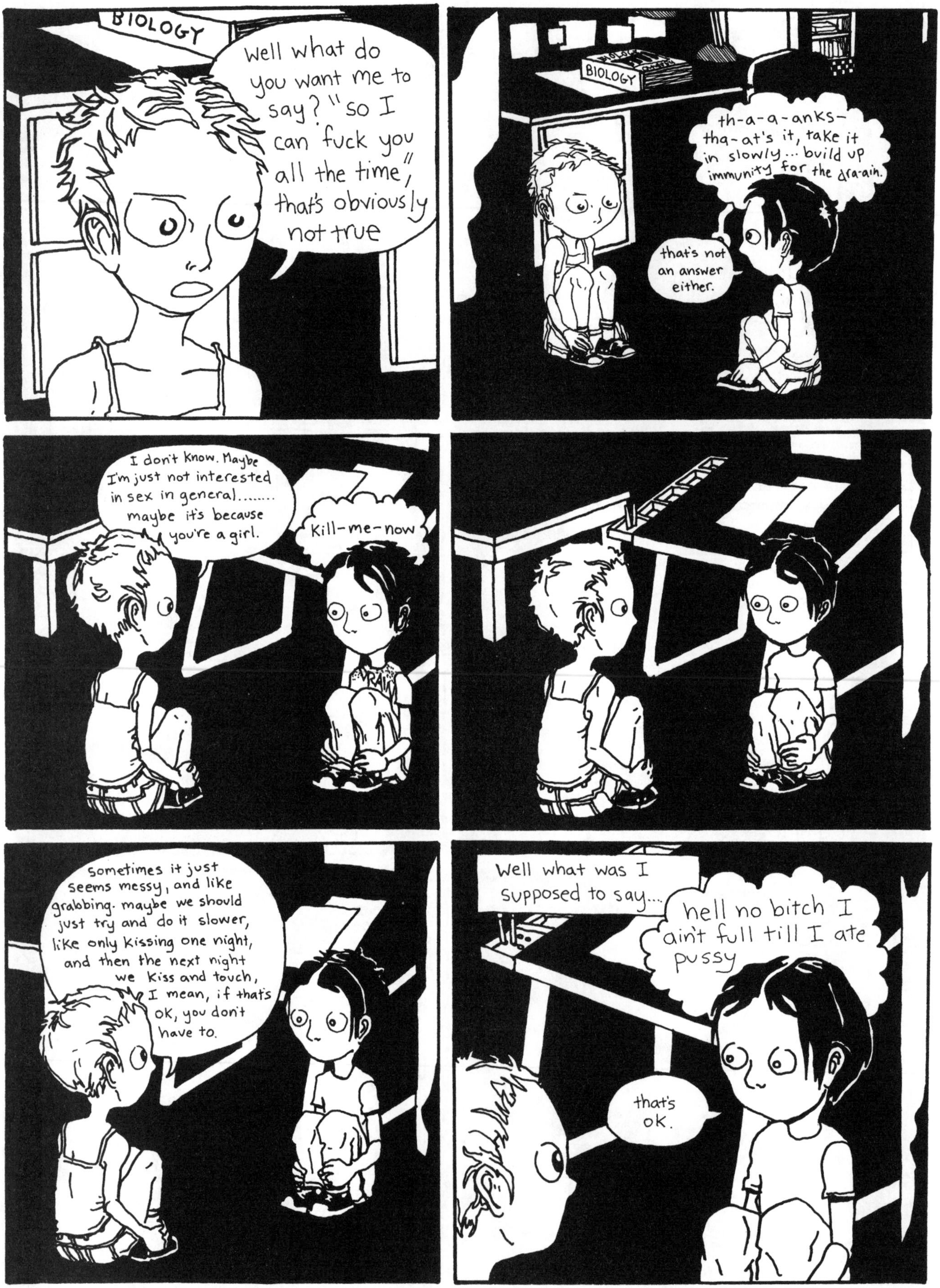
BIOLOGY
Well what do you want me to say? "so I can fuck you all the time", that's obviously not true
BIOLOGY
th-a-a-anks- tha-at's it, take it in slowly... build up immunity for the dra-aih.
that's not an answer either.
I don't know. Maybe I'm just not interested in sex in general........ maybe it's because you're a girl.
Kill-me-now
Sometimes it just seems messy, and like grabbing. maybe we should just try and do it slower, like only kissing one night, and then the next night we kiss and touch, I mean, if that's ok, you don't have to.
Well what was I supposed to say...
hell no bitch I ain't full till I ate pussy
that's ok.

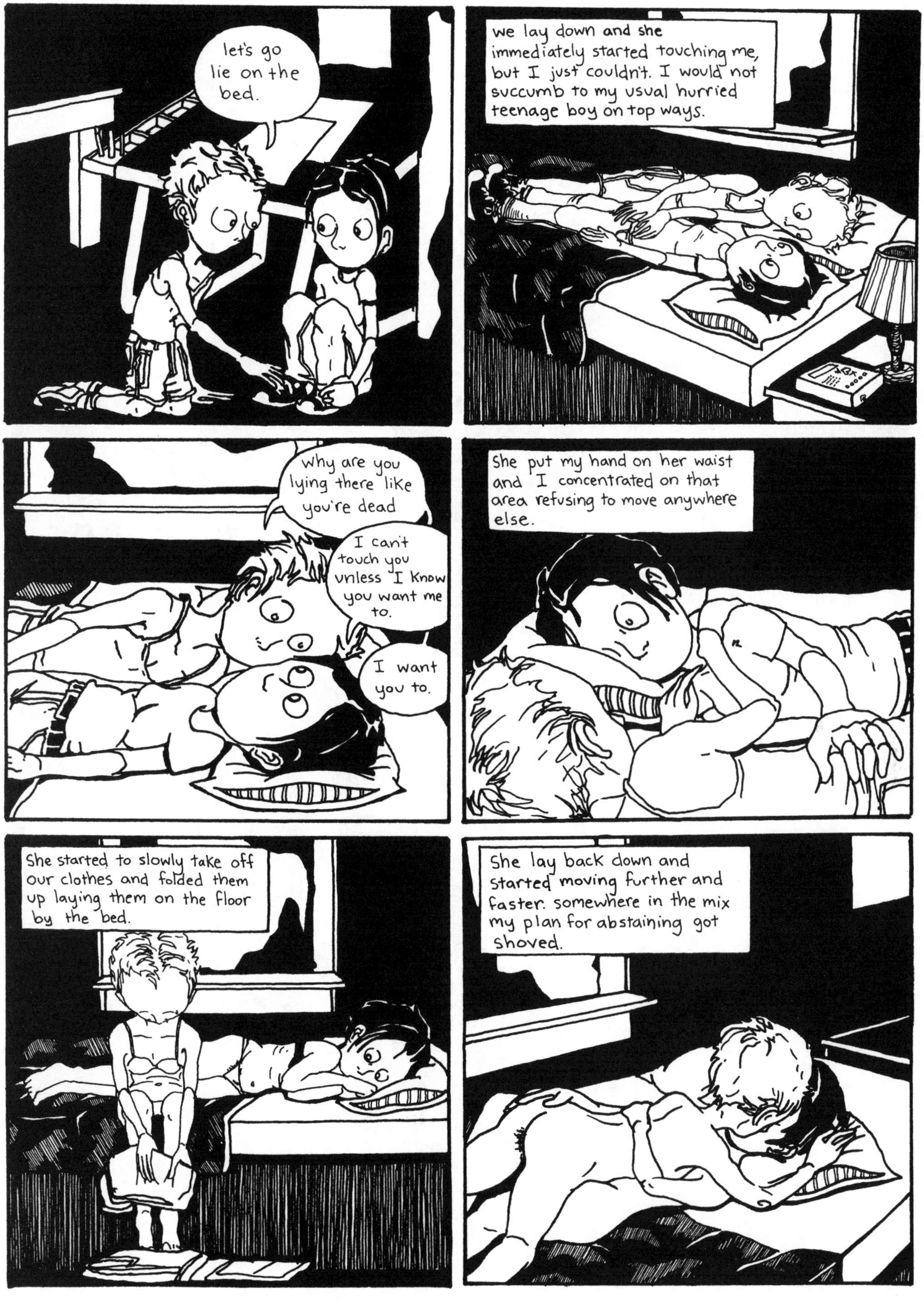

let's go lie on the bed.
we lay down and she immediately started touching me, but I just couldn't. I would not succumb to my usual hurried teenage boy on top ways.
why are you lying there like you're dead
I can't touch you unless I know you want me to.
I want you to.
She put my hand on her waist and I concentrated on that area refusing to move anywhere else.
She started to slowly take off our clothes and folded them up laying them on the floor by the bed.
She lay back down and started moving further and faster. somewhere in the mix my plan for abstaining got shoved.

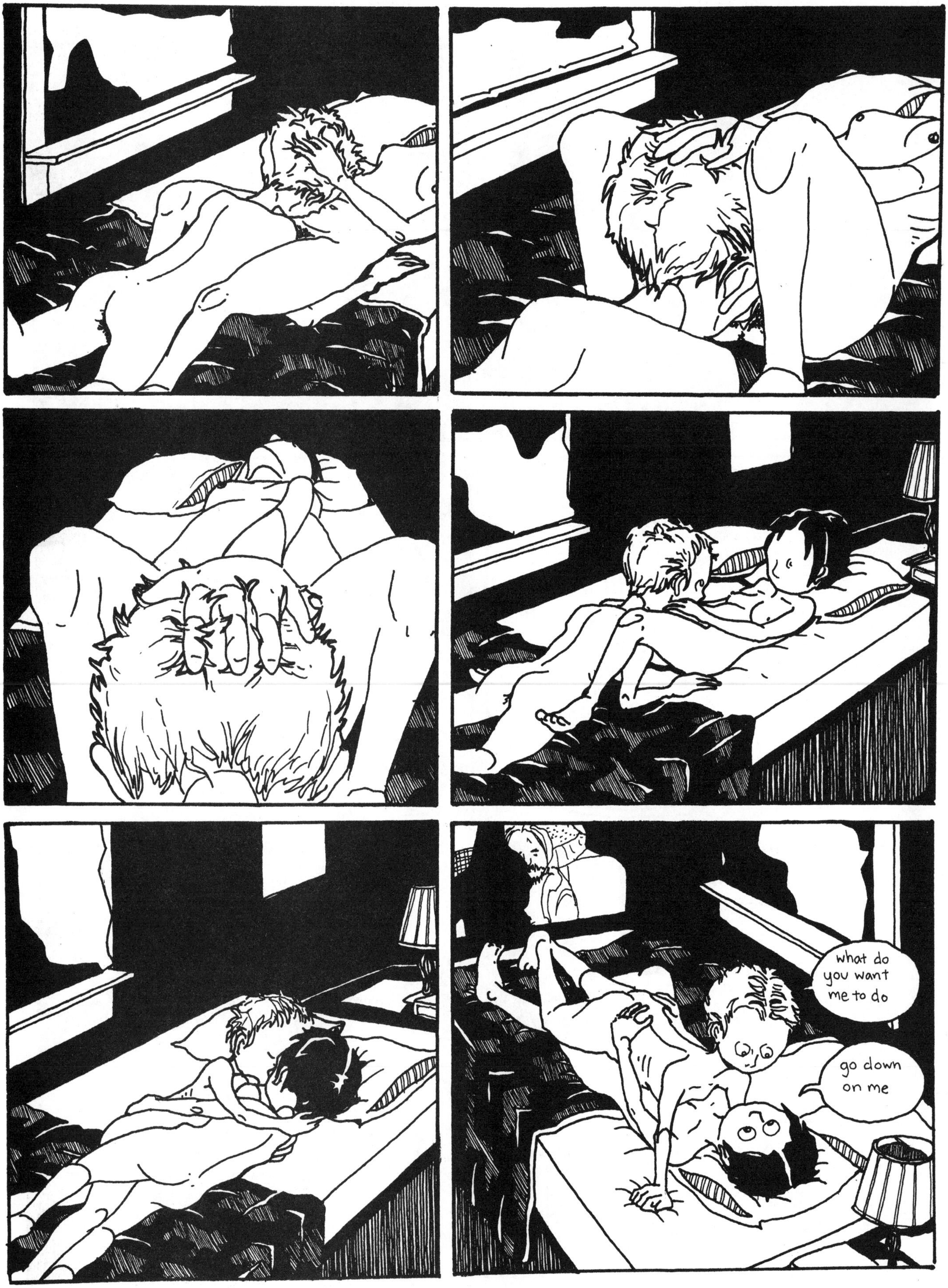
what do you want me to do
go down on me

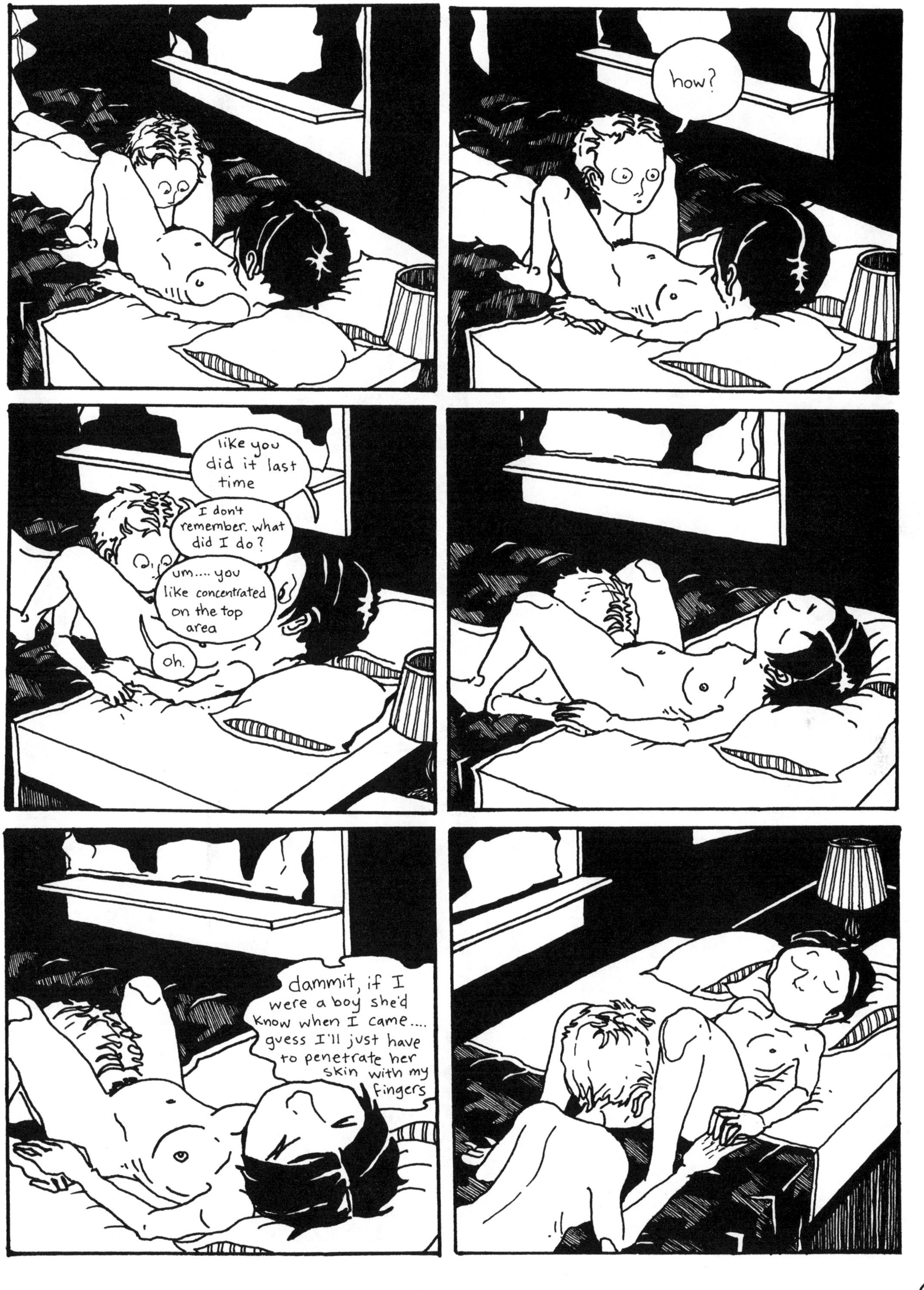
how?
like you did it last time
I don't remember. what did I do?
um.... you like concentrated on the top area
oh.
dammit, if I were a boy she'd know when I came.... guess I'll just have to penetrate her skin with my fingers

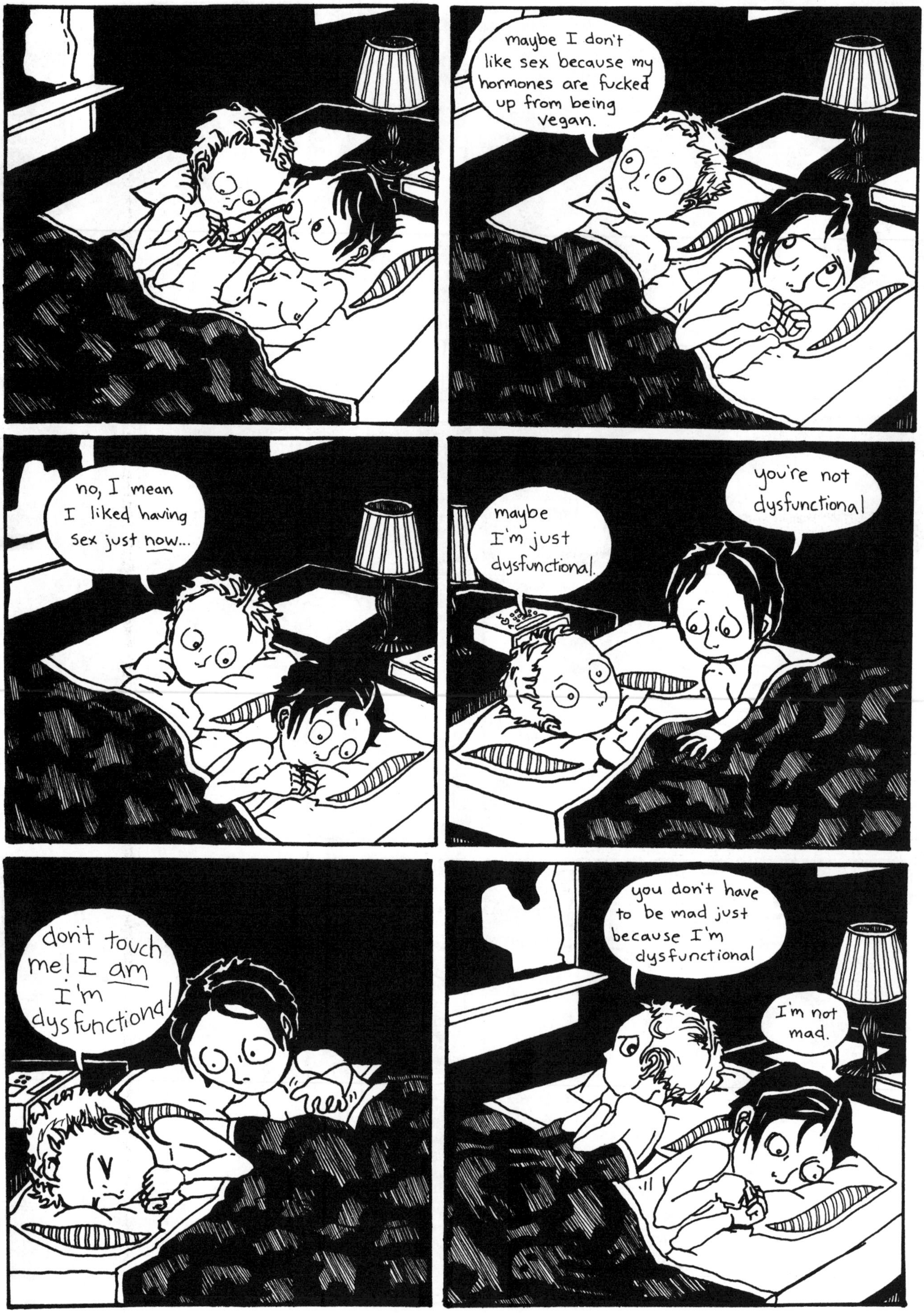
maybe I don't like sex because my hormones are fucked up from being vegan.
no, I mean I liked having sex just now...
maybe I'm just dysfunctional.
you're not dysfunctional
don't touch me! I am I'm dysfunctional!
you don't have to be mad just because I'm dysfunctional
I'm not mad.

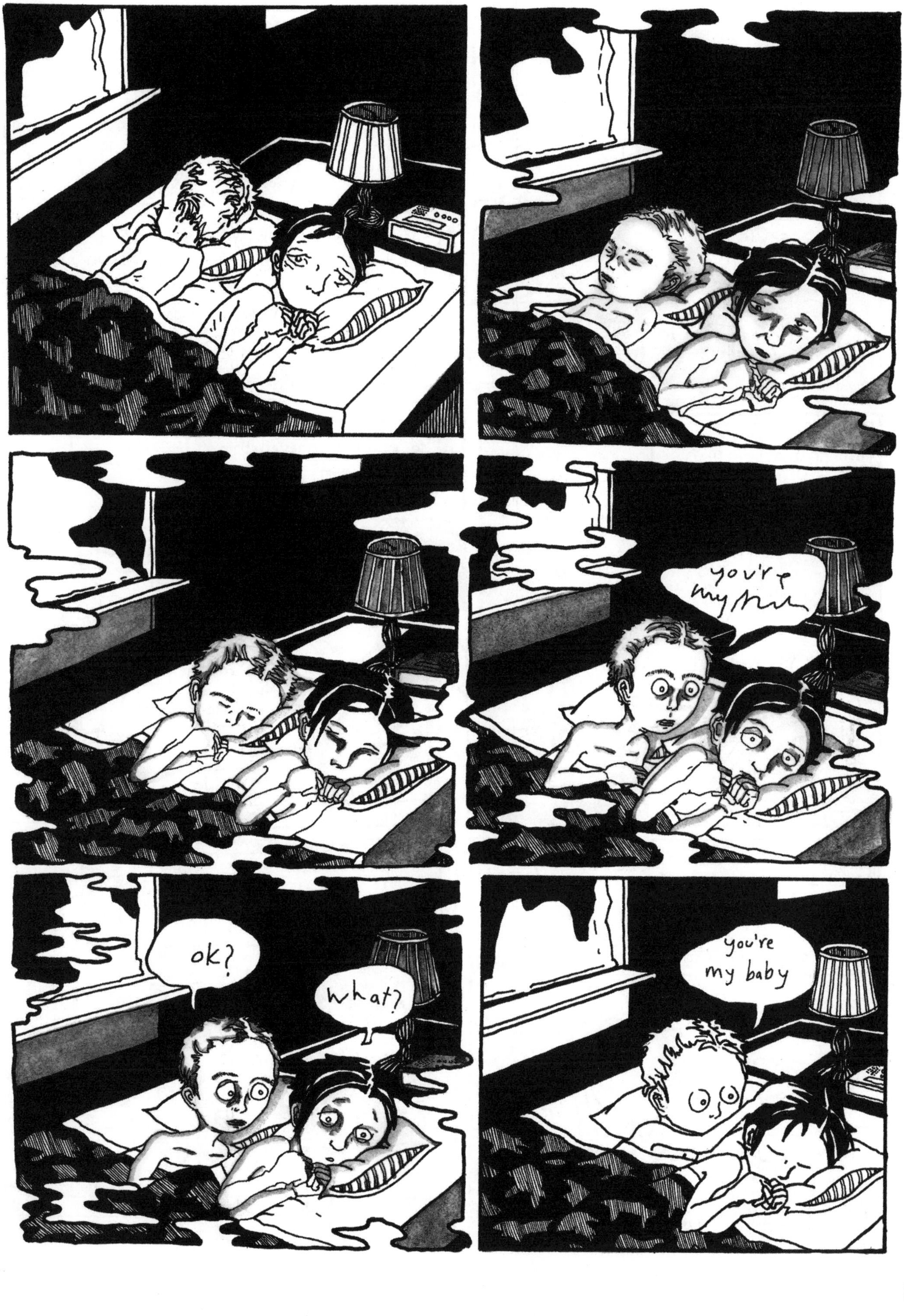
you're
my
ok?
what?
you're
my baby

CHAPTER ★ SEVEN

Ever since the thrill of 6th grade's 90210 Season Finale with Brenda losing her virginity to Dylan and Donna and her dress drunk downstairs.

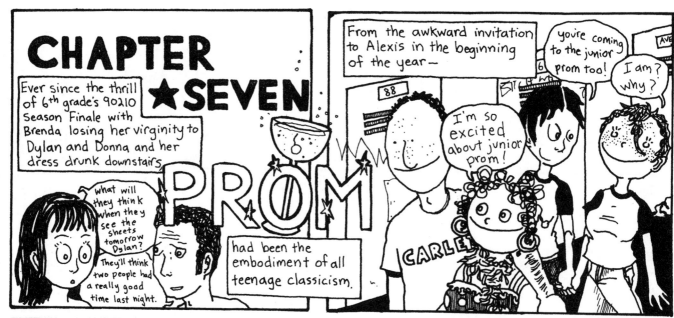

What will they think when they see the sheets tomorrow Dylan?

They'll think two people had a really good time last night.

PROM

had been the embodiment of all teenage classicism.

From the awkward invitation to Alexis in the beginning of the year—

you're coming to the junior prom too!

I am? why?

I'm so excited about junior prom!

CARLE

---

to Maude's short lived dinner and limo plan

yes, my boyfriend's paying for dinner in the city and a stretch limo, and you're invited. I'm wearing a tux.

ECONOMICS

---

to organizing everything properly with Sally—

well if we're going to your senior prom instead of the junior prom you have to ask me.

um, will you go to the prom with me.

I maintained the vision, potential to the 4th degree

---

the date of the prom was May 30 so in late April I began my daily prep of going to the YMCA for 2 hours on the stairmaster and bike machine, drinking 10-12 glasses of water, and eating at very tops one bagel, one tomato, and 3 bites of dinner.

pretty in prom dress sexy for Sally pretty in prom dress

The Evening Post

MORNING EDITION

BIOLOGY

CAMPBELL

---

however, despite my concentrated efforts on its perfection, problems for the best night of my life began to surface from very early on.

Ariel, I know you're just gonna get mad again but I really don't want to go

you promised.

Ariel...

BIOLOGY

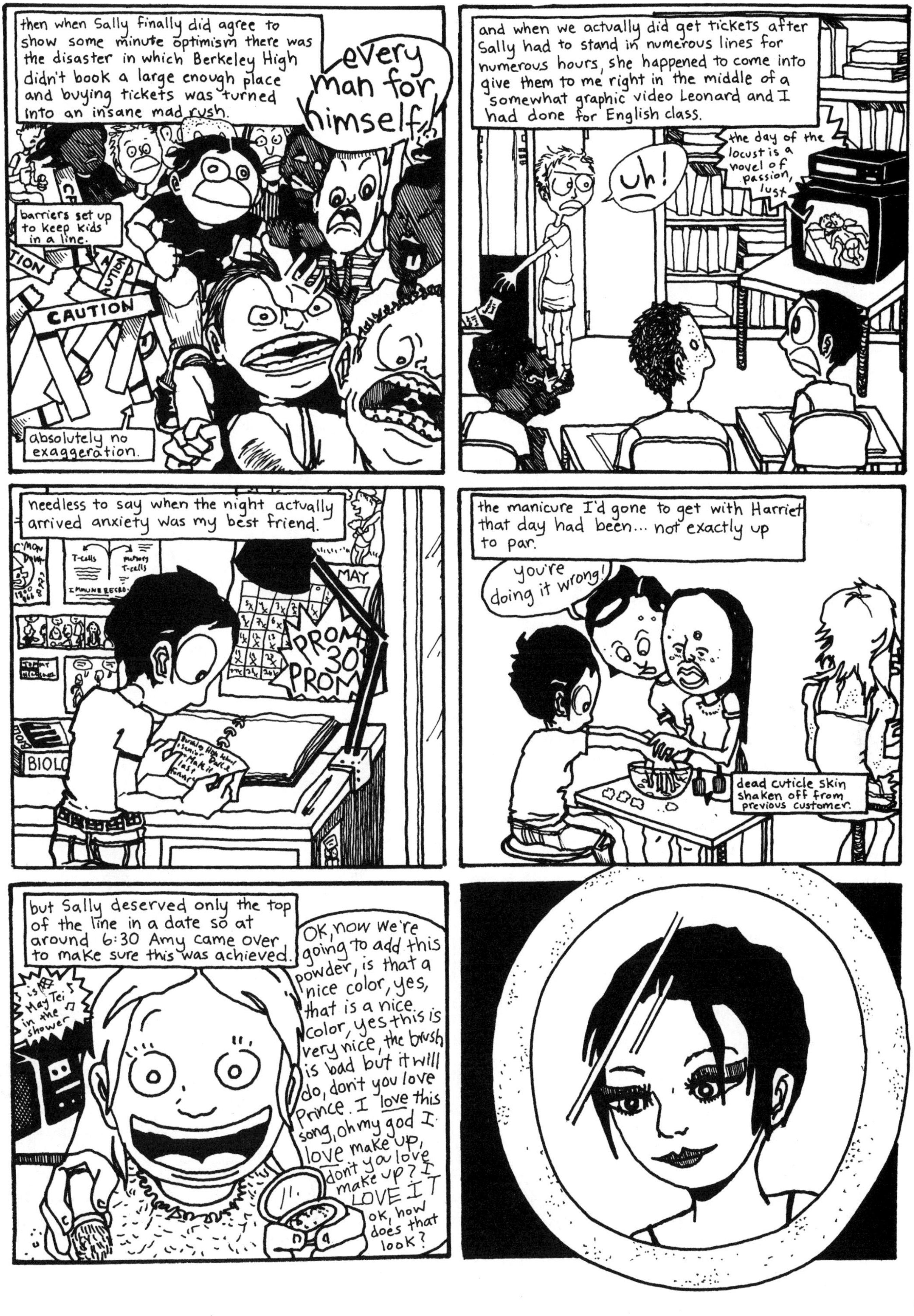

then when Sally finally did agree to show some minute optimism there was the disaster in which Berkeley High didn't book a large enough place and buying tickets was turned into an insane mad rush.
every man for himself!
barriers set up to keep kids in a line.
CAUTION
absolutely no exaggeration.
and when we actually did get tickets after Sally had to stand in numerous lines for numerous hours, she happened to come into give them to me right in the middle of a somewhat graphic video Leonard and I had done for English class.
the day of the locust is a novel of passion, lust,
uh!
needless to say when the night actually arrived anxiety was my best friend.
MAY
PROM 30 PROM
BIOLO
the manicure I'd gone to get with Harriet that day had been... not exactly up to par.
you're doing it wrong!
dead cuticle skin shaken off from previous customer.
but Sally deserved only the top of the line in a date so at around 6:30 Amy came over to make sure this was achieved.
is May Tei in the shower
OK, now we're going to add this powder, is that a nice color, yes, that is a nice color, yes this is very nice, the brush is bad but it will do, don't you love Prince. I love this song, oh my god I love make up, don't you love make up? I LOVE IT
ok, how does that look?

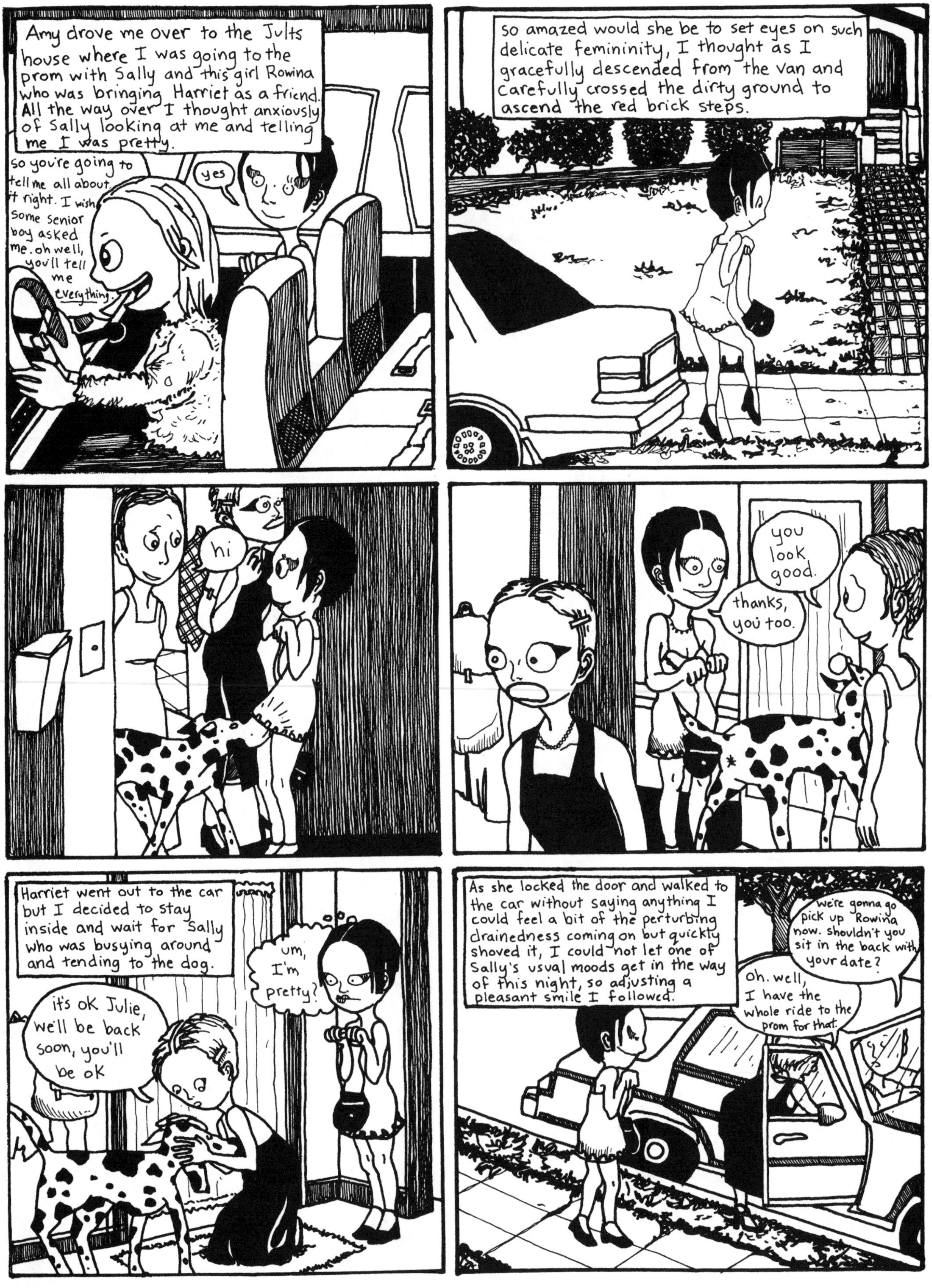

Amy drove me over to the Jults house where I was going to the prom with Sally and this girl Rowina who was bringing Harriet as a friend. All the way over I thought anxiously of Sally looking at me and telling me I was pretty.
so you're going to tell me all about it right. I wish some senior boy asked me. oh well, you'll tell me everything.
yes
So amazed would she be to set eyes on such delicate femininity, I thought as I gracefully descended from the van and carefully crossed the dirty ground to ascend the red brick steps.
hi
you look good.
thanks, you too.
Harriet went out to the car but I decided to stay inside and wait for Sally who was busying around and tending to the dog.
um, I'm pretty?
it's ok Julie, we'll be back soon, you'll be ok
As she locked the door and walked to the car without saying anything I could feel a bit of the perturbing drainedness coming on but quickly shoved it, I could not let one of Sally's usual moods get in the way of this night, so adjusting a pleasant smile I followed.
we're gonna go pick up Rowina now. shouldn't you sit in the back with your date?
oh. well, I have the whole ride to the prom for that.

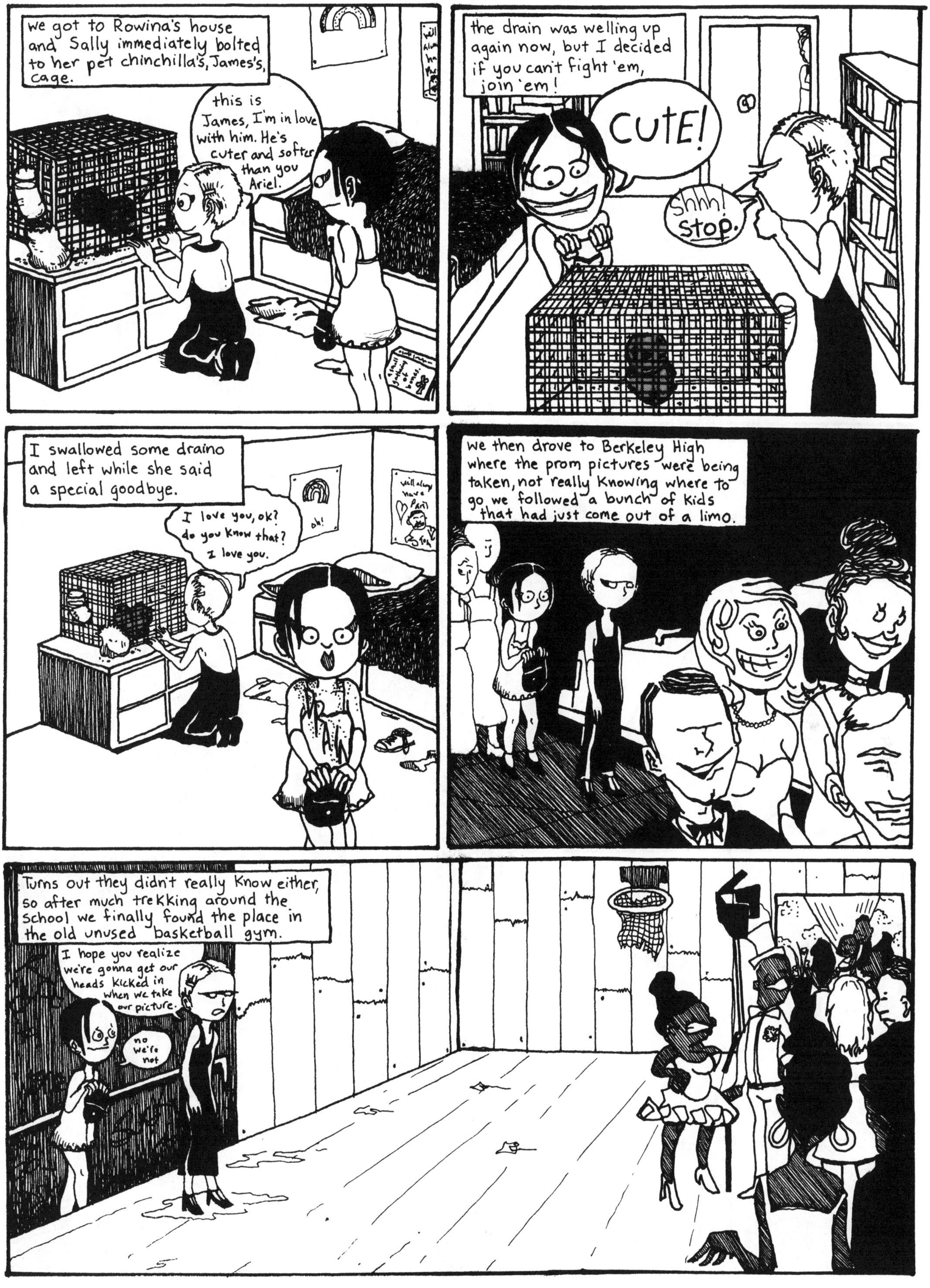
we got to Rowina's house and Sally immediately bolted to her pet chinchilla's, James's, cage.
this is James, I'm in love with him. He's cuter and softer than you Ariel.
the drain was welling up again now, but I decided if you can't fight 'em, join 'em!
CUTE!
Shhh! Stop.
I swallowed some draino and left while she said a special goodbye.
I love you, ok? do you know that? I love you.
we then drove to Berkeley High where the prom pictures were being taken, not really knowing where to go we followed a bunch of kids that had just come out of a limo.
Turns out they didn't really know either, so after much trekking around the school we finally found the place in the old unused basketball gym.
I hope you realize we're gonna get our heads kicked in when we take our picture.
no we're not

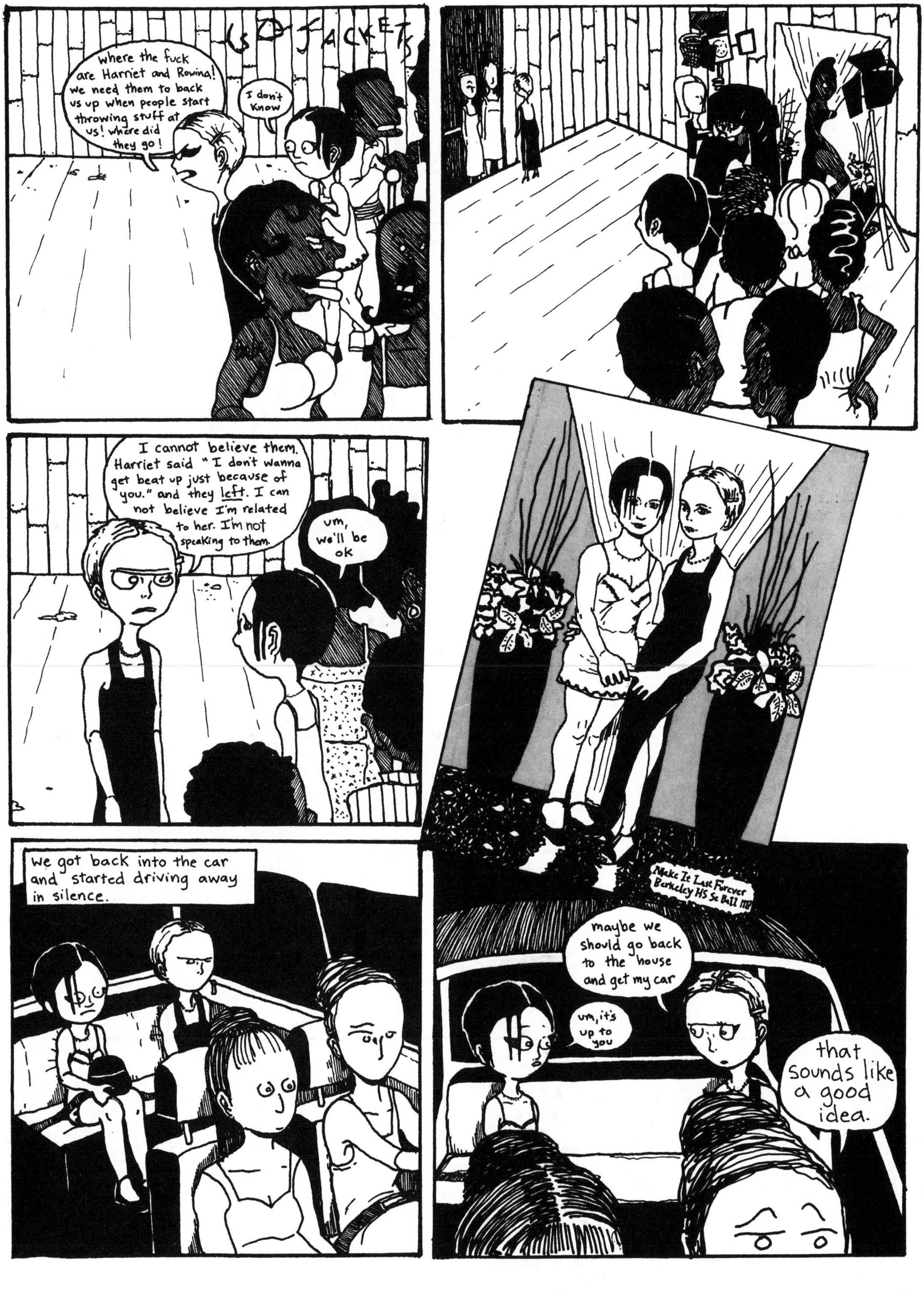

where the fuck are Harriet and Rowina! we need them to back us up when people start throwing stuff at us! where did they go!
I don't know
I cannot believe them. Harriet said "I don't wanna get beat up just because of you." and they left. I can not believe I'm related to her. I'm not speaking to them.
um, we'll be ok
Make It Last Forever
Berkeley HS Sr Ball
We got back into the car and started driving away in silence.
maybe we should go back to the house and get my car
um, it's up to you
that sounds like a good idea.

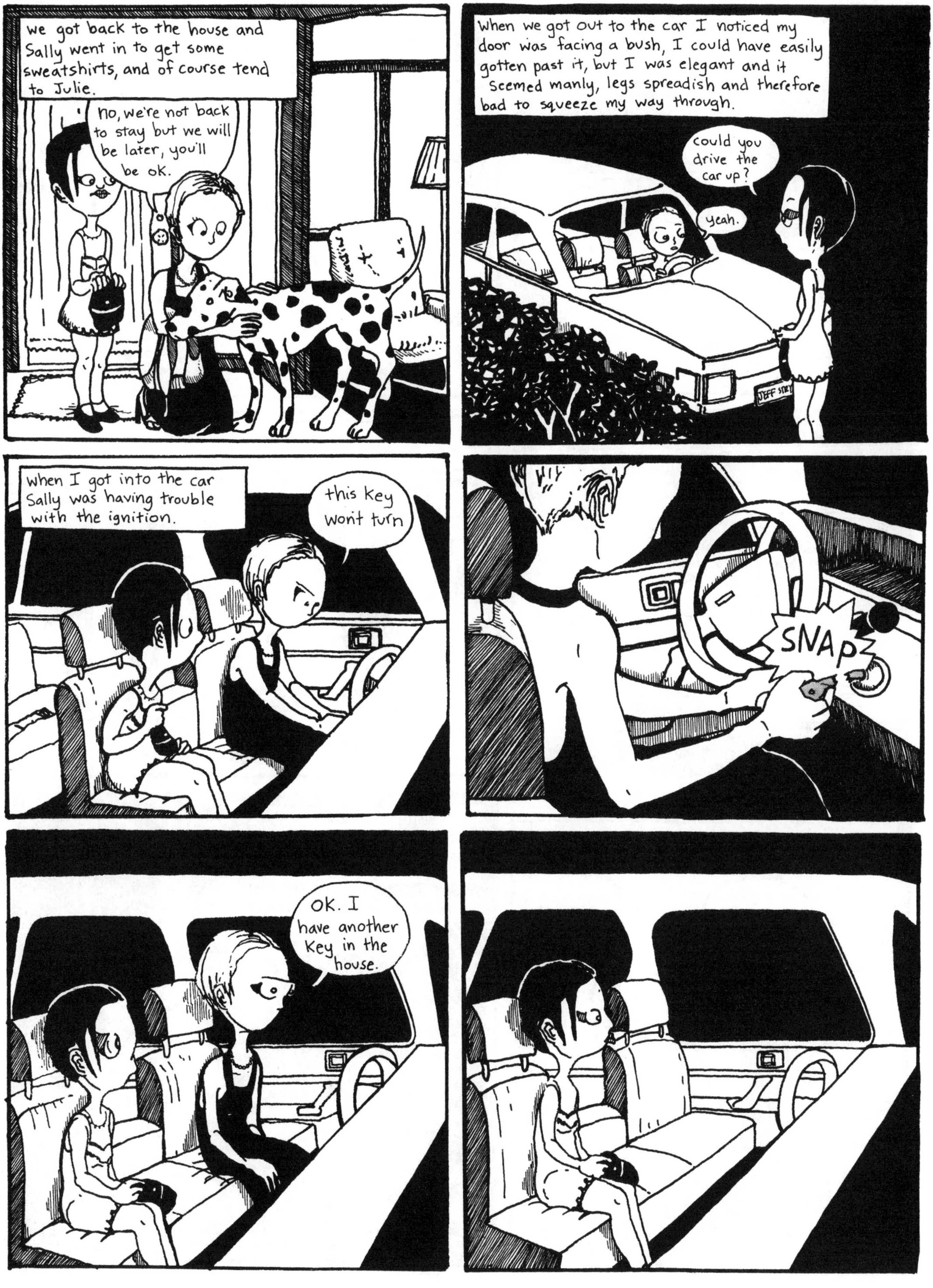
we got back to the house and Sally went in to get some sweatshirts, and of course tend to Julie.
no, we're not back to stay but we will be later, you'll be ok.
When we got out to the car I noticed my door was facing a bush, I could have easily gotten past it, but I was elegant and it seemed manly, legs spreadish and therefore bad to squeeze my way through.
could you drive the car up?
yeah.
when I got into the car Sally was having trouble with the ignition.
this key won't turn
SNAP
OK. I have another key in the house.

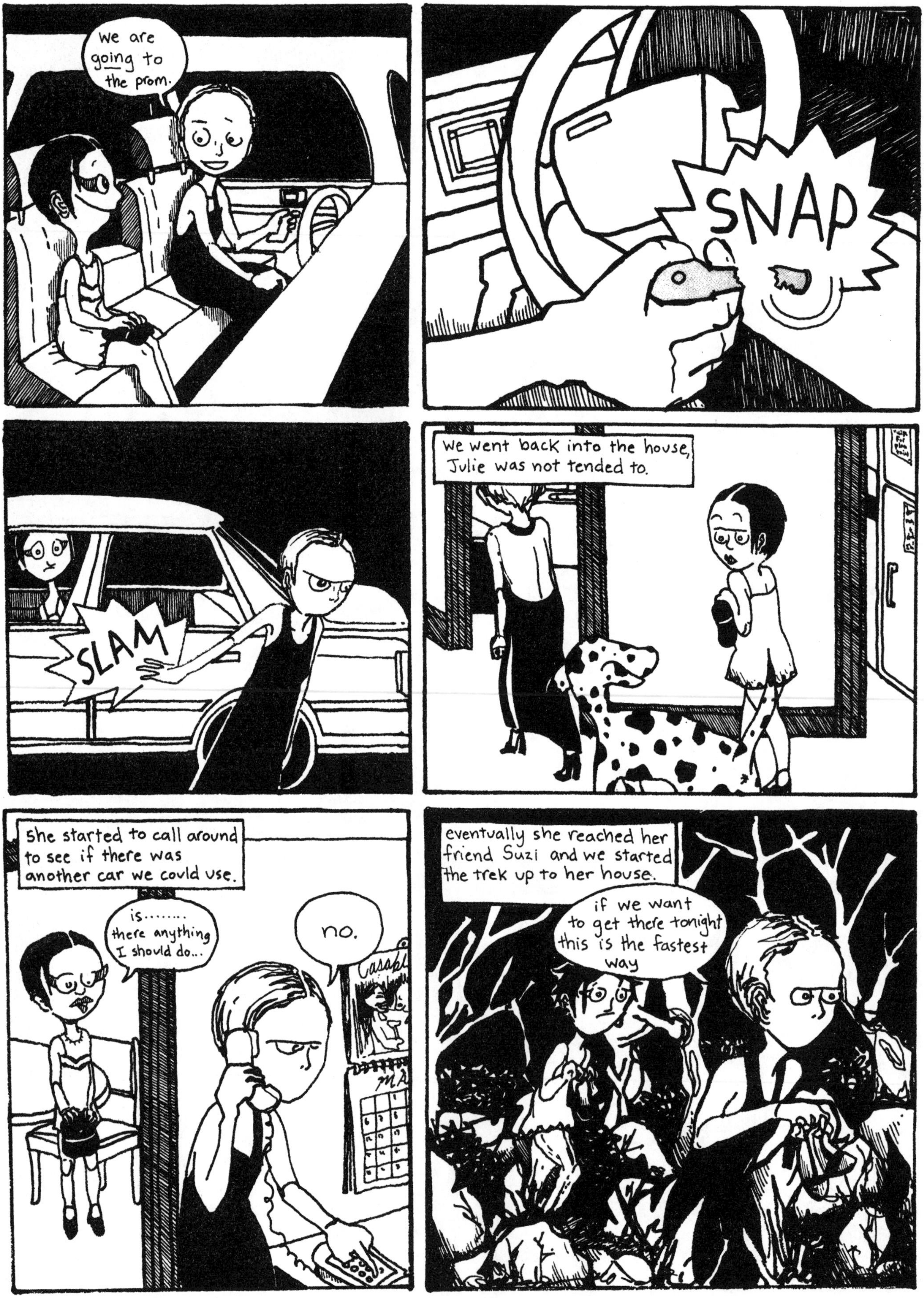
we are going to the prom.
SNAP
SLAM
We went back into the house, Julie was not tended to.
she started to call around to see if there was another car we could use.
is........ there anything I should do...
no.
eventually she reached her friend Suzi and we started the trek up to her house.
if we want to get there tonight this is the fastest way

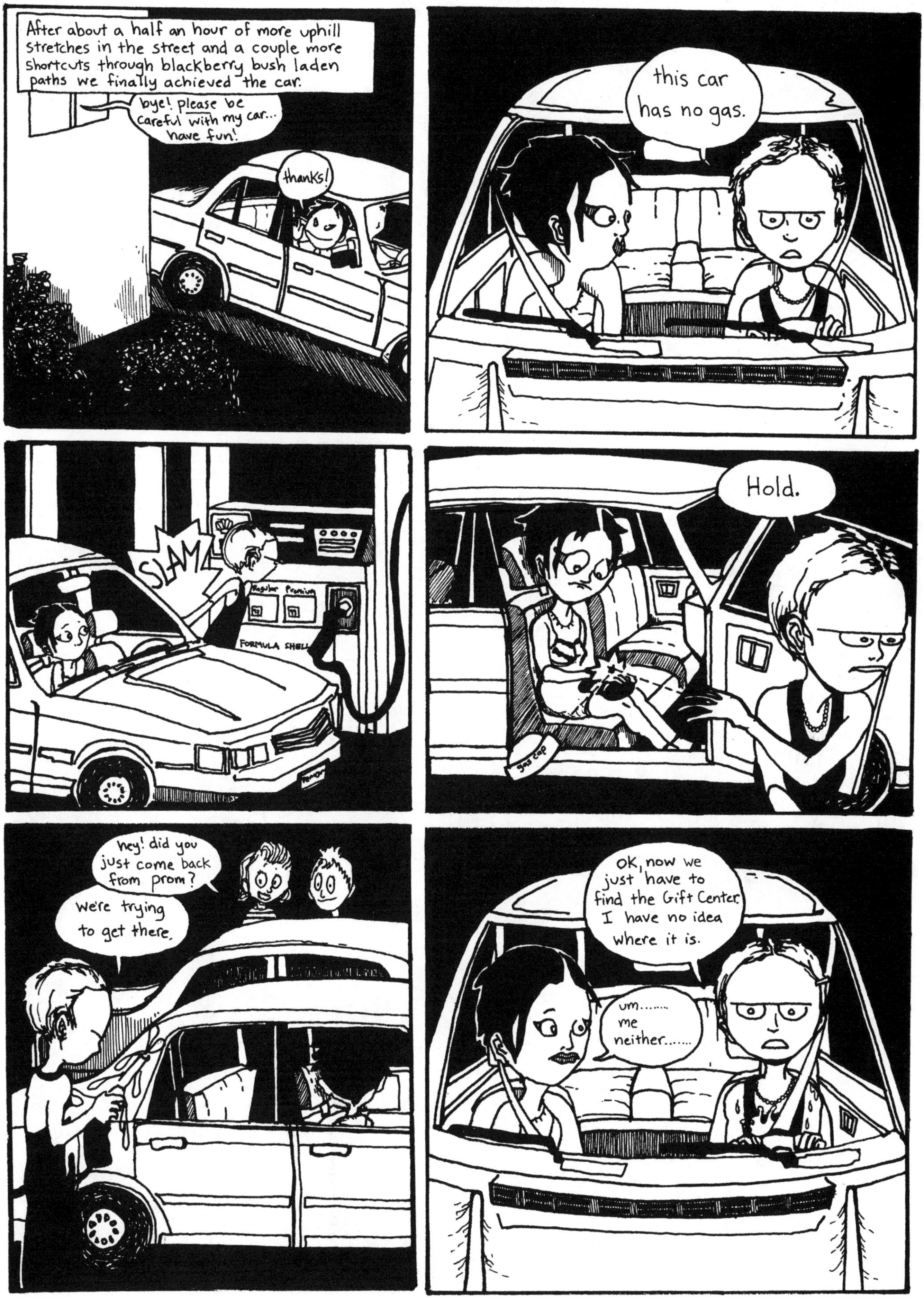
After about a half an hour of more uphill stretches in the street and a couple more shortcuts through blackberry bush laden paths we finally achieved the car.
bye! please be careful with my car... have fun!
thanks!
this car has no gas.
SLAM
Regular Premium
FORMULA SHELL
Hold.
gas cap
hey! did you just come back from prom?
we're trying to get there.
OK, now we just have to find the Gift Center. I have no idea where it is.
um....... me neither.......

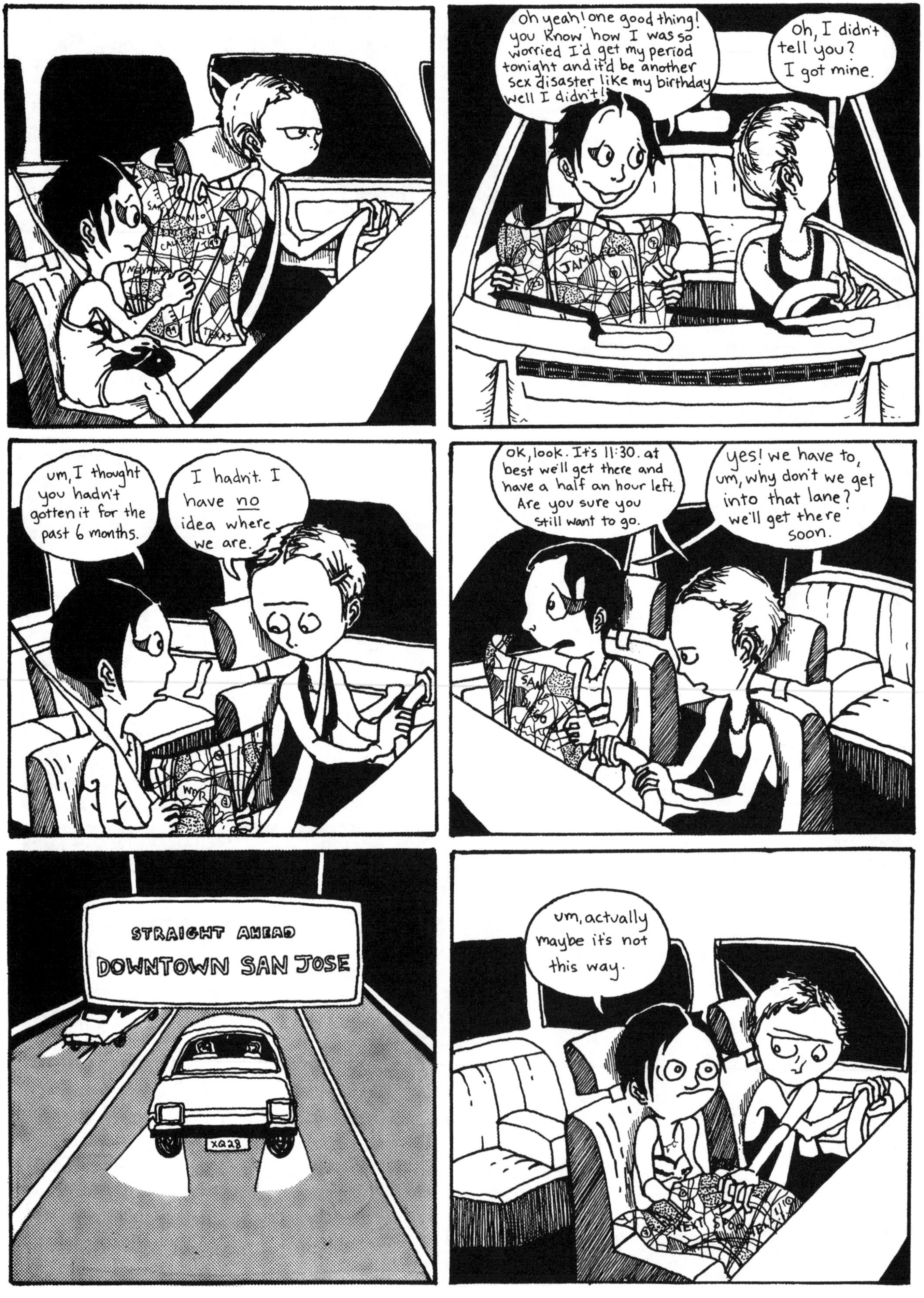
Oh yeah! one good thing! you know how I was so worried I'd get my period tonight and it'd be another sex disaster like my birthday well I didn't!
Oh, I didn't tell you? I got mine.
um, I thought you hadn't gotten it for the past 6 months.
I hadn't. I have no idea where we are.
OK, look. It's 11:30. at best we'll get there and have a half an hour left. Are you sure you still want to go.
yes! we have to, um, why don't we get into that lane? we'll get there soon.
STRAIGHT AHEAD
DOWNTOWN SAN JOSE
XQ28
um, actually maybe it's not this way.

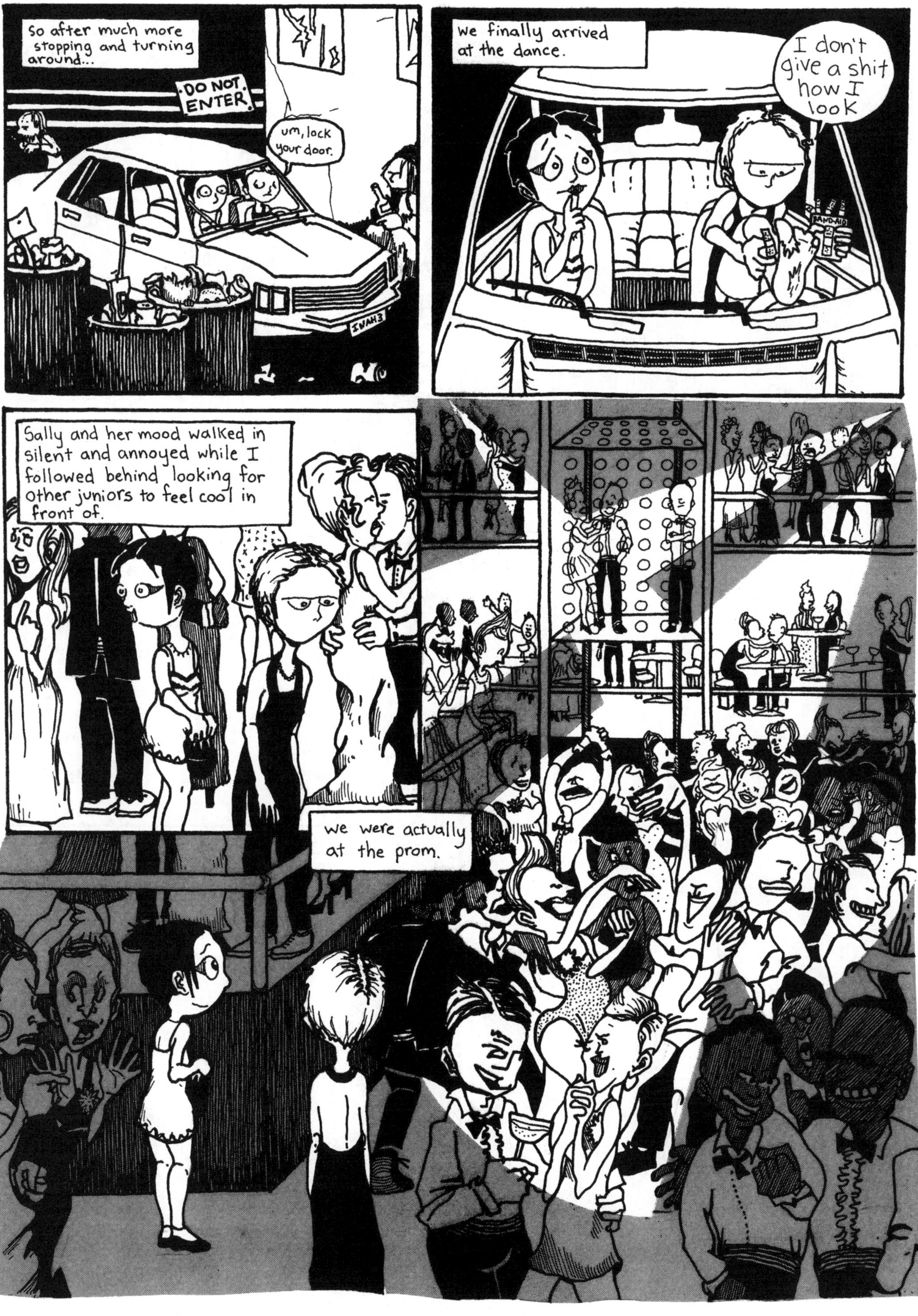

so after much more stopping and turning around...
DO NOT ENTER
IVAN3
um, lock your door.
we finally arrived at the dance.
I don't give a shit how I look
BAND-AID
Sally and her mood walked in silent and annoyed while I followed behind looking for other juniors to feel cool in front of.
we were actually at the prom.

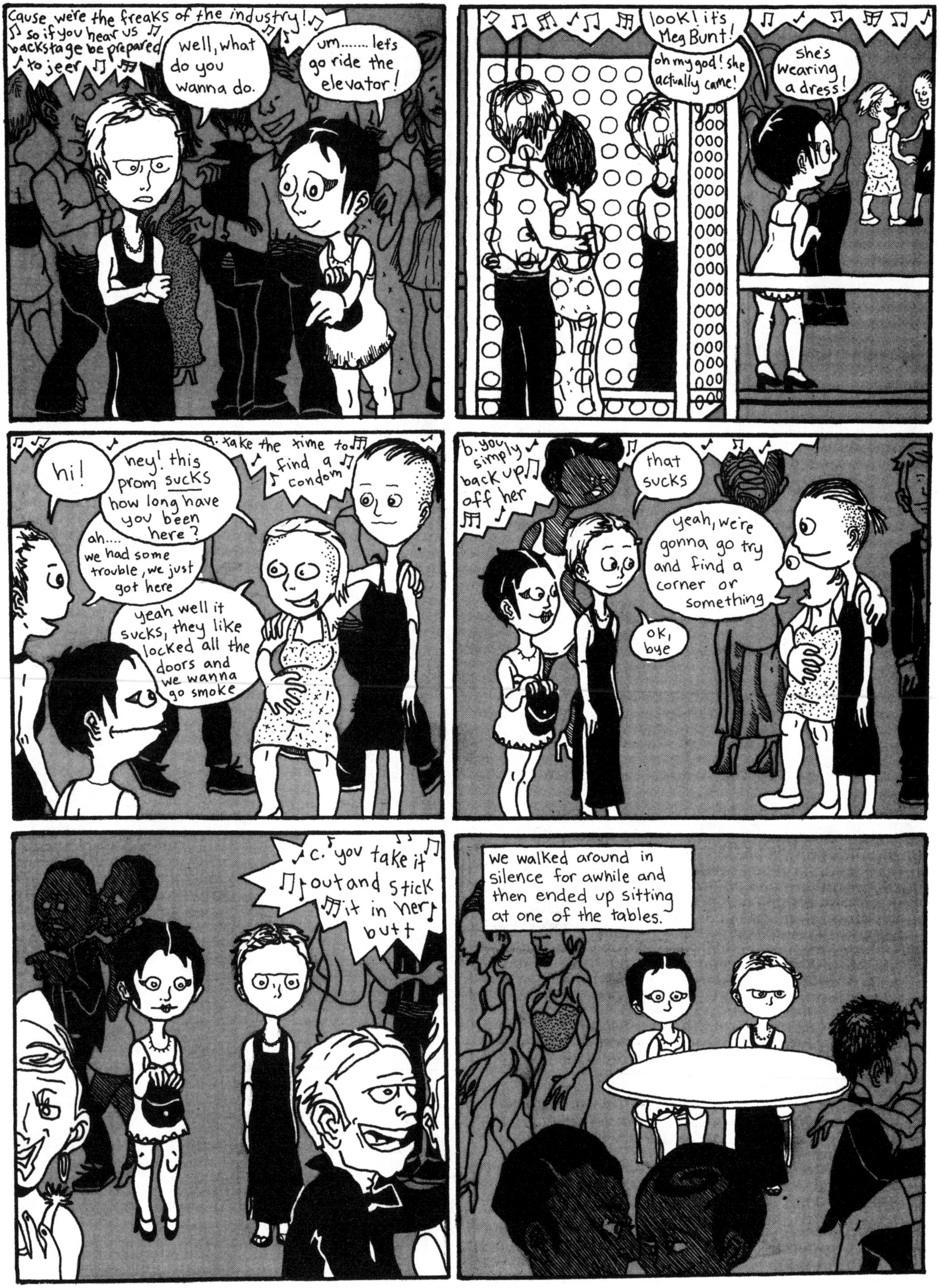
Cause we're the freaks of the industry! so if you hear us backstage be prepared to jeer
well, what do you wanna do.
um....... let's go ride the elevator!
look! it's Meg Bunt!
oh my god! she actually came!
she's wearing a dress!
hi!
hey! this prom sucks how long have you been here?
a. take the time to find a condom
ah.... we had some trouble, we just got here
yeah well it sucks, they like locked all the doors and we wanna go smoke
b. you simply back up off her
that sucks
yeah, we're gonna go try and find a corner or something
ok, bye
c. you take it out and stick it in her butt
We walked around in silence for awhile and then ended up sitting at one of the tables.

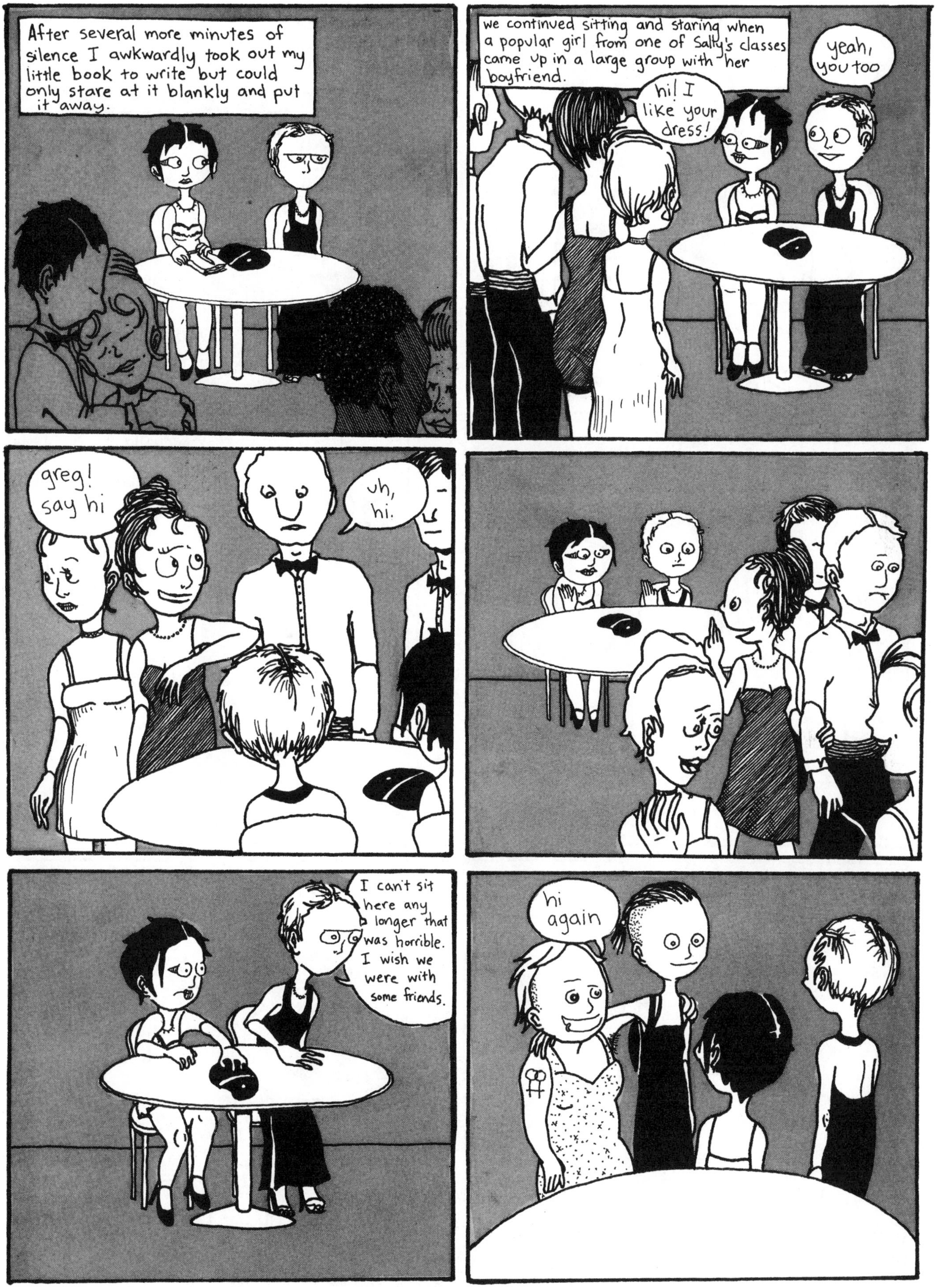
After several more minutes of silence I awkwardly took out my little book to write but could only stare at it blankly and put it away.
we continued sitting and staring when a popular girl from one of Salty's classes came up in a large group with her boyfriend.
hi! I like your dress!
yeah, you too
greg! say hi
uh, hi.
I can't sit here any longer that was horrible. I wish we were with some friends.
hi again

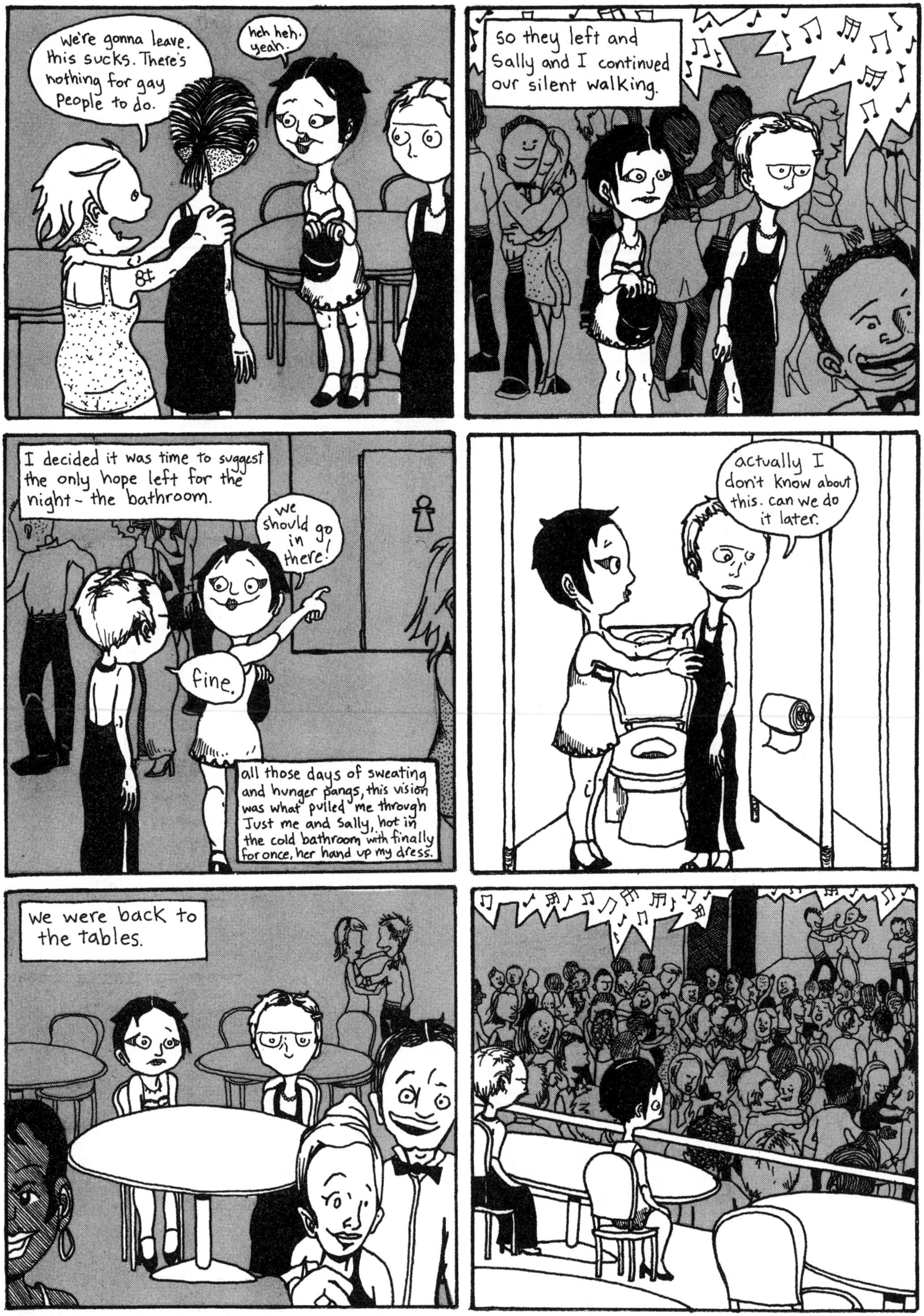
we're gonna leave. this sucks. There's nothing for gay people to do.
heh heh. yeah.
8¢
so they left and Sally and I continued our silent walking.
I decided it was time to suggest the only hope left for the night- the bathroom.
we should go in there!
fine.
all those days of sweating and hunger pangs, this vision was what pulled me through Just me and Sally, hot in the cold bathroom with finally for once, her hand up my dress.
actually I don't know about this. can we do it later.
we were back to the tables.

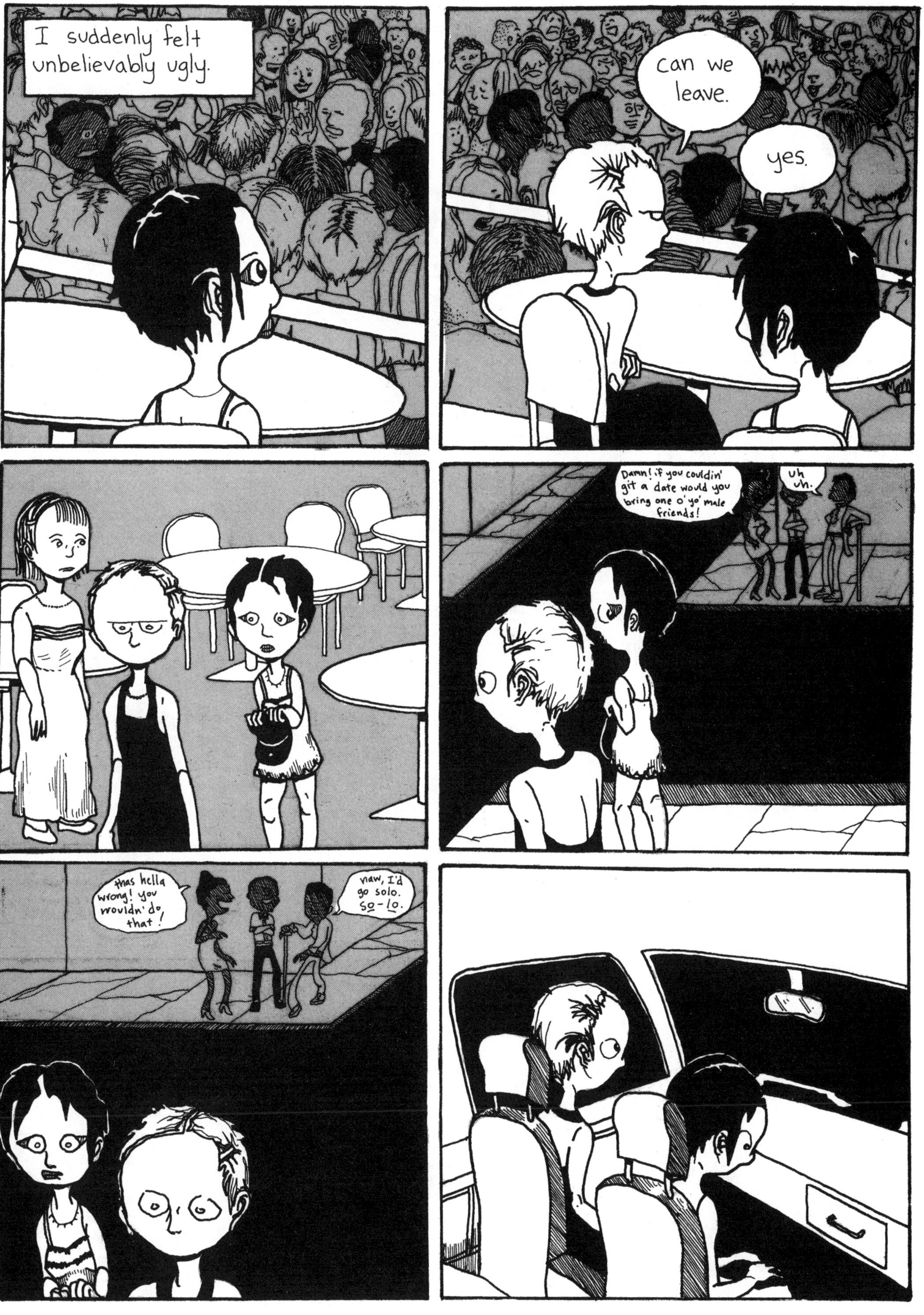

I suddenly felt unbelievably ugly.
can we leave.
yes.
Damn! if you couldin' git a date would you bring one o' yo' male friends!
uh uh.
thas hella wrong! you wouldn' do that!
naw, I'd go solo. so-lo.

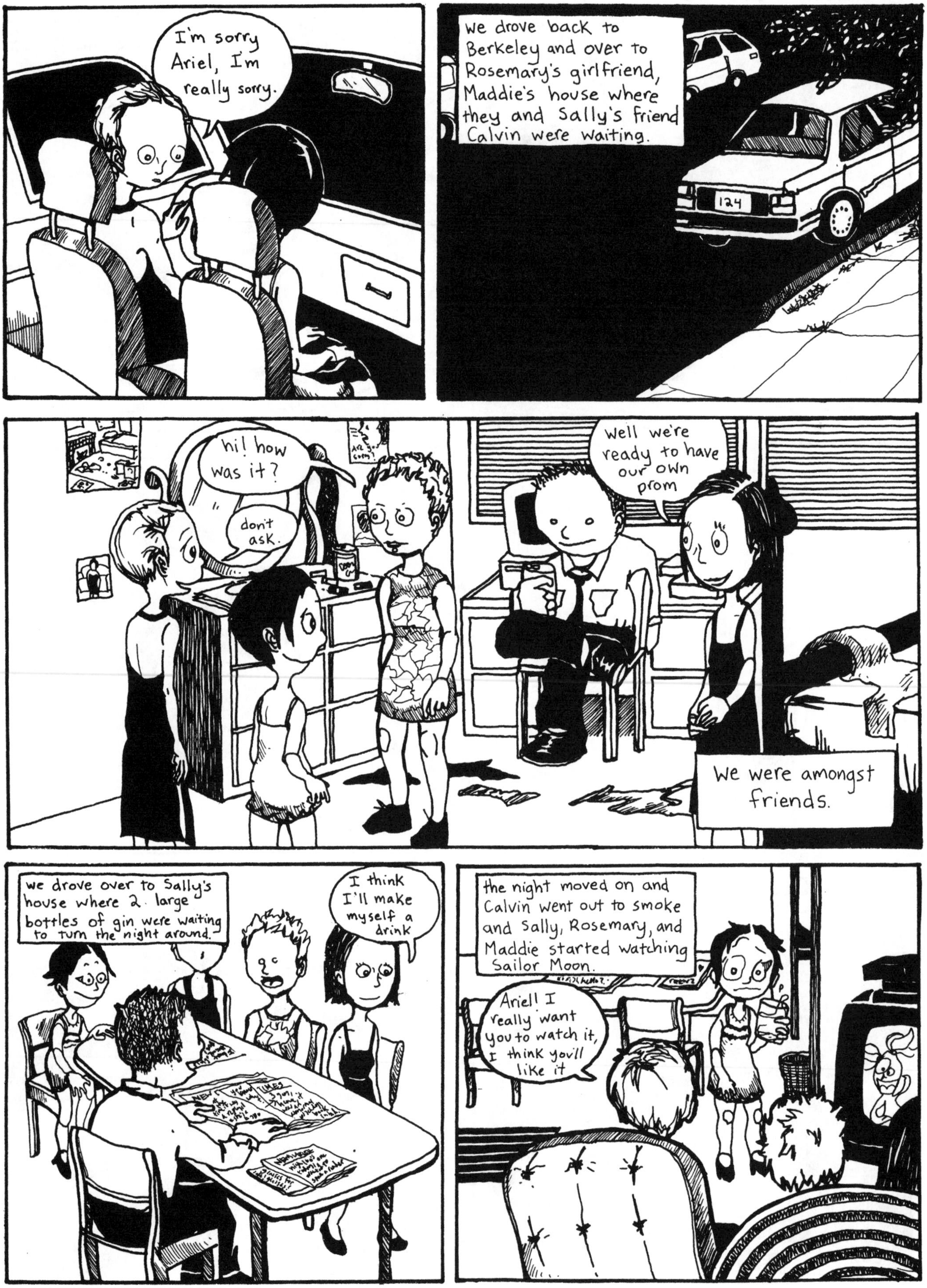
I'm sorry Ariel, I'm really sorry.
We drove back to Berkeley and over to Rosemary's girlfriend, Maddie's house where they and Sally's friend Calvin were waiting.
124
hi! how was it?
don't ask.
Well we're ready to have our own prom
We were amongst friends.
we drove over to Sally's house where 2 large bottles of gin were waiting to turn the night around.
I think I'll make myself a drink
the night moved on and Calvin went out to smoke and Sally, Rosemary, and Maddie started watching Sailor Moon.
Ariel! I really want you to watch it, I think you'll like it

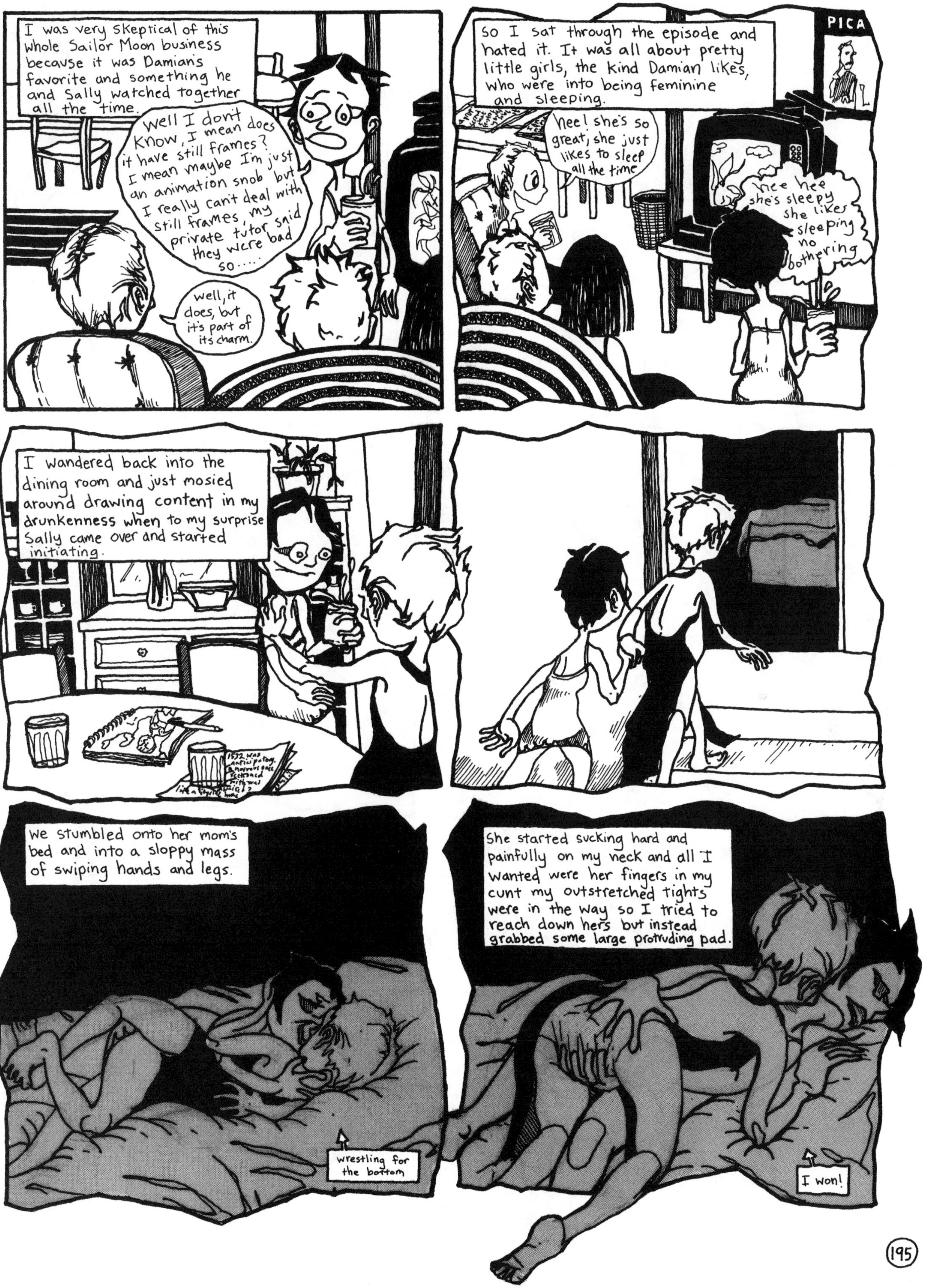
I was very skeptical of this whole Sailor Moon business because it was Damian's favorite and something he and Sally watched together all the time.
Well I don't know, I mean does it have still frames? I mean maybe I'm just an animation snob but I really can't deal with still frames, my private tutor said they were bad so.....
well, it does, but it's part of its charm.
So I sat through the episode and hated it. It was all about pretty little girls, the kind Damian likes, who were into being feminine and sleeping.
PICA
hee! she's so great, she just likes to sleep all the time
hee hee she's sleepy she likes sleeping no bothering
I wandered back into the dining room and just mosied around drawing content in my drunkenness when to my surprise Sally came over and started initiating.
We stumbled onto her mom's bed and into a sloppy mass of swiping hands and legs.
wrestling for the bottom
She started sucking hard and painfully on my neck and all I wanted were her fingers in my cunt my outstretched tights were in the way so I tried to reach down hers but instead grabbed some large protruding pad.
I won!

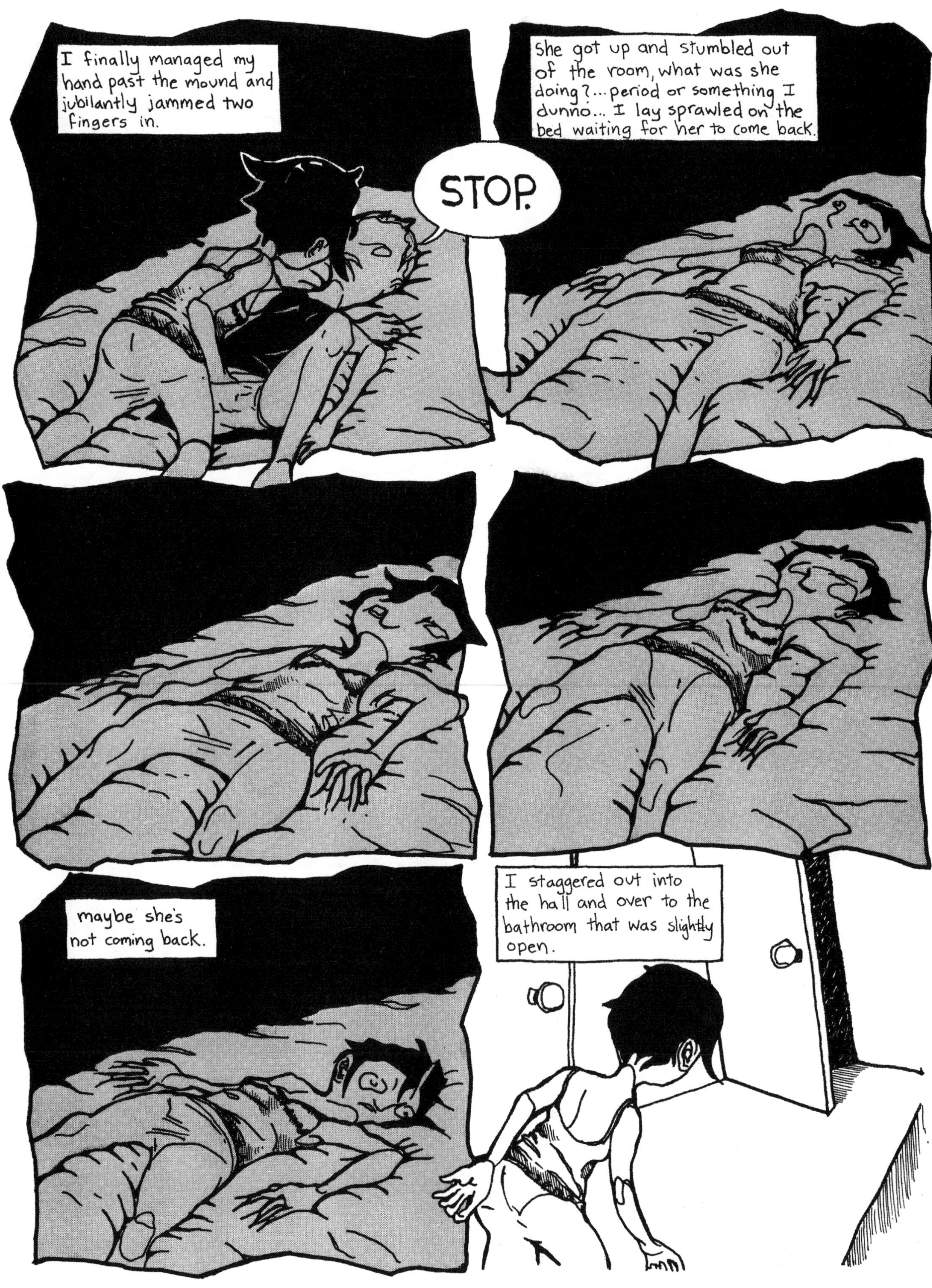
I finally managed my hand past the mound and jubilantly jammed two fingers in.
STOP.
She got up and stumbled out of the room, what was she doing?...period or something I dunno... I lay sprawled on the bed waiting for her to come back.
maybe she's not coming back.
I staggered out into the hall and over to the bathroom that was slightly open.

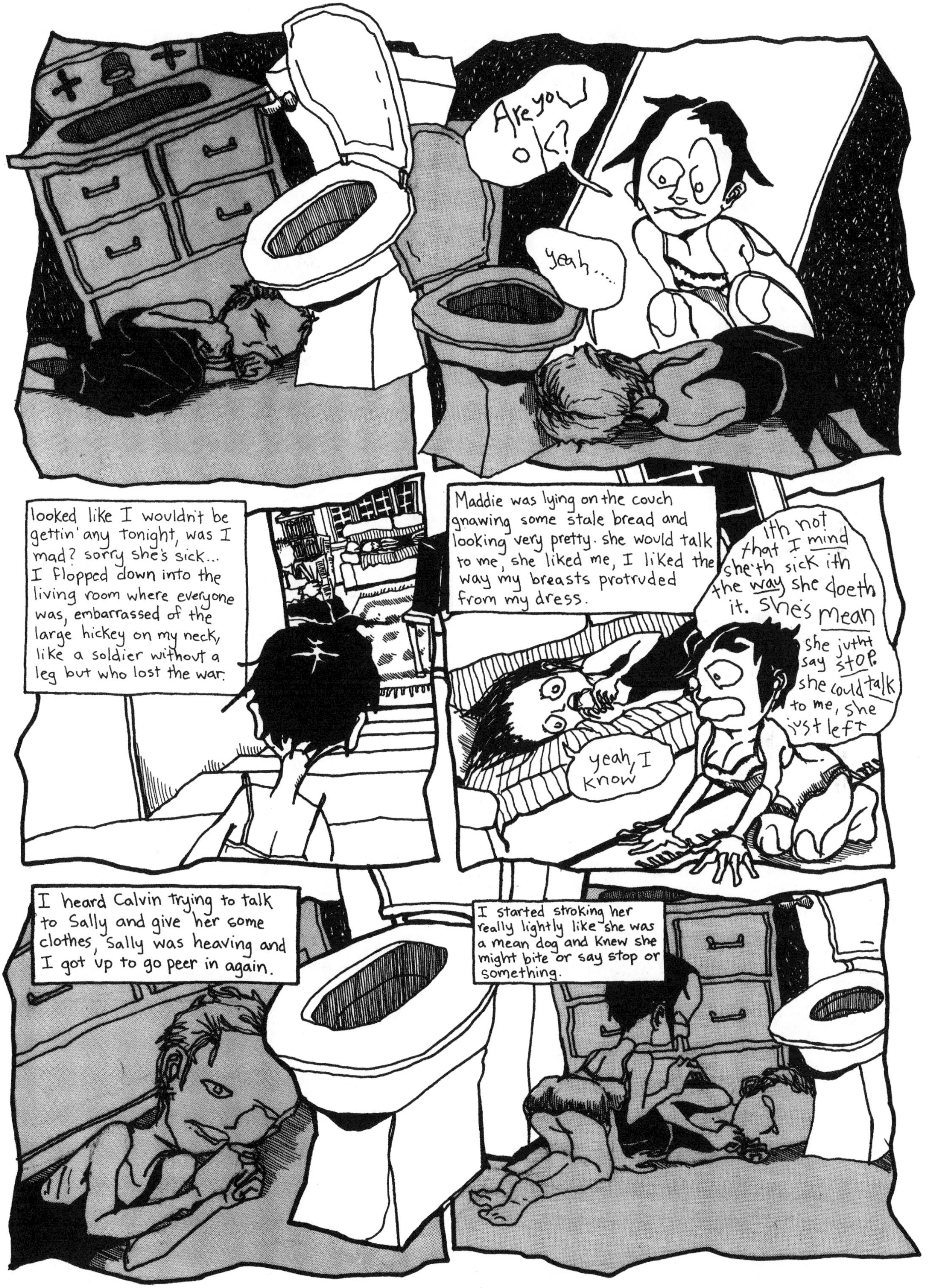
Are you ok?
yeah.....
looked like I wouldn't be gettin' any tonight, was I mad? sorry she's sick... I flopped down into the living room where everyone was, embarrassed of the large hickey on my neck, like a soldier without a leg but who lost the war.
Maddie was lying on the couch gnawing some stale bread and looking very pretty. she would talk to me, she liked me, I liked the way my breasts protruded from my dress.
ith not that I mind she'th sick ith the way she doeth it. She's Mean she jutht say stop. she could talk to me, she just left
yeah, I know
I heard Calvin trying to talk to Sally and give her some clothes, Sally was heaving and I got up to go peer in again.
I started stroking her really lightly like she was a mean dog and knew she might bite or say stop or something.

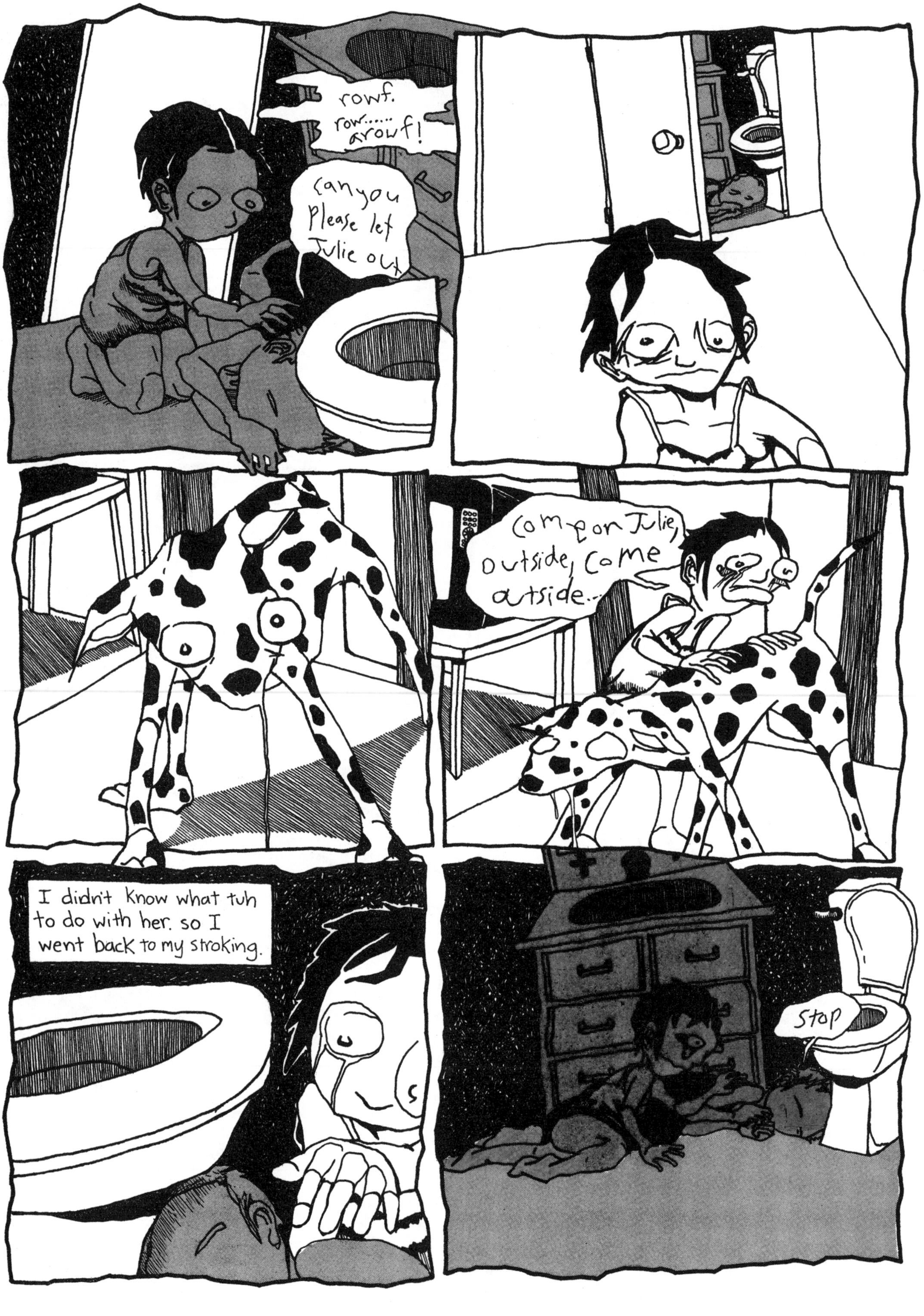
rowf. row...... arowf!
can you please let Julie out
Come on Julie, outside, come outside...
I didn't know what tuh to do with her. so I went back to my stroking.
Stop

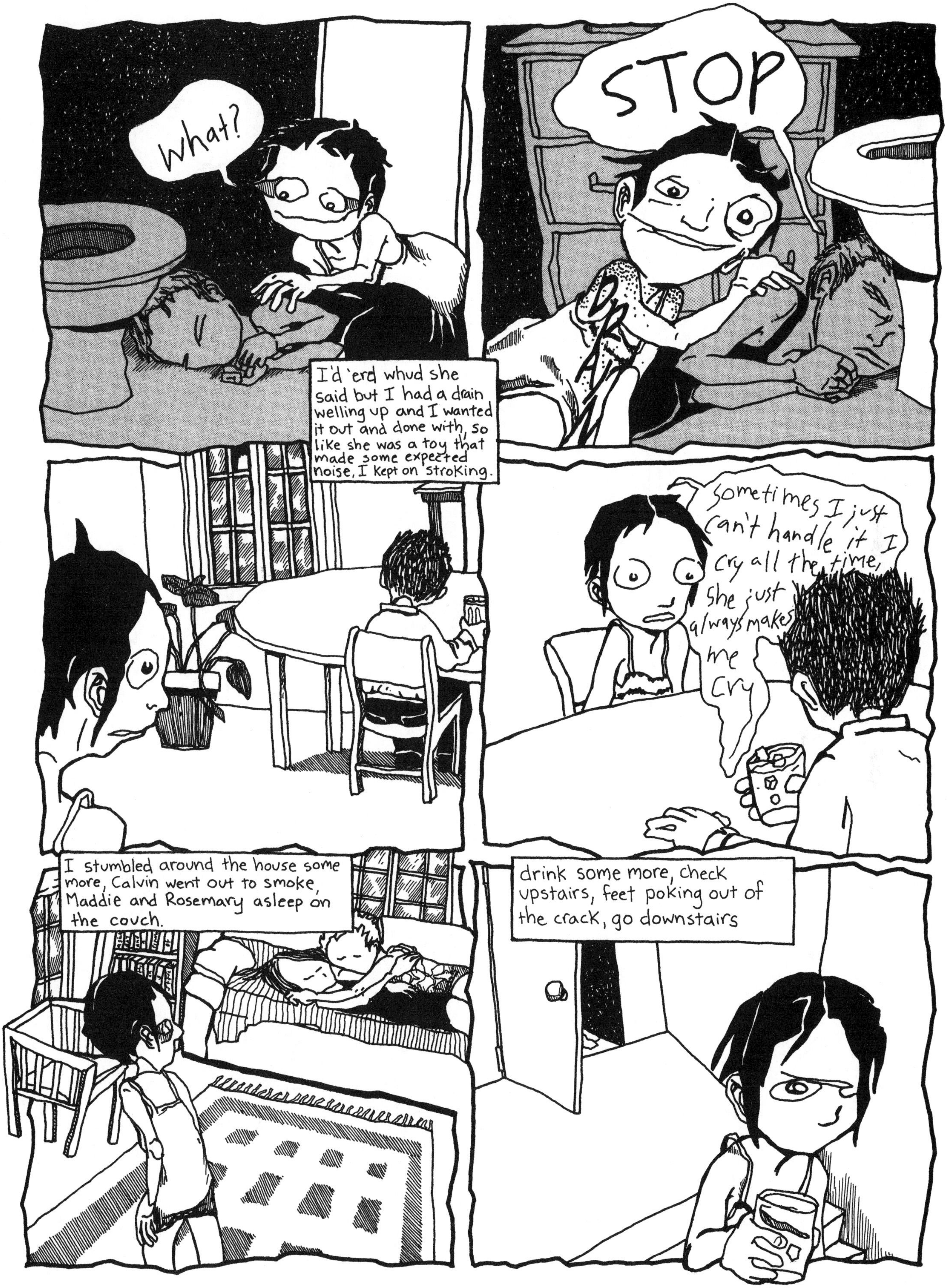

what?
STOP
I'd 'erd whud she said but I had a drain welling up and I wanted it out and done with, so like she was a toy that made some expected noise, I kept on stroKing.
sometimes I just can't handle it I cry all the time, she just always makes me cry
I stumbled around the house some more, Calvin went out to smoke, Maddie and Rosemary asleep on the couch.
drink some more, check upstairs, feet poking out of the crack, go downstairs

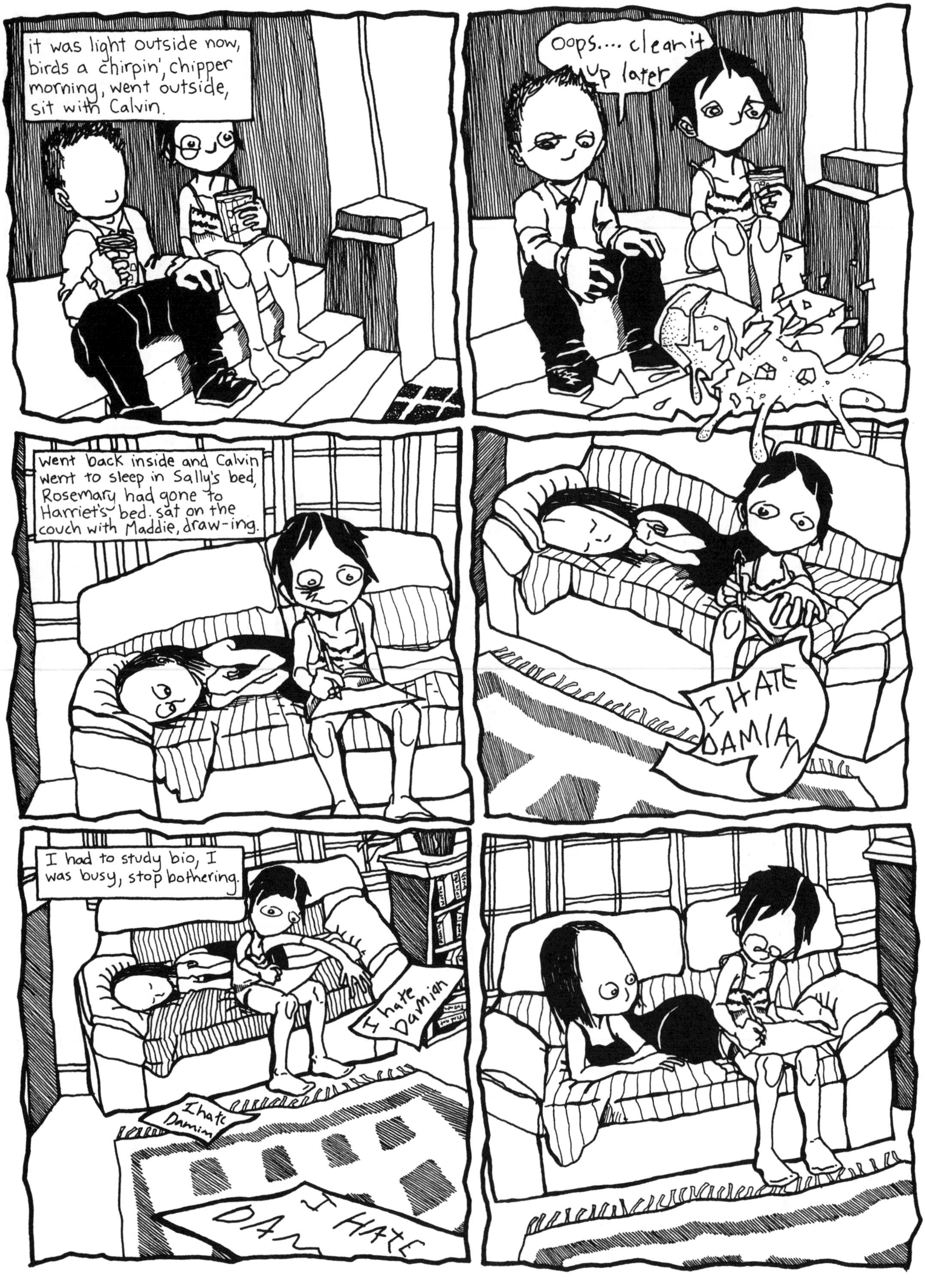
it was light outside now, birds a chirpin', chipper morning, went outside, sit with Calvin.
Oops.... cleanit up later
Went back inside and Calvin went to sleep in Sally's bed, Rosemary had gone to Harriet's bed. sat on the couch with Maddie, draw-ing.
I HATE DAMIAN
I had to study bio, I was busy, stop bothering.
I hate Damian
I hate Damian
I HATE DAM

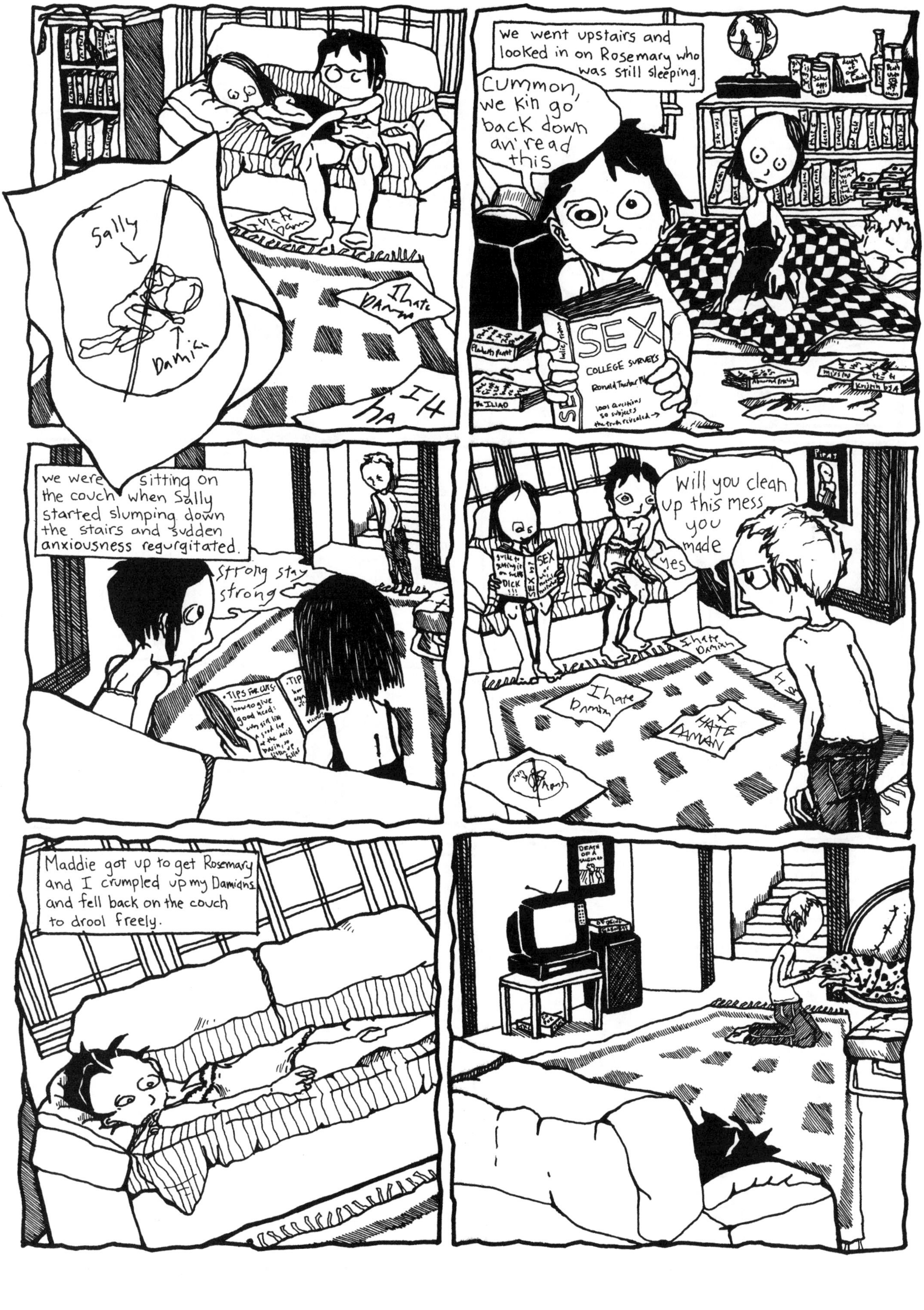
Sally
Damien
I hate Dam
I hate DAMIAN
I H
HA
we went upstairs and looked in on Rosemary who was still sleeping.
Cummon, we kin go back down an' read this
SEX
COLLEGE SURVEYS
Ronald Tucker PhD
1001 Questions
50 subjects
the truth revealed →
The ILIAD
we were sitting on the couch when Sally started slumping down the stairs and sudden anxiousness regurgitated.
strong stay strong
TIPS FOR GIRLS
how to give good head:
DICK
Will you clean up this mess you made
Yes
I hate Damian
I hate DAMIAN
I HATE DAMAN
Maddie got up to get Rosemary and I crumpled up my Damians and fell back on the couch to drool freely.
DEATH OF A SALESMAN

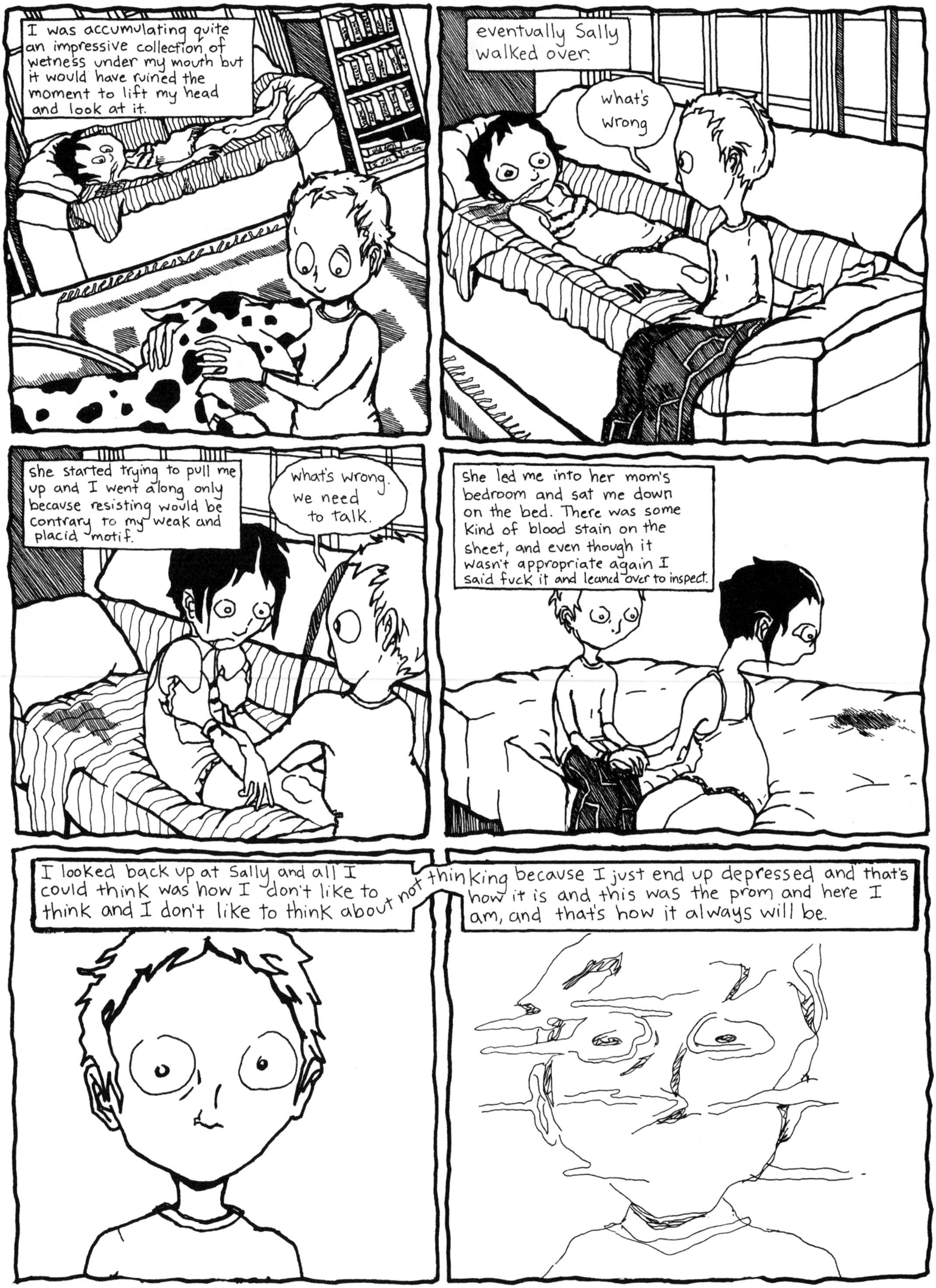
I was accumulating quite an impressive collection of wetness under my mouth but it would have ruined the moment to lift my head and look at it.
eventually Sally walked over.
what's wrong
she started trying to pull me up and I went along only because resisting would be contrary to my weak and placid motif.
what's wrong. we need to talk.
she led me into her mom's bedroom and sat me down on the bed. There was some kind of blood stain on the sheet, and even though it wasn't appropriate again I said fuck it and leaned over to inspect.
I looked back up at Sally and all I could think was how I don't like to think and I don't like to think about not thinking because I just end up depressed and that's how it is and this was the prom and here I am, and that's how it always will be.

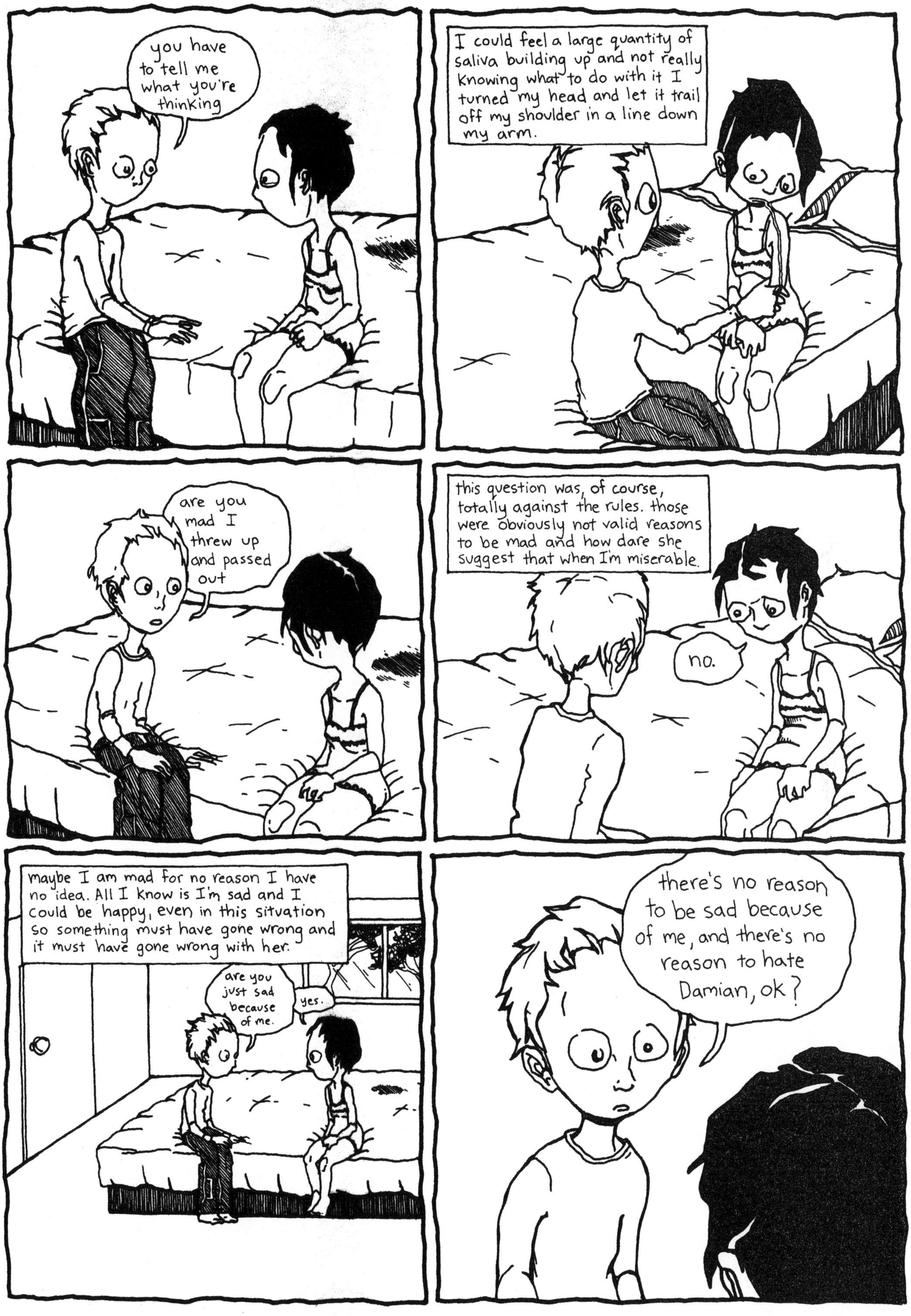
you have to tell me what you're thinking
I could feel a large quantity of saliva building up and not really knowing what to do with it I turned my head and let it trail off my shoulder in a line down my arm.
are you mad I threw up and passed out
this question was, of course, totally against the rules. those were obviously not valid reasons to be mad and how dare she suggest that when I'm miserable.
no.
maybe I am mad for no reason I have no idea. All I know is I'm sad and I could be happy, even in this situation so something must have gone wrong and it must have gone wrong with her.
are you just sad because of me.
yes.
there's no reason to be sad because of me, and there's no reason to hate Damian, ok?

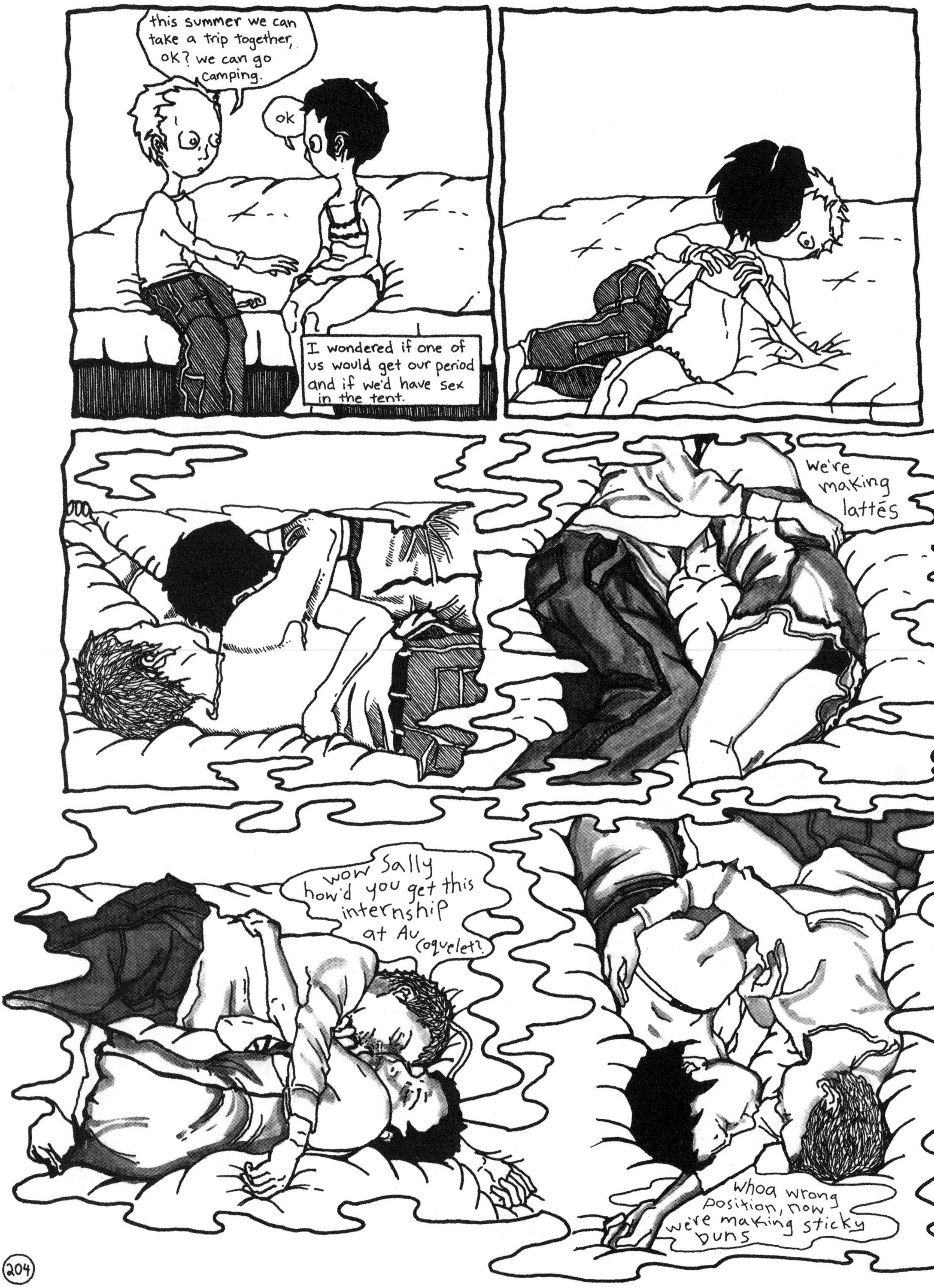
this summer we can take a trip together, ok? we can go camping.
ok
I wondered if one of us would get our period and if we'd have sex in the tent.
we're making lattes
wow Sally how'd you get this internship at Au Coquelet?
whoa wrong position, now we're making sticky buns

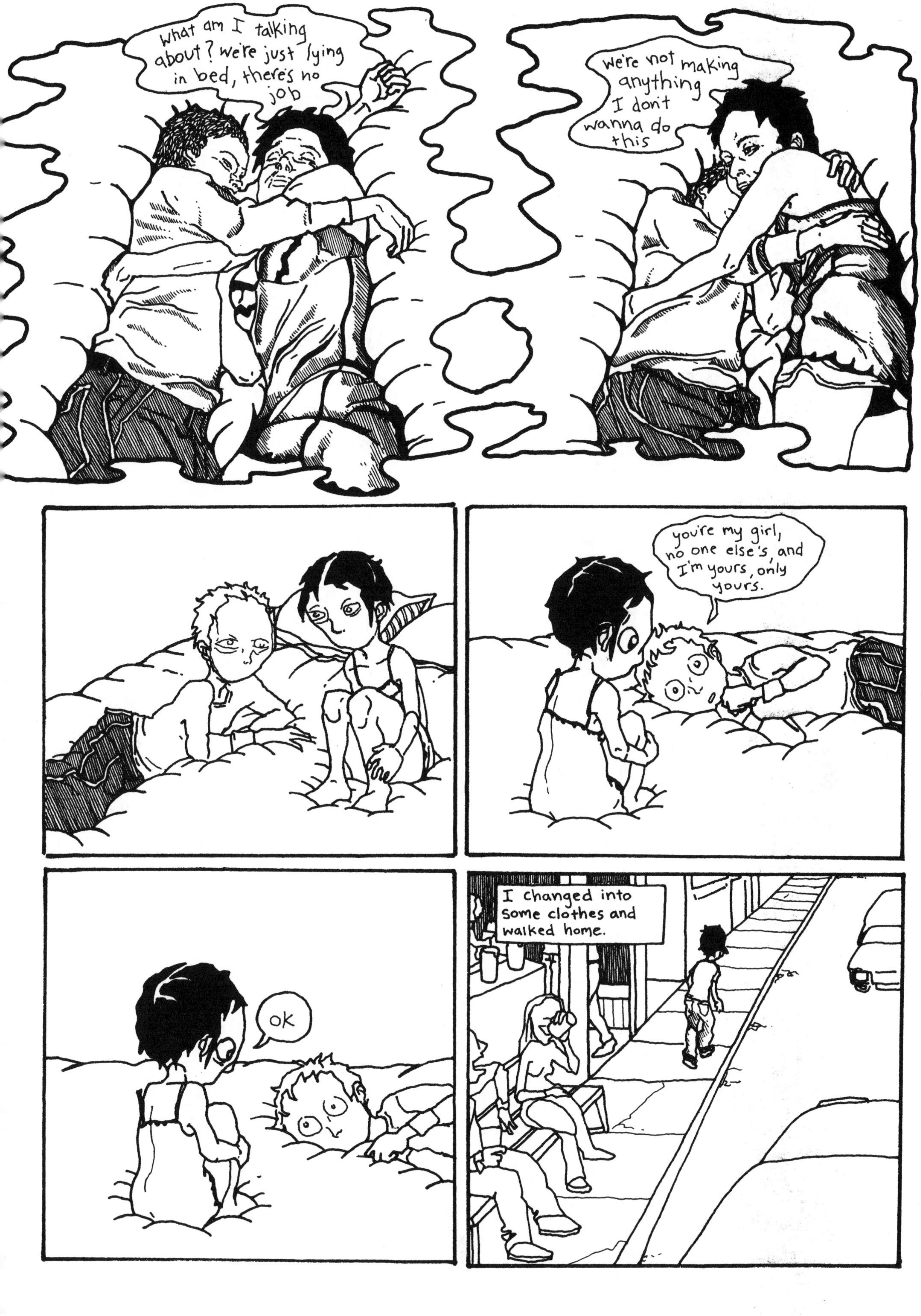
what am I talking about? we're just lying in bed, there's no job
we're not making anything I don't wanna do this
you're my girl, no one else's, and I'm yours, only yours.
ok
I changed into some clothes and walked home.

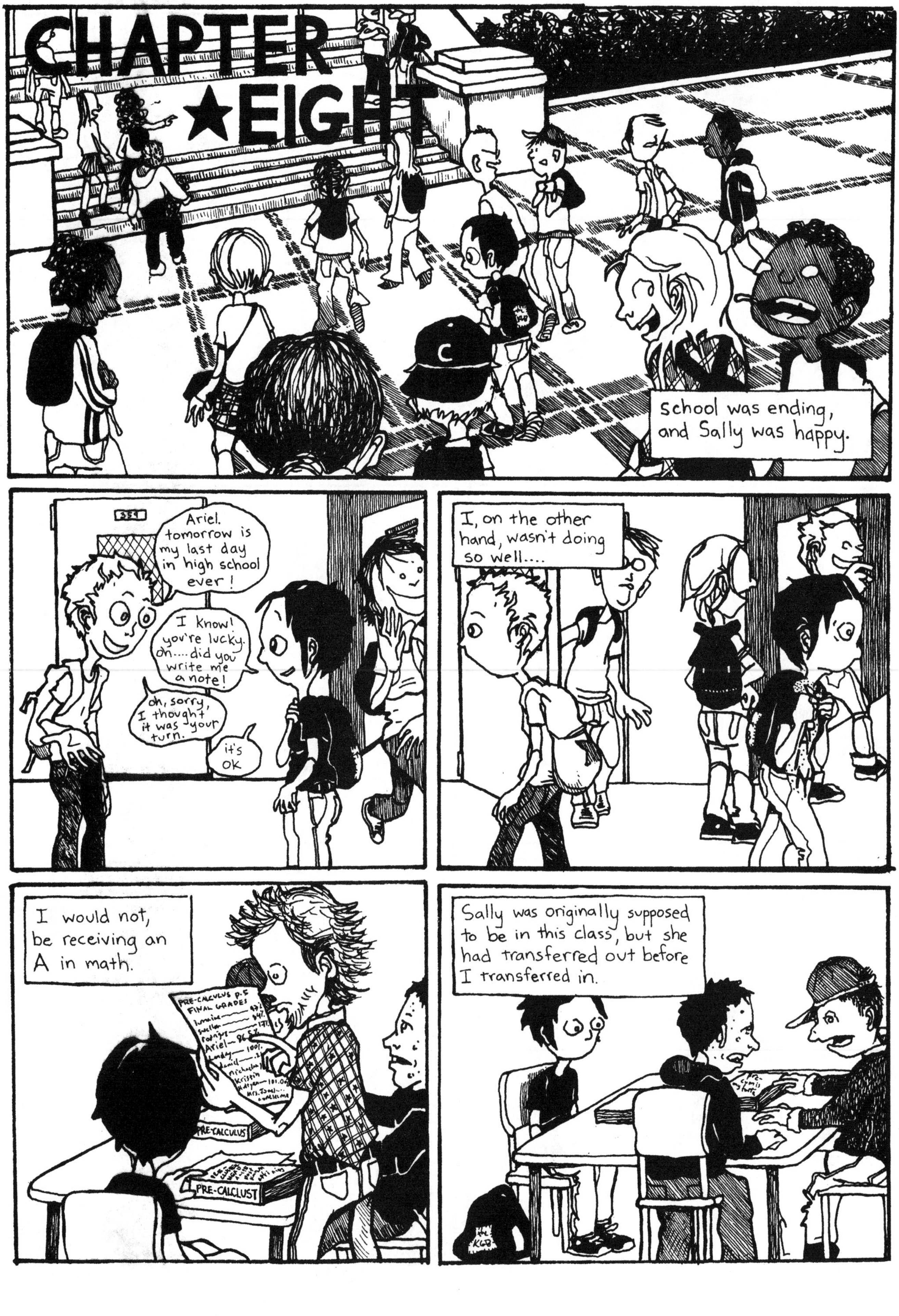

CHAPTER ★ EIGHT
School was ending, and Sally was happy.
Ariel. tomorrow is my last day in high school ever!
I know! you're lucky. oh.... did you write me a note!
oh, sorry, I thought it was your turn.
it's OK
I, on the other hand, wasn't doing so well....
I would not, be receiving an A in math.
PRE-CALCULUS p.5
FINAL GRADES
Ariel — 86.5%
100%
101.0%
PRE-CALCULUS
PRE-CALCLUST
Sally was originally supposed to be in this class, but she had transferred out before I transferred in.

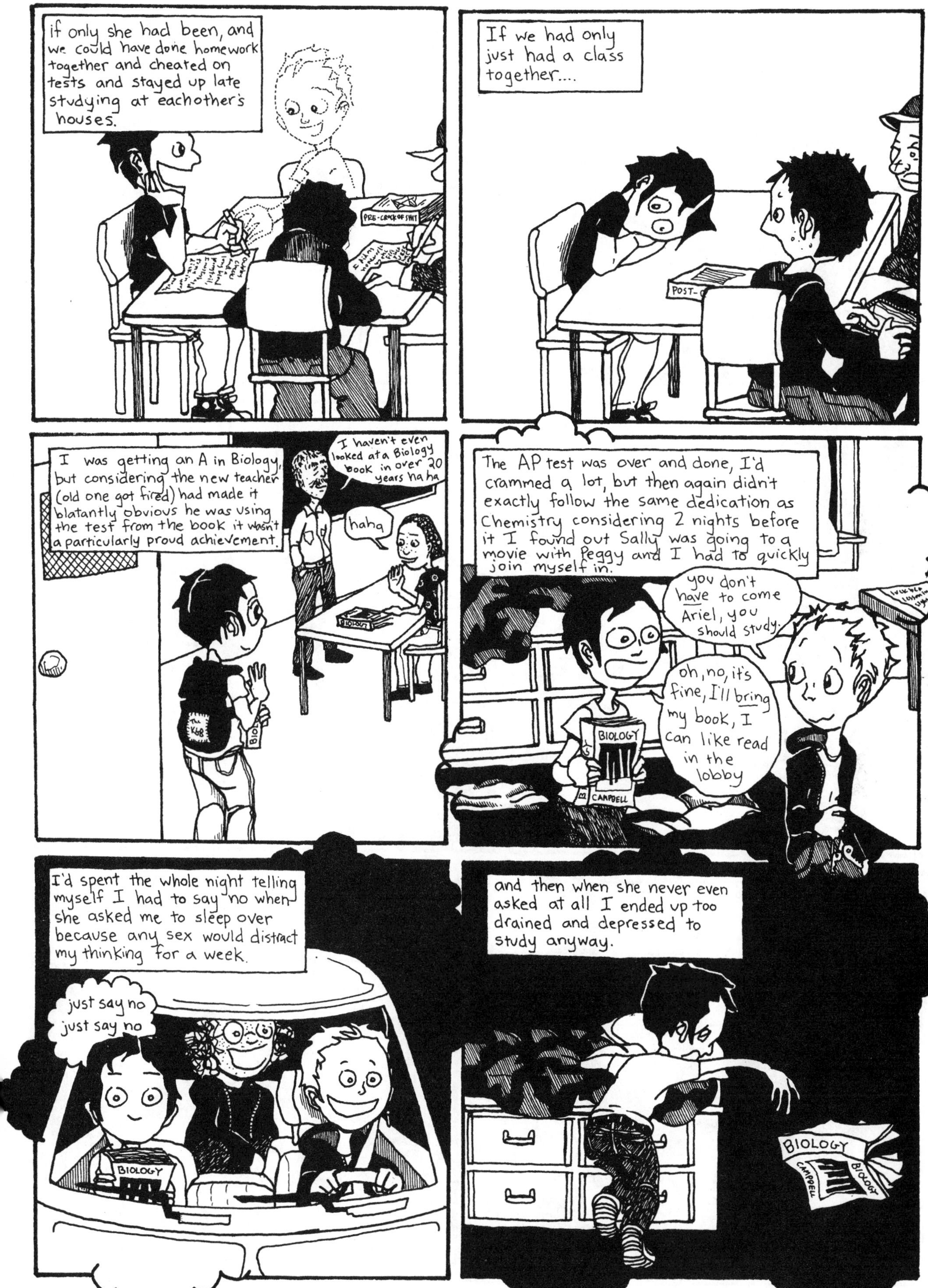

if only she had been, and we could have done homework together and cheated on tests and stayed up late studying at eachother's houses.
PRE-CRACK OF SHIT
If we had only just had a class together....
POST-
I was getting an A in Biology, but considering the new teacher (old one got fired) had made it blatantly obvious he was using the test from the book it wasn't a particularly proud achievement.
I haven't even looked at a Biology book in over 20 years ha ha
haha
The AP test was over and done, I'd crammed a lot, but then again didn't exactly follow the same dedication as Chemistry considering 2 nights before it I found out Sally was going to a movie with Peggy and I had to quickly join myself in.
you don't have to come Ariel, you should study.
oh, no, it's fine, I'll bring my book, I can like read in the lobby
BIOLOGY
CAMPBELL
I'd spent the whole night telling myself I had to say no when she asked me to sleep over because any sex would distract my thinking for a week.
just say no
just say no
BIOLOGY
and then when she never even asked at all I ended up too drained and depressed to study anyway.
BIOLOGY
CAMPBELL
BIOLOGY

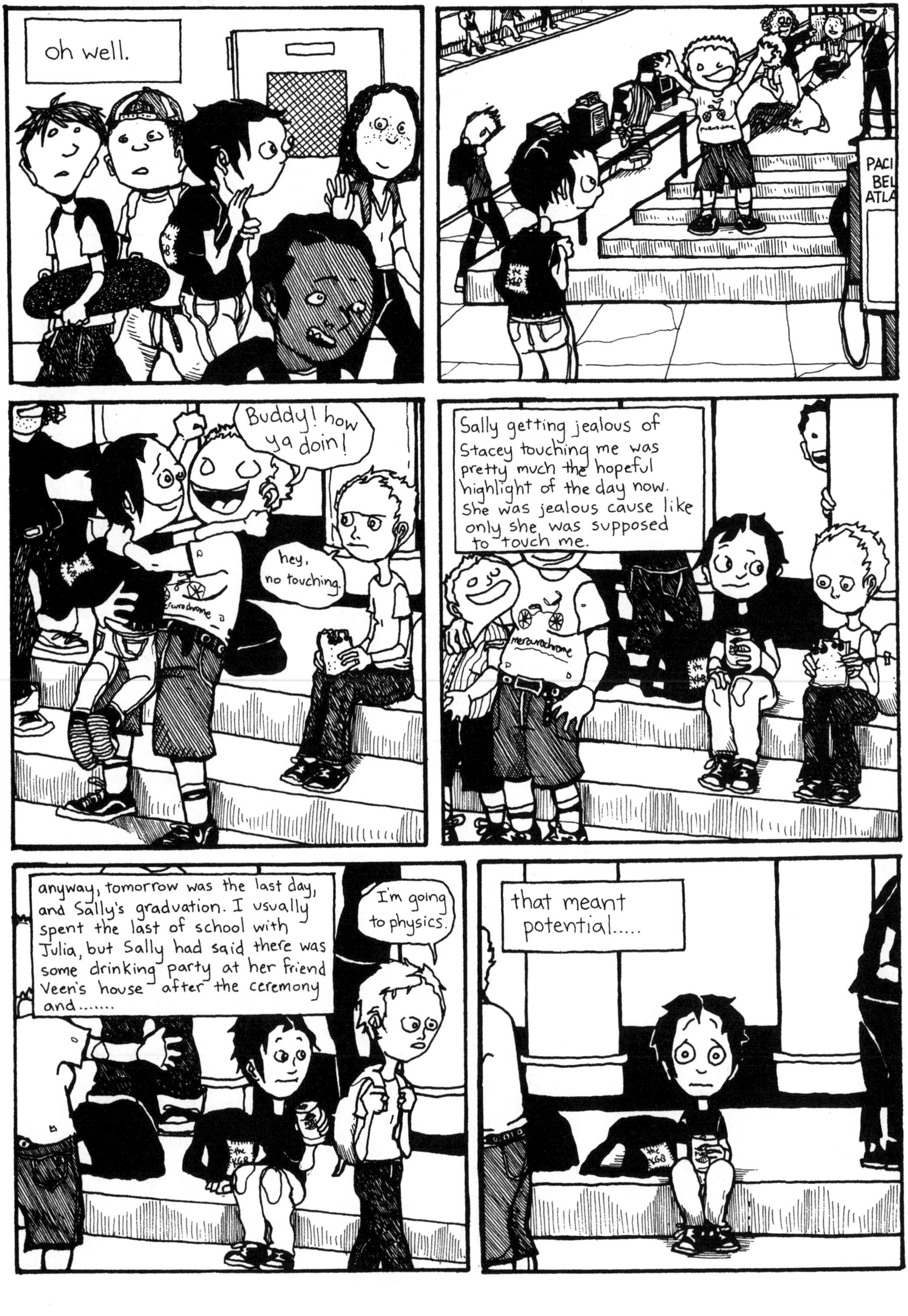
oh well.
PACI
BEL
ATLA
Buddy! how ya doin!
hey, no touching.
mercurochrome
Sally getting jealous of Stacey touching me was pretty much the hopeful highlight of the day now. She was jealous cause like only she was supposed to touch me.
mercurochrome
anyway, tomorrow was the last day, and Sally's gradvation. I usually spent the last of school with Julia, but Sally had said there was some drinking party at her friend Veen's house after the ceremony and.......
I'm going to physics.
that meant potential.....

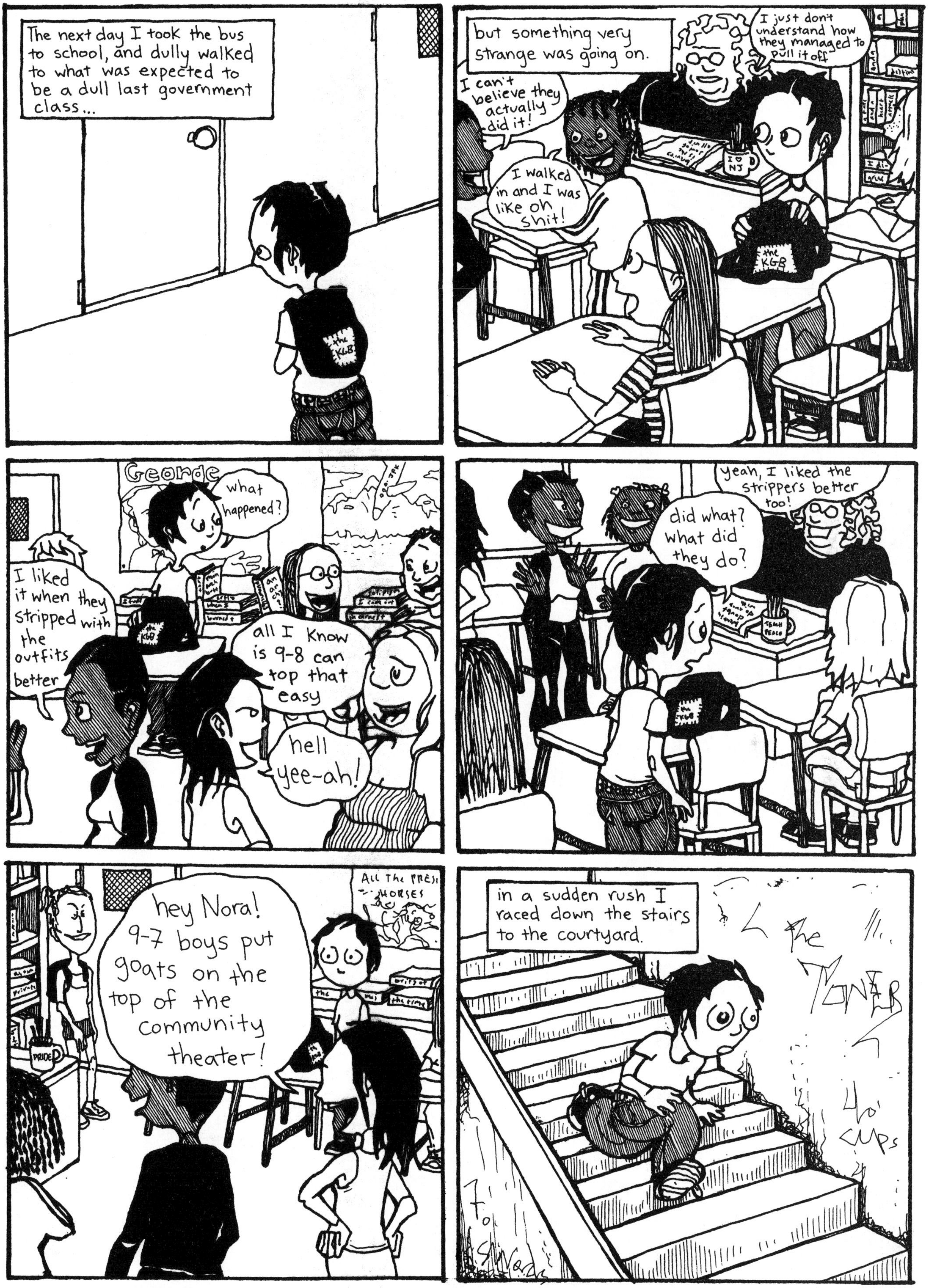
The next day I took the bus to school, and dully walked to what was expected to be a dull last government class...
but something very strange was going on.
I just don't understand how they managed to pull it off
I can't believe they actually did it!
I walked in and I was like oh shit!
what happened?
I liked it when they stripped with the outfits better
all I Know is 9-8 can top that easy
hell yee-ah!
yeah, I liked the strippers better too!
did what? what did they do?
hey Nora! 9-7 boys put goats on the top of the community theater!
in a sudden rush I raced down the stairs to the courtyard.

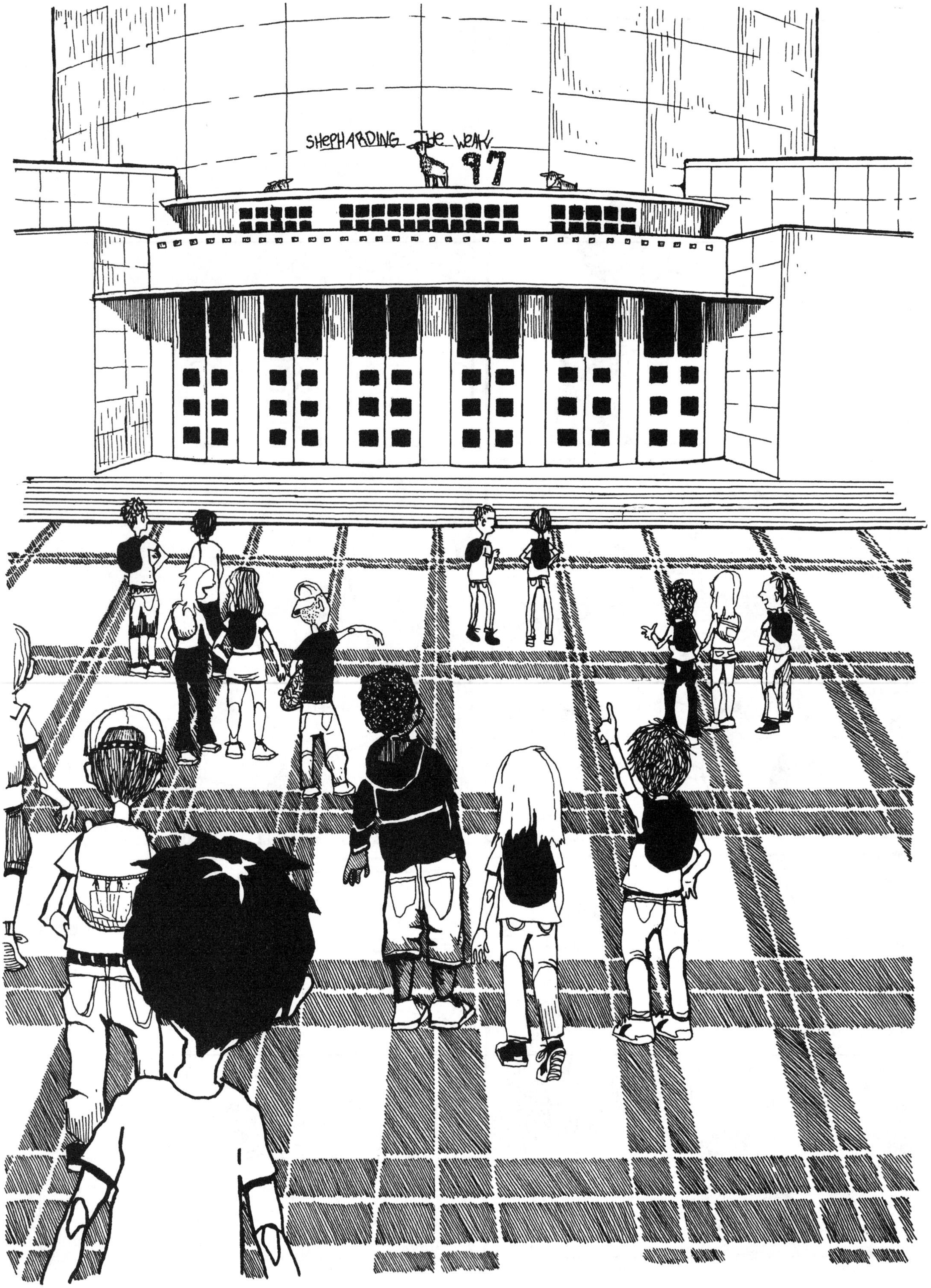
SHEPHARDING THE WEAK
97

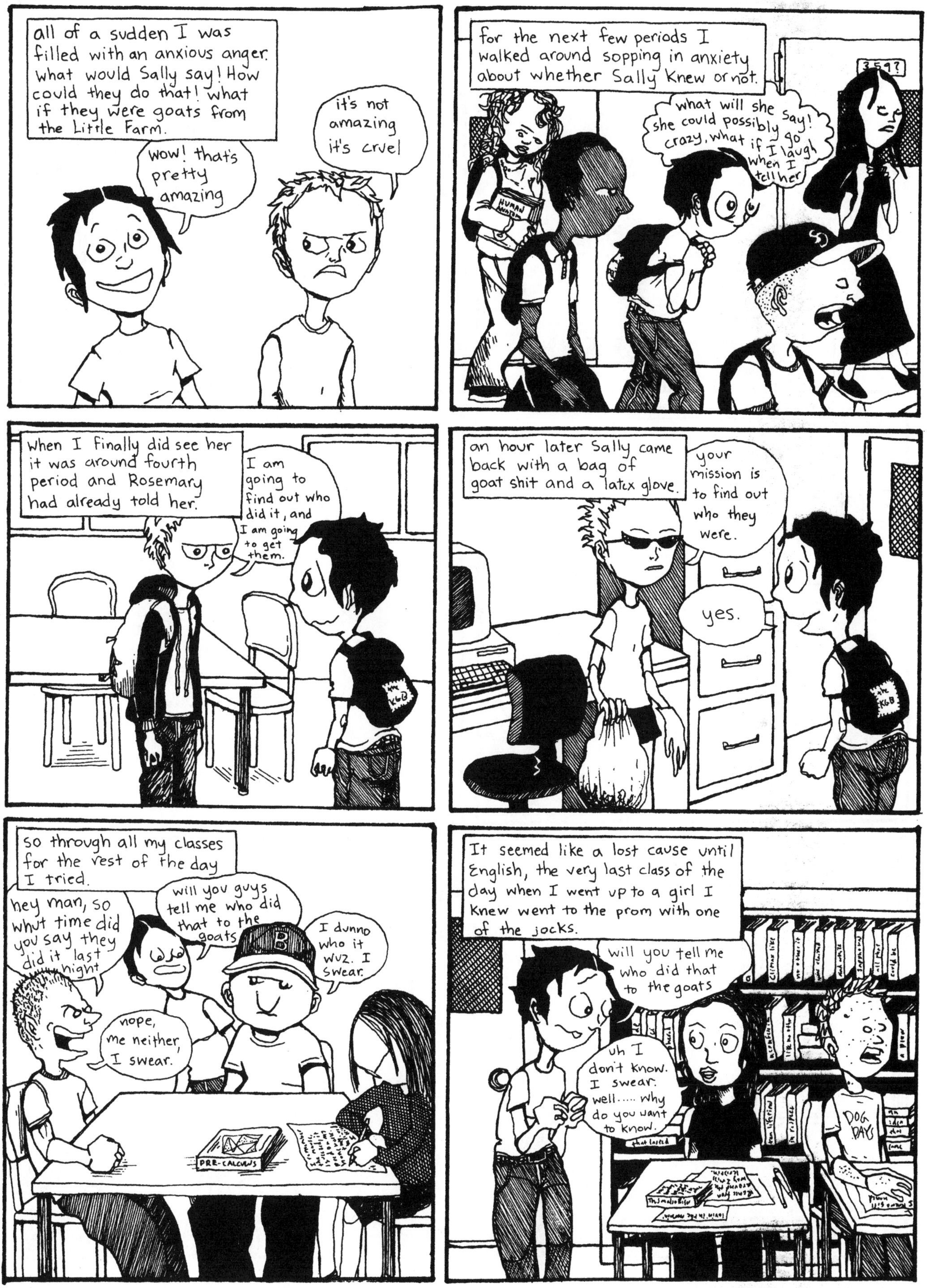
all of a sudden I was filled with an anxious anger. what would Sally say! How could they do that! what if they were goats from the Little Farm.
wow! that's pretty amazing
it's not amazing it's cruel
for the next few periods I walked around sopping in anxiety about whether Sally knew or not.
what will she say! she could possibly go crazy, what if I laugh when I tell her
HUMAN ANATOMY
359?
when I finally did see her it was around fourth period and Rosemary had already told her.
I am going to find out who did it, and I am going to get them.
an hour later Sally came back with a bag of goat shit and a latex glove.
your mission is to find out who they were.
yes.
so through all my classes for the rest of the day I tried.
hey man, so whut time did you say they did it last night
will you guys tell me who did that to the goats
I dunno who it wuz. I swear.
nope, me neither, I swear.
PRE-CALCULUS
It seemed like a lost cause until English, the very last class of the day when I went up to a girl I knew went to the prom with one of the jocks.
will you tell me who did that to the goats
uh I don't know. I swear. well..... why do you want to know.
DOG DAYS

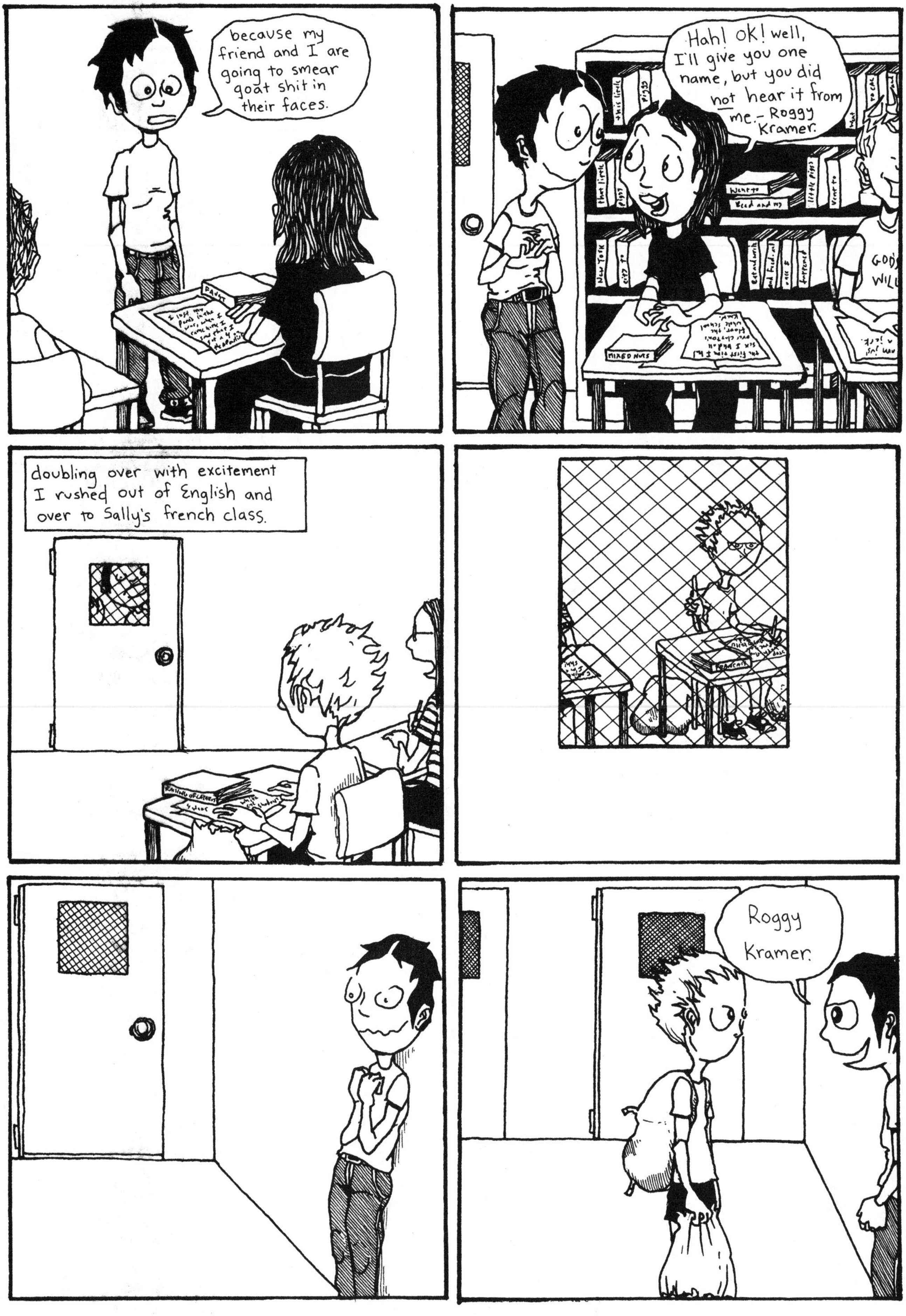
because my friend and I are going to smear goat shit in their faces.
Hah! OK! well, I'll give you one name, but you did not hear it from me.- Roggy Kramer.
doubling over with excitement I rushed out of English and over to Sally's french class.
Roggy Kramer.

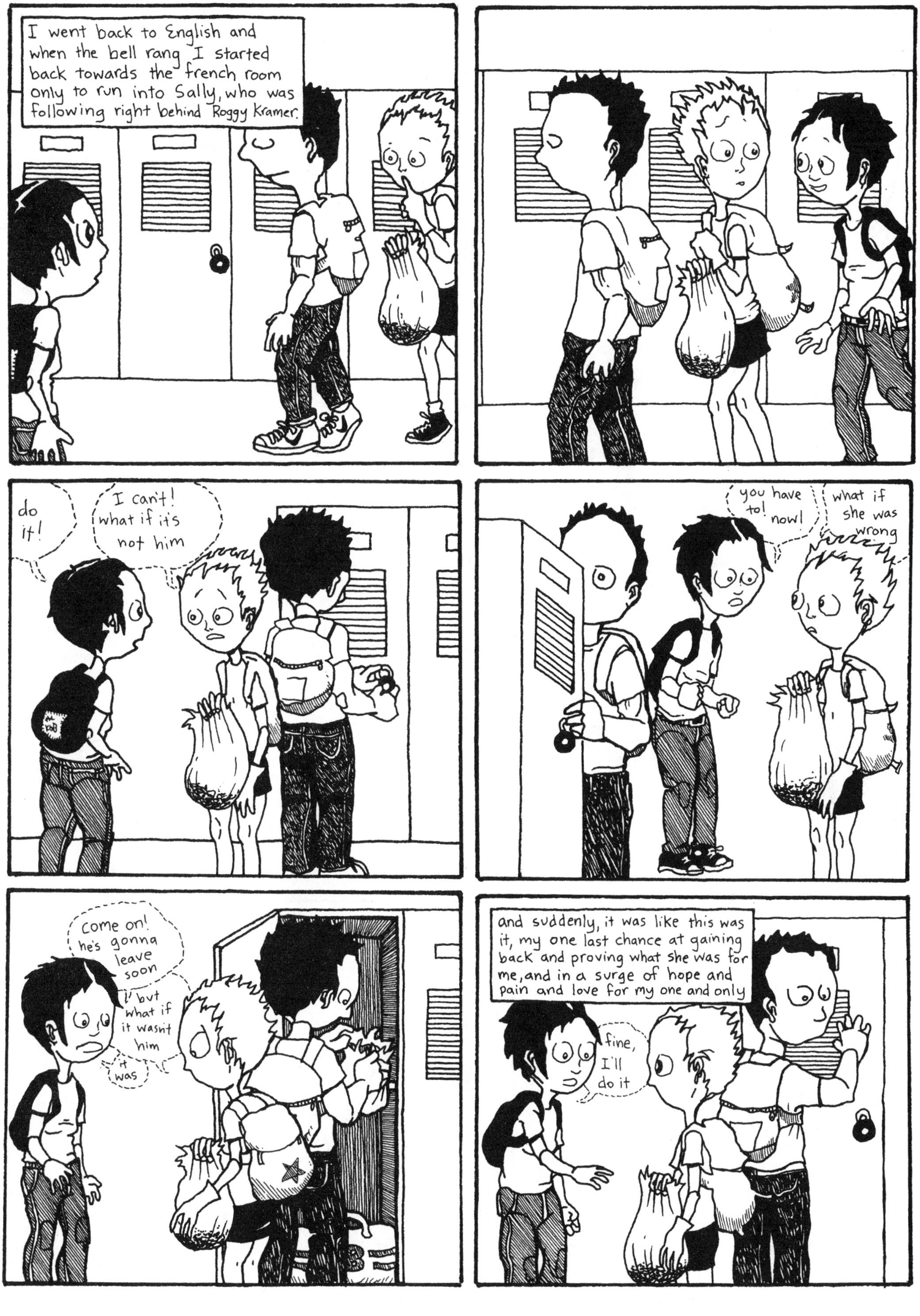
I went back to English and when the bell rang I started back towards the french room only to run into Sally, who was following right behind Roggy Kramer.
do it!
I can't! what if it's not him
you have to! now!
what if she was wrong
come on! he's gonna leave soon
! but what if it wasn't him
it was
and suddenly, it was like this was it, my one last chance at gaining back and proving what she was for me, and in a surge of hope and pain and love for my one and only
fine, I'll do it

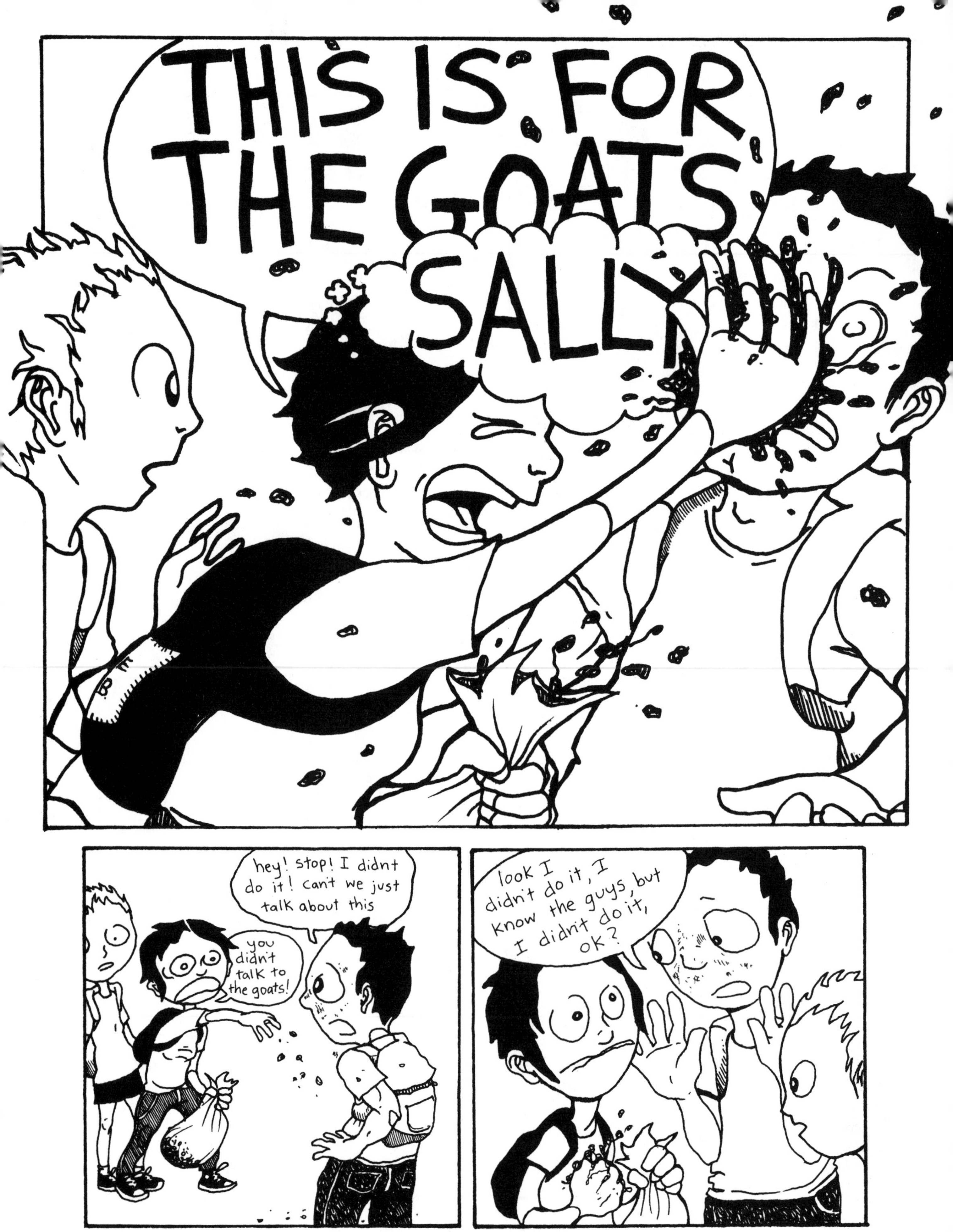
THIS IS FOR THE GOATS SALLY!!!
hey! stop! I didnt do it! can't we just talk about this
you didn't talk to the goats!
look I didn't do it, I know the guys, but I didnt do it, ok?

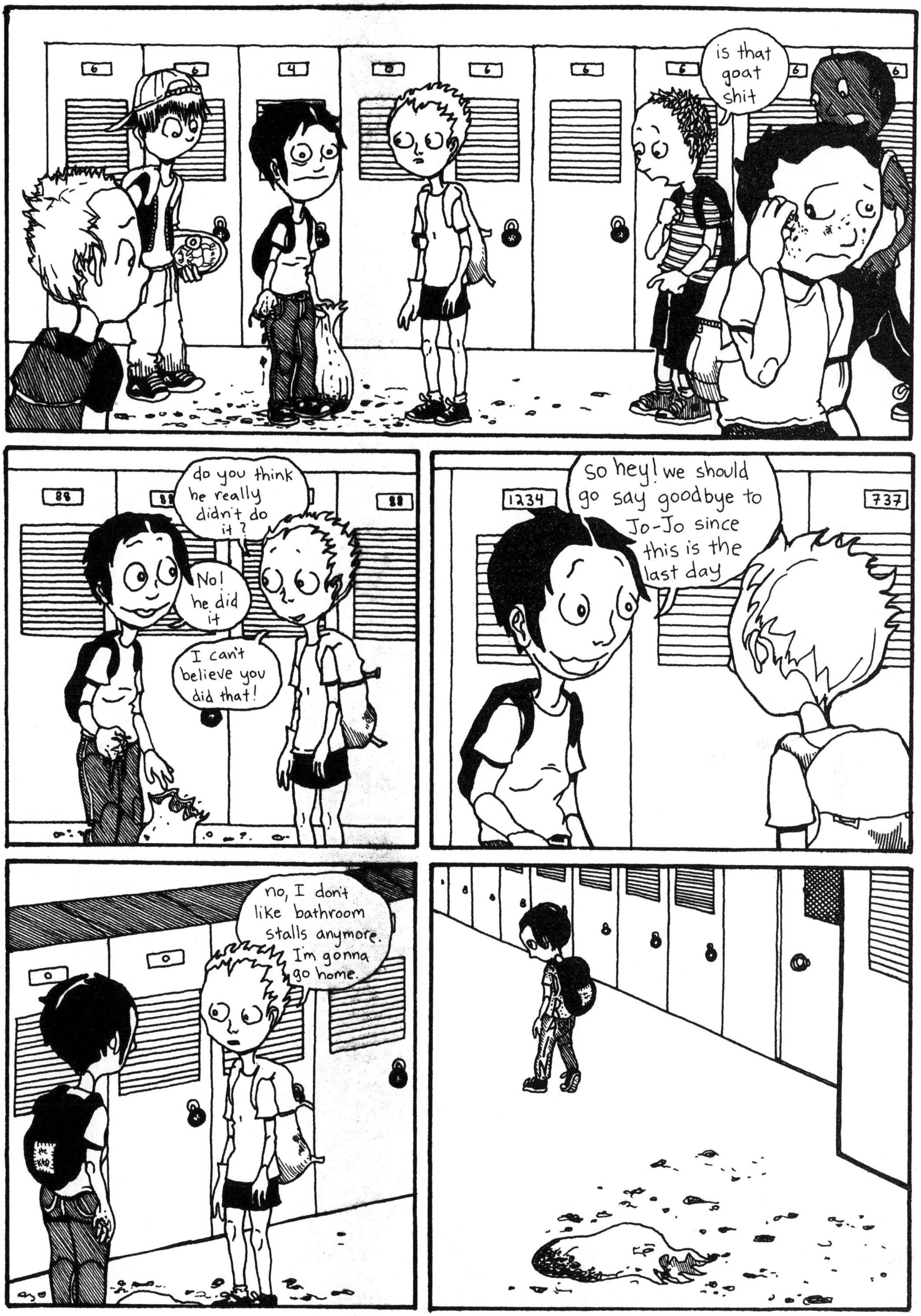
is that goat shit
do you think he really didn't do it ?
No! he did it
I can't believe you did that!
So hey! we should go say goodbye to Jo-Jo since this is the last day
no, I don't like bathroom stalls anymore. I'm gonna go home.

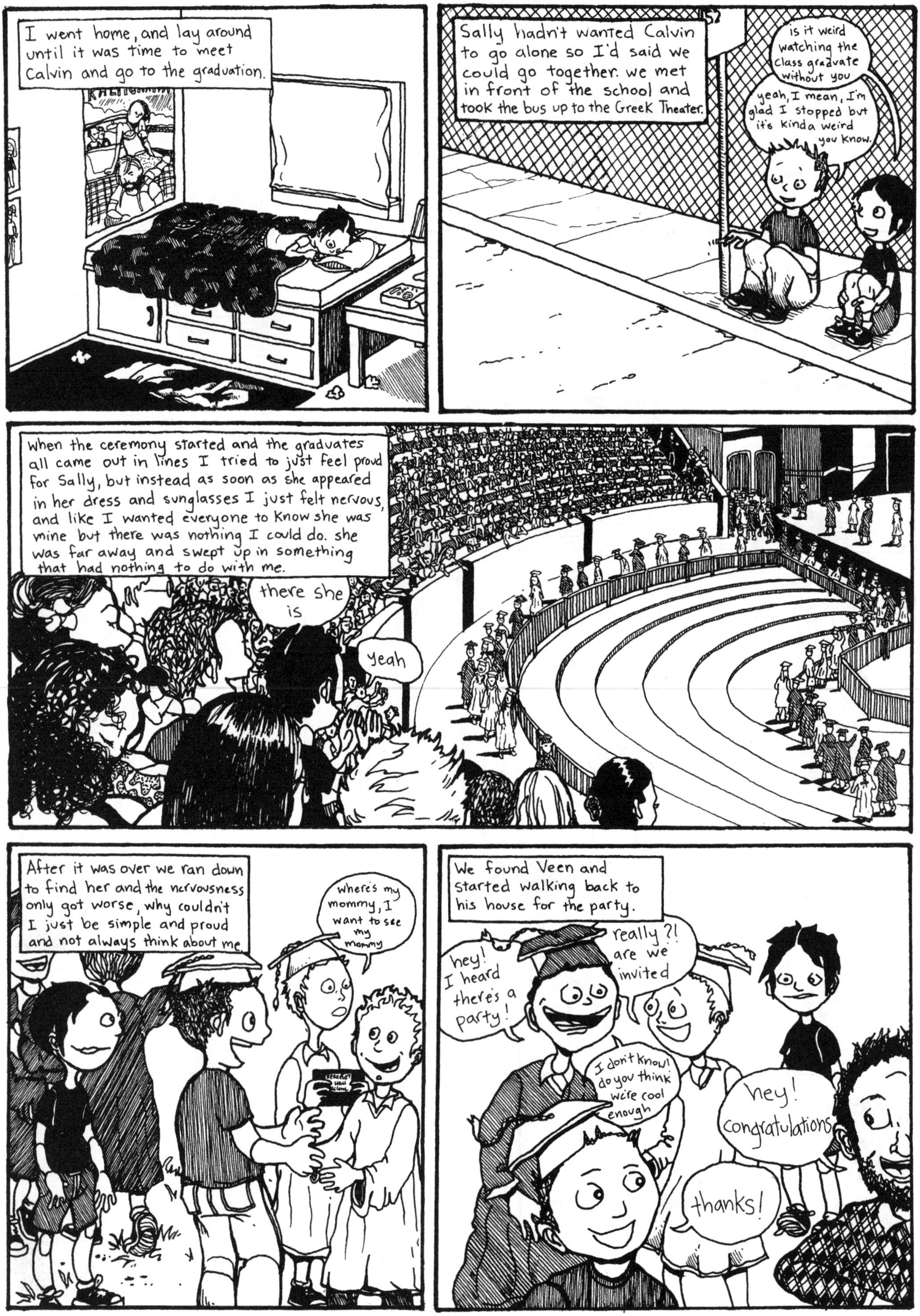
I went home, and lay around until it was time to meet Calvin and go to the graduation.
Sally hadn't wanted Calvin to go alone so I'd said we could go together. we met in front of the school and took the bus up to the Greek Theater.
is it weird watching the class graduate without you
yeah, I mean, I'm glad I stopped but it's kinda weird you know.
when the ceremony started and the graduates all came out in lines I tried to just feel proud for Sally, but instead as soon as she appeared in her dress and sunglasses I just felt nervous, and like I wanted everyone to know she was mine but there was nothing I could do. she was far away and swept up in something that had nothing to do with me.
there she is
yeah
After it was over we ran down to find her and the nervousness only got worse, why couldn't I just be simple and proud and not always think about me.
where's my mommy, I want to see my mommy
We found Veen and started walking back to his house for the party.
hey! I heard there's a party!
really?! are we invited
I don't know! do you think we're cool enough
hey! congratulations
thanks!

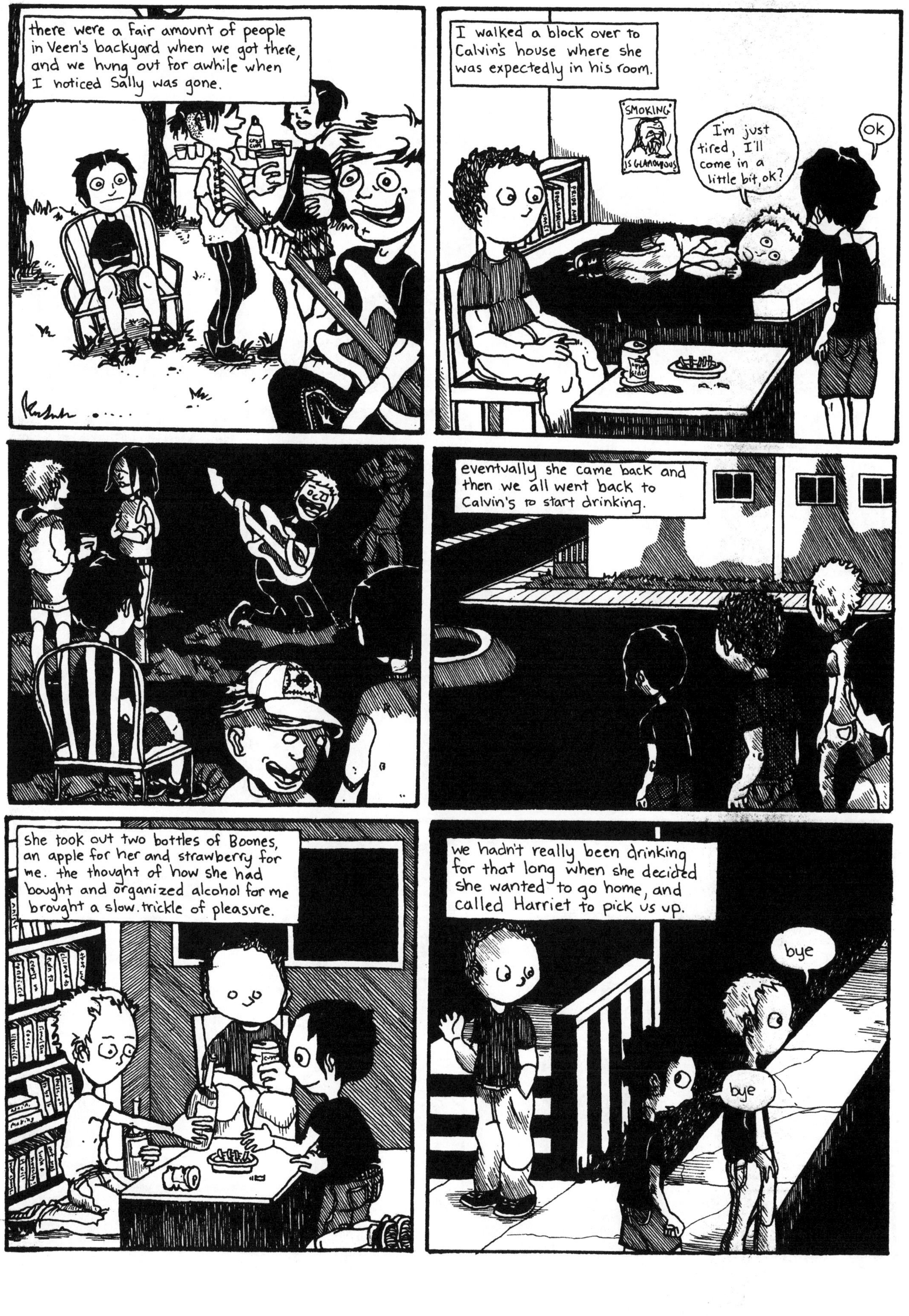
there were a fair amount of people in Veen's backyard when we got there, and we hung out for awhile when I noticed Sally was gone.
I walked a block over to Calvin's house where she was expectedly in his room.
SMOKING
IS GLAMOROUS
I'm just tired, I'll come in a little bit, ok?
ok
eventually she came back and then we all went back to Calvin's to start drinking.
she took out two bottles of Boones, an apple for her and strawberry for me. the thought of how she had bought and organized alcohol for me brought a slow trickle of pleasure.
we hadn't really been drinking for that long when she decided she wanted to go home, and called Harriet to pick us up.
bye
bye

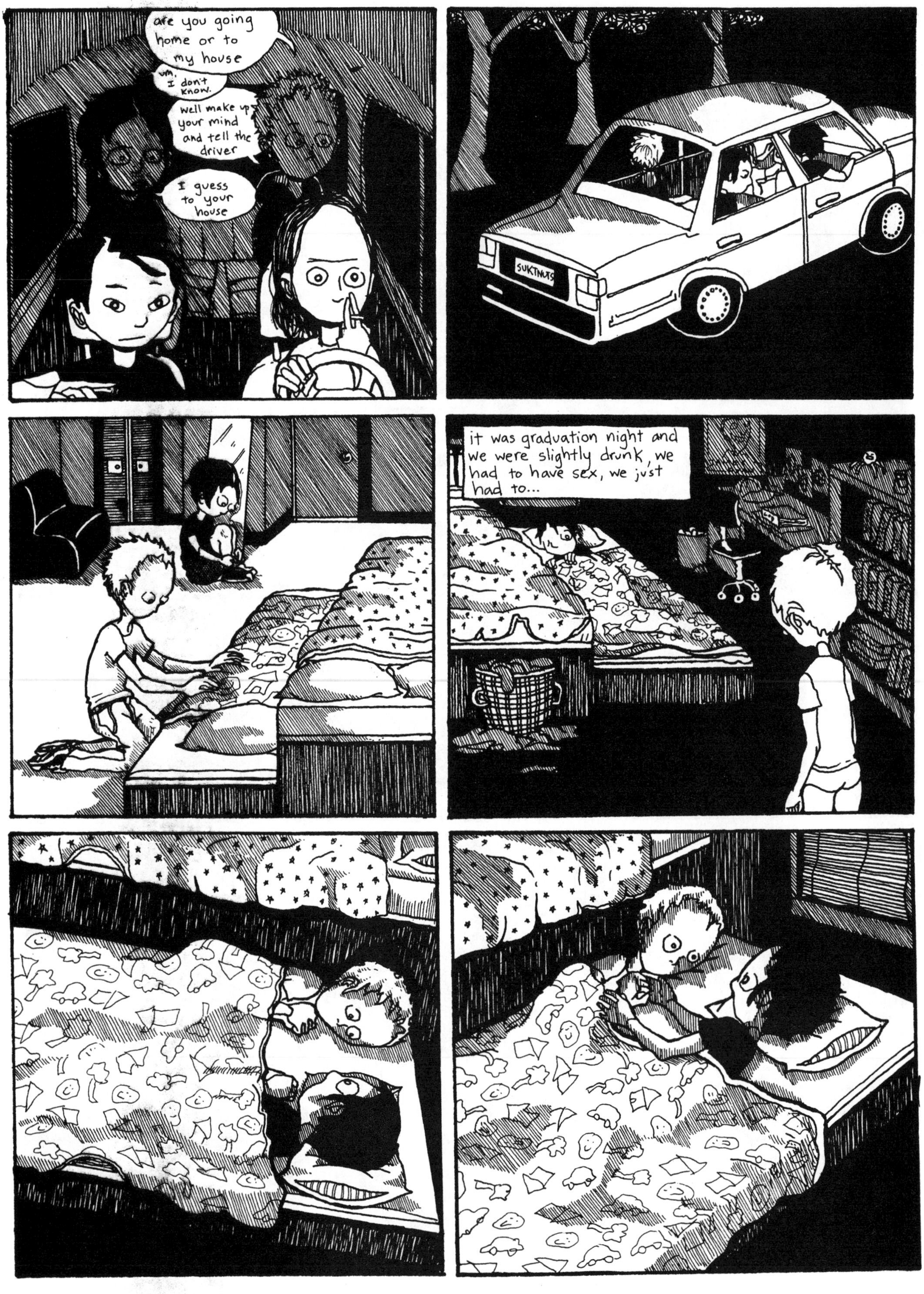
are you going home or to my house
um, I don't know.
well make up your mind and tell the driver
I guess to your house
SUKTNUTS
it was graduation night and we were slightly drunk, we had to have sex, we just had to...

but this was just the way it was.

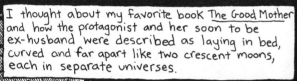

I thought about my favorite book The Good Mother and how the protagonist and her soon to be ex-husband were described as laying in bed, curved and far apart like two crescent moons, each in separate universes.

Ariel

what

nothing

what

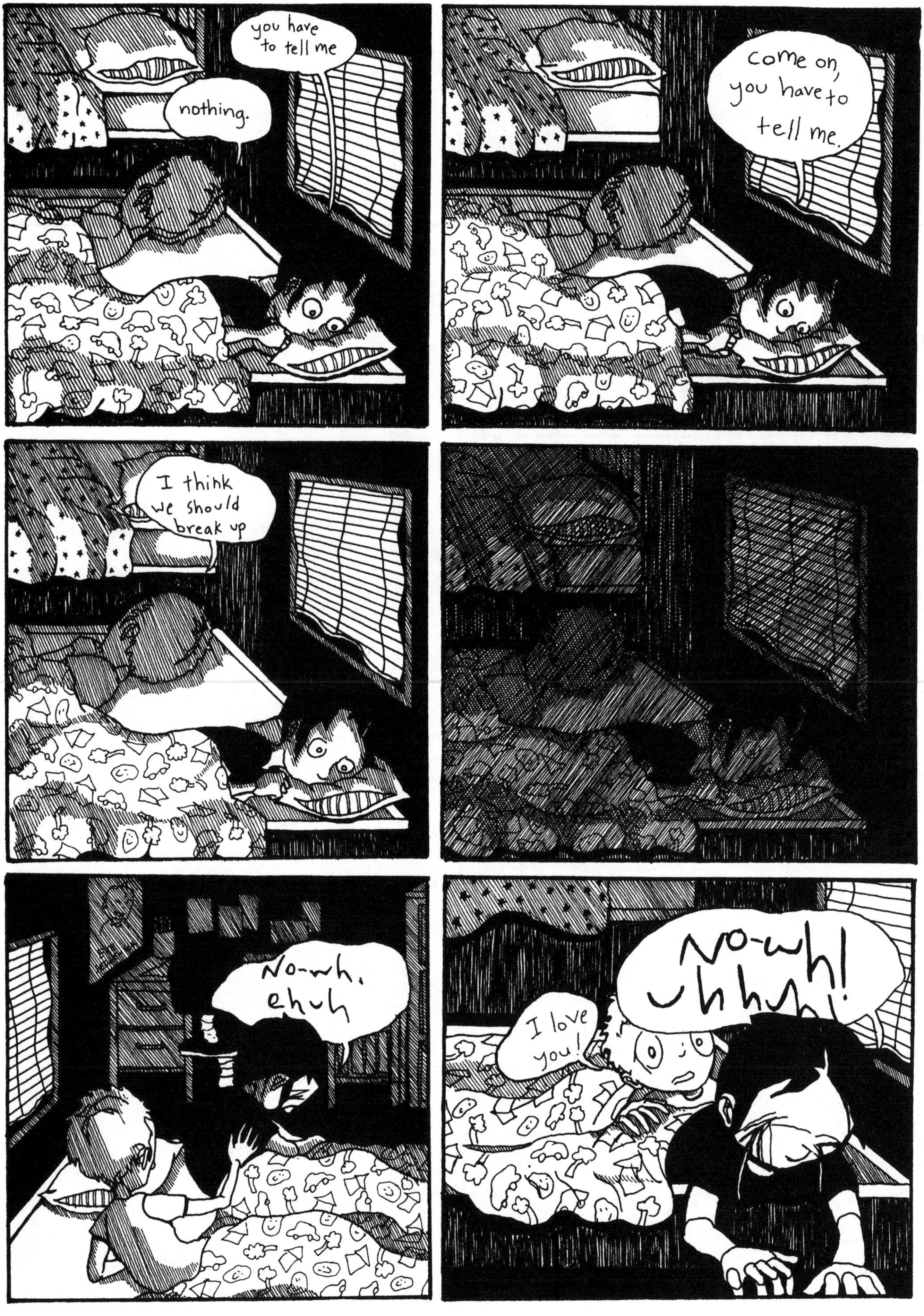
you have to tell me
nothing.
come on, you have to tell me.
I think we should break up
No-uh, ehuh
I love you!
No-uh! uhhuh!

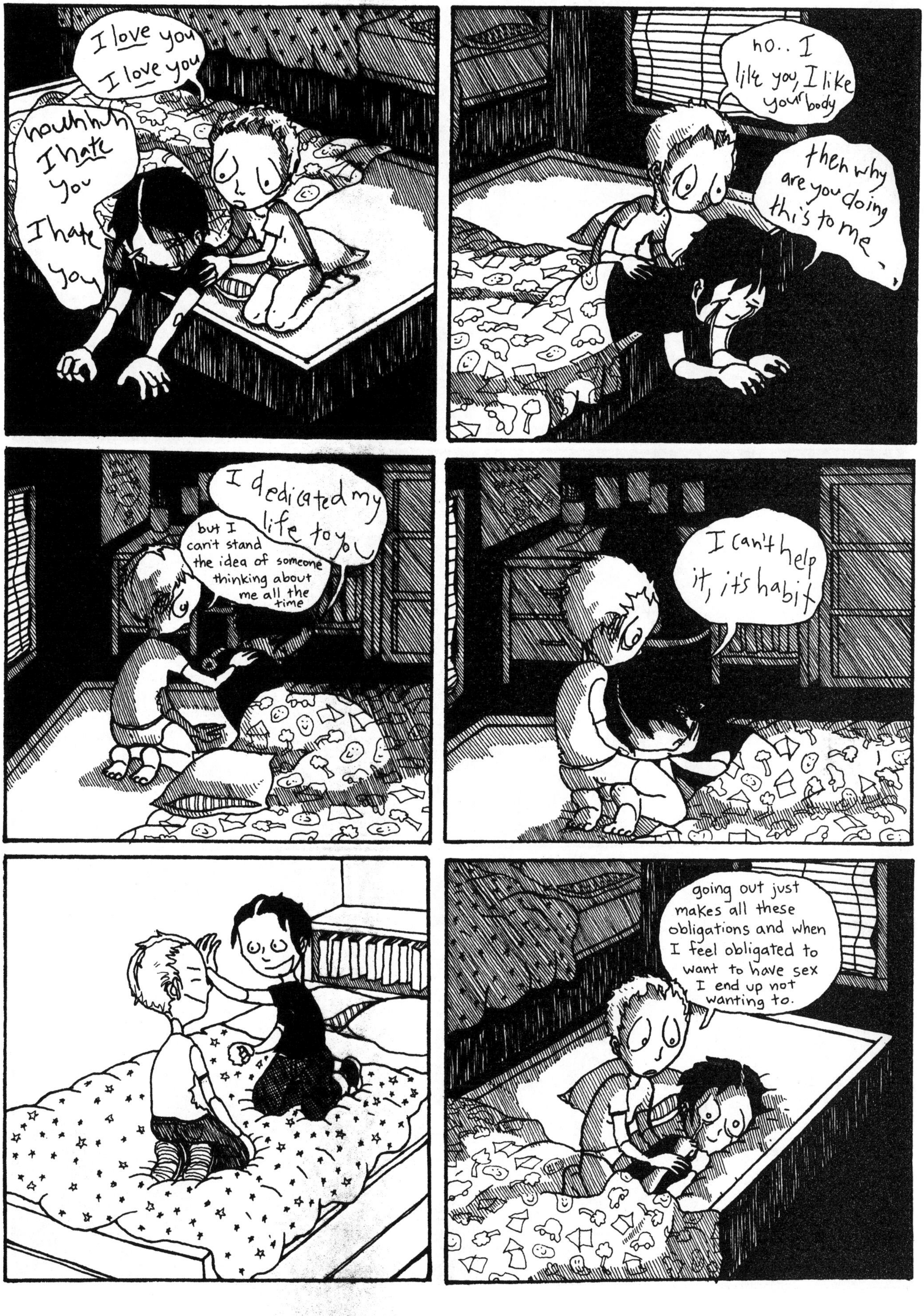
I love you I love you
nouhhuh I hate you I hate you
no.. I like you, I like your body
then why are you doing this to me.
I dedicated my life to you.
but I can't stand the idea of someone thinking about me all the time
I can't help it, it's habit
going out just makes all these obligations and when I feel obligated to want to have sex I end up not wanting to.

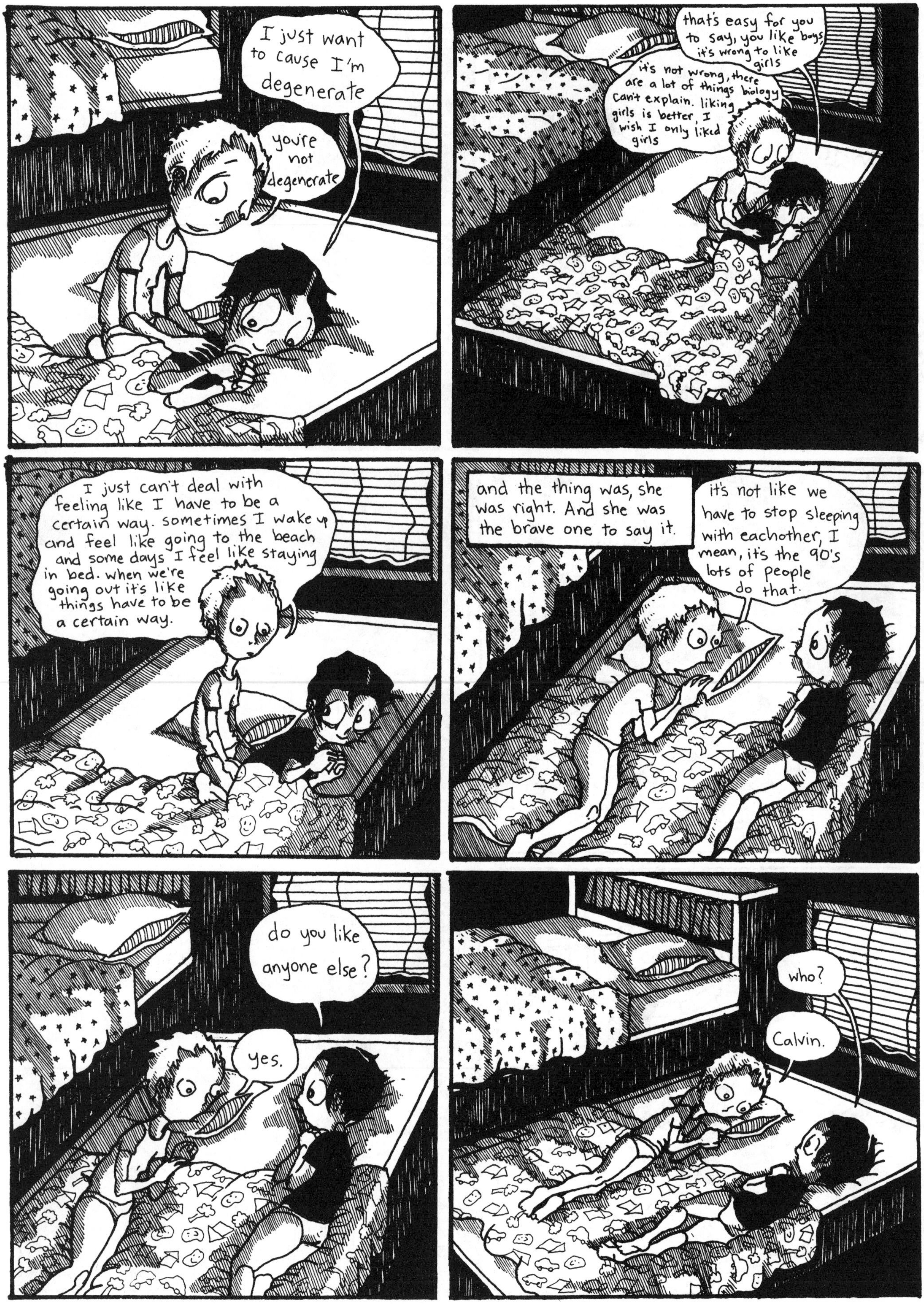
I just want to cause I'm degenerate
you're not degenerate
that's easy for you to say, you like boys, it's wrong to like girls
it's not wrong, there are a lot of things biology can't explain. liking girls is better, I wish I only liked girls
I just can't deal with feeling like I have to be a certain way. sometimes I wake up and feel like going to the beach and some days I feel like staying in bed. when we're going out it's like things have to be a certain way.
and the thing was, she was right. And she was the brave one to say it.
it's not like we have to stop sleeping with eachother, I mean, it's the 90's lots of people do that.
do you like anyone else?
yes.
who?
Calvin.

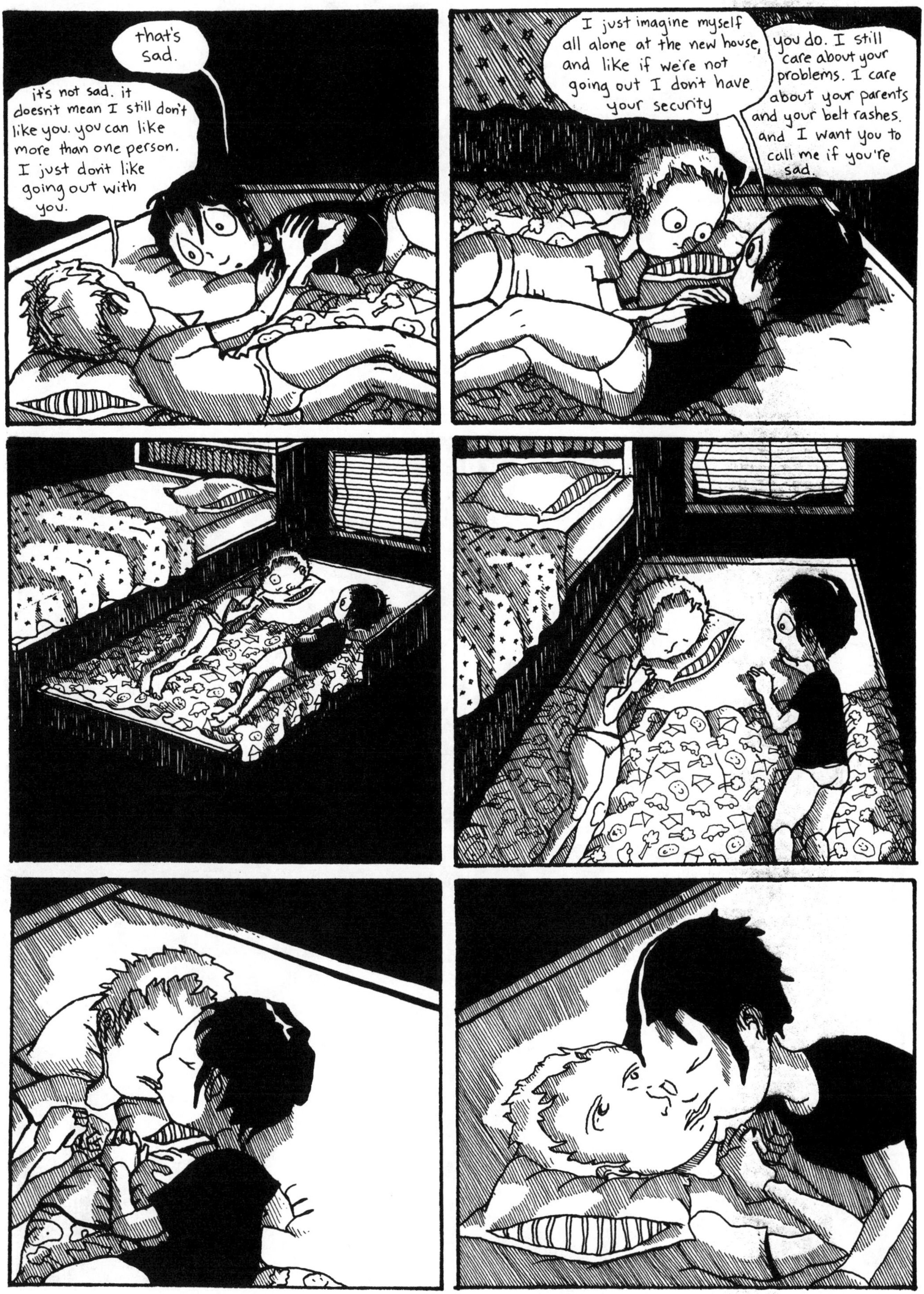
that's sad.
it's not sad. it doesn't mean I still don't like you. you can like more than one person. I just don't like going out with you.
I just imagine myself all alone at the new house, and like if we're not going out I don't have your security
you do. I still care about your problems. I care about your parents and your belt rashes. and I want you to call me if you're sad.

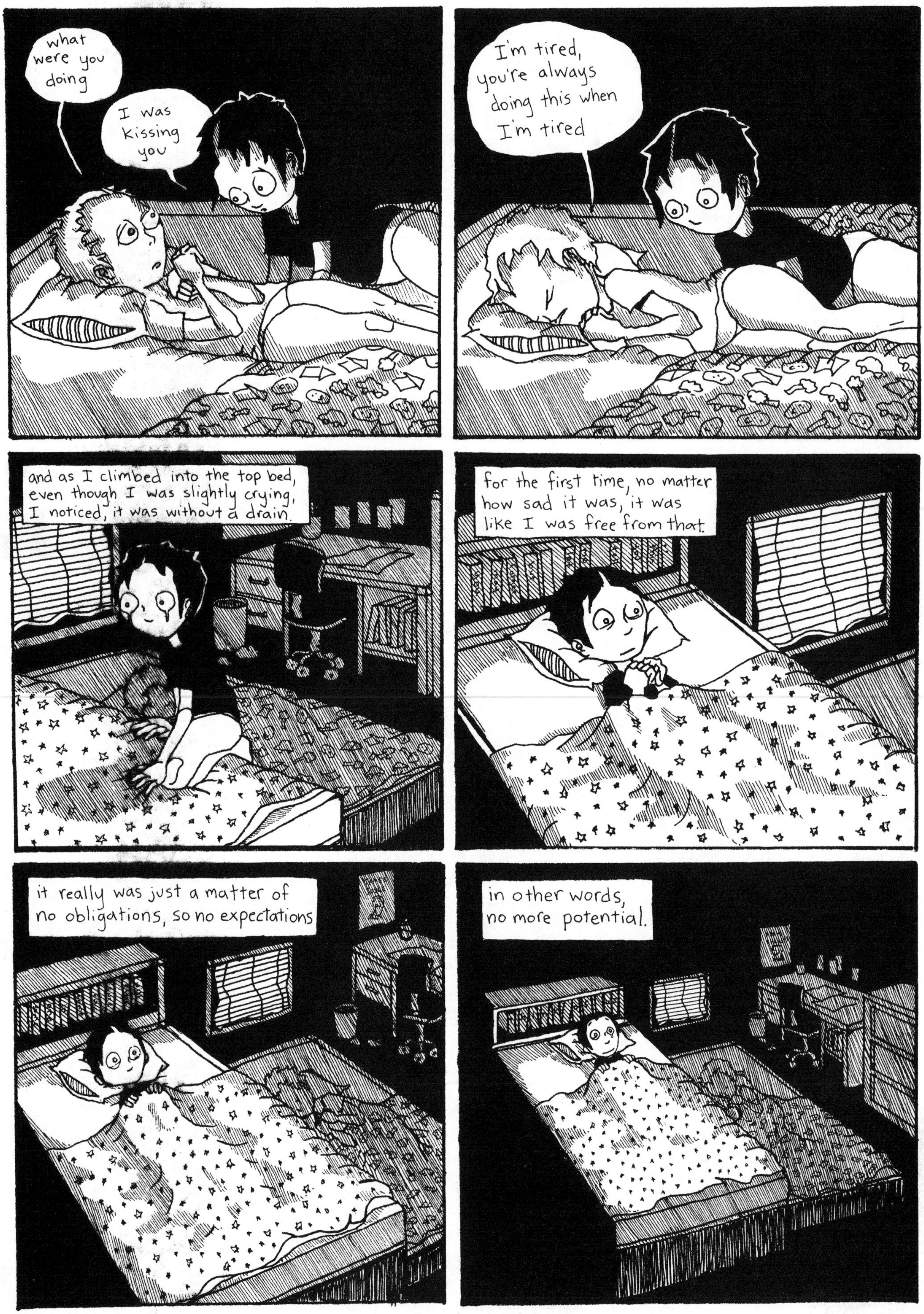
what were you doing
I was kissing you
I'm tired, you're always doing this when I'm tired
and as I climbed into the top bed, even though I was slightly crying, I noticed, it was without a drain.
for the first time, no matter how sad it was, it was like I was free from that.
it really was just a matter of no obligations, so no expectations
in other words, no more potential.

The High School Comic Chronicles of

Ariel Schrag

AWKWARD
AND
DEFINITION
The High School Comic Chronicles of
Ariel Schrag
Author of POTENTIAL

9th Grade

Isn't the girls bathroom just the funnest place to be!
so like guys, I was putting my hand down to masturbate but I kept pissing on my hand! I mean I wanted to see what was goin' on down there, but I just couldn't stop.
bummer
STALLS
Meg peed. But I wasn't exactly in the mood...

10th Grade

when I got out of the shower she had put on the song "16" by No Doubt. the sound of Gwen's voice quickly sent us running back to the bathroom to apply her to our faces.
pass the glitter eyeshadow.
it meant so much to me I could have cried. I'd always been the type that was struggling around for a best friend and to think, this was really truthfully it.
well you're only 16! you poor little thing

POTENTIAL
The High School Comic Chronicles of
ARIEL SCHRAG

11th Grade

Are you ok?
yeah....

"A scathing and meticulously documented autobiographical triumph." —Alison Bechdel, author of Fun Home
LIKEWISE
The High School Comic Chronicles of
ARIEL SCHRAG
Author of POTENTIAL

Coming Soon

12th Grade

startle!

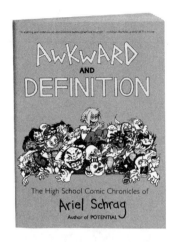

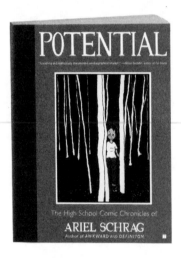

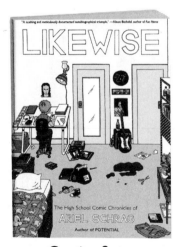

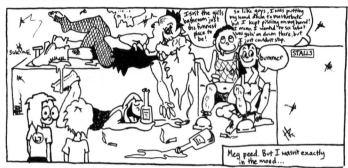

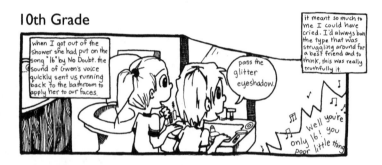

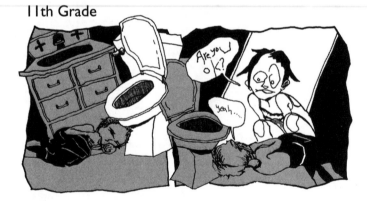

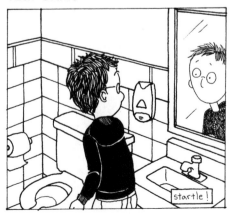

Available wherever books are sold or at simonsays.com

TOUCHSTONE
A Division of Simon & Schuster
A CBS COMPANY